Praise for Aron Ralston's
Between a Rock and a Hard Place

'Here is one man's heroic struggle with the infinite, a searing and compelling read. Aron Ralston tells his agonizing, inspiring tale of survival with all the verve and honesty you'd expect of someone who somehow found inspiration even in the face of a lonely death.'
Benedict Allen

'A gripping book . . . It not only details his entrapment and escape but tells vivid tales of extreme mountaineering prior to that defining misadventure.'
Joanna Walters, *Daily Express*

'Harrowing'
Guardian

'Ralston is superb at evoking the epic beauty of the land, and his description of his ordeal is riveting: think *Touching the Void* directed by Tarantino'
Sarfraz Manzoor, *New Statesman*

'Ralston manages to keep the tension flowing throughout . . . alternating each chapter of angst-ridden, present-tense narrative with a cosier chapter of climbing nostalgia. This lends the book a Hitchcockian rhythm, see-sawing neatly between calm and tension . . . He is somehow able to chronicle the ebb and flow of his thoughts and feelings during his ordeal with an exactness that gives his book the emotional pull of a psychological thriller.'
Craig Brown, book of the week, *Mail On Sunday*

'Ralston is a passionate man who has lived his life resolutely pursuing this passion. His fortitude in his dire predicament was, as he would say, awesome, and from this it is possible to learn much about hope in the face of overwhelming odds.'
Toby Clements, *Daily Telegraph*

127 HOURS:
Between a Rock and a Hard Place

ARON RALSTON

Previously published as *Between a Rock and a Hard Place*

SIMON &
SCHUSTER

London · New York · Sydney · Toronto

A CBS COMPANY

First published in Great Britain by Simon & Schuster UK Ltd, 2004, 2010
A CBS COMPANY

3 5 7 9 10 8 6 4

Simon & Schuster UK Ltd
1st Floor
222 Gray's Inn Road
London
WC1X 8HB

www.simonandschuster.co.uk

Simon & Schuster Australia
Sydney

A CIP catalogue for this book is available
from the British Library.

ISBN: 978-1-84983-390-5

Text permissions appear on page 354.

Credits for insert 1: pg. 1 courtesy of Elias Fallon; all photographs appearing
on pg. 2 of insert, as well as pg. 3 (top and bottom right) are courtesy of the
Ralston family; pg. 4 (bottom right) courtesy of Howard Huang.

Credits for insert 2: pg. 2 (top) courtesy of Kristi Moore; pg. 3 (top and bottom)
courtesy of Greg Funk; pg. 7 (top) courtesy of Eric Meijer; pg. 7 (bottom)
courtesy of Ron Elberger; pg. 8 courtesy of Tony Angelis.

All other photographs are courtesy of Aron Ralston.

Maps by Guenter Vollath

Printed in the UK by CPI Cox & Wyman, Reading, Berkshire RG1 8EX

Passion: That which I suffer, allow, endure, is done to me.

But once your crew has rowed you past the Sirens
a choice of routes is yours. I cannot advise you
which to take, or lead you through it all—
you must decide for yourself—
but I can tell you the ways of either course.
On one side beetling cliffs shoot up, and against them
pound the huge roaring breakers of blue-eyed Amphitrite—
the Clashing Rocks they're called by all the blissful gods.
No ship of men has ever approached and slipped past—
always some disaster—big timbers and sailors' corpses
whirled away by the waves and lethal blasts of fire.

On the other side loom two enormous crags . . .
One thrusts into the vaulting sky its jagged peak,
hooded round with a dark cloud that never leaves—
And halfway up that cliffside stands a fog-bound cavern
gaping west toward Erebus, realm of death and darkness—
past it, great Odysseus, you should steer your ship.
Scylla lurks inside it—the yelping horror,
yelping, no louder than any suckling pup
but she's a grisly monster, I assure you.
She has twelve legs, all writhing, dangling down
and six long swaying necks, a hideous head on each,
each head barbed with a triple row of fangs, thickset,
packed tight—and armed to the hilt with black death!
. . . with each of her six heads she snatches up
a man from the dark-prowed craft and whisks him off.

The other crag is lower—you will see, Odysseus—
Atop it a great fig-tree rises, shaggy with leaves;
beneath it awesome Charybdis gulps the dark water down.
Three times a day she vomits it up, three times she gulps it down,
that terror! Don't be there when the whirlpool swallows down—
not even the earthquake god could save you from disaster.
No, hug Scylla's crag—sail on past her—top speed!
Better by far to lose six men and keep your ship
than lose your entire crew.

—HOMER, *The Odyssey*

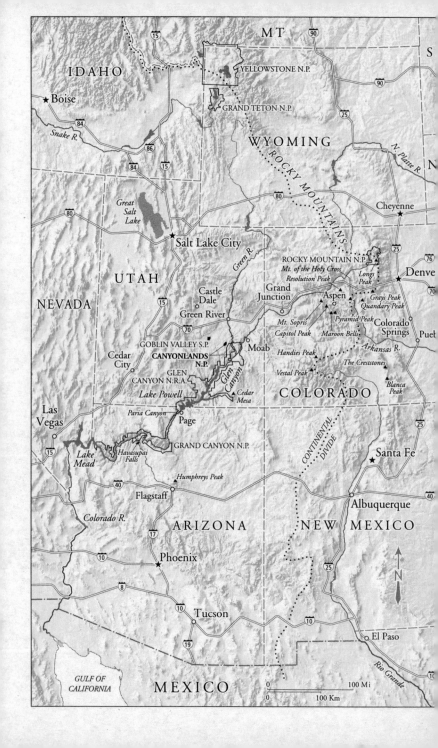

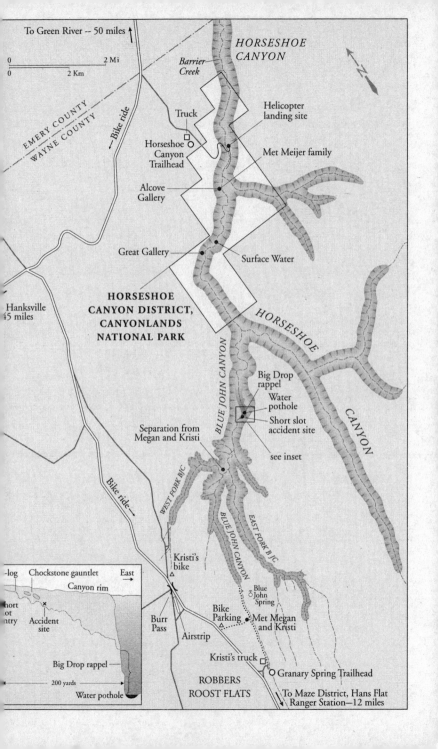

To Green River -- 50 miles

0   2 Mi
0   2 Km

EMERY COUNTY
WAYNE COUNTY

Bike ride

*HORSESHOE
CANYON*

*Barrier
Creek*

Truck

Helicopter
landing site

Horseshoe
Canyon
Trailhead

Met Meijer family

Alcove
Gallery

Great Gallery

Surface Water

**HORSESHOE
CANYON DISTRICT,
CANYONLANDS
NATIONAL PARK**

HORSESHOE

Hanksville
45 miles

BLUE JOHN CANYON

CANYON

Big Drop
rappel

Water
pothole

Short slot
accident site

Separation from
Megan and Kristi

see inset

WEST FORK BJC

Bike ride

BLUE JOHN CANYON

EAST FORK BJC

Kristi's
bike

-log

Chockstone gauntlet   East

Canyon rim

hort
ot
ntry

Accident
site

Burr
Pass

Airstrip

Big Drop rappel

200 yards

Water pothole

Blue
John
Spring

Bike
Parking

Met Megan
and Kristi

Kristi's truck

Granary Spring Trailhead

ROBBERS
ROOST FLATS

To Maze District, Hans Flat
Ranger Station—12 miles

PROLOGUE:
CIRCULATING WITH THE
ROBBERS ROOSTERS

He was a better boatman than a cowboy, and a better cook than a train robber, but John Griffith, with the distinguishing mark of one blue eye and one brown eye, became a favored extra hand with the Wild Bunch, Butch Cassidy's gang, during his time in the Robbers Roost country of eastern Utah. Blue John, as his first employer called him, found entry into the area as a cook for the Harris cattle operation near Cisco, about sixty miles west of Grand Junction. After fewer than two years of legitimate work, the thirty-five-year-old fell in with Jim Wall, alias Silver Tip, and "Indian Ed" Newcomb on a cattle roundup for the 3B outfit in the spring of 1890. The 3B herd ranged the Roost under the infamous foreman Jack Moore, who proffered hospitality to the Wild Bunch during their frequent gatherings in that country bounded by the Dirty Devil, San Rafael, Green, and Colorado rivers. Sometimes dropping into the Roost for the entire winter, to set up a base camp prior to or after a raid, or to help with the 3B stock, the Bunch always had a welcome in the Roost.

Silver Tip, Blue John, and Indian Ed circulated with the Bunch as a trio of second-tier accomplices, contributing their skills to whatever was in the works, be it horse thievery, robbery, or wrangling. In 1898 they helped Moore rope in the remaining 3B cattle of J. B. - Buhr's failing operation before they left for a horse-rustling escapade

in Wyoming. The return trip cost Moore his life in a shoot-out. Early
the next year, as the group returned to the Roost after delivering the
stolen horses to Colorado for sale, Silver Tip, Indian Ed, and Blue
John lifted another batch of the country's choicest horseflesh from
ranches around Moab and Monticello. Not that the Wild Bunch
boys paid much attention to posses—who were careful not to get too
close to the Roost in general—but the outlaws knew that the law was
after them for this most recent spree.

In a side canyon of Roost Canyon, on a late February morning,
Indian Ed climbed across the rocks below the overhang where the
team had spent the night with their cache of stolen goods—two pack
animals and a half-dozen head of horses. Suddenly, a rifle shot split
open the morning stillness, the .38–.55 slug flattening against a rock
before ricocheting to pierce Ed's leg above the knee. He dropped to
the sandy wash and crawled behind brush to the alcove where Blue
John and Silver Tip were exchanging fire with the posse who had
found the outlaws via their tracks and evening campfire. Blue John
kept the posse engaged while Silver Tip sneaked out from the alcove
and climbed to the canyon rim, where he put three shots just over the
heads of the sheriff's men. The posse bolted back down the main
wash of Roost Canyon to their horses and fled at full speed to their
ranches and homes with a tall tale of their shoot-out with the Wild
Bunch.

It was the last time the three bandits worked together or participated in any outlawry. They hung up their rifles and changed their
ways, each peaceably fading into history after shaking things up,
leaving their trails for others to follow. Indian Ed Newcomb healed
his leg and was thought to have returned to Oklahoma, disappearing
into obscurity. Silver Tip escaped from custody after serving two
years of a ten-year sentence in Wayne County, Utah; he eventually
settled in Wyoming to quietly pass the rest of his days. Blue John
Griffith was last spotted in the fall of 1899, departing Hite on the
Colorado River, heading for Lee's Ferry down one of the most beautiful and intimidating stretches of river in the West. While it is spec-

ulated that he quit the river along the way to head for Arizona or even Mexico, he was not seen to arrive at Lee's Ferry and was never heard from again.

Of the three, only one left a permanent mark on the land. Blue John Canyon and Blue John Springs, across the watershed from the site of the fateful ambush attempt, are named for the sometime cook, sometime wagon driver, sometime horse thief who roamed the Roost for a decade just before the turn of the twentieth century.

ONE

"Geologic Time Includes Now"

This is the most beautiful place on earth.

There are many such places. Every man, every woman, carries in heart and mind the image of the ideal place, known or unknown, actual or visionary. . . . There's no limit to the human capacity for the homing sentiment. Theologians, sky pilots, astronauts have even felt the appeal of home calling to them from up above, in the cold black outback of inter-stellar space.

For myself I'll take Moab, Utah. I don't mean the town itself, of course, but the country which surrounds it—the canyonlands. The slickrock desert. The red dust and the burnt cliffs and the lonely sky—all that which lies beyond the end of the roads.

—EDWARD ABBEY, *Desert Solitaire*

FRAYING CONTRAILS STREAK another bluebird sky above the red desert plateau, and I wonder how many sunburnt days these bad-lands have seen since their creation. It's Saturday morning, April 26, 2003, and I am mountain biking by myself on a scraped dirt road in the far southeastern corner of Emery County, in central-eastern Utah. An hour ago, I left my truck at the dirt trailhead parking area for Horseshoe Canyon, the isolated geographic window of Canyon-lands National Park that sits fifteen air miles northwest of the legendary Maze District, forty miles southeast of the great razorback uplift of the San Rafael Swell, twenty miles west of the Green River, and some forty miles south of I-70, that corridor of commerce and last chances (NEXT SERVICES: 110 MILES). With open tablelands to cover for a hundred miles between the snowcapped ranges of the Henrys to the southwest—the last range in the U.S. to be named, explored, and mapped—and the La Sals to the east, a strong wind is blowing hard from the south, the direction I'm heading. Besides slowing my progress to a crawl—I'm in my lowest gear and pumping hard on a flat grade just to move forward—the wind has blown shallow drifts of maroon sand onto the washboarded road. I try to avoid the drifts, but occasionally, they blanket the entire road, and my bike founders. Three times already I've had to walk through particularly long sand bogs.

The going would be much easier if I didn't have this heavy pack on my back. I wouldn't normally carry twenty-five pounds of supplies and equipment on a bike ride, but I'm journeying out on a thirty-mile-long circuit of biking and canyoneering—traversing the bottom of a deep and narrow canyon system—and it will take me most of the day. Besides a gallon of water stored in an insulated three-liter CamelBak hydration pouch and a one-liter Lexan bottle, I have five chocolate bars, two burritos, and a chocolate muffin in a plastic grocery sack in my pack. I'll be hungry by the time I get back to my truck, for certain, but I have enough for the day.

The truly burdensome weight comes from my full stock of rappelling gear: three locking carabiners, two regular carabiners, a lightweight combination belay and rappel device, two tied slings of half-inch webbing, a longer length of half-inch webbing with ten prestitched loops called a daisy chain, my climbing harness, a sixty-meter-long and ten-and-a-half-millimeter-thick dynamic climbing rope, twenty-five feet of one-inch tubular webbing, and my rarely used Leatherman-knockoff multi-tool (with two pocketknife blades and a pair of pliers) that I carry in case I need to cut the webbing to build anchors. Also in my backpack are my headlamp, headphones,

CD player and several Phish CDs, extra AA batteries, digital camera and mini digital video camcorder, and their batteries and protective cloth sacks.

It adds up, but I deem it all necessary, even the camera gear. I enjoy photographing the otherworldly colors and shapes presented in the convoluted depths of slot canyons and the prehistoric artwork preserved in their alcoves. This trip will have the added bonus of taking me past four archaeological sites in Horseshoe Canyon that are home to hundreds of petroglyphs and pictographs. The U.S. Congress added the isolated canyon to the otherwise contiguous Canyonlands National Park specifically to protect the five-thousand-year-old etchings and paintings found along the Barrier Creek watercourse at the bottom of Horseshoe, a silent record of an ancient people's presence. At the Great Gallery, dozens of eight-to-ten-foot-high superhumans hover *en echelon* over groups of indistinct animals, dominating beasts and onlookers alike with their long, dark bodies, broad shoulders, and haunting eyes. The superbly massive apparitions are the oldest and best examples of their design type in the world, such preeminent specimens that anthropologists have named the heavy and somewhat sinister artistic mode of their creators the "Barrier Creek style." Though there is no written record to help us decipher the artists' meaning, a few of the figures appear to be hunters with spears and clubs; most of them, legless, armless, and horned, seem to float like nightmarish demons. Whatever their intended significance, the mysterious forms are remarkable for their ability to carry a declaration of ego across the millennia and confront the modern observer with the fact that the panels have survived longer and are in better condition than all but the oldest golden artifacts of Western civilization. This provokes the question: What will remain of today's ostensibly advanced societies five thousand years hence? Probably not our artwork. Nor any evidence of our record amounts of leisure time (if for no other reason than most of us fritter away this luxury in front of our television sets).

* * *

In anticipation of the wet and muddy conditions in the canyon, I'm wearing a pair of beat-up running shoes and thick wool-blend socks. Thus insulated, my feet sweat as they pump on my bike pedals. My legs sweat, too, compressed by the Lycra biking shorts I'm wearing beneath my beige nylon shorts. Even through double-thick padding, my bike seat pummels my rear end. Up top, I have on a favorite Phish T-shirt and a blue baseball cap. I left my waterproof jacket back at my truck; the day is going to be warm and dry, just like it was yesterday when I biked the twelve-mile loop of the Slick Rock Trail over east of Moab. If it were going to be rainy, a slot canyon would be the last place I'd be headed, jacket or no.

Lightweight travel is a pleasure to me, and I've figured how to do more with less so I can go farther in a given amount of time. Yesterday I had just my small CamelBak with a few bike-repair items and my cameras, a measly ten-pound load for the four-hour loop ride. In the evening, paring out the bike gear, I hiked five miles on an out-and-back visit to a natural arch out toward Castle Valley, carrying only six pounds total of water and camera equipment. The day before, Thursday, with my friend Brad Yule from Aspen, I had climbed and skied Mount Sopris, the 12,995-foot monarch of western Colorado, and had carried a few extra clothes and backcountry avalanche rescue gear, but I still kept my load under fifteen pounds.

My five-day road trip will culminate on Sunday night with an unsupported solo attempt to mountain bike the 108-mile White Rim Trail in Canyonlands National Park. If I carried the supplies I'd used over the three days it took me the first time I rode that trail in 2000, I'd have a sixty-pound pack and a sore back before I went ten miles. In my planning estimates this time around, I am hoping to carry fifteen pounds and complete the loop in under twenty-four hours. It will mean following a precision-charted water-management plan to capitalize on the scarce refilling opportunities, no sleeping, and only the bare minimum of stopping. My biggest worry isn't that my legs will get tired—I know they will, and I know how to handle it—but rather that my, uh, undercarriage will become too sensitive to allow me to ride. "Crotch coma," as I've heard it called, comes from the de-sensitizing overstimulation of the perineum. As I haven't ridden my bike any extended distance since last summer, my bike-saddle toler-ance is disconcertingly low. Had I anticipated this trip prior to two nights ago I would have gone out for at least one long ride in the Aspen area beforehand. As it happened, some friends and I called off a mountaineering trip at the last moment on Wednesday; the cancel-lation freed me for a hajj to the desert, a pilgrimage for warmth to reacquaint myself with a landscape other than wintry mountains. Usually, I would leave a detailed schedule of my plans with my room-mates, but since I left my home in Aspen without knowing what I was going to do, the only word of my destination I gave was "Utah." I briefly researched my trip options by consulting my guidebooks as I drove from Mount Sopris to Utah Thursday night. The result has been a capriciously impromptu vacation, one that will even incorpo-rate dropping in on a big campout party near Goblin Valley State Park tonight.

It's nearing ten-thirty A.M. as I pedal into the shade of a very lone-some juniper and survey my sunbaked surroundings. The rolling scrub desert gradually drops away into a region of painted rock domes, hidden cliffs, weathered and warped bluffs, tilted and tor-tured canyons, and broken monoliths. This is hoodoo country; this is voodoo country. This is Abbey's country, the red wasteland beyond the end of the roads. Since I arrived after dark last night, I wasn't able to see much of the landscape on my drive in to the trailhead. As I scan the middle ground to the east for any sign of my destination canyon, I take out my chocolate muffin from the Moab grocery's bakery and have to practically choke it down; both the muffin and my mouth have dried out from exposure to the arid wind. There are copious signs of meandering cattle from a rancher's ongoing attempt to make his living against the odds of the desert. The herds trample sinuous tracks through the indigenous life that spreads out in the ample space: a lace of grasses, foot-tall hedgehog cacti, and black microbi-otic crust cloak the red earth. I wash down the rest of the muffin, except for a few crumbs in the wrapper, with several pulls from the CamelBak's hydration tube fastened to my shoulder strap.

Remounting, I roll down the road in the wind-protected lee of the ridgeline in front of me, but at the top of the next hill, I'm thrust into battle against the gusts once more. After another twenty minutes pistoning my legs along this blast furnace of a road, I see a group of motorbikers passing me on their way to the Maze District of Canyonlands. The dust from the motorbikes blows straight into my face, clogging my nose, my eyes, my tear ducts, even gluing itself to my teeth. I grimace at the grit pasted on my lips, lick my teeth clean, and press on, thinking about where those bikers would be headed.

I've visited the Maze only once myself, for about half an hour, nearly ten years ago. When our Cataract Canyon rafting party pulled over in the afternoon to set up camp along the Colorado River at a beach called Spanish Bottom, I hiked a thousand feet up over the rim rock into a place known as the Doll's House. Fifty-to-one-hundred-foot-tall hoodoo rock formations towered above me as I scrambled around the sandstone and granite like a Lilliputian. When I finally turned around to look back at the river, I jerked to a halt and sat on the nearest boulder with a view. It was the first time the features and formative processes of the desert had made me pause and absorb just how small and brave we are, we the human race.

Down behind the boats at Spanish Bottom, a furious river churned; suddenly, I perceived in its auburn flow that it was, even at that exact moment, carving that very canyon from a thousand square miles of desert tablelands. From the Doll's House, I had the unexpected impression that I was watching the ongoing birth of an entire landscape, as if I were standing on the rim of an exploding caldera. The vista held for me a feeling of the dawn of time, that primordial epoch before life when there was only desolate land. Like looking through a telescope into the Milky Way and wondering if we're alone in the universe, it made me realize with the glaring clarity of desert light how scarce and delicate life is, how insignificant we are when compared with the forces of nature and the dimensions of space.

Were my group to board those two rafts a mile in the distance and depart, I would be as cut off from human contact as a person could be. In fifteen to thirty days' time, I would starve in a lonely death as I hiked the meanders back upriver to Moab, never again to see the sign or skin of another human. Yet beyond the paucity and the solitude of the surrounding desert, it was an exultant thought that peeled back the veneer of our self-important delusions. We are not grand because we are at the top of the food chain or because we can alter our environment—the environment will outlast us with its unfathomable forces and unyielding powers. But rather than be bound and defeated by our insignificance, we are bold because we exercise our will anyway, despite the ephemeral and delicate presence we have in this desert, on this planet, in this universe. I sat for another ten minutes, then, with my perspective as widened as the view from that bluff, I returned to camp and made extra-short work of dinner.

Riding down the road past the metal culvert that marks the dried-up source of the West Fork of Blue John Canyon, I pass through a signed intersection where a branch of the dirt road splits off toward Hanksville, a small town an hour to the west at the gateway to Capitol Reef National Park. Hanksville is the closest settlement to the Robbers Roost and the Maze District, and home to the nearest landline public telephone in the region. Just a half mile farther, I pass a slanting grassy plain that was an airstrip until whatever minor catastrophe forced whoever was flying there to head back to more tenable ground. It's an indication of how small planes and helicopters are typically the only efficient means of getting from here to there in this country. Some of the time, though, it's not financially worth leaving here to get there, even if you can fly. Better just to stay at home.

The Mormons gave their best efforts to transect this part of the country with road grades, but they, too, retreated to the established towns of Green River and Moab. Today most of those Mormon trails have been abandoned and replaced by still barely passable roads whose access by vehicle is, ironically, more sparse than it was by horse or wagon a hundred years ago. Last night I drove fifty-seven miles down the only dirt road in the eastern half of two counties to arrive at my embarkation point—it was two and a half hours of washboard driving during which I didn't pass a single light or a house. Frontier ranchers, rustlers, uranium miners, and oil drillers each left a mark on this land but have folded their hands in deference to the stacked deck of desert livelihood.

Those seekers of prosperity weren't the first to cross the threshold into this country, only to abandon the region as a barren wasteland: Progressive waves of ancient communities came into being and vanished over the ages in the area's canyon bottoms. Usually, it would be a significant drought or an incursion by hostile bands that made life in the high country and the deserts farther south seem more hospitable. But sometimes there are no defensible answers to explain the sudden evacuation of an entire culture from a particular place. Five thousand years ago, the people of Barrier Creek left their pictographs and petroglyphs at the Great Gallery and Alcove Gallery; then they disappeared. Since they left no written record, why they departed is both a mystery and a springboard for the imagination. Looking at their paintings and standing in their homes, gardens, and trash heaps, I feel connected to the aboriginal pioneers who inhabited these canyons so long ago.

As I grind my way out onto the open mesa, the wind slaps at my face, and I find myself already looking forward to the final hike through Horseshoe Canyon, where I will finish my tour. I can't wait to get out of this demeaning wind.

To judge from what I've seen on my ride, there are few significant differences in this area between Blue John Griffith's day and the present. The Bureau of Land Management (BLM) has graded the century-old horse trail and added scattered signposts, but even the ubiquitous fences that partition the rest of the West are noticeably absent. Perhaps it's the lack of barbed wire that makes this place feel so terrifically remote. I spend a lot of time in out-of-the-way areas—

two or three days a week in designated wildernesses, even through the winter—but most of them don't feel half as isolated as this back road. As I consider this, abruptly, my solitude changes to loneliness and seems somehow more tenacious. While the region's towns may have simmered since those raucous days when the Robbers Roost was earning its name, the outlying desert is still just as wild.

A mile past Burr Pass, my torturous ride into the thirty-mile-an-hour headwind finally comes to an end. I dismount and walk my bike over to a juniper tree and fasten a U-lock through the rear tire. I have little worry that anyone will tamper with my ride out here, but as my dad says, "There's no sense in tempting honest people." I drop the U-lock's keys into my left pocket and turn toward the main attraction, Blue John Canyon. I follow a deer path on an overland shortcut, listening to some of my favorite music on my CD player now that the wind isn't blowing so obnoxiously in my ears. After I've hiked through some dunes of pulverized red sandstone, I come to a sandy gully and see that I've found my way to the nascent canyon. "Good, I'm on the right route," I think, and then I notice two people walking out of view thirty yards downcanyon. I leap down the dune into the shallow wash, and once I'm around the dune's far corner, I spot the hikers, who look from this distance to be two young women.

"What are the odds?" I think, surprised to find anyone else this far out in the desert. Having been inside my head for three hours, and perhaps wanting to shake that feeling of loneliness picked up out on the road, I pause to take off my headphones, then spur myself to catch up. They're moving almost as quickly as I can manage without jogging, and it takes a minute before I can tell that I'm making any distance on them at all. I'd been fully expecting a solo descent in the Main Fork of Blue John Canyon, but meeting like-minded people in far-flung places is usually a fun addition to the experience for me, especially if they can keep a fast pace. In any case, I can hardly avoid them at this point. At another bend, they look back and see me but - don't wait up. Finally, I catch up with them but can't really pass them unless they stop, which they don't.

Realizing that we're going to be hiking together for a while, I figure I should initiate a conversation. "Howdy," I begin, "how's it goin'?" I'm not sure if they're open to meeting a stranger in the backcountry. They answer with a pair of unadorned hi's.

Hoping for something a little more engaging, I try again. "I - wasn't expecting to see anyone in the canyon today."

Even though it is a Saturday, this place is remote, and so obscure I couldn't even tell it was here from the Robbers Roost dirt access road, despite my map that definitively shows the canyon's presence.

"Yeah, you surprised us, sneaking up like that," the brown-haired woman replies, but then she smiles.

"Oh, sorry. I was listening to my headphones, kind of wrapped up in my thoughts," I explain. Returning the smile, I extend an introduction: "My name's Aron."

They relax noticeably and share their names—they are Megan, the brunette who spoke to me and who seems to be the more outgoing one of the pair, and Kristi. Megan's shoulder-length hair whirls attractively around her hazel eyes and rosy-cheeked face. She's wearing a blue zip-neck long-sleeved shirt and blue track pants and carries a blue backpack—if I had to guess, I'd say she likes the color blue. - Kristi's blond hair is pulled back in a ponytail that reveals the sunny freckles on her forehead and her deep grayish-blue eyes. Besides her clothes—a plain white short-sleeved T-shirt with blue shorts over black long underwear—I notice that Kristi has accessorized for the day, wearing small silver hoop earrings and dark sunglasses with faux tortoiseshell frames and a snakeskin-pattern retaining strap. Unusual to have earrings on in a canyon, but I'm hardly dressed to kill, so I skip issuing a fashion citation. Both women are in their midtwenties, and I learn in response to my first question that they both hail from Moab. I briefly work on memorizing their names, and which one is which, so I don't goof it up later.

Megan doesn't seem to mind joining me in conversation. She fires off a story about how she and Kristi overshot the Granary Spring

Trailhead and got lost in the desert for an hour before they found the start of the canyon. I say I think it is easier to navigate on a bike than in a vehicle because the landscape passes more slowly.

"Oh my God, if we'd been on bikes, we'd have dried up in the wind before we got here," Megan cracks, and it serves to break the ice.

The canyon is still just a shallow arroyo—a dry sandy gulch— nestled between two sets of thirty-foot-tall sand dunes. Before the terrain becomes more technical, we ease into a friendly exchange, chatting about our lives in the polarized resort communities of Moab and Aspen. I learn that they, like me, work in the outdoor recreation industry. As logistics managers for Outward Bound, they outfit expeditions from the company's supply warehouse in Moab. I tell them I'm a sales and shop worker at the Ute Mountaineer, an outdoor gear store in Aspen.

There's a mostly unspoken acknowledgment among the voluntarily impoverished dues-payers of our towns that it's better to be fiscally poor yet rich in experience—living the dream—than to be traditionally wealthy but live separate from one's passions. There is an undercurrent of attitude among the high-country proletariat that to buy one's way back into the experience of resort life is a shameful scarlet letter. Better to be the penniless local than the affluent visitor. (But the locals depend on the visitors to survive, so the implied elitism is less than fair.) We understand our mutual membership on the same side of the equation.

The same is true of our environmental sensibilities. We each hold Edward Abbey—combative conservationist; anti-development, antitourism, and anti-mining essayist; beer swiller; militant ecoterrorist; lover of the wilderness and women (preferably wilderness women, though those are unfortunately rare)—as a sage of environmentalism. Remembering an oddball quote of his, I say how he delighted in taking things to the extreme. "I think there was an essay where he wrote, 'Of course, we're all hypocrites. The only true act of an environmentalist would be to shoot himself in the head. Otherwise he's still contaminating the place by his mere presence.' That's a para-phrase, but it's effectively what he said."

"That's kind of morbid," Megan replies, putting on a face of sham guilt for not shooting herself.

Moving on from Ed Abbey, we discover that we're each experienced in slot canyoneering. Kristi asks me what my favorite slot canyon is, and without hesitation, I recount my experience in Neon Canyon, an unofficially named branch of the Escalante River system in south-central Utah. I wax poetic about its five rappels, the keeper pothole (a deep, steep, and smooth-walled hole in the canyon floor that will "keep" you there if you don't have a partner to boost out first), and the Golden Cathedral: a bizarre rappel through a sand-stone tunnel in the roof of an alcove the size of Saint Peter's that leaves you hanging free from the walls for almost sixty feet until you land in a large pool of water and then swim to the shore.

"It's phenomenal, you have to go," I conclude.

Kristi tells me about her favorite slot, which is just across the dirt road from the Granary Spring Trailhead. It's one of the upper forks of the Robbers Roost drainage, nicknamed "Mindbender" by her Out-ward Bound friends. She describes a passage in that slot where you traverse the canyon wedged between the walls some fifteen feet off the ground, the V-shaped slot tapering to a few inches wide at your feet, and even narrower below that.

I mentally add that one to my to-do list.

A few minutes later, just before noon, we arrive at a steep, smooth slide down a rock face, which heralds the first slot and the deeper, narrower sections that have drawn us to Blue John Canyon. I slide fif-teen feet down the rock embankment, skidding on the soles of my sneakers, leaving a pair of black streaks on the pink sandstone and spilling forward into the sand at the bottom of the wall. Hearing the noise as she comes around the corner, Kristi sees me squatting in the dirt and assumes I have fallen. "Oh my gosh, are you OK?" she asks.

"Oh yeah, I'm fine. I did that on purpose," I tell her in earnest, as the skid truly had been intentional. I catch her glance, a good-natured shot that tells me she believes me but thinks I'm silly for not finding an easier way down. I look around and, seeing an obviously less risky access route that would have avoided the slide, I feel slightly foolish.

Five minutes later, we come to the first section of difficult down-climbing, a steep descent where it's best to turn in and face the rock, reversing moves that one would usually use for climbing up. I go down first, then swing my backpack around to retrieve my video camera and tape Megan and Kristi. Kristi pulls a fifteen-foot-long piece of red webbing out of her matching red climber's backpack and threads it through a metal ring that previous canyoneering parties have suspended on another loop of webbing tied around a rock. The rock is securely wedged in a depression behind the lip of the drop-off, and the webbing system easily holds a person's weight. Grasping the webbing, Megan backs herself down over the drop-off. She has to maneuver around an overhanging chockstone—a boulder suspended between the walls of the canyon—that blocks an otherwise easy scramble down into the deepening slot. Once Megan is down, Kristi follows skittishly, as she doesn't completely trust the webbing system. After she's down, I climb back up to retrieve Kristi's webbing.

We walk thirty feet and come to another drop-off. The walls are much closer now, only two to three feet apart. Megan throws her backpack over the drop before shimmying down between the walls, while Kristi takes a few pictures. I watch Megan descend and help her by pointing out the best handholds and footholds. When Megan is at the bottom of the drop, she discovers that her pack is soaking wet. It turns out her hydration-system hose lost its nozzle when she tossed the pack over the ledge, and was leaking water into the sand. She quickly finds the blue plastic nozzle and stops the water's hemor-rhage, saving her from having to return to the trailhead. While it's not a big deal that her pack is wet, she has lost precious water. I descend last, my pack on my back and my delicate cameras causing me to get stuck briefly between the walls at several constrictions. Squirming my way over small chockstones, I stem my body across the gap between the walls to follow the plunging canyon floor. There is a log wedged in the slot at one point, and I use it like a ladder on a smooth section of the skinny-people-only descent.

While the day up above the rim rock is getting warmer, the air down in the canyon becomes cooler as we enter a four-hundred-yard-long section of the canyon where the walls are over two hundred feet high but only fifteen feet apart. Sunlight never reaches the bottom of this slot. We pick up some raven's feathers, stick them in our hats, and pause for photographs.

A half mile later, several side canyons drop into the Main Fork where we are walking, as the walls open up to reveal the sky and a more distant perspective of the cliffs downcanyon. In the sun once again, we stop to share two of my melting chocolate bars. Kristi offers some to Megan, who declines, and Kristi says, "I really can't eat all this chocolate by myself . . . Never mind, yes I can," and we laugh together.

We come to an uncertain consensus that this last significant tributary off to the left of the Main Fork is the West Fork, which means - it's the turnoff for Kristi and Megan to finish their circuit back to the main dirt road about four miles away. We get hung up on saying our goodbyes when Kristi suggests, "Come on, Aron, hike out with us— we'll go get your truck, hang out, and have a beer."

I'm dedicated to finishing my planned tour, so I counter, "How about this?—you guys have your harnesses, I have a rope—you should come with me down through the lower slot and do the Big Drop rappel. We can hike out . . . see the Great Gallery . . . I'll give you a lift back to your truck."

"How far is it?" asks Megan.

"Another eight miles or so, I think."

"What? You won't get out before dark! Come on, come with us."

"I really have my heart set on doing the rappel and seeing the petroglyphs. But I'll come around to the Granary Spring Trailhead to meet you when I'm done."

This they agree to. We sit and look at the maps one more time, confirming our location on the Blue John map from the canyoneering guidebook we'd each used to find this remote slot. In my newest copy of Michael Kelsey's *Canyon Hiking Guide to the Colorado Plateau,* there are over a hundred canyons described, each with its own hand-sketched map. Drawn by Kelsey from his personal experience in each canyon, the technical maps and route descriptions are works of art. With cross sections of tricky slots, identifications of hard-to-find petroglyphs and artifact sites, and details of required rappelling equipment, anchor points, and deep-water holes, the book offers enough information for you to sleuth your way through a decision or figure out where you are, but not a single item extra. After we put away the maps, we stand up, and Kristi says, "That picture in the book makes those paintings look like ghosts; they're kind of spooky. What kind of energy do you think you'll find at the Gallery?"

"Hmm." I pause to consider her question. "I dunno. I've felt pretty connected looking at petroglyphs before; it's a good feeling. I'm excited to see them."

Megan double-checks: "You're sure you won't come with us?" But I'm as set on my choice as they are on theirs.

A few minutes before they go, we solidify our plan to meet up around dusk at their campsite back by Granary Spring. There's going to be a Scooby party tonight of some friends of friends of mine from Aspen, about fifty miles away, just north of Goblin Valley State Park, and we agree to caravan there together. Most groups use paper plates as improvised road signs to an out-of-the-way rendezvous site; my friends have a large stuffed Scooby-Doo to designate the turnoff. After what I'll have completed—an all-day adventure tour, fifteen miles of mountain biking and fifteen miles of canyoneering—I'll have earned a little relaxation and hopefully a cold beer. It will be good to see these two lovely ladies of the desert again so soon, too. We seal the deal by adding a short hike of Little Wild Horse Canyon, a nontechnical slot in Goblin Valley, to the plan for tomorrow morning. New friends, we part ways at two P.M. with smiles and waves.

*   *   *

Alone once again, I walk downcanyon, continuing on my itinerary. Along the way, I think through the remainder of my vacation time. Now that I have a solid plan for Sunday to hike Little Wild Horse, I speculate that I'll get back to Moab around seven o'clock that evening. I'll have just enough time to get my gear and food and water prepared for my bike ride on the White Rim in Canyonlands National Park and catch a nap before starting around midnight. By doing the first thirty miles of the White Rim by headlamp and starlight, I should be able to finish the 108-mile ride late Monday afternoon, in time for a house party my roommates and I have planned for Monday night.

Without warning, my feet stumble in a pile of loose pebbles deposited from the last flash flood, and I swing my arms out to catch my balance. Instantly, my full attention returns to Blue John Canyon.

My raven feather is still tucked in the band at the back of my blue ball cap, and I can see its shadow in the sand. It looks goofy—I stop in the open canyon and take a picture of my shadow with the feather. Without breaking stride, I unclip my pack's waist belt and chest strap, flip my pack around to my chest, and root around inside the mesh outer pouch until I can push play on my portable CD player. Audience cheers give way to a slow lilting guitar intro and then soft lyrics:

How is it I never see / The waves that bring her words to me?

I'm listening to the second set of the February 15 Phish show that I attended three months ago in Las Vegas. After a moment of absorbing the music, I smile. I'm glad at the world: This is my happy place. Great tunes, solitude, wilderness, empty mind. The invigoration of hiking alone, moving at my own pace, clears out my thoughts. A sense of mindless happiness—not being happy because of something in particular but being happy because I'm happy—is one of the reasons why I go to the lengths I do to have some focused time to myself. Feeling aligned in my body and head rejuvenates my spirit. Sometimes, when I get high-minded about it, I think solo hiking is my own method of attaining a transcendental state, a kind of walking meditation. I don't get there when I sit and try to meditate, om-style; it happens only when I'm walking by myself. Unfortunately, as soon as I recognize that I'm having such a moment, the feeling ebbs, thoughts return, the transcendence evaporates. I work hard to set myself up for that fleeting sense of being wholly pleased, but my judgments about the feeling displace the feeling itself. Although it's ephemeral, the general well-being that accompanies such a moment will boost my temperament for hours or even days.

It's two-fifteen P.M., and in the balance of sunshine and thin stratus layers, the day's weather is poised at equilibrium. In the open section of the canyon, the temperature is about fifteen degrees warmer than it was at the bottom of the deep slot. There are a few full-fledged cumulus clouds listing like lost clipper ships, but no shade. I come upon a wide yellow arroyo entering from the right, and I check my map. This is the East Fork. Kristi and Megan definitely chose the correct fork to return. The choice seemed obvious then, but even obvious decisions need to be double-checked in the backcountry. Navigating in a deep canyon can be deceptively complex. Occasionally, I'm tempted to think that there's nothing to it; I just keep going straight. With three-hundred-foot walls fencing me in five feet to either side, I can't really lose the bottom of the canyon, like I can lose the route on a mountainside. But I've gotten disoriented before.

A forty-mile solo trip in Paria Canyon comes to mind. There was a stretch about a third of the way into the canyon when I completely lost track of where I was. I hiked roughly five miles downstream before I found a landmark that indicated an exact position on my map. This became critical, because I needed to find the exit trail before night fell. When you're looking for an entry/exit, sometimes being fifty yards off-route can hide the way. So now I pay close attention to my map. When I'm navigating well in the canyons, I check my map even more frequently than when I'm on a mountain, maybe every two hundred yards.

If we could see the many waves / That float through clouds and sunken caves / She'd sense at least the words that sought her / On the wind and underwater.

The song blends into something atonally sweet but unattended as I pass another shallow wash coming in from the right. On the map, the arroyo seems to correspond with what Kelsey has named Little East Fork, dropping from a higher tableland he labels Goat Park.

The elevated benches and rolling juniper-covered highlands of Goat Park to my right are up above the 170-million-year-old Carmel Formation, a sloping capstone of interlayered purple, red, and brown siltstone, limestone, and shale strata deposit. The capstone is more resistant to erosion than the older wind-deposited Navajo sandstone that forms the smooth ruddy-hued cliffs of the scenic slot canyons. In places, this differential erosion creates hoodoos, freestanding rock towers and tepees, and tall dunes of colored stone that dot the upper reaches of the canyon's cliffs. The juxtaposed textures, colors, and shapes of the Carmel and Navajo rock layers reflect the polarized landscapes that formed them—the early Jurassic Period sea and the late Triassic Period desert. Settling out from a great sea, the Carmel Formation sediments look like solidified mud that dried up last month. On the other hand, cross-bedded patterns in the Navajo sandstone reveal its ancestry from shifting sand dunes: One fifteen-foot-high band in the cliffs displays inlaid lines slanting to the right; the next band's layers slant to the left; and above that, the stratification lines lie perfectly horizontal. Over the eons, the dunes repeatedly changed shape under the prevailing force of wind blowing across an ancient Sahara-like desert, devoid of vegetation. Depending if the sandstone shapes left behind are beat upon more by wind or by water, they look like either rough-hewn sand domes or polished cliffs. All this beauty keeps a smile on my face.

I estimate that the distance I have left to cover is about a half mile until I reach the narrow slot above the sixty-five-foot-high Big Drop rappel. This two-hundred-yard-long slot marks the midpoint of my descent in Blue John and Horseshoe canyons. I've come about seven miles from where I left my bike, and I have about eight miles to get to my truck. Once I reach the narrow slot, there will be some short sections of downclimbing, maneuvering over and under a series of chockstones, then 125 yards of very tight slot, some of it only eighteen inches wide, to get to the platform where two bolt-and-hanger sets provide an anchor for the rappel. Rappel bolts are typically three-inch-long, three-eighths-inch-diameter expansion bolts set in either hand- or cordless-drilled holes that secure a disc of flat metal bent into an L-shape called a hanger. The hangers have two holes, one in the flush section for the bolt to hold it to the wall, and one in the bent lip that can be clipped by a carabiner, a screw-gate chain link, or threaded with a length of webbing. When the bolt is properly installed in solid rock, you can load several thousand pounds on it without concern, but in slot canyons, the rock often rots around the bolt shaft due to frequent flooding events. It's reassuring when there are two bolt/hangers that can be used in tandem, in case one unexpectedly fails.

I have my climbing rope, harness, belay device, and webbing with me for the rappel, and I have my headlamp along to search crevices for snakes before putting my hands in them. I'm already thinking ahead to the hike after the rappel, especially the Great Gallery. - Kelsey's guidebook calls it the best pictograph panel on the Colorado Plateau—and the Barrier Creek style, "the style against which all others are compared"—which has piqued my interest since I read about it on my drive to Utah two days ago.

Gold in my hair / In a country pool / Standing and waving / The rain, wind on the runway.

I'm caught up in another song and barely notice the canyon walls closing in, forming the beginning of the slot, this one more like a back alley between a couple of self-storage warehouses than the skyscrapers of the upper slot. An anthemic guitar riff accompanies me as my stride turns into more of a strut and I pump my right fist in the air. Then I reach the first drop-off in the floor of the canyon, a dryfall. Were there water in the canyon, this would be a waterfall. A harder layer embedded in the sandstone has proved more resistant to erosion by the floods, and this dark conglomerate forms the lip at the drop. From the ledge where I'm standing to the continuing canyon bottom is about ten feet. About twenty feet downcanyon, an S-shaped log is jammed between the walls. It would provide an easier descent path if I could get to it, but it seems more difficult to access via the shallow and sloping conglomerate shelf on my right than by the ten-foot drop to the canyon floor over the lip in front of me.

I use a few good in-cut handholds on my left to lower myself around the overhang, gripping the sandstone huecos—water-hollowed holes in the wall—like jug handles. At full extension, my legs dangle two, maybe three feet off the floor. I let go and drop off the dryfall, landing in a sandy concavity carved deeper than the surrounding floor by the impact of floodwaters dropping over the lip. My feet hit the dried mud, which cracks and crumbles like plaster; I sink up to my shoe tops in the powdery platelets. It's not a difficult maneuver, but I couldn't climb directly up the drop-off from below. I'm committed to my course; there's no going back.

A new song starts up in my headphones as I walk under the S-log, and the canyon deepens to thirty feet below the tops of the sand domes overhead.

I fear I never told you the story of the ghost / That I once knew and talked to, of whom I never boast.

The pale sky is still visible above this ten-foot-wide gash in the - earth's surface. In my path are two van-sized chockstones a hundred feet apart. One is just a foot off the sandy canyon bottom; the next sits square on the corridor floor. I scramble over both blockages. The canyon narrows to four feet wide, with undulating and twisting walls that lead me to the left then back to the right, through a straight passage, then left and right again, all the while deepening.

Colossal flood action has scooped out beach balls of rock from the sandstone walls and wedged logs thirty feet overhead. Slot canyons are the last place you want to be during a desert thunderstorm. The sky directly above the canyon might be clear, but a cloudburst in the watershed even ten or twenty miles away can maul and drown unwary canyoneers. In a flood, the rain falls faster than the ground can absorb it. In the eastern United States, it might take the ground days or weeks to reach saturation and for rivers to flood after many inches or even feet of rain. In the desert, the hard sunbaked earth acts like fired clay-tile shingles, and a flood can start from a fraction of an inch of rain that might come in five minutes from a single storm cloud. Chased off the impermeable hardscrabble, the downpour creates a surging deluge. Runoff gathers from converging drainages and quickly becomes a foot of water in a forty-foot-wide section of the canyon. That same amount of water becomes a catastrophic torrent in a confined space. Where the walls narrow to four feet, the flood turns into a ten-foot-high chaos of churning mud and debris that moves boulders, sculpts canyons, lodges drift material in constrictions, and kills anything that can't climb to safety.

In this meandering section of the narrow canyon, silt residue from the most recent flood coats the walls to a height of twelve feet above the beachlike floor, and decades of scour marks overlay the rosy and purplish striations of exposed rock. The undulating walls distort the flat lines of the strata and grab my attention in one spot where the opposing walls dive in front of each other at a double-hairpin meander. I stop to take a few photographs. I note that the time stamp is a minute slow compared to my watch: The digital camera's screen says it is 2:41 P.M., Saturday afternoon, April 26, 2003.

I bob my head to the music as I walk another twenty yards and come to a series of three chockstones and scramble over them. Then I see another five chockstones, all the size of large refrigerators, wedged at varying heights off the canyon floor like a boulder gauntlet. It's unusual to see so many chockstones lined up in such evenly spaced proximity. With two feet of clearance under the first suspended chockstone, I have to crawl under it on my belly—the only time I've ever had to get this low in a canyon—but there is no alternative. The next chockstone is wedged a little higher off the ground. I stand and brush myself off, then squat and duck to pass under. A crawl on all fours and two more squat-and-duck maneuvers, and I've passed the remaining chockstones. The defile is over sixty feet deep at this point, having dropped fifty feet below the sand domes in two hundred feet of linear distance.

I come to another drop-off. This one is maybe eleven or twelve feet high, a foot higher and of a different geometry than the overhang I descended ten minutes ago. Another refrigerator chockstone is wedged between the walls, ten feet downstream from and at the same height as the ledge. It gives the space below the drop-off the claustrophobic feel of a short tunnel. Instead of the walls widening after the drop-off, or opening into a bowl at the bottom of the canyon, here the slot narrows to a consistent three feet across at the lip of the drop-off and continues at that width for fifty feet down the canyon. Sometimes in narrow passages like this one, it's possible for me to stem my body across the slot, with my feet and back pushing out in opposite directions against the walls. Controlling this counterpressure by switching my hands and feet on the opposing walls, I can move up or down the shoulder-width crevice fairly easily as long as the friction contact stays solid between the walls and my hands, feet, and back. This technique is known as stemming or chimneying; you can imagine using it to climb up the inside of a chimney.

Just below the ledge where I'm standing is a chockstone the size of a large bus tire, stuck fast in the channel between the walls, a few feet out from the lip. If I can step onto it, then I'll have a nine-foot height to descend, less than that of the first overhang. I'll dangle off the chockstone, then take a short fall onto the rounded rocks piled on the canyon floor. Stemming across the canyon at the lip of the drop-off, with one foot and one hand on each of the walls, I traverse out to the chockstone. I press my back against the south wall and lock my left knee, which pushes my foot tight against the north wall. With my right foot, I kick at the boulder to test how stuck it is. It's jammed tightly enough to hold my weight. I lower myself from the chimney-ing position and step onto the chockstone. It supports me but teeters slightly. After confirming that I don't want to chimney down from the chockstone's height, I squat and grip the rear of the lodged boul-der, turning to face back upcanyon. Sliding my belly over the front edge, I can lower myself and hang from my fully extended arms, akin to climbing down from the roof of a house.

As I dangle, I feel the stone respond to my adjusting grip with a scraping quake as my body's weight applies enough torque to disturb it from its position. Instantly, I know this is trouble, and instinctively, I let go of the rotating boulder to land on the round rocks below. When I look up, the backlit chockstone falling toward my head con-sumes the sky. Fear shoots my hands over my head. I can't move back-ward or I'll fall over a small ledge. My only hope is to push off the falling rock and get my head out of its way.

The next three seconds play out at a tenth of their normal speed. Time dilates, as if I'm dreaming, and my reactions decelerate. In slow motion: The rock smashes my left hand against the south wall; my eyes register the collision, and I yank my left arm back as the rock ric-ochets; the boulder then crushes my right hand and ensnares my right arm at the wrist, palm in, thumb up, fingers extended; the rock slides another foot down the wall with my arm in tow, tearing the skin off the lateral side of my forearm. Then silence.

My disbelief paralyzes me temporarily as I stare at the sight of my arm vanishing into an implausibly small gap between the fallen boul-der and the canyon wall. Within moments, my nervous system's pain response overcomes the initial shock. Good Christ, my hand. The flaring agony throws me into a panic. I grimace and growl a sharp "Fuck!" My mind commands my body, "Get your hand out of there!" I yank my arm three times in a naive attempt to pull it out. But I'm stuck.

Anxiety has my brain tweaking; searing-hot pain shoots from my wrist up my arm. I'm frantic, and I cry out, "Oh shit, oh shit, oh shit!" My desperate brain conjures up a probably apocryphal story in which an adrenaline-stoked mom lifts an overturned car to free her baby. I'd give it even odds that it's made up, but I do know for certain that *right now,* while my body's chemicals are raging at full flood, is the best chance I'll have to free myself with brute force. I shove against the large boulder, heaving against it, pushing with my left hand, lifting with my knees pressed under the rock. I get good leverage with the aid of a twelve-inch shelf in front of my feet. Standing on that, I brace my thighs under the boulder and thrust upward repeatedly, grunting, "Come on . . . move!" Nothing.

I rest, and then I surge again against the rock. Again nothing. I replant my feet. Feeling around for a better grip on the bottom of the chockstone, I reposition my upturned left hand on a handle of rock, take a deep breath, and slam into the boulder, harder than any of my previous attempts. "Yeearrgg . . . unnnhhh," the exertion forces the air from my lungs, all but masking the quiet, hollow sound of the boulder tottering. The stone's movement is imperceptible; all I get is a spike in the already extravagant pain, and I gasp, "Ow! Fuck!"

I've shifted the boulder a fraction of an inch, and it's settled onto my wrist a bit more. This thing weighs a lot more than I do—it's a testament to how amped I am that I moved it at all—and now all I want is to move it back. I get into position again, pulling with my left hand on top of the stone, and budge the rock back ever so slightly, reversing what I just did. The pain eases a little. In the process, I've lacerated and bruised the skin over my left quadriceps above the knee. I'm sweating hard. With my left hand, I lift my right shirtsleeve off my shoulder and wipe my forehead. My chest heaves. I need a drink, but when I suck on my hydration-system hose, I find my water reservoir is empty.

I have a liter of water in a Lexan bottle in my backpack, but it takes me a few seconds to realize I won't be able to sling my pack off my right arm. I remove my camera from my neck and put it on the boulder. Once I have my left arm free of the pack strap, I expand the right strap, tuck my head inside the loop, and pull the strap over my left shoulder so it encompasses my torso. The weight of the rappelling equipment, video camera, and water bottle tugs the pack down to my feet, and then I step out of the strap loop. Extracting the dark gray water bottle from the bottom of my pack, I unscrew the top, and before I realize the significance of what I'm doing, I gulp three large mouthfuls of water and halt to pant for breath. Then it hits me: In five seconds, I've guzzled a third of my entire remaining water supply.

"Oh, damn, dude, cap that and put it away. No more water." I screw down the lid tight, drop the bottle into the pack resting at my knees, and take three deep breaths.

"OK, time to relax. The adrenaline's not going to get you out of here. Let's look this over, see what we got." Amazingly, it's been half an hour since the accident. The decision to get objective with my situation and stop rushing from one brutish attempt to the next allows my energy to settle down. This isn't going to be over quickly, so I need to start thinking. To do that, I need to be calm.

The first thing I decide to do is examine the area where the boulder has my wrist pinned. Gravity and friction have wedged the chockstone, now suspended about four feet above the canyon floor, into a new set of constriction points. At three spots, the opposing walls secure the rock. On the downcanyon side of the boulder, my hand and wrist form a fourth support where they are caught in the grip of this horrific handshake. I think, "My hand isn't just stuck in there, it's actually holding this boulder off the wall. Oh, man, I'm fucked."

I reach my left fingers down to my right hand where it is visible along the north wall of the canyon. Poking down into the small gap above the catch point, I touch my thumb, which is already a sickly gray color. It's cocked sideways in the space and looks terribly unnatural. I straighten my thumb with the fore and middle fingers of my left hand. There is no feeling in any part of my right hand at all. I accept this with a sense of detachment, as if I'm diagnosing someone - else's problem. This clinical objectivity calms me. Without sensation, it doesn't seem as much my hand—if it were my hand, I could feel it when I touched it. The farthest part of my arm I can feel is my wrist, where the boulder is pinning it. Judging by appearances, the lack of any bone-splitting noises during the accident, and how it all feels to my left hand, I probably don't have any broken bones. From the nature of the accident, though, there is very likely substantial soft-tissue damage at the least, and for all I know, something could be broken in the middle of my hand. Either way, not good.

Investigating the underside of the boulder, I can touch the little finger on my right hand and feel its position with my left hand. It's twisted up inside my palm, in a partial fist; my muscles seem to be in a state of forced contraction. I can't relax my hand or extend any of my fingers. I try to wiggle each one independently. There's no movement whatsoever. I try flexing my muscles to make a tighter fist, but there isn't even the slightest twitch. Double that on the "not good."

Nearer to my chest along the wall, I can't quite get my left forefinger up to where it can touch my right wrist from below. My little finger can barely slide into the space between the boulder and the wall, brushing my arm at a spot on the lateral side of the knob of my wrist. I withdraw from prodding around and look at my left wrist and estimate that it is three inches thick. My right wrist is being compressed to one sixth its normal thickness. If not for the bones, the weight of the boulder would squeeze my arm flat. Judging from the paleness of my right hand, and the fact that there's no blood loss from a traumatic injury, it's probable that I have no circulation getting to or from my trapped hand. The lack of sensation or movement probably means my nerves are damaged. Whatever injuries are present, my right hand seems to be entirely isolated from my body's circulatory, nervous, and motor-control systems. That's three-for-three on the "not good" checklist.

An inner voice explodes into expletives at the prognosis: "Shit! How did this happen? What the fuck? How the *fuck* did you get your hand trapped by a *fucking* boulder? Look at this! Your hand is *crushed;* it's *dying,* man, and there's nothing you can do about it. If you don't get blood flow back within a couple hours, it's gone."

"No, it's not. I'll get out. I mean, if I don't get out, I'm going to lose more than my hand. I have to get out!" Reason answers, but reason is not in control here; the adrenaline isn't wholly dissipated yet.

"You're stuck, fucked, and out of luck." I don't like to be pessimistic, but the devil on my left shoulder knows better than to keep up any pretenses. The little rhyming bastard is right: My outlook is bleak. But it's way too early to dwell on despair.

"No! Shut up, that's not helpful." Better to keep investigating, see what I learn. Whoever is arguing from my right shoulder makes a good point—it's not my hand I need to worry about. There's a bigger issue. Stressing over the superficial problem will only consume my resources. Right now, I need to focus on gathering more information. With that decision made, a feeling of acceptance settles over me.

Looking up to my right, a foot above the top of the boulder on the north wall, I see tiny wads of my flesh, pieces of my arm hair, and stains of my blood streaked on the sandstone. In dragging my arm down the wall, the boulder and smooth Navajo sandstone acted like a grater, scraping off my skin's outer layers in thin strips. Peering at the bottom of my arm, I check for more blood, but there is none, not even a lone drip.

As I bring my head back up, I bump the bill of my hat, and my sunglasses fall onto my pack at my feet. Picking them up, I see they've gotten scratched at some point since I had them on in the open sunny part of the canyon an hour ago. "Not like that's important," I tell myself, but still I take care to put them on top of the boulder, off to the left side.

My headphones have gotten knocked off my ears, but now, and in my calm, I hear the crowd on the live CD cheering. The noise evaporates as the disc winds to a stop, and the sudden silence reinforces my situation. I am irreversibly trapped, standing in the dimly lit bottom of a canyon, unable to move more than a few inches up or down or side to side. Compounding my physical circumstances, no one who will suspect I am missing knows where I am. I violated the prime directive of wilderness travel in failing to leave a detailed trip plan with a responsible person. Still eight miles from my truck, I am alone in an infrequently visited place with no means to contact anyone outside the fifty-yard throw of my voice.

Alone in a situation that could very shortly prove to be fatal.

My watch says it's 3:28 P.M., nearly forty-five minutes since the boulder fell on my arm. I take an inventory of what I have with me, emptying my pack with my left hand, item by item. In my plastic grocery bag, beside the chocolate-bar wrappers and bakery bag with the crumbs of the chocolate muffin, I have two small bean burritos, about five hundred calories total. In the outside mesh pouch, I have my CD player, CDs, extra AA batteries, mini digital video camcorder. My multi-use tool and three-LED headlamp are also in the pouch. I sort through the electronics and pull out the knife tool and the headlamp, setting them on top of the boulder next to my sunglasses.

I put my camera into the cloth goggles bag I'd been using to keep the grit out of the components, and drop it in the mesh pouch with the other gadgets. Except for the Lexan water bottle and my empty hydration pack, the remaining contents of my pack are my green and yellow climbing rope in its black zippered rope bag; my rock-climbing harness; and the small wad of rappelling equipment I'd brought to use at the Big Drop rappel.

My next thought is to brainstorm every means possible that could get me out of here. The easy ideas come first, although some of them are more wishful than realistic. Maybe other canyoneers will traverse this section of slot and find me—they might be able to help free me, or even give me clothes, food, and water and go for help. Maybe Megan and Kristi will think something's wrong when I don't meet them like I said I would, and they'll go look for my truck or notify the Park Service. Maybe my Aspen friends Brad and Leah Yule will do the same when I don't show up for the big Scooby-Doo desert party tonight. But they don't know for sure that I'm coming, because I -

didn't call them when I was in Moab yesterday. Tomorrow, Sunday, is still the weekend—maybe someone will come this way on his or her day off. If I'm not out by Monday night, my roommates will miss me for sure; they might even notify the police. Or my manager at the shop where I work will call my mom when I don't turn up on Tuesday. It might take people a few days to figure out where I went, but there could be a search out by Wednesday, and if they find my truck, it wouldn't be long after that.

The major preclusion to rescue is that I don't have enough water to wait that long—twenty-two ounces total after my chug a few minutes ago. The average survival time in the desert without water is between two and three days, sometimes as little as a day if you're exerting yourself in 100-degree heat. I figure I'll make it to Monday night. If a rescue comes along before then, it will be an unlikely chance encounter with a fellow canyoneer, not an organized effort of trained personnel. In other words, rescue seems about as probable as winning the lottery.

By nature I'm an impatient person; when a situation requires me to wait, I need to be doing something to make the time pass. Call me a child of the instant-gratification generation, or maybe my imagination was stunted from too much television, but I don't sit still well. In my present situation, that's probably a good thing. I have a problem to solve—I have to get out of here—so I put my mind to what I can do to escape my entrapment. Eliminating a couple ideas that are too dumb (like cracking open my extra AA batteries on the boulder and hoping the acid erodes the chockstone but doesn't eat into my arm), I organize my other options in order of preference: Excavate the rock around my hand with my multi-tool; rig ropes and an anchor above me to lift the boulder off my hand; or amputate my arm. Quickly, each option seems impossible: I don't have the tools to remove enough rock to free my hand; I don't have the hauling power needed, even with a pulley system, to move the boulder; and even though it seems my best option, I don't have the tools, know-how, or emotional gumption to sever my own arm.

Perhaps more as a tactic to delay thinking about self-amputation and less as a truly productive effort, I decide to work on an easier option—chipping away the rock to free my arm. Drawing my multi-tool from its perch above the boulder, I extract the longer of the two blades. I'm suddenly very glad I decided to add it to my supplies.

Picking an easily accessed spot on the boulder in front of my chest and a few inches from my right wrist, I scratch the tip across the boulder in a four-inch line. If I can remove the stone below this line and back toward my fingers about six inches, I will be able to free my hand. But with the demarcated part of the stone being three inches thick in places, I'll have to remove about seventy cubic inches of the boulder. It's a lot of rock, and I know the sandstone is going to make the chipping tedious work.

My first attempt to saw down into the boulder along the faint line I've marked barely scuffs the rock. I try again, pressing harder this time, but the backside of the knife handle indents my forefinger more readily than the cutting edge scores the rock. Changing my grip on the tool, I hold it like Norman Bates and stab at the rock in the same spot. There is no noticeable effect. I try to identify a fracture line, a weakness in the boulder, something I can exploit, but there is nothing. Even if I focus on a small crystalline protuberance in the rock above my wrist where I might be able to break out a chunk, it will be many hours of work before I can remove even that tiny mineralized section.

I hit the rock with the butt of my hand, still holding the knife, and ask out loud in an exasperated whine, "Why is this sandstone so hard?" It seems like every time I've ever gone climbing on a sandstone formation, I break off a handhold, yet I can't put a dent in this boulder. I settle on a quick experiment to test the relative hardness of the wall. Holding my knife like a pen, I easily etch a capital "G" on the tableau of the canyon's north side, about a foot above my right arm. Slowly, I make a few more printed letters in lowercase, "e-o-l-o-g-i-c," and then pause to measure the space with my eyes and lay out the rest of the letters in my mind. Within five minutes, I scratch out three more words, then touch them up, until I can read the phrase "Geologic Time Includes Now."

I have quoted mountaineer and *Colorado Thirteeners* guidebook author Gerry Roach, from his "Classic Commandments of Mountaineering." It's an elegant way of saying "Watch out for falling rocks." As most people who live on fault lines are well aware, the processes shaping and forming the earth's crust are current events. Fault lines slip, long-dormant volcanoes explode, mountainsides turn to mud and slide.

I remember trekking with my friend Mark Van Eeckhout through a field of boulders and coming upon a house-sized rock. We said to each other, "Wow, look at the size of this one!" We'd imagined what a spectacle it would be to see something that size separate from a cliff a thousand feet above and fall, spawning rock slides right and left, crashing with apocalyptic force.

But cliffs don't just form in the middle of the night when no one's watching. I've seen riverbanks collapse, glaciers calve and let loose tremendous icefalls, and boulders plummet from their lofty perches. Gerry Roach's commandment reminds climbers that rocks fall all the time. Sometimes they spontaneously break away; sometimes they get knocked loose. Sometimes they fall when you're so far off you can't even see them, you only hear a clatter; sometimes they fall when you or your partners are climbing below them. Sometimes one will pull loose even though you barely touched it; and sometimes one will fall after you've already stood on top of it . . . when you're using it for a handhold and it shifts . . . when your head is right in the way and you put your hands up to save yourself . . .

It's rare. But it happens. Has happened.

This chockstone pinning my wrist was stuck for a long time before I came along. And then it not only fell on me, it trapped my arm. I'm baffled. It was like the boulder had been put there, set like a - hunter's trap, waiting for me. This was supposed to be an easy trip, few risks, well within my abilities. I'm not out trying to climb a high peak in the middle of winter, I'm just taking a vacation. Why didn't the last person who came along dislodge the chockstone? They - would've had to make the same maneuvers I did to traverse the canyon. What kind of luck do I have that this boulder, wedged here for untold ages, freed itself at the split second that my hands were in the way? Despite obvious evidence to the contrary, it seems astronomically infeasible that this happened.

I mean, what are the odds?

TWO

Beginnings

Mountains are the means, the man is the end. The goal is not to reach the tops of mountains, but to improve the man.

—WALTER BONATTI, *Italian climber*

IN AUGUST 1987, when I was twelve, my family was preparing to move to Colorado from Indianapolis, Indiana, to follow my dad's career. While visiting with a friend of our family in rural eastern Ohio that July, I found an encyclopedic book about the fifty states and looked up my future home. At the time, I had never been over ten miles west of the Mississippi River in my life. Facing this imminent displacement to the West, I wanted to find out what was in store for me. I admit I was prejudiced—I had preconceived images of horseback riders, skiers, and so much snow that it covered the state year-round.

What I found in the book not only reinforced those notions, it terrified me. There was a photo of Pikes Peak, the view from which inspired the song "America the Beautiful," according to the caption. To my twelve-year-old eyes, the peak was so rugged that it seemed a caricature of ferocious nature. I didn't know at the time that there are both a railway and a road to the top of the peak, ending in a parking area beside a restaurant and gift shop. At that point in my life, the great outdoors was a concept limited to the woods behind my house, the dirt-bike course over on the lot near my friend Chris Landis's house, and Eagle Creek Reservoir on the outskirts of Indianapolis. In my world, the outdoors did not include mountains. And it especially did not include mountains fourteen thousand feet tall. Intimidated, I turned the page.

I found people skiing down improbably steep slopes at life-threatening speeds. Though I'd taken my metal-runner Flyer all over the embankments, ditches, and streets of our Indianapolis subdivision, and even ridden a sizable hill in the neighborhood north of our house, I was always able to drag my feet behind me to brake. How do you stop on skis?

I flipped the page again, and this last picture shook me to my core. It was a photo of people cross-country skiing the streets of Denver after a winter storm. There were no vehicles on the roads, just lanes of people on their skis. I slammed the book shut in horror. My imagination went to work completing the scenario. People don't drive anywhere in Colorado, they just cross-country ski. To school, to work, to the grocery store, wherever they went, people travel only on skis, as in some Nordic wonderland. Even in the middle of the summer. To a kid who'd been born in Ohio and spent his formative years as a Hoosier, raised on the holy trinity of basketball, basketball, and Indy car racing, skiing, even on flat ground, was as foreign a concept as riding a camel.

As I developed more of an idea of this place where my family was headed, I came to believe in Colorado as an entire state of skiers, the landscape striated with ski tracks, social groupings segregated by skiing ability. How would I ever fit in if I couldn't ski? I cried to myself in bed every night for a week after I read that book. While sad that we were parting ways, my friends were excited for me to move to Colorado. They told me how much fun it would be to go skiing. They didn't realize that was exactly what terrified me so much. Having noticed my red eyes and sniffles, my parents grew concerned at dinner one night. "It looks like you've been crying. What's wrong?" my dad inquired.

"I'm scared," I lied. I wasn't scared, I was absolutely terrorized by the notion of moving to Colorado.

My dad tried to console me, saying, "I know moving is hard. - We're all leaving our friends behind. You know you'll make new friends, right?"

"Yeah. That's not why I'm scared."

"Why are you scared?"

Once I had explained about the book, my parents smiled, reassured me that it didn't snow *that* much that I would have to ski to get to school, and got me in a better mood. We flew out for a visit before we moved, and aside from the nasty sunburn I got at the water park, I found that Colorado wasn't nearly as inhospitable as it had first seemed. Once we moved for good, I joined the ski club at my middle school, and by the end of my second day on skis that December, I was hurtling down intermediate runs, outracing all my new friends, and even tackling some of the hardest terrain at Winter Park/Mary Jane, the resort that would become my absolute favorite place to ski moguls in the whole world.

My adaptation to my new environment continued the next summer, when I had a seminal outdoor experience on a backpacking trip in Rocky Mountain National Park. The two-week-long trip with other thirteen- and fourteen-year-olds into the park's backcountry marked the first time I would ever carry a heavy load and spend the night more than a few minutes' walk from a house or vehicle. A full season of skiing had assuaged my fear of the mountains. Without knowing it, I was poised on the brink of a love affair.

On the first day of our late-June backpacking trip, I felt so enthused by being in such a grand place as the western side of the park that I leaped and bounded down the trail despite my pack load. My frantic energy quickly earned me the nickname Animal, after the drummer of the Muppet band. Our group's two counselors had their hands full trying to keep me from sprinting off ahead of the group. After lunch they increased my pack burden with the huge bucket of peanut butter that was to feed our group of fifteen for five more lunches, until we were resupplied, but even so I would run up to the next curve along the trail and disappear from sight until I heard one of the leaders shout, "Animal! Wait for us!"

That first evening, as dusk approached, we spread out around our campsite at 9,600 feet elevation in the Big Meadows, each of us with a notepad and the encouragement to write or draw whatever we wanted. I sat in the tall grass in the middle of the meadow, alongside the shallow gravel-bottom stream, and played with the water. After a few minutes on the bank, I watched an adult mule deer amble out from the cover of the trees toward the creek, twitching her ears and shaking her head to shoo away insects. I froze in place, entranced, as the doe paraded out into the meadow, right to left, as I looked to the south. I was at the fringe of our group, since everyone else had stayed closer to the tents. She reached the water, and I leaned back to reach my tablet and cautiously opened the cover, anxious that any rustling might frighten her. For the next five minutes, which seemed like both five hours and five seconds, the doe drank from the creek and I sketched her shape on my notepad, until she turned and walked back into the forest.

When our fifteen minutes of personal reflection time were up, everyone else was quiet and introverted until I bounced into camp with my report of the deer. The other kids were impressed, and I showed off my sketch—it wasn't brilliant art, by any means, but as a souvenir of my awe, it did the job. Two nights later, up at a boulder field of 11,000 feet, I experienced the fun of scrambling on house-sized rocks. We dunked our bodies in a stream pool so cold the snow-banks extended down into the water. That same night I learned a firsthand lesson about not leaving sweaty boots outside the tent when there are porcupines around (they ate the leather uppers, laces, and tongues, reducing my boots to Vibram-soled flip-flops).

The next summer, 1989, I went to an outdoor adventure camp

that ranged across the state, including rock climbing near Estes Park, white-water rafting on the Colorado River out near Grand Junction, and horseback riding at a ranch near Gunnison. I wasn't exactly turning into an expert, but something was growing in me, and four years later, when I headed off for college in Pittsburgh at Carnegie Mellon University, I felt like I'd established an identity in the West. I had become a Coloradoan at heart—a "transplanted native." In Pennsylvania, when I felt homesick, it was for the spaces, sun, and peaks of my western home, and when people asked where I was from, I enjoyed seeing their eyes light up after I told them I was from Colorado. For two years, I was the only student at CMU from Colorado. Lacking fellow Coloradoans with whom I could share my longing for the Rocky Mountains, I pined disconsolately for snowy ski slopes.

I climbed my first fourteener, Longs Peak—one of the fifty-nine mountains in Colorado higher than the magic line of 14,000 feet—in July 1994, with my best friend, Jon Heinrich. Longs dominates the northern half of Colorado's Front Range, northwest of Boulder. At 14,255 feet, the mountain is the sixteenth-highest peak in the state, and one of the most renowned. While its spectacular East Face, known as the Diamond, draws world-class technical climbers to its sheer granite lines, the relatively easy standard hike through the Keyhole allows thousands of scrambling hikers to make the summit each summer. Jon and I gathered advice from Dick Rigo, our friend - Brandon's dad, who had been a Boy Scout leader and who had himself climbed several dozen of the fourteeners. Mr. Rigo told us some basic tenets of hiking high peaks—start early, take water and food, rain gear, a map, and be off the summit by noon to avoid lightning from the almost daily afternoon thunderstorms—most of which we subsequently ignored.

Jon carried a gallon jug of water in his grip; our packs were stuffed with sandwiches, candy bars, and our ski jackets. By the time we reached treeline, the elevation above which trees no longer grow (about 11,000 feet on Longs Peak), we had stripped off our shirts and slathered sunscreen on our chests. We noted our progress compared to the photocopied trail map we'd picked up at the ranger station that morning, marking down the time we reached each landmark. We were going to be a long way behind the record ascent time, but we would easily get back before dark. A broad trail ascended to Granite Pass near 12,000 feet, and in a set of a half-dozen long switchbacks, the route turned back above itself several times to reach the Boulder-field, a half square mile of couch-sized boulders piled over one an-other. We ate a snack under the clear sky at the Keyhole, a steeply sided, jagged notch in the northern ridge of the mountain. Then I climbed up the rocks on the north side of the Keyhole and crawled out onto the overhanging pinnacle some thirty feet above Jon. With my legs dangling over the drop, he took my picture. I came down, Jon climbed up, and I returned the favor.

Even though we were well above 13,000 feet, the most difficult climbing of the day was still to come, with first a treacherous traverse across the granite slabs that slope down the west side of the north ridge, then a steep climb up the Trough Couloir, a five-hundred-foot-high rocky gully, where we encountered a dozen other hikers who were having increasing difficulty breathing under the exertion of scrambling up the couloir (the air near 14,000 feet is about half the density of air at sea level, so the available oxygen is significantly re-duced). Jon suggested we race to the top of the couloir, one at a time, and see how many people we could pass. He went first and eventually passed everyone else in the couloir. While Jon was nearing the halfway point, I started up. Trying to pace myself to overtake a cou-ple before the gully narrowed at a four-foot-high rock step, I felt my breathing escalate, but since I was unacclimated to the altitude, my chest could heave only so much until the fiery sensation in my lungs won and I had to pause at the rock step. Though I still passed all the other hikers, I was several minutes slower than Jon. It was significant to me that it could feel so good to make my body hurt by pushing so hard.

Approaching 14,000 feet under our own power for the first time, Jon and I felt giddy with the promise of making it to the top. But first we rounded an outside corner and were looking up at the Homestretch, a three-hundred-foot-high open dihedral formed at the crease where two sections of the summit walls create an inside corner, like an open book.

The last task before we would stand atop Longs Peak was to scramble up this smoothly polished slab using both hands on the rock. Below us, the rock walls fell away into a two-thousand-foot-deep chasm, from which an occasional wind gust burst, sharpening the psychological edge. Jon and I stopped to watch a summiteer descend the Homestretch above us in his blue jeans. He faced out from the mountain and alternated lowering his feet and scraping his underside down to meet his shoes. His tentative style in such a precarious place concerned us; we joked that if he slipped, he would knock us both off the Homestretch, like bowling for climbers. At a protected spot behind a large flake that had separated from the wall, we passed the man in the flat lee of the protrusion and continued. In another three minutes, we reached the open rocky plateau of Longs Peak and celebrated with an extended hug. Jon made a sign on the back of our map that read "I love you," for his girlfriend, Nikki, and I took a photograph of him holding the paper in the breeze, beaming a hypoxic smile.

Despite our late start, we were off the summit and climbing down the Homestretch before two o'clock in the afternoon. A few clouds were gathering to the northwest, but we'd lucked out with the weather. Once we were down below the Keyhole again, we stopped for another snack and spied an open snow slope to our right, on the east side of the north ridge. I think the idea came to Jon and me at the same moment, because we looked at each other and said, "Let's go slide on the snow!" I don't think either of us knew what glissading was, but we clambered over to the top of the longest stretch of snow, some two hundred yards long, and donned our ski pants. It was a slope steep enough to avalanche, but with midsummer conditions, we were more concerned that we would slide all the way off the bottom edge and go hurtling into the Boulderfield. Jon went first on a thirty-second ride, spraying the softened snow in all directions with his boot heels, hooting with glee. I yelled for him to take a photo of me when I got close enough, and I plopped onto the snowfield and accelerated toward Jon at breakneck speed.

Using the snow groove Jon had created, and with my low-friction nylon ski pants, I quickly surpassed the speed where I could control my descent. Bouncing over buried obstacles, tearing down in a streak, I was going to end up staining some rocks with blood if I - didn't slow down. In fear, I thrust my hands down into the snow at my sides, dug in my heels, and was instantly rewarded with a faceful of heavy wet slush. As the slope angle diminished at the end of the snowfield, I raked my fingers more tenaciously and kicked with my boots until, half blind, I stopped right beside Jon, just a few feet before the rock field. We immediately broke into a bout of exuberant laughter and shouted at each other, "Let's do it again!" Hiking up back to where we'd left our backpacks, I tried to revive my numbed hands, wiping off the ice crystals, and devised a scheme to hold small pointed rocks as brakes this time.

Once we were done terrifying ourselves, we hiked down to Granite Pass and traversed across Mount Lady Washington's eastern flank. Clouds had started to move in by the time Jon and I reached treeline, and we shifted into a run to beat the coming rain. Pounding down the trail in our boots, we christened this first trail-running escapade Rapid Mountain Descent, or RMD for short. By the time we returned to the Land Cruiser, I had been thoroughly infected by the overall experience of climbing my first fourteener and knew that I would be up for more.

I took a weeklong rafting trip with my father in 1993, and enjoyed it so much that two years later, I followed up on my dad's contacts with the rafting companies near Buena Vista, Colorado. Within a week of returning from college after my sophomore year, I got a summer job as a raft guide. In late May 1995, I moved into the motel-cum-boathouse that my employer, Bill Block, used as the base of operations for his company, Independent Whitewater. We were one of the smallest companies on the river, running two or three boats a day compared with some of the larger outfitters, who might have ten times that number. But with three guides, that meant that Pete, my new friend, colleague, and bunkhouse mate, and I worked almost every day. I could have taken off more than the seven days I allowed myself that summer, but this so-called job was so much fun that I rarely felt like doing anything else. Due to a snowpack that reached 400 percent of average levels in the surrounding ranges, the summer of 1995 was the biggest water season in the history of guided boating on the river. Rapids that were normally Class III to IV+ morphed into Class V, the highest runnable grade—and even unnavigable giants—while smaller sets of wave and technical obstacles like the Graveyard and Raft-Ripper disappeared completely. Three people died that season on the stretch of river that we guided—two private boaters and one with another rafting company—and we saw a peak of over 7,200 cubic feet per second in the canyon, nearly four times the average peak and twice the last big-water-year peak. With water like that, I felt like I was missing out when I didn't work a trip.

Even after most of us had taken two half-day trips down through Brown's Canyon, with available equipment and skilled partners abounding in the evenings, guides from other companies and I would load up a van with our hard-shell and inflatable kayaks and drive up the valley to run another excellent section of rapids made even better by the big water. On days when our companies' owners deemed the river too gnarly to run with clients, we would get together an all-guides boat to tackle the most aggressive lines in the canyon, or even do midnight runs under the bright glare of a full moon. The rafting community in the upper Arkansas valley was a culture that rewarded cocksure risk-taking, even when it bordered on the absurd. One afternoon in July, I went with our third guide, Steve, to the hardware store in Buena Vista and bought two inflatable kid-sized pool toys. These kiddie rafts were like three-foot-long rowboats, with twelve-inch-high flotation tubes around the perimeter of the thin, flexible plastic floor. They cost ten dollars each, and river-worthy they were not. We'd been joking about running Brown's Canyon with them ever since Pete had alerted us to their existence, but instead, we drove over to the put-in south of town and dropped them in the ever mighty Arkansas above an eight-mile section of Class I–II rapids, the smallest on the river but sufficiently large compared to our meager craft. Each armed with a personal flotation jacket, a cutoff-milk-jug bailing bucket, and kayak paddle, Steve and I proceeded downstream on our "do not try this at home" mission and successfully ran one of the biggest rivers in the state with our hilariously inadequate dinghies.

In late August, I took three of my best friends, all neophytes on the river, down through Brown's Canyon on a single-raft midnight run. This was much more intense than when I'd gone with other guides on a multiple-boat excursion. The biggest twist was that I'd planned it for the night of the new moon, instead of the full moon. In such darkness, with river, shore, canyon walls and sky all blended into the same inky blackout, navigation was all-important; an unexpected bump could send one of my friends into the river, where he or she would disappear completely in the dark.

In still-water sections, the stars reflected at us from the mirrored surface of the river. Where the stars didn't reflect, that meant there was a ripple, rock, or rapid. At times there was just enough light from above to make out the white-tipped wave crests, but once we entered the canyon, the high walls diminished the ambient light even more, and it became a total memory game for the remaining nine miles to the takeout. Just before the first rapid, Ruby's Riffle, a short Class II, I scraped the front left corner of the raft on a large rock. But after that, through the next thirteen rapids, including some large Class III and technical Class IV sections, we had a completely clean run and an awe-inspiringly surreal experience. When the river was calm, it felt uncomfortable to break the silence. Rather than speak, we looked up. More stars than my friends and I had ever seen floated so vibrantly in front of our eyes that I perceived for the first time that space wasn't a flat blanket but a three-dimensional womb. I thought I could tell that some stars were behind others just by looking at them.

After graduating at the head of my class and receiving my B.S. in mechanical engineering—with a double major in French and a minor in piano performance—in May 1997, I took a job as a mechanical engineer for Intel Corporation, in Ocotillo, Arizona, a far-flung suburb at the southeastern edge of the mega-sprawl of Phoenix. I would eventually transfer first to Tacoma, Washington, in March 1999, and then to Albuquerque, New Mexico, in September of that same year. But it was in 1997, right after graduation, when my long-dormant passions for the wilderness environments of the western U.S. began to blossom. Before I moved to Arizona, I wanted to reward myself for my successes in school and for having found what I anticipated would be a good job, so I planned not just a vacation but a supervacation. It was to be the Road Trip to End All Road Trips. I would start driving my 1984 Honda CRX north, first to the Grand Teton, Yellowstone, and Glacier national parks, then on into Canada, to tour the Banff National Park and Icefields Parkway, over to Vancouver and down into the Cascades, Olympic, and Rainier national parks, finishing the circuit with Crater Lake, Yosemite, and Zion national parks. Thirty days, six thousand miles, ten national parks.

As it turned out, I didn't get very far. Since it was only late May, the snow levels were still high, which confined me to lower-elevation backpacking trips at first. My early-season venture into Phelps Lake in the Tetons rewarded me with a top-rate campsite beside the lake, where at dusk the first night, a cow moose trotted her silhouette in front of the sunset. I saw a pair of bald eagles soaring above a waterfall the next morning, then spied a grizzly bear in the forest near the road the day after that. I drove around and took photographs of the Tetons reflected in the broken windows of abandoned farmhouses in Antelope Flats. That same afternoon, I planned my next excursion, a two-night trip to Bradley Lake, where I intended to place a base camp for an attempt at climbing the Middle Teton, the easiest technically of the major peaks in the park. When I asked the backcountry ranger at the permits station how I could climb one of the Tetons, his disconcerted look foreshadowed the adventure I would have. It was a look that said, "If you have to ask, it's against my better judgment to tell you." He showed me how to get to Bradley Lake on the map under the Plexiglas countertop and explained that the trails were under several feet of snow, concluding with "If you don't have snowshoes, you'll be post-holing up to your waist." I didn't know what post-holing was, but I filled out the permit and kept quiet.

In the early afternoon, I set off hiking with my pack loaded for a three-day solo trip—my first overnight trip alone. I had my camping gear and clothing in my main pack, and my food and cooking supplies in a small purple school pack that I wore on my chest. About a mile in from the Taggert Lake Trailhead, the snowpack was already deep enough that I wallowed with every footstep. Without other bootprints around, I was obviously the first hiker to access this trail in a while, perhaps all winter. I struggled under my heavy pack. Deeper and deeper the snow became as I gained in elevation and moved up onto the rounded moraines left behind from the ice age glaciers. After an hour of slow-moving progress, I was approaching the forest at the crest of the moraine and a significant snowdrift. As my boots sank down several feet with every stride, the jagged ice crystals of the middle snowpack increasingly abraded my shins. In another fifteen minutes, with snow packed in my boots and up my pants legs, I lost sensation below my knees, and the cold wet abuse became less bothersome. After dropping into the snow several dozen times, I changed strategy and crawled up the last twenty feet to the spine of the snowdrift and plopped myself astride the compacted lip of snow. Breathing heavily from the exhausting effort, I looked back over my left shoulder at the series of deep holes I had left and understood then what post-holing meant.

I checked my map and saw that I had about a quarter-mile distance to cover before I reached the south side of Bradley Lake, and then about three quarters of a mile to hike around the lake to get to my campsite. I was at the edge of the forest, where the snow looked to be firmer. There was a short downhill on my right that I slid down on my backside. I stood up only to plunge in up to my waist when I took my first step. "Ohhh, this is going to be a long mile," I said aloud, thinking snowshoes would indeed have been smart, even though I'd never used them.

It took over two hours of toil to reach a short footbridge on the north side of Bradley Lake, fighting my way through the waist-deep snow. Clouds hung above the treetops, and I could see only a few hundred vertical feet up the mountainside to the west, where the evergreens disappeared into the vapors.

A couple hundred yards past the bridge, I found a campsite signpost mostly buried in the snow, twenty feet from the lakeshore. Relieved to have arrived before dark, after the unexpected four-hour slog, I set up my green two-person tent just beyond the sign, on a small patch of dirt and frozen pine needles. My feet ached with the cold. I sat in the doorway of my tent and unlaced my sodden hiking boots. A deluge of melted snow splashed from each boot when I removed them. I was sufficiently tired that I didn't care that my socks dripped water in the tent as I peeled them off my pruned feet. Rubbing the pads of my waterlogged toes, I gave a start at a nearby sound, the breaking of a branch. I listened intently and heard splashes in the lake, coming from the other side of some thick bushes a dozen yards to my left. Maybe it would be another moose coming out at dusk, like I'd seen at Phelps Lake. Intrigued, I leaned forward to peek around the flap of my tent and watched a medium-sized black bear wade out from the foliage hanging a few feet offshore over the shallow lake. He looked to be about two hundred pounds, not over a few years old, and all black.

Hurrying, I grabbed my camera out of my backpack and took a picture. The flash reflected off the bushes, and I worried that it would scare the bear off before I could see him clearly through the brush. However, rather than being startled or running away, he coolly altered course, straight for my tent. One step, two steps, three steps; he was definitely heading for my tent. "Whoa, bear!" I meekly stammered. "Hey, hey, heyyy!" He kept coming, passed the bushes, stepped out of the water, and was closing the distance to my tent. I thought maybe I had been downwind and he hadn't smelled me yet. I tried whistling to alert the lumbering beast of my presence, but I was too frightened to purse my lips properly and only managed to spray spittle onto my camera.

Now just twenty-five feet away, I knew this bear could see me and wasn't coming to pay a social visit. He was looking scrawny and wanted my food for his first big post-hibernation dinner. I had dropped my little purple pack at the tent door and, looking at it there, straight in the sights of the bear, I realized what I had to do. I grabbed the food pack and, escaping the tent with the bear only fifteen feet away, dashed off to my right. My bare feet beat the hard ground as I scampered around the back of the tent and, leaping over a downed tree, landed directly in a snowbank where first my left foot, then my right, punctured the icy crust. Pain seared across my left foot, and when I extracted it from the snow, I saw that I'd cut my arch on a protruding branch of the fallen tree. A glance over my shoulder told me I had no time to spare for first aid. I bounded off into the snowy forest, abrading and numbing my feet as I went.

Scouting the nearby trees for possible food-hanging positions, I - didn't see anything that was at least eight feet off the ground, five feet from a trunk, and strong enough to catch my bag if I tossed it up on a branch. Normally, I would use some string and haul the bag over a high, sturdy limb, but I didn't have time for that tactic now. I circled around clockwise and ended up in front of my tent, then off a few paces to the west. The bear followed my every move in the forest, and I never put more than thirty feet between us. I finally noticed a large tree that had toppled some years ago, leaving a tangle of thick roots jutting into the air. They weren't high enough to be out of reach, but I could at least lash my bag to the roots by the straps and go put on my boots before coming back to find a better spot for the food. I rushed over to the upended tree, wrapped the straps around three gnarled roots protruding four feet in the air, and twisted the bag down behind another root so the bear couldn't easily get to it. I then gingerly pranced back to the tent on my numbed feet.

Sitting in the tent doorway, I briefly checked the cuts on my left foot before cramming on my sopping-wet boots and lighting off to the downed tree once more. In the thirty seconds of my absence, the bear had taken my food bag in his teeth and, yanking it back and forth, shaken the straps off the roots. As I watched the bear easily snap the root to which I had tied the most securely attached strap, I understood I was in dire straits. I had dipped deeply into my energy supply to get to my campsite, and I needed nourishment before I could even attempt to retreat to my car. If the bear made off with that bag, I would be stranded. The bear was already twenty feet along the length of the tree's horizontal trunk, with the purple pack in his jaws, when I came to the conclusion that, with my life possibly at stake, I had to get that bag back—by whatever means necessary. I broke off a yardstick's length of tree root, held it like a club in my left hand, hopped up on the trunk of the fallen tree, and waved my weapon over my head, roaring at the top of my lungs, "Give me my food back, bear!" I'm not sure what response I was expecting, but my body trembled with fear when the bear stopped, turned his head back over his right shoulder, then spun on his hind feet to face me at ten paces. I'd gotten his attention, all right, and now we had ourselves a show-down.

I snarled and shouted, waved my stick in the air, and yelled again, even louder, "Give me back my FOOD!" Like a dog questioning his - master's order, the bear tilted his head quizzically to the left, and I thought I could see his forehead wrinkle. At his pause, I gathered my courage and began stomping on the log. Shouting anew, I took a pounding step toward the motionless bear, then another, and a third, commanding, "You picked the wrong hungry hiker to steal his food—DROP IT!" At the last word, I jumped up and slammed both my boots down on the tree trunk. The bear dropped the food bag, lumbered off the side of the log, and started off into the forest. I could hardly believe it. I yelled after him, "Shoo, bear!" and went over to my purple backpack. Before I picked it up, I threw my broken root after the bear; it crashed into some pine branches over his head, and he scampered off to the west.

Five minutes later, I had my camping stove heating a pot of lake water. I anxiously waited for it to boil, imagining that the bear would return any minute. Two minutes after the water finally boiled, I'd set a personal record for the fastest-ever consumption of a bowl of ramen-noodle soup. I inspected the little rucksack while I packed my food, bowl, and stove into it, and saw four distinct holes from the - bear's teeth. By the time I had hoisted the pack into a safe location, night had fallen, and I cowered back at my tent, the bear winning some revenge via my psychological taxation. With the darkness blinding me, I lay in my sleeping bag, fear provoking paranoia every time the faintest forest sound reached my ears. For seven hours, whenever a leaf fell to the snow, a pine needle dropped into the lake, or a tree creaked in the breeze, my imagination launched like a screaming dragster, accelerating from zero to death-by-bear-mauling in a split second. Splash, a fish jumped in the lake, and instantly my mind responded, "OhmyGodthebearisbackhe'sgonnaeatmeI'mgonna die!" as I held what I was certain would be my last breath. The terror - didn't ease until well after three in the morning, when I finally caught some uneasy shut-eye.

After starting late the next morning, I managed to wade through the hip-deep snow up Garnet Canyon to an elevation around 10,500 feet. The ever present rain clouds obliterated the landscape. I knew I was in the cirque where I had to make a critical route-finding decision, and I couldn't see a single landmark. It was too late in the day to find my way by trial and error, so I went down in the trench I'd excavated on my ascent. Two hours later, I arrived at the edge of Bradley Lake and tramped in the rain back to my campsite, where I faltered at the sight of the wreck that had been my tent. The rain fly had been ripped off, two of the four poles were snapped, the front access flap was torn completely open, and my sleeping bag was floating in the lake. "What in the hell?" I exclaimed, inspecting the contents of my tent, thoroughly soaked and slimed with mud. "That bear," I thought. "He came back while I was climbing and ransacked my stuff trying to get to my food." But the food pack was untouched in its spot in the tree, beyond the bear's reach. Standing over the wreckage, I could only think that the bear had done all this out of spite. I got the purple food pack down, fished my sleeping bag out of the lake with a branch, and packed away my gear. With everything soaking wet, I couldn't stay the night, and it would be dark by the time I hiked back to my car—but that's what I would have to do. With seventy pounds of sodden gear weighing me down, my food pack on my chest like the day before, I started on my way out and immediately noticed the bear tracks overlying my old footprints. Mr. Bear had followed me into my campsite like a hunter on the scent.

At the far side of the little footbridge, where the snow was deeper, I could see how the bear had intersected my post-holes from the north. With my eyes, I retraced his tracks as they went up a thirty-foot-high hill . . . to where the bear was sitting next to a pine tree, watching me. "Ho-ly shit . . ." My voice trailed off as the reproachful anger I'd pent up against the bear in the last half hour switched back to the familiar strain of terror. All I could do was keep hiking, hope I didn't founder in the snow, and pray that the bear would leave me alone. I pulled my drenched map from my pocket and held it with my compass in my left hand: no room for mistakes now.

I left the trail after about fifty feet and stumbled to the hilltop south of the bear. He hadn't yet moved. I imagined he was sitting there grinning as I struggled to escape him. I surveyed the snowpack from the hill, and it seemed to be shallower to the east; I reasoned I could make an off-trail shortcut directly to the highway and avoid wallowing in the drifts at the top of the moraine. Crossing the ridge-line of the hill, I descended to a hollow in the forest and looked back over my left shoulder. The bear was gone. He'd dropped off the other side of the hill toward the lake. Relieved, I walked about fifteen paces, then checked behind me again, just as the bear sauntered over the hillcrest in my tracks, a mere thirty feet away.

For ten minutes, I blazed a heading to the east, alternately glancing at the compass, orienting the map to my surroundings, and peering over my left shoulder at the bear. He closed in to within twenty feet behind me a couple of times, and I was ever more nervous about finding my way, avoiding deep snow, and trying to guess what the bear would do to get at the food bag strapped to my chest. Navigating in such stressful circumstances was very difficult, and I shortly became disoriented; the terrain no longer matched what I was expecting from my judgment of the map. It took me a minute to get back on the correct bearing, compensating for the declination between true north on my map and the magnetic north shown on my compass. Then, surmounting a short rise, I found myself looking down at a lake. I wasn't counting on a lake. But there, between my position and the snowy lakeshore, were some footprints. Aha! My spirit leaped at the discovery. Navigating would be no issue, and I might even find some other people to help me scare away the bear. I tromped through the snow to the boot track, and then it hit me: "Those are *my* footprints . . . and this is Bradley Lake . . . I've gone in a complete circle!" My heart sank in disappointment.

The bear was ten paces behind me; to this point, he had stopped when I stopped. But now he came down the hill toward the trail and my stance. I felt like giving up, throwing my food bag to him—damn the regulations not to feed the bears—and, most strongly, I wanted to cry.

The bear was only fifteen feet away when again something changed in my demeanor: My despair turned to anger. "Leave me alone!" I shouted right in his face. Again he stopped. Recalling the most visceral threat I'd ever heard in a movie, I adapted a few lines from *Pulp Fiction* and continued, "I'm gonna get some hard pipe-hittin' rangers to come out and get medieval on your ass! They're gonna tranquilize you and ship you off to Idaho!" I resorted to waving my arms over my head and growling, but this was old news to the bear. He cocked his head like he'd done the night before during our standoff on the log. Spying an exposed stone in the conical dip surrounding a pine tree a few feet to my left, I reached into the tree well and grabbed the softball-sized rock to carry for self-defense, then hurriedly moved to the south, retracing my old tracks.

The bear followed me, too closely now, stalled only at intervals by my shouting. I figured I would hit the bear with the rock if he came within ten feet of me. I wouldn't be able to throw it much farther than that with the packs and their straps confining my range of motion. I focused on keeping myself upright, though the snow got deeper and was noticeably weaker than it had been the day earlier, due to the rain that was still falling. At one point, I broke through the crust and sank in up to my hips. I was good and stuck and couldn't pull myself out. The bear seemed to understand his opportunity and narrowed our separation to a mere twelve feet from my head to his snout. As I groped for purchase in the snow, my arms flailed, and my feet stayed stuck. I twisted left at the waist and rolled onto my back over my right shoulder, popping my legs out of their holes. Like an upturned turtle, I was weighted down by both the packs on my torso. I was frightened the bear would attack and maul me while I was on my back; I was very vulnerable. Shakily standing on the unstable crust, I faced the looming bear and raised the stone projectile to my shoulder like a shot put and, with a heave, let fly my only defense. The bear and I both watched its lobbing arc end in a snowy crater to the right of his left shoulder. I had missed. The bear stayed put.

I checked the closest tree well and found two smaller rocks. Rearmed, I made for the moraine, lunging fifteen steps along the trail in my day-old post-holes, until I broke through again at a spot that had previously held my weight. We repeated the same routine—I flopped onto my back, the bear got way too close, I stood up and threw a rock at him. This time, however, my rock found its mark on the animal's rump, and like a rocket, he launched up the nearest pine tree to his left, bounding in three dynamic leaps to thirty-five feet. My jaw sagged, and my eyes rolled up in their sockets; I'd never seen a large animal move so athletically in my life. At that display of power, I knew I would sooner pin the Ultimate Warrior in a wrestling match than outfight this bear if he attacked. But I also realized I'd bought some time. I reloaded with the same rock and turned south once more. After thirty seconds, I heard branches cracking and looked back to see the bear coming down the tree. Immediately, I plunged back into the snow, and we established what became our little ballet. My part: fall, roll, stand, throw; the bear's part: climb, wait, descend, follow. Time after time, we repeated our dance. As I got closer and closer to the moraine, I added shouts and curses to intimidate the bear, hoping to buy myself more time in the deeper snow. The bear, of course, had no issues with the snow at all, his four paws distributing his weight more broadly on the snowpack's crust than my two ever could.

I topped out on the moraine's main drift, crawling as I'd done the day before, and hungrily eyed the clear dirt trail a half mile in the distance. The bear hadn't relaxed his determination at all, continuing to follow me even within a distance of fifteen feet. Moving downhill off the moraine was faster going for me, and as the snowpack depth decreased, I picked up my pace. Twenty minutes later, at the edge of the snowpack, I stopped and waited for the bear to come closer. He had lagged relatively farther back, with thirty feet separating us, on the downhill section. Within ten seconds, he was within striking distance of my tiring arm—a meager fifteen feet—so I threw the first rock at his head and missed high, but the second one struck home behind the bear's neck on his left side. He yelped and sped off to the closest tree. This time I changed the pattern of our maneuvers and followed him to the base of the tree and removed my packs. There were plenty of rocks around, and I proceeded to unleash my vengeance by pounding the bear's rump—at least every third attempt—with baseball-sized stones. I shouted and yelled in anger at the bear, finding release from the strain and terror he'd put me through over the last twenty-four hours. After he climbed so high in the tree that I missed on five consecutive throws, I knelt and put my packs on again and strode back to the muddy trail and on toward my car, not looking back anymore.

I was done with Wyoming and rain and post-holing, and most of all, I was done with bears. The prospect of continuing on my planned trip to Glacier National Park—home to even more bears than the Tetons and Yellowstone and, due to its higher latitude, more snow than I had already encountered—was totally unappealing. I stopped at the ranger station to alert the park staff of my experience. The rangers told me they had heard of this kind of stalking behavior from other national parks (probably Glacier, I thought, putting the final nail in that coffin), but mine was the first report from the Tetons. They also told me that if you were to shout at a bear, wave your arms, stomp aggressively toward it, and then hit it with rocks, nine times out of ten you could count on being mauled. Score one for my guardian angel, I figured. I headed into town, where, after finding a motel room to dry my things out, and calling my parents to let them know what had happened and that I was coming home the next day, I went to several restaurants asking if I could get a bear flank steak, but there was none to be had. And, before going to bed, I did not go to see either of the two movies playing at the theater in Jackson— *Jurassic Park 2* (dinosaurs stalk Jeff Goldblum) or *The Edge* (a bear stalks Anthony Hopkins).

THREE

The Night Shift

We know that the condemned man, at the end, does not resist but submits passively, almost gratefully, to the instruments of his executioner.
—EDWARD ABBEY, *Desert Solitaire*

I GLANCE AT MY WATCH; it's 4:19 P.M. I have been trapped for an hour and a half, hammering my knife against the boulder for about half that time. There will be daylight until around nine P.M., but I already have my headlamp over my blue cap. Though it's not on right now, I'm glad I brought the lamp on this day trip. As with my knife, I usually wouldn't carry it on what should have been a short outing. That warning in Kelsey's guidebook about checking for spiders and snakes was helpful, not because I've seen any creepy-crawlies, but because it suggested bringing a light. I've already used it to throw light up into the half-inch gap where my squashed wrist is caught, to further examine my hand from every angle.

One of the more important concerns I've been trying to address is how much of the boulder's weight my wrist is supporting. If it's holding barely any weight, the amount of rock I need to remove is less. The more the boulder is being propped up by my hand and wrist, the more it will settle as I remove weight-bearing material. In fact, for me to get my hand free in that case, the rock will have to settle completely onto the wall. Unfortunately, there's a good probability that since there's a gap between the stone and the north canyon wall immediately below *and* above my wrist, the boulder is not resting cleanly on the wall. The rock will settle; I'll be working on a subtly moving target. I can only guess how much this will affect my chances of freeing my wrist, so I table the question and return to scraping and pecking at the boulder with my knife.

I try not to think about the fact that I am stuck. Though it's an irrepressible reality, thinking about it doesn't help my situation. Instead, I concentrate on finding small weaknesses in the face of the boulder just above and to the left of my trapped right wrist. My earlier instincts led me to etch a demarcation line above the softball-sized volume of rock that I have decided I must eradicate to gain my freedom. I'm speculating on a flaw in the rock's structure, in a slight concavity that's above the bulge almost six inches from my wrist; the demarcation line runs through this concavity. I start at my line, high on the face of the rock but a few inches below the top, and hack downward, attacking as near to my mark as I can manage. Tapping, then pounding, my multi-tool's three-inch stainless-steel blade against the stone, I try to hit the same spot with each strike.

Everything else—the pain, the thoughts of rescue, the accident itself—recedes. I'm taking action. My mind seems determined to find and exploit any seams or natural cleavage of the chockstone to hasten the removal of material. Every few minutes, I pause to look over the boulder's entire surface to make sure I'm not missing a more obvious target.

But the going is imperceptibly slow. I unfold the metal file from the tool, and for five minutes, I use it to etch the boulder. It works only marginally better than the knife, and only when I turn it on its side and saw down at the line. The rock is clearly more durable than the shallow rasps of the file. When I stop to clean the file, I see the grooves are filled with flecks of metal from the tool itself. I'm wearing down the edge without any effect on the chockstone. I inspect the boulder again, and noting the nonuniform coloring, its relative hardness compared to my knife and the walls, and its similarity to the chockstones of the gauntlet up above, I realize this boulder isn't strictly sandstone. It seems to have come from the darker-colored layer within the Navajo sandstone that formed the overhanging lip a hundred yards upstream near the S-log at the head of this lower slot canyon, the one I'd hung from before dropping irreversibly into the sand about two hours ago.

"That's bad news, Aron," I think. "The rock layer formed that ledge because it's more erosion-resistant than the rest of this canyon. This chockstone is the hardest thing here." I wonder if it wouldn't be faster to carve out the wall instead of the boulder, and decide to give that a try. Switching from the file back to the three-inch blade, I strike the multi-tool against the wall above my right wrist. The knife skitters across the pink sloping canyonside. Very close to stabbing myself in the arm at every blow, I conclude the geometry is prohibitive—I can't slash at the wall in the right spot because my arm is in the way.

I pause to rest my left arm and hand and brush a little pulverized grit from my right forearm. I can't see any change in the boulder's position. I return to hacking at my target line in the concavity. Tick, tick, tick . . . tick, tick, tick. The sound of my knife tapping at the rock is pathetically minute, but all the same, it resounds through the canyon. I can strike the rock only so hard, otherwise my knife skitters off and I bash my knuckles, or I miss my target. I'm hoping to loosen the crystals around a gray knob in the chockstone and remove a quarter-sized chip in one piece. It will be an uplifting and measurable gain, but even the tiny bulge seems to be an impregnable safe. No matter what I try, I can't crack it.

Another hour has passed. It's six P.M. now, a little over three hours since the accident. It's still warm, but a few degrees off the high temperature of 66 degrees back at three-thirty, according to the watch looped on my left pack strap. I blow some dust off the area I've been assailing with my multi-tool and look for any discernible sign of progress. I get my eyes in close to the rock and inspect the mineralized characteristics of my target zone, wondering again if there might be a place with a less durable crystal structure. Considering my negligible progress, the question is more theoretical than practical. The only way I'm going to drill my way free of this stone is if a geologist's pick magically materializes in my hand.

I feel like I'm in the most deadly prison imaginable. My confinement will be an assuredly short one with only twenty-two ounces of water. The hiker's minimum for desert travel is one gallon per person per day. I think again about how long I might last on my scant supply—until Monday, maybe, Tuesday morning at the outside. Escape is the only way to survive. In any case, the race is on, and all I have is this chintzy pocketknife to blast my way through this boulder. It's akin to digging a coalmine with a kid's sand shovel.

I become suddenly frustrated with the tiresomeness of pecking. My mind runs the analysis on how much rock I've chipped away (almost none) and how much time it's taken me to do it (over two hours), and I come to the easy conclusion that I am engaged in a futile task. As I debate my remaining choices, my stress turns to pessimism. I already know I won't be successful in an attempt to rig an anchor for a pulley system. The rocks forming the ledge are six feet above my head and almost ten feet away; even with two hands, that would be an impossible chore. Without enough water to wait for rescue, without a pick to crack the boulder, without an anchor, I have only one possible course of action.

I speak slowly out loud. "You're gonna have to cut your arm off." Hearing the words makes my instincts and emotions revolt. My vocal cords tense, and my voice changes octaves.

"But I don't wanna cut my arm off!"

"Aron, you're gonna have to cut your arm off." I realize I'm arguing with myself and yield to a halfhearted chuckle. This is crazy.

I know that I could never saw through my arm bones with the blunted knife, so I decide to keep trying to free myself by pecking away at the boulder. It's futile, but it's the best of my current options. As I hit the rock, I imagine the early evening sun projecting ever longer shadows across the desert. The blue of the sky deepens while I carve unproductively for the next hour, taking infrequent and brief breaks. My understanding of the engraving above my right arm, "Geologic Time Includes Now," changes from Gerry Roach's intended warning to a spur of motivation. It becomes a hopeful reminder that, like an agent of geologic time, I can erode this chockstone, perhaps enough to free my hand from the obdurate handshake of the sandstone block. However, the stone has rapidly dulled my knife. I reconfigure the tool to expose the file again, and continue sawing down along the line I've etched above the grayish bulge at the near edge of the concavity.

While I'm filing, I think about the first time I visited Utah. I'm not sure what brings it to mind. Perhaps it's in response to the nagging question of how did I get here, how did I end up stuck in this place? That first trip was with my family on spring break in 1990, my freshman year in high school. We went to Capitol Reef, Bryce Canyon, and Zion Canyon before swinging south to the Grand Canyon. I - wasn't that thrilled by the idea. The weeks before we left, all my friends were excited for their skiing trips or vacations to Mexico. Me? I was going to Utah with my parents.

Fortunately, our family friend Betty Darr from Ohio was with us. She was the most well-read person I'd ever known, and her passion for reading was surpassed only by her love for the outdoors—two qualities that make for an excellent traveling companion. She was also one of the most positive, insightful, and caring people I've ever had the pleasure to call my friend. Betty had contracted polio when she was a little girl in the 1930s, and it paralyzed her from the waist down. I don't know if it was because of her battle against polio that she was so positive, or whether it was because she was so positive-minded that she overcame the challenges posed by her paralysis, but Betty found the light and good in every person, and she loved everyone. She spent several days a week volunteering at the county jail, where she helped prisoners learn to read and write, bringing them her magazines and working with them one-on-one. Her humanity saw in them their potential; nothing else mattered.

Betty had used arm crutches and a total leg-and-back brace every day since the polio, though sometimes she scooted around her rural Ohio house on her behind, dragging her legs and using her arms and hands to propel herself backward. She had a specially outfitted car that she could drive using hand controls. While we were visiting the national parks, she used an electric wheelchair to get around—she called it her Pony—or else my dad would carry her ninety-pound frame to the nearer spots that didn't necessitate the Pony. Sometimes, when Betty drove her Pony, she encountered hills too steep for its electric motor. My sister and I fought over who got to help push Betty. At Bryce Canyon, I won and was pushing Betty in her Pony up the final hill to the lookout. With my arms outstretched and head level with my shoulders, I was staring down at the battery tray under the chair when I heard Betty exclaim, "Oh, look at this, Aron!"

I looked up and almost let go of her. We were at a sweeping vista encompassing hundreds of orange and pink sandstone towers filling a three-hundred-foot-deep canyon that plunged directly in front of us and stretched for a half mile to either side of the lookout. I was stunned, and can trace my fascination for canyons back to the emotions I felt at that viewpoint. I wanted to race down into the canyon, touch the towers that seemed like they would topple at any moment, and follow every path that laced around the formations until I became lost in the maze. I imagined myself standing atop the tower called Thor's Hammer, and then, with superhuman ability, bounding to the top of the next pinnacle, and from there to the next. When it was time to go, I left with an empty feeling in my soul. At fourteen, I didn't understand why I felt this way, but I had met a calling in my life, though it would remain unfulfilled for a long time.

Two days later in the trip, we arrived at the Grand Canyon after dark and checked in to our room at the lodge. We got up at five-thirty in the morning to watch the sunrise from the South Rim.

Since we'd come in at night, I hadn't seen the canyon itself yet, so I was grumbling, "Why do we have to do this?" It was cold, and I hated having to get up so early. We took the comforters from our beds in the hotel room and loaded the five of us into the minivan for the five-minute drive west to the overlook. I tried my best to fall back asleep in the backseat, and I almost managed to convince my dad to let me stay in the van while everyone else went to the guardrail. But Betty won me over with her subtle encouragement: "We'll be right over at the benches when you're ready to see the sunrise." My mom and sister took the comforters while my dad carried Betty over to the viewpoint. Without the van heaters on, I got chilled in just a few minutes, so I walked over to my family and crawled under the blankets next to my sister.

I had never before sat and watched a sunrise for the sake of it, and I wasn't at all prepared for how majestic it would be. There stood forty miles of the mile-deep, fifteen-mile-wide wonder of the Grand Canyon, running from our toe tips to the growing horizontal rainbow at the horizon. The rock strata of the inner canyon changed from dark umbers and black shadows to immense bands of pastel yellow, white, green, and a hundred shades of red in the mysterious chemistry of twilight. At last, a blazing crescent burst over the distant desert palisades at the epicenter of the rainbow, and the canyon exploded in an array of dozens of temples, buttes, gorges, and pyramids, brought into glowing contrast with the encompassing canyon walls by the sunrise's glowing rose-colored light.

I didn't know it, but that sunrise was a dream come true for Betty, one she never counted on seeing because of the thousands of miles of challenging travel it involved for her to get to the canyon. She taught me something that I must have learned despite my bratty crankiness, for I have returned to that spot and dozens of others across the West just to watch a sunrise. It wasn't all I would learn from Betty; her positive attitude and zest for life was so instilled in me that I developed a passion and urgency to experience and discover the world that borders on obsession.

*   *   *

The Grand Canyon is a distant memory now. Because I'm stuck down in this hole, I'll miss the sunrise. During a break around seven P.M., I set the knife on top of the boulder where my scratched sunglasses have been perched. I lift my shoulders, stretch my left arm above my head, shake out my stiff hand, and sigh. Flexing my fingers, I look at my left hand with a degree of awe—my hand and fingers are swollen to nearly twice their regular thickness from the crushing blow they received during the accident, when the boulder smashed my left hand before ricocheting. The swelling has so disfigured my fingers that my knuckles no longer rise above their constituent bones. There are no veins visible on the back of my hand, just this balloon at the end of my arm. Perhaps the strangest thing is that I don't feel any pain from the injury, but it could well be that my situation is distracting me. So many other things are wrong with my circumstances that the swelling isn't important enough to warrant attention.

My left thigh hurts more than my swollen hand, and after I inspect under the leg of my shorts, I understand why. The skin covering my lower quadriceps is bruised and abraded in a dozen places above my knee. These injuries happened while I was struggling to lift the boulder right after I became trapped. There are a few small clots but no active bleeding. I ripped through my shorts in five places where they were pinched between my leg and the underside of the boulder. The lower right corner of the pocket is ripped open enough that I can see the loop of my half-inch-diameter bike-lock key ring protruding through the fabric.

It seems important that I keep track of those keys. If, by whatever miracle gets me out of here, I end up back at my bike, I'll need to be able to unlock the U-lock through my back tire. I reach to take the keys out of the torn pocket and put them in my backpack, but in the second before I withdraw my hand, the ring snags on my pocket lining and I fumble the keys. They fall into a hole between the rounded rocks near my left foot. "Damn!" I shout. They are not only out of my limited reach, but they've slipped down a narrow crack where it would be difficult to retrieve them even if I were free.

I roll my shoulders to the left, maximizing my extension, but I can only barely touch the top of the rock by my left sneaker. Dropping my feet down into the sand downcanyon of the rounded stones, I can touch this same rock more easily, and I see a faint glint of the odd-shaped keys in the sandy hole. Still, my trapped wrist prevents me from moving the planted rock or reaching into the hole. At that moment, a vague memory of a TV program that showed a man with no hands using his toes to type at a keyboard gives me the idea to use my bare foot to reach in under the rock and extract the keys. Once I get my running shoe and sock off my left foot, I step back down into the sand and begin dredging short twigs, desiccated plant stems, and other debris out from the space under the left side of the rock near the wall.

Even cleared out, the hole is too small for my size-ten foot. But I'm not discouraged; this challenge takes on an added significance. The goal of getting my keys back symbolizes the larger struggle against my entrapment. I seize upon another idea. I retrieve one of the longer sticks that I pulled out from the rocks. It's a sagebrush stem about two feet long, thin and brittle, and with a convenient bend near the skinny end that might allow me to hook the key ring. I turn on my headlamp to cast some extra light into the hollow and dip the hooked end of my stick down into the hole. The stick easily catches the keys, but it flexes and snaps when I try to fish them up through the gap. Kerplink! The keys jingle against each other as they land back in the sandy fissure. "Damn," I mutter.

Without the hook, I can only swat at the keys with the broken end of the stick, but I manage to flick them a few inches closer to my toes. I still can't quite reach the ring with my foot, so I insert the stick between my big and second toes and thread it into the hole from the side. Peering down into the hole with my headlamp, I guide the stick with a series of delicate, jerking movements until it pokes about two inches through the ring loop. Tugging, I extract the keys with the stick until they slip off the end. They're not all the way out, but I've moved them close enough to the crevice's exit that I can drop the stick and claw at the sand with my toes, grasping the keys in a foot-fist. Not wanting to accidentally drop them again, I lift my left leg until I can reach under my foot with my left hand. Success! It's the first victory of my entrapment, and it is sweet. I tuck the keys into an accessory pocket on the right side of my shorts and zip it shut.

After I put my sock and my shoe back on, not bothering to tie the laces, I decide to try a new approach to pecking at the boulder with my knife. Selecting a softball-sized stone from the pile below my feet, I maneuver it to the top. Now that it's in reach, I stretch and grab the rock—not without a spike of pain from my trapped wrist—and set the ten-pound stone on top of the boulder next to my knife. I've already discounted the idea of smashing a smaller rock directly against the chockstone, as all the available rocks are of the softer pink sandstone, like the walls. Instead, I plan to use the rock to pound my knife into the chockstone, like a hammer and chisel.

In preparation, I balance my knife so the tip fits in the slight groove I've carved in the concavity on the upper right side of the boulder, just above my right wrist, and lean the handle against the canyon wall. I grip the hammer rock tightly to ensure I will accurately hit the head of the knife and bring the hammer down in a gentle trial tap. I'm afraid the rock will kick the knife off the backside of the boulder or down into the rocks beneath my feet. My chiseling setup is as stable as I can manage, but it doesn't instill much confidence, so I tap the knife carefully a second and third time just to test if it will skitter away. It stays put, but I need to hit harder.

Here goes . . . I drive the hammer rock into my knife with ten times more force than that last tap. Karunch! The rock detonates in my hand, splitting into one large and a half-dozen smaller pieces, leaving me with a handful of crumbling sandstone as shrapnel flies up into my face. The force of the blow knocks my knife off the chockstone, and it bounces off my shorts, hitting the sand half a yard in front of my right foot. "I can't win here, nothing's working," I think, but my thin discouragement is thankfully fleeting.

I lick my lips and taste the coating of pulverized grit that has stuck to the dried sweat on my face. My knife is out of reach for my left hand, and nudging it with my foot only buries it in the sand. (At least I know I can get it back.) Taking note of the crushed rock that's all over the chockstone and my right arm, I sigh. I drop the rest of the hammer rock in front of my feet, attentive to my knife. I take off my left shoe and sock again, grab the multi-tool in my outstretched toes, and retrieve it easily.

"Come on, Aron, no more stupid stuff like that," I chastise myself, knowing I won't be trying the hammer-chisel approach again. - "That's the last thing you can afford, to lose your knife." Somehow I know it will be vital to my survival. Even though I'm certain it's far too dull to saw through my arm bones, I might need it for other things, like cutting webbing, or maybe making my backpack into a kind of wearable jacket to keep me warmer at night.

It's going on eight o'clock, and a breeze is blowing softly down-canyon. Every few minutes, the wind accelerates, flicking sand over the ledge above me into my face. I bow my head to protect my face beneath the brim of my hat. This keeps most of the dust out of my eyes, but I can feel the grit on my contacts. After huddling from a half-dozen cycles of the breeze, I catch myself not doing anything or even thinking about anything; I'm in a fleeting daze that dissolves when I become aware of it. Coming back around to my current situation, I look at the broken-up dirt and rock pieces covering my right arm. Using my fingers, then my knife, to get to the more confined spots around my right hand, I brush off the dirt. With pursed lips, I puff the last dust particles off my hand. It's ridiculous, this compulsion to keep my arm clean, but being tidy is one of the few means by which I can exert even a small degree of control over my circumstances.

I resume my excavation as darkness seeps from my penumbral

hole and spills into the desert above me, turning dusk to night. I turn my headlamp back on and pick a new target on the chockstone—a beige-pink heart of sandstone ringed by hard black mineral features. This spot is two inches above my wrist, so I am cautious with my strikes until I can chisel out a starter hole that allows me to jab harder at the chockstone. I establish a rhythm, pecking at two jabs per second, pausing to blow away dust once every five minutes. Time slips past. I can see a tiny measure of progress as a small salmon-colored flake emerges beside the shallow trough I'm carving out of the chockstone. If I'm right, I might be able to dig out enough material around this pastel nugget so that I can pop it out as a single chip.

I slip into the flow of intent action. Before I know it, three hours are gone, and it's nearly midnight. I have isolated the little flake on three sides—left, top, and bottom—by a channel about an eighth of an inch wide, and I'm ready to pry it off the boulder. Not wanting to accidentally break off the tip of my knife blade, I switch my multi-tool to the file. The file is not only thicker and sturdier, it's also somewhat more expendable. With the file tip positioned in the in-cut groove, I lever the handle toward the rock and watch for the flake to come flying for my eyes, holding my breath. I feel my tool biting into my palm just as the flake crumbles and breaks away. Yes! A dime-sized piece of rock pops off the chockstone and falls onto my trapped wrist. It's not as big as I could have hoped, but I'm pleased that my strategy paid off with at least a little progress. With the flake removed, I've exposed some softer rock that I can extract more easily. Pecking for another hour eradicates almost as much stone as what came off in the flake. I save the largest chips that fall on my trapped arm, setting them side by side on the top of the boulder. My collection grows as I enlarge the minute crater, but as my line of chips increases, so does my fatigue. The aching pain of my arm nags at my mind too much for my grogginess to matter; I need to work at getting out of here while I have my strength. Besides, even if I wanted to sleep, I couldn't. The penetrating chill of the night air and occasional breezes urge me to keep attacking the rock to generate warmth, and when my consciousness does fade, my knees buckle and my weight tugs on my wrist in an immediate and agonizing call to attention.

Perhaps because of my growing fatigue, a song is playing over and over in my head. The melody is from the first Austin Powers movie, which I watched a few nights ago with one of my roommates, and now just a single line of the ending credits' chorus is repeating on an infinite loop.

"Yeah, that's not annoying at all, Aron," I say sarcastically. "Can't you get something else on the juke?" It doesn't matter what else I try to hum—even some of my favorite standbys—I can't free myself from the mind-lock of Austin Powers.

Taking a break, I extract from my main pack the rope bag, my harness and climbing hardware, CamelBak pack, and water bottle, then strap the large backpack on my back for the first time since the afternoon. I figure—correctly—that the pack's padding will help me retain my body heat. I remove the CamelBak's blue water reservoir and slide its empty pack alongside my pinned arm. I can get the inch-thick insulation only a few inches past my elbow, because the boulder has my arm pressed tight against the wall from my wrist to my middle forearm. But with the small pack in place, most of my arm and shoulder is held off the cold slab. I remove my rope from its bag, leaving it neatly coiled, and stack it on a rock sitting on the canyon floor in front of my knees. With the rock padded by the rope, I can bend my knees forward and lean in to the rock, easing the weight on my legs a little. I still can't relax, but now I can change my position from time to time and stimulate the circulation in my legs.

It's just before one-thirty in the morning when I open my water bottle for the second time and have a small sip. I've been thinking about having a drink for at least two hours, but I was purposefully delaying until I made it halfway through the night. Four and a half hours down, four and a half to go. The water is expectedly refreshing, a reward for having gone so long since those first extravagant gulps some eight hours ago. Still, I worry. I know that the remaining twenty-two ounces are the key to my survival. But it's a puzzle as to how much I should drink or conserve and how long I should try to make it last. Mulling it over, I settle on a plan to have a small sip every ninety minutes. It will give me something to gauge the time, something to look forward to as the night advances.

With fatigue buckling my knees periodically, I decide to construct a seat that I can use to completely take my weight off my legs. Getting into my harness is the easy half of the equation. Stepping into the leg loops, I pull up the waist belt and weave the thick webbing through the buckle; with the limited dexterity of my single hand, I skip the usual last step of doubling back the belt—a precaution necessary for climbing safety but more protection than I need in my current situation. Now comes the hard part: getting some piece of my pared arsenal of climbing gear hung up on a rock overhead, something suspended substantially enough to hold my weight.

I have my eye on a crack system that starts on the south wall, about six feet above and to the left of my head. The crack is actually a gap between the wall and the eight-foot-diameter chockstone suspended six feet in front of me. This is the boulder forming the twelve-foot drop-off that I reached at the end of the chockstone gauntlet, the one I was descending when I stepped onto the chockstone that pinned my wrist. I hadn't taken much time to look closely at this chockstone earlier, but now I see two features that might help me in building an anchor. One is the crack, tapering from the upper gap to a pinch point that unfortunately flares open toward me; the other is an apparent horn that I might use as an anchor if I could lasso my rope or a piece of my yellow webbing around it. But how can I fabricate a block to throw into the crack and pull it down until it catches at the pinch point? There are two options: either clipping a few of my carabiners together in a wad on a knot in my rope; or tying a knot directly into the rope or onto a piece of webbing to jam the knot itself in the constriction. In either case, it will be very difficult to toss the apparatus with enough precision for it to slip into the crack and catch at the pinch point.

Still, it's worth a try. First I unwrap about thirty feet of my climbing rope. At the end, I tie a series of overhand knots to make a fist-sized block. With some extra rope stacked on top of the chockstone, I cast the fist up at the crack, but it bounces off the wall. I realize the combination of my left hand's awkward throwing abilities and the nature of the rope to fall short as it lifts more of its own weight are an unforgiving mix. I will have to make the perfect toss. Perhaps it will be easier with a heavier lead. I decide to add three carabiners from the climbing supplies on my harness to a figure-eight knot, replacing the rope fist.

Each toss takes two minutes to set up, and my first dozen tries fall short, bouncing off the wall or the face of the chockstone, or slipping out of the crack before the carabiners can wedge tightly. I refine my procedure of stacking the trailing rope so it unfurls with as little drag as possible, and my accuracy improves. Of the next dozen tries, five of them land my carabiners in the crack, but each time they pull free. I add a fourth carabiner to my improvised grappling device. With a brilliantly lucky throw on my next try, the carabiner bundle hits the wide mouth of the crack and drops into the pinch point, and with a tug at just the right moment, the block wedges tight. I test the constriction's strength and watch the carabiners bite into the rock. I'm worried that the sandstone pinch point will break and let the 'biners loose, but the metal links jam hard against one another, and the rock holds the stress without a problem. As a wave of happiness washes over my tired mind, I tie another figure-eight knot on a loop of the anchored rope that drapes back over the chockstone near my waist, and I clip myself to the system. With two adjustments of the knot to cinch my harness a little higher and keep my weight from tugging on my arm, I finally lean back and take some weight off my legs. Ahhhhh. I relax for the first time, and my body celebrates a victory over the strain of standing still for over twelve hours.

I take my water bottle from its perch and have a small sip right at three A.M. My respite is complete but disappointingly short—just fifteen minutes until the harness restricts the blood flow to my legs and

I have to stand again. There is the risk that if I sit too long, I will cause damage to my legs or cause a blood clot to form. Long before that danger manifests, the harness makes my hamstrings ache where the leg loops hold my weight. I alternate standing and sitting, establishing a pattern that I repeat in twenty-minute intervals.

In these coldest hours before dawn, from three until six, I take up my knife again and hack at the chockstone. I can chip at the rock either standing or sitting. I continue to make minimal but visible progress in the divot. After sips of water at four-thirty and six A.M., I take stock of the rock I've managed to eliminate during the past fifteen hours of tiring work. I estimate that at the rate I've averaged, I would have to chip at the rock for 150 hours to free my hand. Discouraged, I know I will need to do something else to improve my situation.

Just after eight o'clock, I hear a rushing noise filtering down from the canyon above me, a wind swoosh that pulses three times. I look up as a large black raven flies over my head. He's heading upcanyon, and with each flap of his wings, echoes filter down to my ears. At the third flap, he screeches a loud "Ca-caw" and then disappears from my window of the overhead world. It's still clammy cold in the depths of the canyon fissure, but I can see bright daylight on the north wall seventy feet above me. Broken strands of stratus clouds float by. I turn off my headlamp. I have made it through the night.

Around nine-thirty A.M. a dagger of sunlight appears behind me on the canyon floor. The light blade is teasingly close but still three feet behind my shoes. I haven't yet fully rewarmed from the night's chill, and I yearn for even a small touch of sun on my skin. After five minutes, the dagger has stabbed toward my heels enough that when I step down next to the hole where I dropped my keys, stretching my body until my arm pulls at my wrist, I can extend my left leg behind me so the sunshine caresses my ankle and lower calf. For ten minutes, I hold still, alternating between stretching out my left and then my right leg as the sunlight moves across the canyon floor. Like a yoga pose, this sun stretch welcomes a new day. The question crosses my mind of how many mornings will I be here to perform this matinal rite, but I push it back and relish the soothing warmth on my calves. Climbing up the north wall above my right leg, the light dagger bends and warps over the sandstone undulations until it ascends above my leg's reach. Watching the beam scale the last three feet to where a suspended chockstone blocks it from my view, I realize it is the only direct sun I will get during the day.

With the sunlight's presence, my emotional status lifts, and I feel rejuvenated for a time. Taking advantage of this positive infusion, I take up my knife and begin another two-hour cycle of pecking at the rock. I speculate on the odds of being found and the timing of when outside efforts will initiate a potential search. It looks bleak from every angle. Kristi and Megan barely know me. When I didn't show up at their truck late yesterday afternoon, they probably thought I blew them off. They don't know what my truck looks like, either, so even if they went over to the Horseshoe Canyon Trailhead, they - wouldn't know if my vehicle was there or not. Since I didn't confirm with Brad and Leah that I would see them at the Scooby party, they - wouldn't be alerted to a problem. My roommates will miss me, but they don't know where I am. If they should get so concerned to notify the Aspen police, the authorities won't do anything until Tuesday night, at the earliest, once I'm overdue by over twenty-four hours.

It seems more probable to me that my manager at the Ute Mountaineer will call my parents to find out why I haven't shown up for work. At that point, maybe they'll get the police to poll my credit-card companies for my recent purchasing history and track me to Moab. This thought causes me to mentally slap myself, thinking about the purchases I made—I used my credit card only for gas in Glenwood Springs, where the highway from Aspen meets the interstate. I could have gone either east or west from there. I used my debit card to get groceries and top off my gas tank in Moab before I drove in to Horseshoe. Or did I? Maybe I used my credit card. Now I can't remember. I hope it's part of the missing-person's procedure to check debit purchases, too.

If the police notify the National Park Service and the NPS initiates a general search on Wednesday, they're unlikely to find my vehicle right away—the commanders will focus on the areas closer to Moab first. I saw a sign at the trailhead notifying visitors that rangers lead weekend tours down into Horseshoe Canyon to the major pictograph panels; the best shot for a ranger to find my truck will be when they come back to Horseshoe on Saturday, if they're looking for it by then. A lucky strike, or more thorough second-stage canvasing, might mean they pinpoint my truck in the first day of searching, Thursday, and by the time they sweep the canyon and move all the way through Blue John, it'll be Friday.

Friday, then, before someone pops his or her head over that chockstone ten feet in front and above me.

Friday.

But that's at the earliest. Sunday's more likely to be the day the searchers get to me, given the rangers' schedule. Sunday, a week from today.

Without water, people die in a lot less than a week. I'll be shocked if I survive until Tuesday morning. There's no way I'll make it to Friday. No way.

And I'll be mummified by Sunday.

FOUR

How to Become a Retired Engineer in Just Five Short Years

Deep Play: whereby what [one] stands to win from a gamble can never equal the enormity of what [one] will lose.
— JOE SIMPSON, *Dark Shadows Falling*

IN THE YEAR after my encounter with the stalking black bear in the Grand Tetons, I selected three climbing projects that would come to occupy my entire recreational focus: I would climb all of the Colorado fourteeners; I would climb all of them solo in winter (something that had never been done before); and I would ascend to the highest point in every state in the U.S. In late June 1997, I started my job at Intel, which seemed like a piece of cake compared to being hunted by a winter-thin bear.

Compensating for the banality of my new career in mechanical engineering, I created adventure in my life by exploring Arizona's vast variety of public lands—canyons, mountains, volcanic cones, meteor craters, deserts, and forests. I met my friend and mentor Mark Van Eeckhout through a college classmate. We both worked at the same clean-room facility in southern Phoenix, and over lunch we would plan out hiking and camping trips.

My college girlfriend, Jamie Zeigler, gave me Edward Abbey's book *Desert Solitaire,* which fanned my passion for desert adventure.

I became a founding member of the Intel Adventure Club in 1998 when four of my friends from work, including Jamie Stoutenberg and Judson Cole, drafted a plan to hike across the Grand Canyon twice on consecutive days. Starting from the South Rim, we would descend five thousand feet in seven miles via the South Kaibab Trail to cross the Colorado River near Phantom Ranch, then continue fourteen miles on the Bright Angel Trail to the North Rim, climbing six thousand feet up to our campsite. After resting, we would turn around and do it in reverse, North Rim to South Rim. We called it the Rim-to-Rim-to-Rim, or R^3 for short.

Just before the trip I was reading Jon Krakauer's book *Into the Wild*. The story of young Chris McCandless dropping out of mainstream society to travel around the country entranced me with dreams of living out of the back of a truck and "rubber tramping" across the U.S. I was so caught up in the adventures of Alex Supertramp, Chris's nom de voyage, that I carried the book with me across the Grand Canyon on the R^3 trip. One passage in particular—from a letter that Chris sent to an older friend he'd met on the road—read like a manifesto:

> So many people live within unhappy circumstances and yet will not take the initiative to change their situation because they are conditioned to a life of security, conformity, and conservatism, all of which may appear to give one peace of mind, but in reality nothing is more damaging to the adventurous spirit within a man than a secure future. The very basic core of a man's living spirit is his passion for adventure. The joy of life comes from our encounters with new experiences, and hence there is no greater joy than to have an endlessly changing horizon, for each day to have a new and different sun.

I wanted to taste that joy, to experience that passion for adventure, to cast away the security of my job and let my spirit roam. This meant I needed to get educated on outdoor living; I needed to gain experience before tackling major expeditions; and I needed to be prepared and mitigate risks. Even more directly, I needed to get a truck and then leave my job. But I had a ways to go before I would be ready to do that.

Another of Krakauer's books, *Into Thin Air,* captured my imagination in the winter of 1998. It documented the Mount Everest disaster, in which eleven people died, so compellingly that I felt transported to 26,000 feet on the South Col with Neal Beidleman's group of lost climbers, just a few hundred yards from Camp IV, wondering what I would do in their place. Exhausted from summit day, pounded by the hellion winds of a blizzard, out of oxygen, and frostbitten—would I lie there dying? Would I leave the others to save myself? Would I go back to find them if I made it to camp? How would I behave in a situation that caused me to summon the essence of my character? The tragedy inspired me to test myself. I wanted to reveal to myself who I was: the kind of person who died, or the kind of person who overcame circumstances to help himself and others. Not only did I want to go to the Himalayas to climb a major peak, I wanted to explore the depth of my spirit.

And so it was that on March 8, 1998, I set out for a solo winter climb of Humphreys Peak, the highest point in Arizona. Mark lent me snowshoes, an ice axe, and the mountaineering reference *Freedom of the Hills,* telling me that I needed to master the ice axe techniques it described. Orienteering north from the Snowbowl ski area five miles northwest of Flagstaff, I snowshoed through the pine trees for two hours, following the 10,000-foot contour until I entered a meadow at the base of a long snowfield. From there, I took Mark's ice axe in my hand and climbed over 2,500 feet up the moderate slope to the summit ridge, where I left the snowshoes smothered in storm. In places, the clouds were so thick that I couldn't see the drop-off on the right-hand side of the ridge, so I stayed safely to the left, which was, conversely, more exposed to the wind. After a half hour of hiking along the rock-strewn rim of the ancient high volcanic crater, I was shivering hard from the ice-cold blast, but I eventually found the summit, where I squatted behind a hand-stacked wall of rocks at 12,633 feet. Three distant clashes of thunder and lightning collapsed in the clouds to the south.

I couldn't stay on the summit and risk getting hit by a lightning bolt, but I didn't want to leave the protection of the rock wall, either. For a fleeting moment, I empathized with that huddling group of lost climbers on the South Col. Here in my own winter whiteout, I was confused, stressed, and lethargic, and I understood a little more personally how the temptation to wait until things got better could, in extremis, turn into deadly apathy. Collecting myself, I stood up from behind the windbreak to face the storm. Staring into a feature-less blanket of hazy gray and bracing myself against the wind, I checked my compass to pick a ridgeline to descend. My ascending footprints had been obliterated in seconds.

Forcing my way down, I kept my eyes searching for Mark's snow-shoes. I had left them on the ridge at the top of the snowfield, mark-ing the turn where I would descend into the trees and get out of the storm. Above the gale, I noticed a hissing sound coming from my pack. I stopped to check it out and saw small blue sparks discharge between the metal tips of my ski poles. Idiotically, I had lashed them onto my pack so that the tips were three feet above my head, and they were attracting lightning. I dropped the pack and dove onto a patch of snow faster than I had ever moved on a mountainside. Panting, I dragged my pack beside me as I scooted off the ridge on my belly. When I felt safe to stand up, I ran for my life. After a minute, I slowed down when a momentary break in the clouds showed me Mark's snowshoes just above. I ditched my pack to retrieve them and made it back to my truck two hours later without further incident.

There are patterns to my climbing style that first sprouted on this ascent of Humphreys Peak—traveling by myself, climbing through storms, making solid route-finding decisions in demanding situations, and getting lucky around lightning. This climb was also a confidence builder for me: My awareness was heightened, and in that awareness I felt more deeply alive.

*   *   *

After my adventure on Humphreys Peak, Mark and I spoke often about my plan to solo-climb all the fourteeners in Colorado in winter. Mark knew I was too inexperienced to tackle such a risky project, but he also knew that I was intent on getting the project going. He taught me the basics of rock climbing, rope work, avalanche awareness, and snow travel. We went on beginner-level climbing excursions around central Arizona, took trips to the indoor rock climbing gym in Tempe, and over Labor Day weekend of 1998, Mark led my friend Howard and me on my first multi-pitch alpine rock climb on Vestal Peak in the San Juan Mountains of Colorado.

Vestal Peak was especially memorable, as Mark taught us to handle the fear we felt before and during the climb of the two-thousand-foot-high slab of granite that tops out at nearly 14,000 feet. Halfway up the center of the north face, the soles of both my climbing boots blew out within minutes of each other, the stitching of the heels just disintegrating under the stress of the ascent, leaving me with the equivalent of massive flip-flops for the upper part of the route.

Despite my failed equipment, we reached the summit, and I was even longing for more, wishing the climbing weren't already over. At the top, Mark introduced me to his favorite summit ritual of kippered fish and crackers, a tradition that we continue on every shared mountaintop. We took photos together, my beaming smile through a mouthful of half-chewed fish was a genuine expression of how giddy I felt to be at the top with my best friends, having overcome fear that day.

When my sister started college in the fall of 1998, she moved to a part of northwest Texas that could give a prairie dog a case of the doldrums. Wanting to share the exhilaration I was discovering through the outdoors, I invited her to come with me to one of the most beautiful places I've ever seen—the waterfalls of Havasupai Canyon, just southwest of Grand Canyon National Park. In the language of the native peoples who have lived in the canyon for a hundred genera- tions, Havasupai means "people of the blue-green waters," for the waterfalls of the lower canyon. There are four major falls, the tallest of which leap over two-hundred-foot cliffs into deep turquoise pools filling the canyon from wall to wall.

My sister and I arrived at the trailhead on Thanksgiving Day, 1998, and hiked ten miles down from the plateau into Havasupai Canyon to pass the village of about two hundred residents. Since there is no road to the village, everything is brought in on small heli- copters and trains of pack burros. The Havasupai village has the dis- tinction of housing the only post office in the United States that is still served by burros. Residents have a community landline phone, plumbing, and sufficient electricity to power the reggae music that pushes past Bob Marley tapestries hung in the windows of every third government-issued trailer home. Most of the younger residents forgo the subsistence farming that the overgrown plots in front of their homes suggest their parents and grandparents pursued.

Beyond the village and Navajo Falls, the least dramatic but widest of the four waterfalls, we came to the Havasupai Falls and camping zone in the early afternoon. Havasupai is the trademark waterfall that pours its luminous flow over a 150-foot drop of maroon travertine draperies into a deep pool warmed by the sun. It's a magical place that sees a heavy load of traffic from hikers and campers, though the Havasupai manage the use to concentrate the impact upstream of the largest of the cascades, 220-foot-high Mooney Falls. We chose a campsite in the middle of the zone and left our packs and gear to ex- plore farther downcanyon.

Within minutes of venturing beyond our camp, we came to the brink of Mooney Falls, its beauty and flamboyant color freezing us in our tracks. It was a full minute before either of us even muttered "Wow." We looked down on islands of lush green grass, towers of brilliant yellow cottonwood leaves reflecting the dazzling sun, sand-

bars strewn with bleached white tree trunks, and the uniquely flowing rock formations of cherry-red travertine that decorate the canyon
in hanging curtains under a wall-to-wall cerulean sky.

Below Mooney, which we descended by a system of tunnels,
chain ropes, and downclimbing, a faint trail disappeared into tall
thickets of grasses that sprang from the sandbars. We waded down
the streambed for another three miles and came to Beaver Falls, a
group of interlaced and terraced pools that receives only a small fraction of the visitors as the upper falls. Here the travertine builds up
dams across the stream that form horseshoe-shaped pools, each
spilling over into the next. The falls drop about fifty feet and are
spread out along a two-hundred-foot-long corridor in the canyon.
They reminded me of the thermal pools my family had visited in Yellowstone almost a decade earlier. Five miles past Beaver Falls, the
creek drops into a narrow channel where the turquoise waters of
Havasupai spill directly into the often muddy-brown torrent of the
Colorado River at the bottom of the Grand Canyon. My sister and I -
didn't have time to go all the way to the river, so she sat on a rock
above Beaver Falls while I balanced my way across the dams to reach
the west shore of the creek. In my wet sandals, my footing was un-
sure, but I made it over to a rock shelf alongside the dams that was
guarded by a barrier of prickly-pear cactus. I needed to go upstream
on the shelf, somehow bypassing the garden of four-foot-high cacti,
to gain a wider series of dams where it would be easier to cross back to
the east side. The best strategy looked to be climbing about ten feet
up the rock wall above the shelf and traversing over the cacti. I went
for it, despite doubts that my sandals would grip the steep, wet
travertine.

Perched a body's length above the largest of the prickly-pears after
five moves from right to left, I pinched a hold with my left hand that
stretched my body into an X. As I shifted my weight onto my extended left foot, the travertine broke off, and the resulting jolt of my
body on the knob I was holding in my right hand caused it to disin-

tegrate as well. Suddenly, I was slipping down the travertine slide on the toe tips of my sandals, facing the rock. I had enough time to spot the prickly-pear closing in on my ass. The branches and paddles were naturally arranged in a curve close to the wall, with two separate cacti at the shelf's lip. In my brief downward glance, the prickly-pear bushes turned into a grotesque smile, like a ravenous oversized fly-trap about to enjoy an overdue meal. Just before my heels met the top of the cactus, I sprang off the wall, turning a half rotation in midair to clear the tallest part of the spiny plant.

My feet hit the sand straddling a three-foot-high branch of the pear-shaped paddles—the nose of the smiling face. The landing would have been safe, except that my momentum had pushed my body into a crouch to absorb the fall's energy. Spine-covered pear paddles met the sensitive soft tissue of my inner thighs. Recoiling from dozens of impalements, I burst back into the air. I stood bow-legged on the shelf above the travertine dams and aqua pools like a dismounted cowboy. My sister's shout, "Are you okay?," allowed me to defer looking down for another five seconds while I replied, "Yeah . . . but I fell on a cactus."

I twisted and maneuvered my way out of the cactus garden, then dropped my shorts. The fabric of my gray long underwear was polka-dotted with red spots of blood. At the center of each crimson bull's-eye was a half-inch-long barbed cactus needle. I plucked for twenty minutes and removed the most offensive thorns, then took off my long underwear to hunt for the smaller, more hairlike spines. Extracting them one by one, I lost count somewhere past a hundred. Nearly an hour later, Sonja shouted over the water noise for me to pull my shorts back on—there were other hikers approaching. I stuffed my gray tights into my pocket and crossed the dam to see who was coming. These were the only other people we had seen below the village. They were two gregarious guys about my age, also from Phoenix, heading down to camp at the Colorado River. I wanted to see the lower part of Havasupai, but as my sister had little desire to make the sixteen-mile round trip, I arranged to meet Jean-Marc and Chad at the river by ten the next morning to make the return trek together.

Sonja and I returned to climb the Mooney Falls tunnels in the fading light. For our dinner back at camp, we laid out some pre-cooked turkey on crackers to go with our main course of macaroni and cheese. Even for backcountry cuisine, it was basic fare, but we - weren't there to celebrate a big traditional Thanksgiving dinner—we were most thankful about being with each other in such an inspiring place. After a chocolate bar each for dessert, we hung our food to protect it from the ring-tailed cats and raccoons and crawled onto our open-air tarp, the two lone occupants of the half-mile-long campground. My sister rolled over and fell asleep as I sat with my headlamp and tweezers for about forty-five minutes, trying to extract the remaining prickly-pear barbs from my inner thighs. It eased my embarrassment to know that no one was watching my peculiar ritual of awkward stretching, rubbing, plucking, prodding, and grimacing— my tweezers and I had the canyon to ourselves. It would be a full week before I found and removed the last spine, a fine hair impaled in my left buttock, while watching football on television in my town home in Chandler.

By seven A.M. the next morning, I was descending the canyon by headlamp, downclimbing the ropes and chains at Mooney Falls, splashing through the streambed, and hiking swiftly through the grasses and reeds bordering the sandbars and creek banks past Beaver Falls. I was exactly on time for the rendezvous at the Colorado River, where Jean-Marc and Chad offered me some of their coffee, freshly brewed on their backcountry stove. We hung out on the slate ledges along the downriver side of the Havasupai outlet, overlooking the comparatively monstrous Colorado, and scoped out swimming possibilities along the south shore of the river. Chad waded out through the confluence zone of Havasupai Creek to get a picture of the mixing line where the translucent waters first met the rushing madness of the Colorado's black-opal current.

What possessed me to follow Chad out into the water, pass him to climb onto the last rock at the upstream edge of a powerful eddy, and then cannonball into the Colorado River, fully clothed, without a life jacket . . . Well, it seemed like a good idea at the time. Chad did get a funny picture of me, balled up in midair and unthinkingly bound for disaster, but had he and Jean-Marc not acted as fast as they did in the ensuing moments, it would have been the last picture anyone ever took of me, silly or otherwise. As I plunged in and came to the surface, I gasped at the unexpected temperature of the river—a hypothermic 50 degrees—over twenty degrees colder than the tropically warm Havasupai Creek.

My thick long-sleeved shirt and pants became ten-pound weights, and my running shoes dragged my feet plumb as the current swept me along the edge of the fifteen-yard-long eddy. Kicking off my shoes, I swam hard and fought my way into the eddy within five feet of shore in deep water. I noticed I was no longer getting any closer to solid ground. The circular eddy current was too strong to overcome. As I made stroke after stroke, I watched the shore move past. Chad and Jean-Marc were watching me and called out, "Aron, do you need help?" My pride replied, "Nah, I'll make it," as I took in my first swallow of river water.

Chad must have heard panic in my voice, because he dashed up the ledge behind the short beach to their campsite, thirty feet away, as I recirculated upstream in the eddy. Pushed from shore by the eddy current, I was quickly caught by the main current and the cycle began to repeat itself. As I attempted to unbutton my long-sleeved shirt to alleviate the drag, I instantly submerged and couldn't get more than a single button undone before I needed air. The icy grip of the Colorado constricted my chest, making my breathing a shallow and rapid gasping. After swallowing three gulps of water and immersing a second time, I abandoned the shirt removal. Downstream of the eddy, the canyon walls rise straight from the water in two-to-three-hundred-foot cliffs for a thousand yards until the river turns right and disappears at the corner. I knew if I were swept past the Havasupai Creek eddy, I would drown long before I had another chance to get out of the river, and indeed it would be another hundred river miles until the current would spit my remains onto a beach at the upper end of Lake Mead. A newspaper headline flashed in front of my eyes: IDIOT ENGINEER DROWNS IN GRAND CANYON, BODY RECOVERED IN LAKE MEAD.

I thrashed at the water, straining for the eddy. At the farthest downstream edge, I broke through the eddy line and cried out, "Help! Help!"

Chad was up on a ledge returning from the campsite. "Jean-Marc, here!" Chad tossed a coiled accessory cord to Jean-Marc, who was fifteen feet away from me.

"Aron, grab hold!" He threw out the line, but it fell in the eddy, upstream of my position, and quickly floated out of my reach.

"Unnnggh," I grunted. I continued to swim as hard as I could manage toward the shore. The cold was crippling me, numbing my legs, my arms, and my core. Jean-Marc retrieved the cord and tossed it out again, but the eddy current had already swept me past the beach and out into the overwhelming force of the Colorado. Concentrating on the eddy line, I kicked my lethargic legs and pumped my arms freestyle. I didn't see Jean-Marc hand the cord off to Chad, but when I broke into the eddy again five seconds later, Chad had already thrown the coil and was shouting, "Aron, grab it! Get it! It's right there!"

I reached to my right and brought my hand down on the thin black line as it drifted limply in the eddy. Chad yanked on it to reel me in, and I lost my sodden grip on the cord. The crush of disappointment nearly drowned me. Certain I wouldn't survive another recirculation, I pleaded, "Help! Throw it again!"

My strokes were desperate but weak. The toss had to be perfect. Any mistake here and I was dead. Three seconds later, the line came back and draped over my right shoulder. A miracle! I grabbed at it with both hands, wrapping my left wrist in the line twice as my body wilted. With one last breath, I let my head drop into the water and felt the tension increase on the cord, biting into my wrist, but I didn't care. My only thought was a hope that the line wouldn't break. First my hands, and then my arms and chest brushed up onto the sand, and Jean-Marc was grabbing me under my shoulders. I felt sick, cold, blown out, and apathetic. I was safe at last but exhausted beyond concern. A voice spoke: "Oh my God, are you breathing?"

I nodded. "Thank . . . you . . . ." I huffed between choked breaths, my head buried between my outstretched arms, face in the sand.

"Jesus, you almost died!" Jean-Marc was upset and stressed out, but Chad was calm.

"It'll be okay. You're safe. How do you feel?"

"I'm cold." I paused and shuddered. "I think . . . I swallowed . . . a lot of water." Rolling over to sit up, I slowly drew my legs out of the eddy and held my bloated stomach, groaning over the ache, wanting to puke, but I was too faint to summon the energy.

It took a full five minutes of rest, staring at the eddy where I nearly took my last lungful of air, before I could stand up. Chad offered me a dry sweatshirt, and I paced around in lurching stumbles, trying to restore my equilibrium. Even dry, I was still chilled and needed to get moving. However, nauseated from the river water, I could barely hold my balance. Jean-Marc spotted me when I climbed up the slate ledge to our earlier perch, and I had to sit and take a break while they packed away their camping supplies. We were relaxing, and the aftermath of the adrenaline made us all a little slaphappy.

"I can't believe how lucky that last toss was." I was dumbstruck at how a matter of seconds and inches had saved my life.

"I can't believe you were like 'No, I don't need any help—I'm drowning, but I'll be OK,' " Chad teased me.

I looked up and smiled, and we giggled. "Are you ready to go? I need to get my metabolism fired up."

"Yeah, we're ready," Jean-Marc said. "Get your shoes on."

"Oh. They're gone. I had to kick them off when I was in the river.

I'm gonna hike back in my socks." My shoes were halfway to Mexico by now, and my sandals were back at Havasupai Campground.

"It's eight miles, man. Here, take my sandals off my pack." Chad leaned over, and I undid the Velcro loops. The rubber sandals were too big, but they were better than nothing.

The more we walked, the better I felt. I warmed up, and my stomach absorbed the river water. We rehashed the rescue, I asked if Chad had gotten the picture of me, and he confirmed, "It was you in the middle of 'Yeee-haw' jumping off the rock."

"Well, then, it was worth it. As long as you got the picture," I said sarcastically and grinned. Secretly, I was pleased to know that I'd have a souvenir of one of my stupidest moments ever.

As we headed back to our camp, Jean-Marc mentioned he had a bottle of Stolichnaya up at their gear stash above Mooney Falls, and all of a sudden, it was the only thing the three of us could think about. We sped the remaining three miles upstream, hopping over logs, splashing and slipping in the creek, in an hour-long dash for the Havasupai happy hour. We eagerly guzzled most of Jean-Marc's vodka, then found Sonja as it was getting dark, to join up for a swim in the large pool below Havasupai Falls. Telling and retelling the story of my near-drowning, we waded up under the falls to reemerge in the moonlight like creatures from the Blue Lagoon. After polishing off the vodka, our group of four stumbled out of the water well past dark. We crafted a faux distress note to stick in the bottle before sending it over Mooney Falls toward its destiny. We imagined it making a journey all the way to Lake Mead, where a Jet Skier would find our message: "Help! We're at Havasupai Campground. Send more vodka immediately! Emergency! [signed] Jean-Marc, Chad, and Aron, November 29, 1998."

An hour later, when we'd called it a night, Sonja and I got into our sleeping bags. Lying there next to my sister, I told her what it had been like at the Colorado. All comedy aside, I said, "I was scared, Sonja. I saw headlines reporting my death. I thought I was a goner." We cried together, then drifted off to sleep. The next morning, we packed up our gear for the ten-mile hike back to my car, then posed together for a final picture next to Havasupai Falls, happy to have each other. It became one of my favorite photos of the two of us.

By December 1998, I hadn't yet climbed any winter fourteeners. Indeed, I'd climbed only seven total, and all of those in summer conditions. I planned to start with the easier, nontechnical peaks at the beginning of the winter 1998–99 season. Even these least demanding mountains would require safe snow-travel knowledge and winter-weather experience. On the last training trip Mark and I did before I left for my winter vacation, we attempted Engineer Mountain in southwestern Colorado, near Durango. Conditions were rough, due to a ground blizzard whipping snow into fifty-foot visibility conditions. About a third of the way in, we bailed on the climb and spent the late morning and early afternoon digging snow-study pits to practice evaluating the snowpack. Mark showed me how to check the snow layers for hardness, cohesion, and avalanche potential, something that would become routine for me as part of my fourteener project.

Two days later, after one of my best days skiing ever—in three feet of powder at Wolf Creek—Mark and I drove down into Alamosa in my fully laden sports coupe to get a motel room and recuperate from our binge of snow recreation. We had skied together regularly in the big snow year of 1997, usually camping out in zero-degree weather in the back of his Tacoma in ski-area parking lots, sitting on his tailgate eating hot oatmeal straight from his camping-stove pot, and watching the other skiers arriving. This time was even more special because Mark was moving to work in Alamosa for the winter.

In the morning, we parted ways, and I drove north toward Fairplay, in central Colorado. My plan was to attempt a winter solo of Quandary Peak before I visited my parents for Christmas. Quandary's easy winter access and short ridgeline route makes it the easiest winter fourteener, and one with a low exposure to avalanches, an ideal proving ground to test my winter skills and solo methods. December 22 dawned clear and cold, but with a jet-stream wind blowing hard across the high peaks. I had bought Mark's old snowshoes from him, and as I strapped them to my waterproof leather hiking boots, I jittered with childlike excitement, feeling that it wasn't just another hike. This ascent of the 14,265-foot Quandary represented the first stage of a substantial commitment, an engagement to my project. I stood at the threshold of the forest, arms wide, balancing on that moment when preparation changes into performance.

The wind in my face occupied my attention for most of the gentle ascent. I tried to keep my head bent and my goggles from frosting over on the inside as I trudged in the snow up to the elevation where the trees grow more horizontally than vertically. I quickly left behind even these stumpy juniper shrubs. Higher up, the wind scoured the snowpack down to the rock-strewn tundra. I left my snowshoes on the broad ridge at a knoll somewhere above 12,000 feet. I looked to the southwest, where the nearby Lincoln group of fourteeners was clearly visible. The wind cut through my goggles' ventilation ports, making my eyes tear up; snow-frosted summits swam in my vision under the azure sky.

As I put more and more of the atmosphere and its contaminants below me, the sky sank along the color wheel from Mediterranean blue to solid cobalt to indigo dye. I imagined I could hike until the sky went black, and to me, for a few hours, the sky in my world was a different color than just about everyone else's. I thought about the chance that I was the highest person in Colorado, and it seemed extremely likely—virtually no one climbs fourteeners in the winter. Given that it's the off-season for the other high mountains of North America, I figured there were fairly good odds that I was the highest person on the continent, too.

Windchill temperatures were in the negative twenties, and I'd completely spaced on my plan to keep a few food items in my pants pocket. At the summit, I found that my storebought water bottles had frozen through completely, and my chocolate bars were frost-nipped inside their packages. They weren't edible, though I sucked on one like a Popsicle until I had licked the chocolate coating off the peanut core.

Descending with the wind at my back, I nearly took flight from the mountaintop, as I ran in bounding leaps to my snowshoes. Relief from the physical stresses of the climb gave me a chance to celebrate my accomplishment. I put on the snowshoes and thought back over the day, especially about what I could do better to keep my food and water thawed during the climb—it wouldn't always be such a short trip that I could get away without eating and drinking. In fact, hunger was gnawing in my stomach, and my tongue felt sticky in my mouth. I needed refreshment and was discouraged that I'd carried around the deadweight of my frozen food and water without gaining from it.

I returned to my car and drove two hours down to Denver and my parents' house, bursting with the exhilaration of a successful start to my project. There would be many more successes and opportunities for improving my performance on the winter solo climbs, but that one held me all year, until I climbed my second winter four-teener in December 1999. In the interim, I moved to Washington State with my engineering job, which provided me mountaineering opportunities that pushed my skills to the next level. My speed increased to where I could climb over 3,000 vertical feet in an hour with a twenty-pound pack; I became proficient in using crampons on snow, ice, and rock; and I went out with climbing partners to practice crevasse rescue and roped-team glacier travel techniques as we prepared for multiple ascents of the Cascades' glaciated peaks—Mount Rainier, Mount Baker, and Mount Shuksan. During the six months I spent in Washington, there wasn't a single weekend of good weather (by the end of summer, the world record for annual snowfall had been set on Mount Baker), but neither was there a single weekend that I didn't go mountaineering. I discovered that if I waited for the weather, I'd never do anything, so I coped with soggy clothes, a mildewed tent, cold nights out in the middle of summer, and less than rewarding summit views from the inside of clouds.

On Mount Rainier, I learned what it meant to sit in an exposed bivouac after my partner Paul Budd and I had made a traverse over the summit, ascending via the Kautz Ice Chute route and then—because of our shortage of ice screws and a nasty lightning and snow storm—descending via the standard Disappointment Cleaver route. With our camping gear, food, and water supplies at 11,000 feet on the opposite side of the mountain, we shivered at 10,000 feet for eight hours as a ten-degree chill drained our bodies' warmth. During that epic, we climbed over 15,000 feet vertical in twenty-four hours (we had to reclimb the peak to retrieve our gear) and went sixty-six hours without sleeping due to the storms.

Paul and I had put forth a monstrous effort that showed new depths to my strength; these came to bear the next weekend, when I returned with my friend Judson Cole from Arizona and we climbed the regular Disappointment Cleaver route in a single push, going from the Paradise base area to the summit and back in fourteen hours. On an endurance-climbing kick, I joined a group of three companions from the ACME Mountain Club for an ascent of the North Face of Mount Shuksan, one of the most beautiful mountains in the world and still one of the greatest climbs I've ever done. But the approach to the climb was proof of the adage "If you want to get to heaven, you have to go through hell." Our team bushwhacked through such heavy forest undergrowth that it ripped one of my ice tools completely off my backpack without my even noticing. I lost our only map as well, as I slipped with every second step on the sloping hillside coated in two-inch-thick slide alder branches. Thankfully, we knew the route well enough from having memorized the description that we were able to keep going, despite gaining only a - mile's progress in almost eight hours of hiking through the night.

By morning we were exhausted from the heinous approach. After reorienting ourselves in the daylight, we reached 5,000 feet on the north shoulder of the mountain and collapsed for an hour-long nap. At noon, we rousted ourselves and roped up for protection against falling into a crevasse while we climbed the mountain's upper glaciers. A thousand feet up, in the middle of the ramp connecting the two glaciers of the North Face, as my rope-mate Bruce and I were spread across an avalanche debris field, we heard a distant rumbling far above us.

Our partners ahead started screaming at us to run. Without looking at what the other was doing, Bruce and I ran three steps away from each other, and the rope drew taught, comically jerking us to a halt. It was a moment that we recounted later in bellyaching guffaws, but it brought me to the brink of a roiling panic at the time. I turned back toward Bruce. "THIS WAY!" I yelled over the increasing but still invisible thunder, and gave a rough tug on the rope.

We both sprinted forward across the snowfield in a blinding terror. With heavy mountain boots, crampons, and forty-five-pound packs, moving quickly proved to be a nightmare. Time slowed; it felt like we were running in place. Suddenly, the noise got louder and then stopped, as though I'd stepped into a soundproof room. I shot a look back over my shoulder.

From an ice cliff hanging above and halfway across the traverse, a boulder the size and shape of a motor coach hurtled into the air, spinning and wobbling violently like a punted football. The sight brought me to a horrified stop as I screamed for Bruce. "RUN! KEEP RUNNING!" I couldn't tell if he was clear of the boulder's landing zone yet, and we had only about two more seconds before we both found out the hard way.

In those last elongated seconds, Bruce didn't even look up—he just sprinted harder toward me. I grabbed the rope, whipped it downhill, and pulled it in as he ran, trying to keep it from tangling in his crampons. A brilliant fury of adrenaline contorted Bruce's face as the gargantuan boulder ended its meteoric flight in a mammoth explosion of snow fifty yards uphill and—thank the heavens—forty yards behind Bruce. With its momentum only partially absorbed, the boulder slid across our tracks like a derailed train car, accelerating until it careered over the edge of the crevasse lip at near-highway speed.

The sound died away. None of us could believe how quickly the whole sequence had played out. Bruce didn't see the boulder at all; he was still running when it dove off the glacier. We were safe from the near-miss and regrouped in a cyclone of backslapping.

"You sure nobody needs to change underwear?" one of the other guys jested. We had been shaken and wanted to rest, but we were each equally determined to keep going and make our high camp before we ran out of afternoon light.

After they had led for three hundred vertical feet, the other rope team turned over this more difficult work to Bruce and me. Still recovering from his emotional expenditure, Bruce wasn't up for kicking steps, hammering in snow pickets, and carrying the psychological burden of being in front. I collected the pickets, borrowed an ice hammer to temporarily replace my lost second tool, and set off from the others, who would follow once I was a rope length above them. Stabbing the front points of my crampons into the stable late-summer snowpack, I held my ice tools like daggers, with my fists wrapped high around the handles.

I fell into a cycle of motion, first plunging my right axe into the crust above my shoulder, then kicking my right foot through the crust and compressing a step. As I stood on my right foot, the sequence continued on my other side. When I started, I had nearly two thousand feet of virgin white mountainside rising steeply above me. Without landmarks, the unbroken field slipped by indeterminately. Even the horizon of the glacier's upper slopes rolling back out of sight above me seemed fixed at an unapproachable distance. My one indication of progress was the occasional shout from Bruce that let me know we'd climbed another rope length, and it was time to pound in another picket. At his signal, in a smooth series of motions, I would draw a two-foot-long T-section metal post from my pack's quiver, hold it against the slope, and strike it with the hammer on the back of my right ice tool until it was nearly buried. Clipping the rope through the adjoining carabiner protected Bruce and me against a fall. Our second team used the same pickets, then removed them as the last man passed each snow stake.

To my left, the slope swept down to the same hanging ice cliff where we had watched the boulder perform its airborne display. I drew myself inward, focusing my mind on efficiently regulating my - body's motions. My climbing patterns took on an unbreakable rhythm, plunging an axe, kicking twice with my foot, switching sides, plunge, kick, kick, plunge, kick, kick. It was a waltz that I danced with the mountain for an enchanted hour.

As the sun dropped into a thin cloudbank forty miles out over Puget Sound, light refracted in the prism of ocean vapors, and Mount Shuksan put on her finest evening gown. I glanced over my right shoulder to watch the lights of Victoria illuminate the coastline of Vancouver Island. As the sunset spilled claret wine over the jagged Picket Range and the border peaks of the North Cascades, I found it harder and harder to lean in on my axes, until finally, I stood up and walked ten yards without kicking steps. I was at the top of the glacier, close to 9,000 feet above sea level. Staring ahead, I admired the black pyramid of Mount Shuksan's symmetrical summit jutting up from the surrounding snowfields. As the rope allowed, I walked over to a convex roll in the white plateau that commanded views of Mount Baker, Puget Sound, the North Cascades, and southern British Columbia, and made an executive decision that this would be our campsite for the night. If the afternoon's exquisite climbing had been a reward for the torture of the previous night's bushwhacking, then the tranquil splendor of this campsite was due return for the boulder's terror. My run-down teammates arrived one by one with compliments for my step-kicking and campsite selection, and we went to work making ready for dinner and rest.

Our adventure on Mount Shuksan wasn't over. Since we hadn't yet topped out on the mountain—and indeed were on the opposite side of the summit pyramid from the fastest route to the top—we had a long day ahead of us when Sunday dawned bright and clear. Circumventing the black pyramid's ramparts on the east and then the south, we were forced to skip going up the final five hundred feet to the peak's high point so we could scout the three major gullies that dropped off the west side of the mountain's southern glacier. Without the map, we had little certainty of our descent, and though we found our way down the steepest climbing of the trip—through an ice tunnel at a glacial bergschrund (a crevasse created where the head of a glacier pulls away from the adjacent rock), down the vertical rock of the Fisher Chimney, and up a grueling finish to reach the Mount Baker ski area—it was dark again before we were off the mountain.

A week after the Mount Shuksan climb, I moved to New Mexico with my job and immediately joined the search-and-rescue (SAR) group to which Mark had belonged for five years. The Albuquerque Mountain Rescue Council, the top team in the state for technical rock rescues, provided me unparalleled training and experience and introduced me to nearly every one of my climbing partners of the next three years. Living in Albuquerque also allowed me closer access to the peaks in Colorado where I spent an average of five days climbing each month, year-round.

With my summer of big-mountain adventures in Washington, and more time for training in the Colorado mountains, I had gained a significant amount of experience that prepared me for a full slate of winter fourteener ascents during the winter of 1999–2000. However, I was still at the mercy of the mountain gods. Greater-than-100-mph winds blasted me on the summit plateau of Mount Bross on December 22, repeatedly knocking me over. The entire time I was crawling and fighting for my balance, unbeknownst to me, the metal frame of my headlamp was conducting the heat off my forehead into the bitter windchill, leaving a Gorbachevian crimson frostbite mark centered between my temples. I joined my family that evening in

Denver with a ridiculous purple brow that faded to a brown splotch, like the stain of a mild sunburn, after four days.

In the three days after Christmas that year, I surmounted five fourteener summits; two days later, I rang in the millennium in the Everglades of Florida with about twenty of my friends (and eighty thousand other fans) at my fiftieth Phish show. The band played continuously from midnight until dawn, nearly eight hours, in an incomparable marathon set. Later in the spring, four of my friends and I decided to go to Japan that summer to see the band play an entire tour of small venues; while we were there, we also hiked to the top of Mount Fuji, the first time I'd ever been to the highest point of a country.

Before the winter of 2000 was over, I soloed another six winter fourteeners back in Colorado, including the moderately technical Kit Carson Mountain and Blanca Peak, both in the southern Sangre de Cristo Range. On January 16, 2000, after nabbing the first documented ascent of the millennium on Blanca and its easier sister summit, Ellingwood Point, I descended briskly on a thin snowfield that barely covered some underlying boulders. At about 12,000 feet, I broke through the snow crust up to my right knee for about the hundredth time—I was bruising and scraping the front of my shins from bashing into the leading edge of the crust each time I stumbled—but this time I couldn't pull my leg out of the hole. I yanked and yanked without reward; a rock had shifted under the snow, trapping my foot at the ankle. There wasn't much pressure against my foot, but the boot was stuck fast, and I couldn't budge the rock from my forward-leaning position. I would have to dig away the snow, then move the rocks to get my boot out, which would be easier if I weren't lodged in place. Wriggling my hand down into the hole, I released my shoelace, yanked my foot out of the boot, and rolled over onto my right side, trying to keep my sock-covered foot out of the snow. Fifteen minutes later, I had my boot once more. The experience gave me cause to wonder what might have happened if not just my boot but my leg had been stuck, or if I'd twisted my ankle or even broken my leg. Could I have survived a night in the open? I had a 30-degree sleeping bag compressed in the bottom of my pack, and a stove and fuel, but nighttime temperatures were cold enough that I had my doubts. Shrugging off the accident as a brief delay, I nevertheless avoided two other shallowly buried boulder fields during the remainder of the descent.

Over the course of the winter, I learned about the concept of deep play, wherein a person's recreational pursuits carry a gross imbalance of risk and reward. Without the potential for any real or perceived external gain—fortune, glory, fame—a person puts himself into scenarios of real risk and consequence purely for internal benefit: fun and enlightenment. Deep play exactly described my winter solo fourteener project, especially when I would begin a climb by heading into a storm, accepting malevolent weather as part of my experience on that trip. Suffering, cold, nausea, exhaustion, hunger—none of it meant anything, it was all part of the experience. The same went for the joy, euphoria, achievement, and fulfillment, too. I found that I could not set out with the intent of having a particular experience—safety precautions and risk management aside—my goal instead was to be open to what that day was giving me and accept it. Expectations generally led to disappointment, but being open to whatever was there for me to discover led to awareness and delight, even when conditions were rough. Mark Twight, an American alpinist with an extraordinary history of success and misadventure at the most extreme level of mountaineering, wrote in a climbing essay, "It doesn't have to be fun to be fun." Precisely.

In my next two winter fourteener seasons, I would tackle increasingly difficult ascents; however, I had saved the most technical and remote peaks for the second half of the project. With time, I became more efficient with my climbing and camping methods and equipment, and made gains with my fitness and acclimatization, which allowed me to attempt longer and more strenuous routes. I always established an itinerary and communicated my expected return time to my parents or roommates, and chose routes and adjusted my schedule to minimize avalanche exposure—the deadliest objective hazard of the project.

By the end of 2002, I had completed thirty-six of the fifty-nine fourteeners in four winters. My achievements were greater than the numbers—I was consistently creating for myself new experiences that no one else in the world was having. It was common when I signed in at trailhead registers to see that the last entry before mine was three, four, or sometimes five months old. On the occasions when I would return to a summit in the summer, my entry would be the only one in a seven- or eight-month period. With the solitude that came from being in places four months removed from others' presence, I felt a sense of ownership of these cold high mountains, these buried alpine tarns, these sound-dampened forests; and a sense of kinship with the elk, deer, beaver, ermines, ptarmigans, and mountain goats. The more I visited their home, the more it felt like mine.

In the willow thickets of Mount Evans's west bowl, I almost stepped on a snow-white ptarmigan that cooed and hopped out of my way at the last instant. Bending down to the bird, I fell into a trance in its ink-drop eyes. The universe expanded; neither of us moved. I felt a connection with that little puff of feathers on its matching snow pillow that seemed to surpass my bond with my own species. With our coexistence in the wintry landscape, we shared more than I did with the other humans who would never journey into this world. I took a picture to show my friends, but despite my explanation, they saw only the ptarmigan, not the connection.

These places, and the experiences I had in them, were mine and mine alone. The senses of solitude, ownership, and place that I felt on these trips were creating a private world that, by definition, was impossible to share. Nevertheless, I tried. I took photographs and posted online albums of my trips; however, the images failed. They were unsuccessful because they were removed in time and location from what I went through to be *in* that place *at* that time. To a person sitting in an office or a living room, a picture of a winter mountain sunset is just a picture. To me, it was the experience of taking the picture. For instance, after snowshoeing for eight hours with my fifty-pound pack up Cottonwood Creek Valley, through an un-tracked forest of bottomless powder, past frozen cascades, I attained the 13,000-foot pass between Electric and Broken Hand peaks. From a vantage worthy of an Albert Bierstadt painting, I watched the red sunset light of the millennium's first winter solstice transform Crestone Needle's snow-plastered rock ribs into a purple mountain so majestic I cried at its beauty. A picture couldn't do the experience justice—no matter my photographic talents, I couldn't make the viewer feel the transcendent combination of depletion, fatigue, hy-poxia, elation, and accomplishment that I felt in reaching such a sub-lime vista at that twilit moment.

The further along I got with my solo winter fourteener project, the larger this private world grew, and the more it intertwined with my sense of self. Climbing fourteeners in the winter by myself wasn't just something I did; it became who I was. I didn't hold any delusions about the difficulty of the project relative to world-class climbing routes, or compare myself with elite alpinists, but each time I scaled another high peak, I explored and developed another part of me.

I left my first swooping backcountry ski tracks on Mount -Harvard's lower south face with my telemark skis, the only traces of human passage that peak would see for six months. I saw three wolves run a half mile in three feet of powder across a wide-open meadow at 11,000 feet on the west side of Mount Massive—even more impressive than their power and grace was the fact that prior to that day in March 2002, wolves had been extinct in Colorado for over six decades. I stared into storms and met their fury with inten-sity and jubilation, growing icicles on my face on Humboldt Peak and spreading my arms like wings in the wind on the summit of -Torreys Peak. I basked in the sun spray of a perfectly calm and unnaturally warm noon atop Mount Yale and froze in my maximum-thickness down parka on Mount Sneffels.

As my passion and dedication to the outdoors deepened, my time in the mountains left me with a singular desire to move back to Colorado and pursue my development from a home in the high country. I was altogether burned out on working in a large corporation. Then, in the spring of 2002, the opportunity came up for me to climb Denali with a group of über-athletes. But without the required vacation time to go on the trip, I had to make a choice between following my bliss and keeping my job at Intel. In the end, it didn't even feel like a sacrifice to quit my job, sell most of my household goods, and pack my outdoor toys into my three-year-old Toyota Tacoma pickup truck (complete with rubber-tramping topper for camping). On my last day of work, Thursday, May 23, 2002, I wrote an e-mail to all my friends, announcing my new start, quoting Goethe: "Whatever you can do, or dream you can, begin it. Boldness has genius, power, and magic in it."

Most of my colleagues encouraged me in my transition, but there were a few who could scarcely believe what I was telling them—that I was quitting, didn't have another job lined up, and wasn't going back to school. It just wasn't something that Intel engineers did. But at twenty-six, after a modest career of five years, I officially retired. "Holding a corporate job" joined "living east of the Rocky Mountains" on a two-item list of things I vowed never to do again in my life. Thus began a journey that would take me to the summit of Denali, the highest mountain in North America, through thirty-eight states and Canada in six months, and end in a little place called Aspen, Colorado, elevation 7,890 feet.

FIVE

Day Two: Failing Options

Desert dawn
Rise up early, lift your song
On the breath of life that rises from the
Glowing stone
Feel the rock of ages, smooth against your skin
Smell the breath of flowers dancing on the wind
Dancing on the wind.

—STRING CHEESE INCIDENT,
with lyricist Christina Callicott, "Desert Dawn"

As THE MORNING HEATS UP, I no longer have to unproductively hammer my knife into the rock just to stay warm. My aching grip cries out for a change of routine, so I leave the hacking and chipping for another time. Even without sleep, I feel an increased energy from the ambient light in the canyon. It boosts me in the same way that dawn has done when I've hiked through the night. Today, though, there is no end in sight. This isn't a climb with a final pitch or an endurance hike that will be over after a set length of time. My struggle against the boulder is open-ended. I will be here until I solve this problem or I die.

From desert survival stories I've read, I know dehydration can kill you by slightly variable mechanisms, but fundamentally, they all entail your organs not receiving adequate nutrients to the point that they shut down. Some people expire once their kidneys fail and their body's own toxicity kills them; other people last until their heart collapses. Under exertion in hot environments, dehydration can lead to overheating, and you effectively cook your brain. Whatever way death might come to me, convulsions and severe cramping will most likely herald it. I start to speculate . . .

I wonder what kidney failure will feel like? Not good, probably. Maybe like when you eat so much you get cramps in your back. Only worse, I bet. It's gonna be a rough way to die. Hypothermia would be better, if it's fast onset. At least then I could slip off in mind numbness and not feel it. The temperature didn't dip that low last night, though, only about 55 degrees. Not cold enough for severe hypothermia. Maybe death by a flash flood would be better? Not so much. Is it better to go out with a scream cut off by a wall of muddy water, to fade silently into a cold-induced coma, or to have the final experience of the gasping spasms of heart failure? I don't know . . .

But I'm ready for action, not for dying. It is time to get a better anchor established, one that I can use to rig a lifting system and try to move the boulder. If I can rotate the front of the chockstone up, maybe as much as a foot, I can pull out my hand, though that's a long way to move a rock this size. Maybe I can budge the boulder backward enough to ease its grip and create a two-inch gap—that's all I need to get the thicker pad of my thumb out of its trap. I know it's going to hurt worse than the accident itself, because it will be slow and self-inflicted. The hand is done for; I've already written it off. But what happens when blood starts circulating in it again? Will it carry the decay back into my bloodstream and poison my heart? Medically, I'm uninformed about the potential threat involved, but spreading toxins seems like a logical result if I'm able to suddenly free my hand. It's a risk I accept, and one I can only hope to face.

My first move in attempting to create a second anchor is to unclip my stowed fluorescent yellow webbing from its carabiner on the back of my harness and unwrap the tidy chain of storage loops. I untie the knot holding the two ends together and string the twenty-five-foot length back and forth across the top of the chockstone, trying to keep it stacked neatly apart from the ropes of my current harness support system. Facing upcanyon from my manacling point, I guess at the contours and edges that may or may not exist on top of the chockstones that form the shelf above and in front of me. I wasn't paying close enough attention to their shape when I was up there yesterday afternoon. It appears to me that a shallow triangular horn sticks out in the middle of the shelf nearly six feet over my head. Perhaps if there is a substantial enough in-cut feature on the back of the horn, a strand of webbing could catch and drape over each side of the horn without pulling over the top of it.

My attempts to toss the webbing up over the horn founder; the material doesn't have sufficient heft for me to throw it in the air accurately. When I can get it high enough, the yellow fabric pulls itself off the horn, almost bouncing off the rock like it's somehow become spring-loaded. I puzzle over a solution and decide to tie the currently unused end of my climbing rope to one end of the webbing and try throwing the rope over the horn, then drawing the webbing over the horn with the heavier leader. The next dozen attempts—each a prolonged and tedious effort of recovering and reorganizing the rope and webbing, and getting my body back into position so I can try again—all fail as well. I can get the rope over the horn, but as the knot slides over the top, it loses precious centimeters. Subsequently, the webbing is too far forward on the point of the shelf to securely catch on the smooth sandstone. Time after time, the webbing pulls free and falls to the sand on the other side of my chockstone.

A fissure on the right side of the horn catches my eye. Maybe I can slip the webbing into that slot and give it a better angle to slide around the back of the horn more steadily. The next time I throw and pull the rope, right as the knot is about to crest the horn, I put the rope leader in my teeth and gently twitch the webbing. It responds by slipping back into the slot. Aha! This time, I tug the knot over the - shelf's lip. I can see the difference in how the webbing drapes farther over the back of the salmon-colored horn. Slowly reeling in the leader, I know I've got a workable setting for my anchor. Untying the knot connecting rope and webbing, I slip a metal rappel ring over the yellow strap and tie a series of overhand knots in the webbing until it hangs in a loop with the ring at the bottom. I tug on the loop with my left hand, tightening the knot and testing its placement around the outcropping. The webbing doesn't creep at all as I apply more and more of my body weight. It's set.

Checking my watch, I note that it's already after eleven on Sunday morning. I've spent two hours just getting the anchor reconfigured, but the endeavor has been an unqualified success so far. My prescribed sip of water enhances my feeling of satisfaction. I'm using discipline well, and I'm pleased with myself over the accomplishment of setting an anchor from below—and single-handedly at that—around an unlikely feature.

Good work, Aron. Now all you've got to do is move the boulder. Don't stop now.

Cutting my climbing rope about thirty feet from one end, I loop one end of the short piece around my chockstone and tie it to itself. Next I thread the other end up through the rappel ring—I can just reach the ring with my left hand. Without expecting any movement of the boulder, I yank on the rope. Sure enough, nothing.

Well, at least the anchor is holding.

I need to fashion a pulley system to create some mechanical advantage. With the single bend in the rope, I'm not lifting the boulder with as much force as I'm pulling on the line. Friction at the rap ring is actually making this setup a mechanical *disadvantage* system. Unfortunately, I don't have any pulleys with me; I do have carabiners, though they'll have a much greater friction loss. Attempting to tear down the 'biner-block anchor that I was previously using to suspend my harness, I flip the rope again and again until the jumbled mess of interconnected links unwedges from the crack.

Time lapses unnoticed for me now; I'm wholly attuned to my endeavor with the rope system. I call upon my training in search and rescue and design a scheme in my mind that will replicate the technical hauling systems we use to evacuate immobilized patients from vertical rock faces. The Albuquerque rescue team taught me two standard systems, and I choose between them, deciding on a Z-pulley system with an additional redirection of the haul line. Modifying the typical system layout for my space and equipment constraints, I add Prusik loops of tied runners clipped to carabiners to connect the rope back to itself. With two such changes in direction, I've theoretically tripled the force applied at the haul point—a mechanical advantage ratio of 3:1. Due to my improvisations, the friction in my system is probably halving that advantage, but 1.5:1 is still better than 0.5:1, like my first attempt.

Still, the system is too weak. The boulder ignores my efforts. At the end of the haul line, I tie a set of slipknots that slide onto stopper knots, creating foot loops. Stepping into the loops makes me about two feet taller in the canyon, and though I'm in an awkward position due to my stuck hand, I can now put most of my body weight into service on the haul line. I've probably tripled or quadrupled the force that I could apply when I was gripping the rope with one hand. The haul line is taut, even through the bends at the carabiners, and my system is working as designed. However, because I'm using a dynamic climbing rope, meant to stretch and absorb the energy of a climbing fall, I lose much of the force I'm exerting on the haul line. Flailing through hours of taxing work, and several unsuccessful iterations of raising the anchor webbing a few inches by tying another knot above the rap ring, I never once budge the rock. I'm doing the best I can with my available materials. Maybe I could rig a 5:1 system—I have enough carabiners and webbing—but I would need another foot of space between the anchor and the rock to fit all the bends of the larger system. Discouraged from the effort and the lack of measurable progress, I stop for a break and glance at my watch. It's after one o'clock in the afternoon, and I'm sweating and panting.

Suddenly, I hear distant voices echoing in the canyon. My mind swears in exhilarated surprise, and my breath abruptly catches in my dry throat.

Could it be? It's the right time of day—a group would get to this part and be able to return out to the West Fork or to Horseshoe Trailhead in daylight. And just like you figured, the odds are better that others will come through on a weekend day. After all, that's how you came to be here yesterday afternoon.

Even reasoning it through, I'm afraid I may be delusional, that the sounds are in my head. Holding my breath, I listen.

Yes! The noises are distorted and far off but familiar: shoes scrabbling on sandstone. It's probably a group of canyoneers descending the first drop-off, back at the S-log.

"HELP!"

The caterwauling echoes of my shout fade in the canyon. Forcing myself not to breathe, I listen for a reply. Nothing.

"HELLLP!"

The desperation of my quivering shout disturbs me. Again I hold my breath. After the dying fall of my shout, there is no returning sound besides the thumping of my excited heart. A critical moment passes, my hopes evaporate, and I know there are no people in this canyon.

My morale slumps in a pang, like the first time a girl broke my heart. Then I hear the noises again. This time I know better and I wait. The echoes I took to be approaching canyoneers resolve into the scratchy sounds of a kangaroo rat in his nest in the debris jammed around the suspended chockstone above and behind my head. I rotate and see his tail whip across a pile of twigs as he disappears into his hole.

In that moment, I promise myself that I will yell for help only once a day. Hearing my voice's shaky timbre nearly panicked me, and to yell out any more often would undermine my effort to maintain a calm and clearheaded demeanor. Rationally, I know there will be no one coming down this canyon until perhaps the next weekend, when the search teams will be scouring the backcountry for my body. Since my voice can be heard fifty yards away at most, and the nearest people would be five to seven miles away, it serves no positive purpose to shout myself scared.

*   *   *

Around two o'clock, I reconsider my status and my options. Waiting, chipping, and lifting have all played out unsuccessfully. For the first time, I seriously contemplate amputating my arm, thinking through the process and possible consequences. Laying out everything I have on the surfaces around me, I think through each item's possible use in a surgery. My two biggest concerns are a cutting tool that can do the job, and a tourniquet that will keep me from bleeding out. There are two blades on my multi-tool: The inch-and-a-half blade is sharper than the three-inch one. It will be important to use the longer blade for hacking at the chockstone and preserve the shorter blade for the potential surgery.

I instinctively understand that even with the sharper blade, I won't be able to saw through my bones. I've seen the hacksaws that Civil War–era doctors used for amputating patients' legs and arms in battlefield hospitals, and I don't have anything that could approximate even a rudimentary saw. I've made an assumption that I want to amputate as little of my arm as possible. This unstated parameter leads me to think strictly in terms of cutting through the bones of my forearm, as opposed to going through the cartilage of my elbow joint. The latter possibility never occurs to me, preemptively eliminating the likeliest method.

A vivid memory from a movie of a heroin user shooting up, with a length of surgical tubing wrapped around his arm, gives me the idea to experiment with a tourniquet of tubing from my empty Camel-Bak. I cut the tubing free from the reservoir and manage to tie it in a simple knot around my upper forearm, just below the elbow. The placement comes to me without consideration of the pressure points nearer my biceps. I'm thinking I will have to twist the tubing so tightly that it will permanently damage part of my arm; therefore, I should put it as close to the cutting site as possible. The knot in the tubing is loose, and I can't cinch it down even after redoing it three times: The plastic material is too stiff to allow a small knot that would stay snug around my arm. I look around for a stick to put in the tourniquet, but there aren't any thick enough for my needs. To tighten the tubing will require a force that would snap any stick I can reach.

So much for that idea.

I have a piece of purple webbing knotted in a loop that I untie and wrap around my forearm. A five-minute effort yields a doubled knot, but the loops are too loose to stop my circulation. Again, I need a stick . . . or I can use a carabiner and twist the loops tighter with that. I clip the gate of my last unused carabiner through the loops and rotate it twice. The webbing presses deeply into my forearm, and the skin nearer my wrist takes on the pallor of a fish belly. I've fashioned an effective tourniquet, and seeing my makeshift medical setup working brings me a subtle sense of satisfaction.

Nice work, Aron.

What else will I need? Basic first aid says to put direct pressure on a wound, so I'll need something to wrap the end of my arm, minimizing any blood flow that sneaks past the tourniquet. The cushioned crotch of my biking shorts would make a good absorbent pad, and with the four feet of unused yellow webbing that I could cut from the anchor, I can secure the shorts around the end of my arm. Then I can stick my stump into my CamelBak mini-backpack, and with both straps around my neck, the pack will act like a sling, immobilizing my arm across my chest. Perfect.

Despite my optimism, there's a darker undercurrent to my brainstorming. Though my mind is working on the amputation scenario, the operation is still only a theoretical possibility. I'm thinking, *"If I cut off my arm, how will I stop the blood loss?"* and *"If I cut off my arm, how will I pad and sling my stump?"* Because my knife is too dull, the rest of the plan is no more than an idle mental exercise. Until I figure out how to cut through the bones, amputation isn't a practical choice; it's more a point of theory that allows me to follow through on all my options. I wonder about my courage level and how my mental state will change if I can solve the riddle. As a test, I expose the shorter blade of my multi-tool and hold it to my skin. The tip pokes between the tendons and veins a few inches up from my trapped wrist, indenting my flesh. The sight repulses me.

What are you doing, Aron? Get that knife away from your wrist! What are you trying to do, kill yourself? That's suicide! I don't care how good a tourniquet you have, you've got too many arteries in your arm to stop them all. You'll bleed out. You slice your wrist, and it's as good as stabbing yourself in the gut. If you manage to get through the bones and free yourself, say you make it down as far as the rappel. That tourniquet won't make a damn difference—the rescuers will find your depleted body sometime next month, pecked clean by buzzards down in that canyon. Cutting your arm off is just a slow act of suicide.

I feel vaguely ill and drop my left hand, allowing the knife to ease away from my skin. I can't do it. Maybe I'm not ready to pursue amputation any further at the moment. Maybe that argumentative voice is right, though, maybe it is suicide. I'll have to be a lot more strung out to go through with the amputation. Who knows, maybe some random person will come along tomorrow. All I can be certain of at this point is that, should the need arise for a prolonged and nasty operation—such as hacking through my bones like I was doing to the chockstone—my fortitude will have to be at an all-time high. I shudder at the thought, my eyes close softly, and my mouth gapes open. I can picture my blood spilled on the canyon walls, the torn flesh and ripped muscles of my arm dangling in gory strands from two white bones pockmarked with divots, the result of my last efforts to chisel through my arm's structural frame. Then I see my head drooped to my sagging torso, my body lifelessly hanging from the knife-nicked bones. It's like watching the closing sequence of a film, but it doesn't fade to black. It's my waking nightmare, a premonition that causes me to set my knife down on the chockstone's shelf and retch.

Slowly, I blink. My vision blurs in a nauseating swirl, but then it stabilizes and my equilibrium returns. With the sickening surgical practice session over, I review my situation. I no longer have any options that I haven't already examined and tabled as ineffective or deadly. Even though I've followed each potential scenario through its preliminary stages, I can't presently go further with any of them. I'm stymied at every turn. I'll die before help arrives, I can't excavate my hand, I can't lift the boulder, and I can't cut off my arm. A sinking depression hits me for the first time. The optimism that has graced me for the last day is gone, and I feel lonely, angry, and scared. I whimper to myself: "I am going to die." Probably in another two days, not that it matters when.

I will die here.

I will waste away here.

I will shrivel up, slumping here with my arm trapped in this place, when dehydration decides to stop toying around and finally kills me.

Why do I even bother drinking my water? It's only prolonging my ordeal. Dismally, I wish for a flash flood to end it all. The thought of intentionally slitting my wrists fleetingly dashes in and out of my mind. My despair turns to adolescent anger. I hate this boulder. I hate it! I hate this canyon. I hate the morgue-cold slab pressing against my right forearm. I hate the faint musty smell of the greenish slime thinly glazing the bottom of the southern canyon wall behind my legs. I hate the breezes that blow grit in my face and the dim half-light of this claustrophobic hole where even the sandstone looks menacing.

"I . . . hate . . . this!" I punctuate each word with slaps of my left palm against the chockstone as tears well in my eyes.

The echoes of my anguish reverberate up the canyon and vanish into the afternoon. Then another voice, this one inside my head, speaks coolly.

That boulder did what it was there to do. Boulders fall. That's their nature. It did the only natural thing it could do. It was set up, but it was waiting for you. Without you coming along and pulling it, it would still be stuck where it had been for who knows how long. You did this, Aron. You created it. You chose to come here today; you chose to do this descent into the slot canyon by yourself. You chose not to tell anyone where you were going. You chose to turn away from the women who were there to keep you from getting in this trouble. You created this accident. You wanted it to be like this. You have been heading for this situation for a long time. Look how far you came to find this spot. It's not that you're getting what you deserve—you're getting what you wanted.

Understanding my responsibility for my circumstances placates my anger. My despondency remains, but I stop striking out against the rock. One thought in particular circulates over and over in my mind: "Kristi and Megan were angels sent to save me from myself, and I ignored them." Everything happens for a reason, and part of the beauty of life is that we're not allowed to know those reasons for certain, though on this question, my conviction grows. They might not have had wings and harps, but Kristi and Megan came into my life to fulfill a purpose. They were trying to spare me from my accident. I am convinced that they somehow knew what was going to happen to me. Again and again I think about Kristi's last question— "What kind of energy do you think you'll find down there?"—and about their repeated urgings, but my stubbornness and ambition had closed my brain in a lock. I did get myself into this. Somehow, in some convoluted way, it's what I've been looking for in my life. How else did I come to be here? We create our lives. I don't fully understand why, but little by little I get that somehow I've wanted something like this to happen. I've been looking for adventure, and I've found it.

I remember the conversation Megan and I had about a time when she'd gotten lost on Cedar Mesa, a region of southeastern Utah littered with canyons and ancient cliff-dwelling ruins. She and a friend had huddled over a fire of juniper branches through the long night. In return, I told her the story of when I, too, got lost on Cedar Mesa, coming out from a canyon after dark. Unable to find the footprints we'd counted on following back to my truck, my friend Jamie Zeigler and I had stumbled around disoriented for an hour. By a stroke of luck, we found my vehicle on the open mesa top. Then I told Megan about an episode in February when my friend Rachel

Polver and I attempted a twenty-mile circuit of Chute and Crack canyons in the San Rafael Reef of central Utah. Fifteen miles into the loop, we came to a sandstone slide that Rachel couldn't ascend. For an hour, I tried boosting her, coaching her, pulling her, even letting her stand on my back, but she couldn't get up the ten-foot rise in the slot. We went back the way we'd come until we found a 150-pound log that we then carried two hundred yards back up the canyon to use like a ladder. The entire conversation about being stuck and lost in canyon country had been an unwitting presentiment of my entrapment. After all that talk, I should have known that I was jinxing myself and gone with Kristi and Megan.

Such thoughts are ridiculous, but the fatigue of being awake for thirty-two hours has assuredly started to cloud my mind. I feel sluggish and stupid, the sleep deprivation exaggerating my depleted condition. Before I slip into some sorely needed perversion of a nap and hurt my arm, I clip my daisy chain into the rap ring suspended on the anchor and adjust it to take the weight off my legs again. The numbers on my watch silently change to 2:45 P.M.

I don't know if I was purposefully waiting for an occasion to pull out my mini-DV camcorder and record some videotape, but just after three P.M., I decide to video myself for the first time. Using my now-standard procedure for taking off my backpack, I slip the strap through its friction clasp and swing the ruck around to my knees. Besides the burritos, my cameras are the only useful items left in the pack. I still have the CD player, the battery collection, and the empty CamelBak reservoir jumbled in the bottom, but everything else is in use. Turning on the palm-sized unit, I flip the digital screen around so I can ensure that I'm in the viewfinder and press the record button before setting it on top of the chockstone.

Just start at the beginning. Assume whoever sees this will find it after - you're dead. You can leave it out on top of the rock with an etching in the wall, "Play me," and an arrow or something pointing at the camera. Maybe it will be separated from your body in a flood. Tell them everything.

I begin. "It's three-oh-five on Sunday. This marks my twenty-four-hour mark of being stuck in Blue John Canyon above the Big Drop. My name is Aron Ralston. My parents are Donna and Larry Ralston of Englewood, Colorado. Whoever finds this, please make an attempt to get this to them. Be sure of it. I would appreciate it."

I take long blinks and rarely check the camera's screen. I'm unkempt from four days of scruffy facial-hair growth since the last time I shaved at home in Aspen. But what really makes me avert my glance is the haggard look in my eyes. They are huge, wide-open bowls reflecting the harrowing stress I've been through in the last day. Loose rolls of flesh sag and tug at my lower eyelids.

My slurred words come listlessly between labored breaths. I struggle to enunciate clearly.

"So . . . I was hiking Blue John Canyon yesterday . . . Saturday . . . at about two-forty-five to three, somewhere in there, I got to where the lower section of Blue John slots up again. Did some free downclimbing . . . not too bad . . . got to the second set of chockstones. And that's where I am still right now. Because one of the chockstones pulled out as I was pulling on it, climbing off of it, and it slid down, smashed, and trapped my right hand."

Picking up the camera, I point it first to where my forearm and wrist disappear in the horrifyingly skinny gap between the chockstone and wall. Then I pan the camcorder up over the pinch point to get a view down on my grayish-blue hand.

"What you're looking at there is my arm, going into the rock . . . and there it is, stuck. It's been without circulation for twenty-four hours. It's pretty well gone."

I swing the camera up to the anchor webbing and rap ring.

"The ropes you see are set up to give me a seat so I don't have to stand up all the time. I was not rappelling at the time of the accident, although I did get my harness on afterwards, and I've been sitting.

"I've been putting a lot of effort into staying warm. I have very, very little water. I had less than a liter when I got here. I have about a third of a liter now. At that rate I will be out before morning."

Another breeze sweeps over me, and I shudder uncontrollably for five seconds.

"My body's having a difficult time controlling its temperature.

"Unnhhhh . . . I'm in deep stuff." I wince, grimace, and choke on the weight of my words.

"Nobody knows where I am except for two girls that I met yesterday while hiking Blue John. Kristi and Megan of Moab . . . with Outward Bound there. They went out the West Fork of Blue John, and I continued on.

"I had ridden my bike, which is still parked and locked—the keys are in my pocket here—about a mile southeast of Burr Pass, at a tree - that's about a hundred and fifty yards off the side of the road, the left side of the road as you're heading southeast. It's a red Thin Air, Rocky Mountain. It'll still be there."

The breeze picks up, and I squint into the gust, trying to keep grit out of my eyes. Wind noise obliterates my voice on the tape, so I stop recording. After gathering my thoughts, I start the tape again to explain my options.

"So the way I see it . . . there's kind of four things happening. Ummm, I'm shuddering. Unnhhh . . . I tried to move the rock with the rigging. I set an anchor and put some foot lines in so that I could stand in them and try to move the rock. It wouldn't budge."

Shaking my head in defeat, I yawn, battling the fatigue that comes in waves.

"I tried chipping away at the rock. The progress I made in twenty-four hours, with a *lot* of work, it would be a hundred and fifty hours, if ever. I think part of the problem is, is that my hand is actually supporting the rock. Which means every time I chip away part of the rock, it moves a little bit and settles onto my hand again. I can't feel it happening, but microscopically, it seems to be, because the little gap over here between the rock and the wall—right there—is actually, well, at least I think it's gotten smaller as I've been working on it. So, there you can see the chip marks under the rope. I removed a lot of that rock where the rope is right now. And even some you can't see anymore because my arm is now covering it. Again because the rock moved."

Pausing to lick my dry lips, I try to swallow, then give a long and despondent sigh. When I rehash my situation, I hear the downheartedness in my voice. The failure of my options trounces my spirit into dejection.

"So, those two things out, the third thing left was to cut my arm off."

I grimace. My face wrinkles into a contortion that takes ten seconds to straighten out before I can continue with a wholeheartedly dejected explanation.

"I worked a tourniquet up and got into place a couple times with all my plans and what I was going to do . . . but it's pretty much suicide. It's, uh, four hours from here to my vehicle. It would be . . . if at all possible—because of the fourth-class climbing involved—to go back out the way I came in, it would be about four hours that way, to where I don't have a vehicle, well, I have a bike, but . . . um . . . To go out the West Fork, it would be a couple hours later . . . er, less . . . two hours, maybe two and a half hours, but again, fourth-class climbing, which would probably be impossible with one hand. Between the blood loss and my dehydration, I think I'm ruling that out. I think I would die if I cut off my arm.

"Umm, the fourth thing that could happen is someone comes. This being a continuation of a canyon that's not all that popular, and the continuation being even less so, I think that's very unlikely that that will happen before I retire from dehydration and hypothermia.

"It's odd . . . The temperature is sixty-six degrees, at least it was yesterday at this time; I think it's a degree or two colder than that now. It got down to fifty-five overnight, which wasn't bad. I spent a lot of time shivering, though. When I would wake up, I would chip at the rock . . . I didn't really wake up, I sat and I tried to sleep."

I begin my familiar recitation of the most likely rescue scenario.

"So, either somebody notices I'm missing because I don't show up at the house for the party on Monday night or I don't show up for work on Tuesday, but they don't really know anything more than I went to Utah. I think maybe my truck will be found. I think it will be Wednesday, Thursday, at the earliest when someone figures out where I might be, what I've done, and gets to me. That's at least three days from now.

"Judging by my degradation in the last twenty-four hours, I'll be surprised if I make it to Tuesday."

I know with a sense of finality that I'm saying goodbye to my family, and that regardless of how much I suffer in this spot, they will feel more agony than me. After a long pause, I stumble through an explanation, trying to apologize to my family for what I know they will go through because of my disappearance and demise.

"I'm sorry."

With tears brimming, I stop the tape and rub the back of my knuckles across my eyes. I start the tape once more.

"Mom, Dad, I love you. Sonja, I love you. You guys make me proud. I don't know what it is about me that's brought me to this. But this is . . . what I've been after. I go out looking for adventure and risk so I can feel alive. But I go out by myself and I don't tell someone where I'm going, that's just dumb. If someone knew, if I'd have been with someone else, there would probably already be help on the way. Even if I'd just talked to a ranger or left a note on my truck. Dumb, dumb, dumb."

I stop the tape for the last time and I turn off the camcorder, then pack it away. As I said on the tape, my best option is to wait for a potential rescue. My strategy shifts. I need to stay warm, manage my water intake, and most importantly, conserve my energy. Rather than trying to actively extricate myself, I am now waiting to be found.

SIX

Winter Rhapsody

Eventually, I sickened of people, myself included, who didn't think enough of themselves to make something of themselves—people who did only what they had to and never what they could have done. I learned from them the infected loneliness that comes at the end of every misspent day. I knew I could do better.

—MARK TWIGHT, "I Hurt, Therefore I Am"

I WAS NEVER LUCKIER than in the twelve months following my retirement from corporate life.

For our 2002 Denali expedition, I was privileged to join the elite adventure racers of Team Stray Dogs—Marshall Ulrich, Charlie Engle, and Tony DiZinno. I assisted our team leader, Gary Scott, with everything from early trip preparations, food orders, and flight reservations, to cooking and cleaning after meals, building shelters, carrying loads, and making decisions during the climb. Besides being an ultra-fit team of people who were flexible and learned quickly about high-altitude glacier climbing, the Stray Dogs taught me valuable lessons about group dynamics. From my experiences on that trip, I easily figured out that I enjoyed leading groups and teaching people about the outdoors.

When I was back in Colorado after the Alaska trip, my interest in mountain guiding solidified. I especially enjoyed showing off the wild places of the West. I led a camping and peak-bagging trip near Aspen with two of my less experienced friends from Chicago. Friends from Florida saw wilderness for the first time when they came with me to the Utah desert of the Escalante. I carried equipment on an expedition with the renowned Colorado landscape photographer John Fielder, an ambassador of the wilderness who takes people places through the medium of his pictures. He instilled a desire in me to take people there in person.

I decided I would go back to Denali in 2003 to climb the West Buttress with some of my friends from New Mexico, Colorado, and California. Gary Scott, our team leader in 2002, holds a record for the fastest ascent of the mountain; in 1985 he climbed from Kahiltna Base Camp at 7,200 feet to the 20,320-foot summit in eighteen and a half hours. I knew I could move fast on the mountain, and after I had climbed with Gary, the siren lure of his record called to me to go even faster. I put together a plan to follow our 2003 team's climb with an attempt at a solo speed ascent, hoping to complete the first sub-twenty-four-hour round trip on the mountain. I spent the next year getting into the best shape of my life.

In November 2002, I moved to Aspen and immediately found a sales job at the Ute Mountaineer. When I wasn't telemark and cross-country skiing, mountaineering, or snowshoeing, I was talking about telemark and cross-country skiing, mountaineering, and snowshoeing at the Ute with customers (but always saving the best stories for my colleagues and managers). Besides having a home base from which I would train for and climb nine of the most challenging four-teeners in the state that winter, I was surrounded by an entire town of like-minded friends.

One of the enjoyable challenges of my winter was maintaining a balance between going out on the town, going out to dinner parties, going out to see music, and keeping up my training. Fairly often, I would squeeze in a three-hour cross-country ski session between my split shift, skin up one of the four ski mountains of Aspen/Snowmass on my telemark skis before work, or head out on an evening snow-shoe run after work, then catch up with some friends at a club until late. When the music wasn't happening in Aspen, my friends and I might head to Vail or pull a big drive down to Denver or Boulder and back in the same night. There was never a routine, nor a dull moment.

I was loving the ski-town life. My townie friends and I would make almost daily references to "living the dream." We employed all sorts of tricks, favor exchanges, and bartering to ensure a high quality of life in Aspen, despite our meager wages in a place that has one of the most expensive costs of living in the world. We had free two-day-a-week ski passes from our jobs, but we figured out how to ski five days a week by earning our turns—hiking to the upper lifts where passes - weren't scanned. I quickly learned where I could go to find untracked snow when I couldn't be the first one out on a powder day. "If you - can't ski first, you gotta ski smart," I would say to folks I met riding the chairlifts before squireling off into the trees to a favorite stash.

Outside the ski areas, boundless public lands yielded infinite opportunities for free outdoor recreation. While it's hard to beat free, we scored discounts and deals wherever we could in town: pro deals on top-quality gear, cafeteria pals we could count on for a "good-guy discount," friends who would organize lavish dinner parties, bouncers and bartenders who would give us the nod for the familiar-face freebie. It didn't hurt that we were getting the best snow in five years.

As soon as winter officially began, my attention narrowed, and I focused on my upcoming solo fourteener climbs. The routes and mountains started at an advanced level and got more and more desperate as the winter progressed. Besides the blessings of my job, my roommates, my friends, and the social and musical scene, I was also lucky to have a guardian angel who apparently didn't mind putting in some long hours when I traveled into the backcountry.

My climbing efforts commenced on the day after Christmas,

when I scaled and skied two adjacent fourteeners—Castle and Co-nundrum peaks—twice taking what backcountry guru and guide-book writer Lou Dawson calls "the journey through the valley of death."

Avalanche exposure increased significantly over the New Year, so by January 9, camped below the north face of the picturesque North Maroon Peak, I had to change my itinerary from the standard route on North Maroon. Instead, I climbed Pyramid Peak by its West Face route, despite a storm that blew dangerous amounts of fresh snow into the steep-faced west amphitheater at 13,800 feet. Avalanche hazard was at volatile levels, waiting for a human trigger named Aron to step onto the wrong part of the slope.

Descending the summit ridge, I contorted my body over my gloved hands, poised on loose mudstone slats, to make a difficult downclimbing maneuver through a fifteen-foot-high band of cliffs. When my grip came loose, I fell four feet to land flat-footed on a three-foot-wide shelf. Wobbling directly above a second cliff, I stead-ied myself before easing down another ten feet onto the upper perimeter of the wind-loaded amphitheater's snowfield. From there, it was a heart-stopping descent all the way to treeline. To avoid the unstable zones that had filled in with a foot-thick layer of avalanche-prone snow as I climbed above them, I had to take inefficient devia-tions from my ascent path. I made a safe return, sometimes pushing snow down onto a slope below me to make it avalanche in a loose slide of spindrift before I continued down myself. I had never taken a fall on a winter climb. I'd been fortunate to land safely—a backward step from the ledge would have sent me on a fast ride into the sweet spot of the bowl, most likely injuring me as I triggered a massive slide—but I was spooked and gave every hazard an extra margin on the way down.

Starting with the experience on Pyramid Peak's summit ridge, I went on a month-long streak of climbing fourteeners in January, with close calls on all of them. On my approach to Mount of the Holy Cross, I got caught after dark at 13,000 feet in bitterly cold temperatures due to an incorrect route description for traversing Notch Mountain. Bivouacking on a two-foot-wide snow ledge, I was just below the notch that separates the two 13,200-foot summits, but above a sickening drop into a fifteen-hundred-foot-long steep snow couloir. My intent in hunkering down was to replenish my body's energy with hot Gatorade and instant mashed potatoes. Twelve miles of travel had brought me to the top of the northern summit of Notch Mountain, but without a tent, I was planning to reach a rock-walled shelter on the southern summit before dark. However, deeply drifted snow and the guidebook that had said to traverse the east side of the southern summit, when it meant the *west* side, had slowed me down and used up all of my energy reserves, as well as my water. By the time I was certain I was headed the wrong way, I was too tapped to regain the notch where I would be on track again.

A finicky fuel-bottle O-ring then nearly cost me everything. Unbeknownst to me, the rubber gasket had gotten pinched at the fuelline insertion hole, and for five minutes, fuel spilled into the snow when I opened the valve. I unwittingly lost three quarters of my fuel before I figured out why the stove was burning so weakly. I had popped the troublesome O-ring in my mouth and was flattening it out with my tongue when I saw the storm coming in from the west. I knew I had to get to the shelter, but I needed energy first, and without water, I couldn't eat anything—I had to get the stove working properly. The thought occurred to me then that there are many shapes to the thing that separates life from death. Sometimes it's obvious: the distance that separates you from a lightning bolt, the seat belt that restrains you when you hit a deer at 80 mph, the actions of a friend whose quick reflexes save you from drowning in the Colorado River. Other times it's subtle, even imperceptible: the microscopic string of DNA that enables your body to fight off an infection you - don't even know you've contracted, a decision to climb a different mountain and thereby miss being hit by a rock that assails the route you aren't on. We go through life ignoring these subtleties because there are a million things we survive every day without recognizing we were ever at risk. Then we have a close call, and we become acutely aware of what that fraction of an inch or that split second means. I knew my stove was my salvation from the ledge and quite probably the link that would get me off the mountain. I had to fix the fuel-line seal.

Extracting the three-millimeter O-ring from my mouth, I examined the deformed section. While I was handling it, my deteriorated state caused me to fumble the critical piece into the dark. One of those subtle lifelines had just become terrifyingly obvious. I was horrified to think I had bobbled the O-ring off the ledge. With my headlamp illuminating the ground, I sifted my bare fingers through the concealing snow and found the little black rubber seal. Five minutes later, the stove roared as I melted snow, and I knew I had a fighting chance.

The longer I struggled through the storm, the more difficult the traverse got. I couldn't remove my goggles because of the blinding wind and blowing snow, but nor could I see in the dark with the mirrored lenses eliminating more than half of the visible light from my headlamp. I left my goggles on but lifted them periodically to hunt for the most efficient route. An hour into the steep traverse, with unseen slopes dropping away to my right, I crossed at the top of a slab-laden snowfield below an ice-plastered rock cliff in fifteen-foot visibility. I tried moving up the rock but made only forty feet of progress before the technical nature of the terrain overcame my confidence. I backed off to find an easier way. Though I had grown accustomed to scrambling up complex terrain in my flexible-toed telemark ski boots, my skills weren't up to the challenge of climbing fifth-class vertical ground in the dark with a heavy pack. Another hour of searching through the cliffs for a reasonable exit onto the southern summit wore me down, and by the time I reached the rock shelter and found it filled with snow, I was too exhausted to do any shoveling. I laid out my sleeping bag, crawled in, and passed out.

The next morning, the storm had passed, but I doubted my chances at twice traversing the Halo Ridge of Mount Holy Cross. Because of the route's layout, I would have to climb over the three intermediary high points—each above 13,200 feet—to reach the main summit, then return over those same subpeaks. Back at the shelter, I would have to reverse the entire approach over both summits of Notch Mountain to get back to my vehicle. In sum, there were nine peaks above 13,000 feet that I would have to climb before returning to my skis and the nine-mile descent. Due to my stove fiasco the previous night, I had only enough fuel to melt two liters' worth of water, less than half of what I would need. Without enough water, I - wouldn't be able to prepare my oatmeal and protein shake for breakfast, and would therefore have to ration my five candy bars—my only remaining ready-to-eat food, and again, only half of what I needed— until I returned to my truck.

Outside, the calm sunny weather and dramatic surroundings infused me with confidence. Before I knew it, in five hours, I had rounded the halo to arrive at the top of Mount Holy Cross, where I could easily discern the ski areas and major summits of the Elk Range surrounding Aspen to the southwest. On the climb, I had to rely on fitness, acclimatization, and pacing to keep from spiking my energy demands. I found if I could avoid unnecessary power moves and maintain a consistent output, my endurance would get me through. An hour after topping out, I was retracing my telemark boot prints along the gentle ridge that would take me back to the boulder field of Holy Cross's southern satellite summit. At a horseshoe-shaped set of rocks about twenty feet to the windward side of a steeply dropping cornice, I stepped into a shallow post-hole I'd made on my ascent.

Suddenly, a splintering noise erupted from the snow ahead of me. I leaped instinctively to my right and the protection of solid ground. Splitting the snow along the inside boundary of the horseshoe of rocks, a fast-moving crack traced a semicircle from the far side of the snowfield toward the spot where I had stepped a second before. As I hopped over the rocks to the safety of the nearby tundra, the entire snowfield tore away and disappeared. Aside from the initial rupture, the cornice collapse didn't make another noise. I walked over boulders to the southern edge of the hole I had created and cautiously peered down the underlying cliffs. Five hundred feet below the ridge, the wreckage of the fallen cornice lay strewn on the snow slopes above the frozen shore of the Bowl of Tears Lake. I eased back from the drop-off and considered the fate I'd escaped. The image of my pulverized body smashing against the cliffs amid a jumble of snow blocks flashed briefly in my mind. "There's no way I could have survived that fall," I thought. "I'd be down there with my head bashed in, under a ton of cornice debris." The most frightening aspect of the collapse was that I hadn't recognized the cornice on my ascent. Overhanging cornices are highly prone to collapse—it's their nature. With a hundred yards' progress up the ridge, I looked back and saw my footprints marching straight into the abyss.

Back over the intermediate peaks and the two summits of Notch Mountain with my reloaded backpack, I got to my stashed skis at dusk and skied the remaining nine miles and four thousand vertical feet under the silvery light of the moon. At about nine P.M., speeding down the wide track of the summertime approach road, I spooked an elk in a sloping treeless area. It dashed off into the forest, plowing through four to five feet of powder with little strain. Remembering my clumsily slow pace pushing skis up through the forest in the same snow, I gave a moment's appreciation to the elk's prowess, though I knew how lumbering it would seem to a pack of hungry wolves.

On Tuesday of the week following my thirty-mile trip on Mount Holy Cross, my roommate Brian Payne ended up in the ICU after a serious skiing accident left him in critical condition. Minutes after I arrived at Aspen Valley Hospital to visit Brian, I found out my friend Rob Cooper was also there, to undergo surgery for a snowboarding accident that had crushed his right arm, wrist, and hand. Brian spent five days in the ICU and another five days in recovery, with a collapsed lung, a crushed kidney, and six ribs broken in twenty-two places. Rob stayed for two weeks. I visited Brian and Rob twice more before I left on Thursday night to drive to Boulder for a pair of climbs on Longs Peak, shorter but more technical than Halo Ridge. Although my primary concern was for their well-being, their accidents also reminded me how lucky I had been on my recent trips.

Just as Holy Cross had been the last fourteener of the Sawatch Range for my completion list, Longs Peak would be my last summit of the Front Range. I met my friend Scott MacLennan for a team attempt on the north-face cables route (named for the cableway built in the 1930s to assist hikers up the most direct ascent of the upper mountain). Horrendous storm winds hindered our approach, but we arrived in the Boulderfield and our advance camp location by nightfall. Unfortunately, Scott suffered ill effects of the 12,600-foot altitude, compounded by yet another malfunctioning stove. I warmed a foil packet of lentil stew on my stomach, but it was insufficient to properly restore our bodies' reserves for the climb. As rest had not alleviated Scott's altitude woes by morning, we prudently abandoned our trip and returned for hot food and recuperation in Boulder.

The next morning, a Saturday, Scott dropped me off at the same trailhead, with a plan for him to return in ten hours. I hiked up the trail alone, prepared for my solo attempt. Longs Peak is unusual in that it is so windswept that it is best climbed without skis. Up at 13,000 feet, as I rounded the Keyhole for the first time in eight years, I saw that the windward slabs and towers of the west face and north ridge were coated in thick layers of rime. Wind accelerates over the peak, chilling the air below the dew point, and then frost condenses on every exposed surface as the supercooled water vapor slams into the upper mountain. Ice mushrooms pillow from the ridgeline features most exposed to the westerly storm winds, especially along the rock rib extending to the west of the top of the Trough Couloir and the Narrows. My ascent took me over the same route by which I'd climbed the peak as my first fourteener.

Since I still hadn't put on my crampons or removed my second ice tool from my pack, I chose a route that avoided the too-thin verglass on the Homestretch in exchange for two hundred feet of steep snow, connecting a series of ledges that ended in a vertical-walled chimney with a short overhanging finish. Pressing my legs against the right wall with my back against the left wall of the chimney, I removed my pack to make the final squeezing moves out the top around the overhang. My climbing skills were up to it, but my basketball skills failed me.

I tried to hurl my pack over the blockage onto the summit. It was a bad idea. My throw was weak, and instead of landing on the foot-ball-field plateau beyond, my pack hit the overhang and careened out to my left. Still off balance from the throw, I twisted around in time to watch my pack bounce over my head, clear of the wall. Free-falling for a hundred feet, the pack cratered into the snow to the left of my ascent tracks, then slid downhill, gathering speed toward a two-thousand-foot chasm. I watched in disbelief as the pack miraculously jerked to a stop, caught in a two-foot-wide crack in the middle of a rock slab.

My amazement at this stroke of luck dissolved as I realized my crampons and ice tool were now unavailable for my planned descent of the Homestretch. I topped out around the overhang, walked over to the highest discernible point on the plateau, and took a few photos. Dangling my legs from a huge boulder above the Diamond—the well-known east face of Longs—I set aside my dejection and enjoyed the tremendous drop-off below my feet. But in the back of my mind, all I could think about was how I would retrieve my pack.

A few minutes later, I walked over to the Homestretch. Lips tight and forehead wrinkled, I dropped through the first five moves facing out from the mountain into the storm clouds. I quickly encountered loose snow cloaking a treacherous layer of smooth ice that trans-formed the only usable footholds into slippery smears. I turned my body to face the rock slab to my right, my left boot hunting for pur-chase. Watching my foot and trying to ignore the chasm that men-aced in the background, I brushed some snow off a small protrusion that supported my boot sole when I weighted it. Three more down-climbing moves, tapping my axe's pick into the half-inch-thick smear of ice for a grip, and I reached an inset section protected behind a boulder. I turned outward again and, keeping my bottom in contact with the slab, scooted down onto another tiny snow patch coating the underlying rock.

I needed to descend another thirty feet to a pair of thin detached flakes of rock that stuck out an inch where they had separated from the adjoining slab. They enticed me with the prospect of encouraging handholds for a twenty-foot-long swing to my right. I had two options: Moving to my left as I faced down the slab, I could make a few easy moves that would leave me with a fifteen-foot-long slab traverse back to my right, which would be exposed, but it was clear of snow and ice; or I could go straight down a snow groove to the right of the slab, following the usual ascent/descent route, and skip the exposed slab traverse.

Go with the snow; there's no handholds on that slab; it's too risky.

The first four times I moved my feet down into the furrow of snow, I managed to find solid footholds and made comfortable downward progress. Still facing outward with my rear end on the snow, I extended my arms out to either side of the groove and pressed my hands against the grayish-brown granite, palms down. My ice axe dangled from its leash around my left wrist, clanging against the rock each time I rocked my upper body forward to relocate my hands farther down the rock. After easy gains for about ten feet, my left boot heel skittered on some ice hidden beneath the snow. Lowering myself until my right foot bent all the way under my buttocks, I stretched my left foot farther down the furrow, but it skidded off at every attempt. I could really use those crampons.

I took the head of my ice axe in my left hand and planted the pick side into the snow until it struck rock. Weighting the axe, I was then able to extend my left foot another six inches, though without finding an ice-free foothold. This would be child's play with some metal spikes on my feet. Just at the point when I was berating myself for dropping my pack, I made a mistake. I pivoted too far forward on my right haunch, flattening the sole of my right boot on the snow. It peeled out of its divot, and I fell. Instinctively, I rolled over onto my stomach and grabbed the ice-axe shaft with my right hand. I was in the self-arrest position, but my torso slipped below the axe, both my feet skidded onto the rock slab, and my weight fell on the ice pick too abruptly. It jerked out of its placement, and I slid down the last of the snow onto the forty-degree rock slab. Gaining speed, I could feel the crystals of granite grab at my waterproof pants under my knees. From inside my closed eyes, I saw the maw of the chasm rear up behind me, and I gasped. "This is it," I thought. "I don't have a chance."

Trying to drive the axe into the slab to make myself stop, I rotated my shoulders until the full weight of my torso pressed into the axe, grinding it in a hideous squeal of steel on rock. I spent as much energy squinting my eyes shut as I did gripping the axe; I couldn't bear to witness the rock slip away faster and faster until gravity grabbed me by my collar and I tumbled backward down the ever more precipitous face, bouncing like a rag doll into the two-thousand-foot void.

The axe screeched for another moment, and then it caught on something, and I jolted to a stop. The fact that I was no longer falling stunned me into momentary paralysis. Still holding my breath, I opened my eyes cautiously, certain that even the twitching of my eyelids would end this intermission and cause me to break free, plummeting me to my death. I saw first that I was still on the featureless slab, having slid only about two body lengths down the rock. What was holding me in this improbable position? Tilting my head to the left, I peeked under the shaft of my axe. My gaze zeroed in on the tip of my pick . . . and saw nothing. To all appearances, I had ground the pick into the granite with such pressure that I welded it straight onto the bare rock. There was no other obvious explanation. No shelf, no knob, no lip, no ledge, no crack; just the microscopically featured granite, rough as unfinished concrete, that had cropped up directly

in the path of my pick and snagged me from the clutches of imminent doom. In disbelief, I gave in to my body's need for oxygen and
took a series of panting breaths. It was a full minute before I moved,
and then only my head, to peer over my left shoulder toward my escape route.

I don't know how I got out of the self-arrest position and to a secure shelf behind a boulder to my left, but soon I was standing on my
feet, looking over the rest of my descent. What I do know is that I
never once looked at the chasm, centering my attention instead on
the remaining traverse below the two flakes. Soon after reaching the
first flake, I discovered more ice under the twenty-five-foot-long
snowfield. Desperately overgripping the in-cut upper lip of the flake
with my right hand, I swung my axe in my left hand, using the adze
to chop footholds for the front tips of my boots in a descending traverse across the ice. In ten minutes, I had crossed this last obstacle of
the Homestretch and rejoined my ascent tracks, eventually reaching
the fissure where my bag was lodged. Immediately, I retrieved my
crampons from my pack and strapped them onto my boots, then re-
crossed the slab. I was at last equipped for my descent, and down I
went to Scott, waiting for me at the trailhead.

With two technical routes and three long-distance routes in four
weeks—including skiing the northeast bowl of Snowmass Mountain, another Elk fourteener—I felt ready for the biggest challenge of
my project: solo climbing Capitol Peak. In my experience, Capitol
has the longest stretch of difficult climbing of all the fourteeners, as
technical as Longs and Pyramid put together, and is as dangerous as
the Maroon Bells (aka the Deadly Bells). But I knew the approach, I
knew the snow conditions, and I was at the top of my fitness and acclimatization. The peak is known for the Knife Ridge; a hundred-
yard-long ridge at 13,500 feet that drops fifteen hundred feet away to
the east, down steeply corniced flutings that end high above the
Pierre Lakes Basin, and twenty-five hundred feet down the west side

to Capitol Lake. While the exposure gives the Knife Ridge its infamous reputation, the most arduous sections of climbing come after the ridge, on the upper pyramid of the peak.

On February 7, 2003, I woke to sub-zero temperatures at my advance camp on the frozen rocky perimeter of Moon Lake. Ascending in the hyperborean conditions, I skinned on alpine-touring gear until the grade became too steep for my ski skins to hold on to the slope. Still below 13,000 feet, I removed my skis, mounting them on my backpack, and wallowed through bottomless powder, trenching six- and even eight-foot-deep troughs up the forty-degree snow slopes to the 13,600-foot-high subsidiary peak, locally known as K2. Stashing my skis at K2 in anticipation of the long powder-field descent, I continued across the Knife Ridge with crampons strapped to my randonée boots. Halfway across, I came to a disturbing section of the precipitous ridgeline, which was broadly corniced on the left-hand side. Due to prevailing westerly winds, snow had solidified in a cantilevered lip extending from the east side of the ridge.

I had been straddling the apex of the ridge to move across it, but at the overhanging snow cornices, I had to add to my technique, moving forward now with my ice axe poised to latch on to the rock rib if I should tumble off my saddle position. While I was safely perched with my weight balanced on either side of the knife-blade ridge, the cornices continually broke away from under my left leg, vacating space in a startling silence. Each collapse jolted me onto the Knife Ridge's edge under my crotch. An accompanying sense of airiness frightened me, as I knew without looking that coffee-table-sized sections of compacted snow were dropping from under my left buttock in muted free fall. I focused on the rhythm of placing my right crampon in a convenient crack on the west side of the ridge, then humping my body forward another six inches or a foot. Soon enough, I was across the Knife Ridge. Euphoric with the rush of having completed the daunting traverse, I pulled my digital camera out of my jacket for a self-portrait. The huge smile on my face said it all.

I dug my way up the final five hundred feet. At twelve-forty-five

P.M., I summited Capitol Peak and fulfilled a dream of five years. My entire project had been building to the day that brought me safely to the top of the mountain, my forty-third winter solo fourteener. It was the test piece of the project. With a second traverse of the Knife Ridge still to follow on the descent, I hustled off the high point after recording an exultant video and snapshot footage from the summit, and returned to my skis at the top of K2. As the day grew longer, I dropped into the freezer-box shadows of the upper mountain and had to periodically remove my gloves to knock ice from their linings. All the trenching and wallowing in the snow on the ascent had soaked the gloves and packed them with snow that quickly solidified into ice with the dropping afternoon temperatures.

Skiing off K2, I worried less about my hands than the stability of the snow. The powder turns I laced down the face of K2 joined those first S's of Mount Harvard on a short list of my favorite backcountry ski descents. By the time I arrived back at my Moon Lake campsite, however, I knew something wasn't right with my hands—they wouldn't warm up again, no matter what I tried. Holding them over my lit stove, I melted my liner gloves in the flame without feeling any warmth in my fingertips. Tearing the molten fabric off my hands, I saw for the first time the eggshell-white pallor of my fingers and thumbs. Not good.

I hastened my departure from camp without preparing any food. I wasn't so much afraid of frostbite; I accepted what had happened and wanted to minimize any further tissue damage. I had climbed a peak in a style that, over the course of the last thirty hours, had completely satisfied my yearnings for mountain experiences. That I had attained partial- and full-thickness frostbite on eight of my fingers, including both thumbs, was part of that adventure. While I didn't understand the depth of the damage at the time, I put on a dry set of liner gloves and kept my barely functional hands protected from the cold for the seven-mile ski descent.

When I arrived home in Aspen, instead of going to the hospital (which is what I should have done), I treated myself for the frostbite.

To start with, I took four tablets of extra-strength pain-reducing medication to prepare me for the next part of the procedure. I waited a half hour for the pills to take effect, filled the kitchen sink with hot water, and experimented with how fast the steaming faucet had to run to maintain a consistent hot-tub temperature in the plugged washbasin. Standing alone, I held both my hands in the basin for an hour, watching my fingertips change from white to black, red, orange, and green, obscenely screaming out at the throbbing pain. At times I had to seize my right wrist with my left hand to keep from yanking it out of the water—it was more damaged and caused me more agony. My roommates were all out of the house, and our neighbors must have been gone, too, or they may well have notified the police of a murder in progress. Over the hour, I hoped again and again to see blisters form under the skin of my fingers. Blisters meant the underlying tissue would probably recover, though never fully regain its original circulation; whereas no blisters meant the cold damage was severe and I could lose portions of those fingers. One after another, excruciating blisters bubbled up at the end of each finger, back to the first knuckle on most of them. I was thankful for the fiery swelling.

I subsequently decided I would take five weeks off from solo mountaineering, allowing my hands to heal from the frostbite, even though I had two peaks left in the Elk Range—the Maroon Bells. There was plenty to occupy me until my fingers grew new layers of protective skin: Phish was touring the West for the first time in three years; I had a hut trip planned with some friends from New Mexico; and there was lots of in-area telemark skiing to be done with my Aspen pals. But even this "downtime" wouldn't be free of risk.

Two weeks after my ascent of Capitol, I headed over to a mountain range just east of Mount of the Holy Cross to join six friends from the Albuquerque Mountain Rescue Council and five of their relatives on an annual backcountry ski trip. This year's destination was the

Fowler-Hilliard Hut on Resolution Mountain above Camp Hale. We met in Leadville and divvied up food and drink loads to be carried in our packs to the hut. The 10th Mountain Division huts are named for the World War II ski infantry who fought the infamous Battle of Riva Ridge in Italy. Their main training camp for two years was Camp Hale, halfway between Leadville and Vail. Many of the war veterans returned to Colorado, where they helped propagate the postwar ski-area development boom with their passion for skiing and familiarity with the region. The ski areas of Breckenridge, Vail, and Aspen were some of the largest of the 10th Mountain veteran enterprises. While the backcountry huts weren't established until the 1980s, they are dedicated to the memory of individuals whose love for country took them overseas to protect the freedom that I find most glorified in the mountains.

After five hours plowing through two feet of fresh snow along the six-mile approach to the hut, we settled into our weekend home and ate gourmet appetizers of oysters, spicy hummus, clams, and kippered fish on crackers, and drank three rounds of hot cocoa and schnapps. Spying out the hut's picture windows, I lusted to take some turns in the east bowl of Resolution Peak directly in front of the hut. When talk turned to action, two of my Mountain Rescue colleagues, Mark Beverly and Chadwick Spencer, joined me in buckling up our boots and preparing our avalanche safety equipment for the short ascent.

Our threesome skinned up to Resolution Peak on the wind-scoured northeast ridge, starting at 4:50 P.M. and summiting the 11,950-foot peak just after 5:15. Darkness was coming quickly, but while Mark and I waited for Chadwick to arrive, we took a five-minute break to survey the ridgeline of the Continental Divide to the east and the Eagle River watershed and Mount of the Holy Cross to the west. Beyond the White River National Forest, only thirty miles away (but a three-hour drive from the trailhead), was my home in Aspen. I recounted my solo winter ascent of Holy Cross for Mark, and the night ski off the 12,000-foot saddle when I'd seen the elk in the meadow. I also spoke of the hairball adventure I'd had with my emergency bivouac en route to the rock shelter and the contrasting triumph I'd felt at surmounting the Halo Ridge.

Even though this was our first trip together, I knew Mark was one of the best climbers on our rescue team. I admired his technical climbing and rescue rigging skills, advanced medical training, and guiding experience. In sharing the details of one of my recent climbs, I think I was trying to impress him, as he had impressed me with his Canadian ice-climbing trips. He surprised me when he responded with an accepting but seemingly unmoved reply: "I can't be excited for you, Aron. I don't do climbs like that. But I think it's great for you—as long as you're happy."

"Yeah, I am. I'm living my dream."

Mark was saying that he didn't aspire to do winter solos, and it seemed like he was making sure I was doing them for the right reasons—climbing not for bragging rights, or the perceived admiration of others, but because it made me happy. It was a subtle check that I had cleared in myself a long time back, but I was grateful for his reminder.

Once Chadwick joined us, we posed for a group portrait with Elk Ridge behind us. Skiing off the rock-strewn summit, Mark led us back down the wind-packed ridge, a safe but unappealing ski descent because of the thin, icy snow. After I slipped and fell to avoid an exposed tree root, I called out to Mark: "Hey, this sucks! I'm gonna head over to the powder." I had borrowed a set of new powder skis from the Ute in Aspen and was itching to try them out in the untracked bowl. It had been a year since I had first freed my heel and started telemark skiing. Chadwick had given me some of my first pointers on technique, and I was excited to show him how much I'd improved. Leaving the ridge, I skied out to my right onto the softer snow, which got deeper and deeper the farther I traversed across the top of the forty-degree bowl.

Mark stopped slightly downhill from me on the ridge. Chadwick was behind me, traversing to the right, parallel and uphill from my tracks. None of us called out to dig a snow-study pit to check the snow stability and the likelihood of an avalanche, but I felt confident in the snowpack from having been out climbing and skiing the back-country all winter. Success on the fourteener climbs and providential salvation from the string of close calls had bred in me a cavalier atti-tude toward the real avalanche danger. We spread out in the standard routine to expose one skier at a time to potential slide terrain. I ar-rived at the top of the lowest-angle fall line that started at thirty-eight degrees and eased off to about thirty-two degrees above a cluster of twenty fully grown pine trees.

"I'm gonna ski here. Are you coming down?" I said to Chadwick, who was close enough that we could talk in normal tones. Mark was still a hundred yards away over on the ridge.

"I don't know. How are you going to get back to the hut? It looks like you'll have to skin back out."

"I'm not going to go past those trees. I'll stop there, then traverse back left to the hut."

Mark shouted over that he wasn't going to ski the bowl. He'd go down the ridge. I yelled out, "Okay! Watch me!" to let my partners know I was dropping into the bowl. I felt a little nervous but didn't pause to pinpoint whether it was about the avalanche danger or wanting to ski well in the deep powder. Moments later, as I took my first three sweeping turns, the sweet sensations of plowing through billowing snow replaced my timidity. I sped up and quickened my rhythm, popping shorter-radius turns on the lower-angled slope, and hooting as I passed the uppermost trees on my right. With another 1,500 vertical feet of the bowl below the trees luring me to keep ski-ing, only the fatigue in my legs made me stop. I turned and yelled back to Chadwick, three hundred vertical feet above me, "Yaaa-hooo! That was great! The snow is awesome! Come on down!"

Lurching in the powder, Chadwick followed my tracks, falling twice on the steeper part near the top as Mark watched from the ridge. I had my camera out, taking pictures as Chadwick settled into the easier slope, matching his turns to my tracks. Breathing hard, Chadwick forced out his last turns and stopped next to me. "Wow, that was a lot of work. I could barely turn, the snow was so deep."

"Yeah, but it was great, huh? You looked good on that last part. I got a couple pictures of you. Check it out, how our tracks slink down like that. It's like we're heli-skiing." I yelled up to Mark, "Come on— it's great!"

Chadwick and I stood at the edge of the trees, looking up to Mark traversing into the bowl just below our entry tracks, bouncing on his skis. He was ski-cutting the snow, trying to preemptively trigger a slide by simulating the impact of his weight as he compressed in a turn. Seemingly satisfied at the snow stability, Mark made three turns in the upper slope, fell, tumbled over, and stood up, still skiing but sitting back on his skis. He recovered and finished his run smiling. Exhausted, Mark plopped down into the snow about thirty feet from the trees instead of turning to a stop. A hollow whoomph escaped from the snow under Mark, and we each jumped through our skin— hearing the whoomph of collapsing snow often means you've triggered an avalanche. But the snow around us remained in place without fracturing. Relieved, Chadwick joked, "Did you hear that? - Mark's butt just whoomphed."

"Ha! Hey, Chadwick, drop forward on your knees—I want to get a picture of you in the snow."

A diesel engine—or maybe it was the whispered roar of a jet plane—sounded above us.

As I lined up Chadwick in my viewfinder and depressed the shutter release, I noticed a swirling cloud of thick airborne spindrift over his head. Then the diesel rumble registered in my ears, and in the same fraction of a second that I realized the growling and the spindrift were related, I was shoved hard from behind my right shoulder, lifted from my feet, and slammed downhill onto the slope on my left side. My world went black.

Accelerating from zero to thirty as if a truck had hit me, I opened my eyes to a dense soup of white. I knew immediately that I was sliding downhill headfirst, buried in a teeming mass of snow, but several seconds passed before I understood that I was being carried away by an avalanche. I opened my mouth and sucked in a mist of snow that lined my throat, choking me. Spitting out the snow, I waited until I saw a patch of sky through the avalanche, then inhaled deeply and held my breath. I fought the pull of the current, trying to rotate my body to get my head uphill so I could swim against the roiling white flood, but my skis dragged through the accelerating debris, anchors shackling my feet above me. Relaxing to save my oxygen until another window opened in the suffocating tide, I silently wondered when my life would start flashing through my mind; fortunately, it never did. My next thought was "So this is what it's like to be in an avalanche." I was expecting to be rolled over in a terminal somersault, but I simply continued to slide on my left side. Several more seconds dragged on. I needed to breathe again. I waited for a chance, but there was no blue window this time. I gasped and filled my mouth with snow.

Then I sensed the deceleration as the avalanche slowed, and I yanked my arms to get them above the snow. Because of the ski poles tethered to my wrists, only my right hand came up. It ripped free from my glove, with my forearm and elbow interred in the stiffening snow, like the rest of my inundated body. As I stopped sliding, I jerked my head up and thrust my hips forward, arching my back like a scorpion. I was peering down the hillside, eye level with the rubble. The thought struck me: "I'm alive!"

My torso heaved relentlessly for air. The asphyxiating conditions of the avalanche and a mouthful of compacted snow had starved my body of oxygen. Spitting out the snow, I continued to hyperventilate but managed to yell out, "I'm okay! I'm okay!" between overwrought gasps. The avalanched snow had promptly consolidated, encasing me in an unyielding cast that constricted my chest and held my body motionless except for my right hand and my head. Brushing away what little debris I could from in front of my face, I looked to my left and saw the hut; to my right, the hillside. Avalanche debris was everywhere, but I saw no sign of either of my partners. "Chadwick! Mark!"

Above me, Chadwick screamed in response. "Aron! Mark!"

I craned my head as far to the left as I could and caught a glimpse of Chadwick about a hundred feet upslope. "I'm okay! Are you okay? Where's Mark?"

"I don't know!" Chadwick sounded scared, and the shouting - wasn't helping.

"Are you free?"

"Yes, not yet, I'm digging my feet out!" Chadwick had somersaulted in the avalanche several times, but landed on his feet and stood up as he came to a stop. He had already unclipped his shovel from his backpack and was excavating his boots and ski bindings as I continued to yell for Mark.

"Chadwick, can you see anything of Mark?"

"No!"

My goggles, shovel, and camera were gone, torn off me during the tumult. My probe poles and right glove were gone, too, buried in the debris. I was hoping Mark might have lost some equipment and that a visible trail of gear would suggest his location, but neither of us could see any personal effects amid the debris field.

"Switch your beacon to search and come dig me out. We'll need both of us to find Mark," I shouted. Protocol might suggest that Chadwick should try to find Mark by himself, but I couldn't unbury myself enough to get to my beacon and switch it to search mode. Until I could do that, Chadwick's beacon would be receiving my transmission on top of Mark's, making it difficult to pinpoint him.

Within two more minutes, Chadwick was at my side, digging out my left hand. "Stay with me, Aron!" Chadwick was very emotionally shaken. I reassured him that I was okay and directed him to dig at my legs and then to free my boots from the ski bindings.

Rolling out of my hole, I stood up and saw the extent of the vast slide. It hushed my voice. "Oh my God, Chadwick. Look at it." Five hundred vertical feet above us, a gargantuan fracture cut across the top of the bowl, as high as a two-story house on the right. Blocks the size of refrigerators littered the mountainside; a few monstrous chunks were as big as railroad cars. At first glance, the slide looked to be several hundred feet from side to side. Then I saw how it continued to the left, behind the island of trees where we'd been blindsided, arcing almost a half mile to the far southeastern ridge. Untold thousands of tons of snow had crashed down the hillside. My knees weakened at the scale of the avalanche. That two of us were coherently mobilizing a rescue, after a slide of this magnitude had swept us two city blocks down the mountain, was almost unimaginable. But where was Mark?

Chadwick was still surveying the bowl when I ran down to a terrace in the hill thirty feet below us. The rollover blocked our view of the lower snowfields. At the edge, I scanned the debris for any visual clues, but there were none—the avalanche had swept down the bowl another thousand feet below our position, all the way to the creek. With my beacon set to search mode, I frantically wished for a signal, but there was no feedback on the display. I shouted back to Chadwick, who had started moving to the right and was over a hundred feet away from me. "What's your range?"

"I don't know."

"Switch your beacon to transmit." I wanted to identify how far apart we could be and positively pick up a transmission. With Chadwick transmitting and my beacon receiving, we could establish our working range.

"Do you get me?" he yelled. I could hear the desperation in both our voices.

"Not yet—come back toward me now."

"Okay! I'm coming! I'm coming!"

"There; thirty-eight!" My beacon had picked up Chadwick's frequency at thirty-eight meters. "Switch back to search!" We had a range of just over a hundred feet and a slide path over two-thousand-feet wide. If we could trust our beacons to consistently perform at the working range with a minimum overlap in our search pattern, it would take us five trips up and down the length of the slide zone to cover the whole debris field. But there was no time for that.

Think, Aron. Think.

"Chadwick! We were together at the top. Look where you and I ended up. We're in line. Mark should be in that same line. Is he above us or below us?"

Chadwick didn't respond. I ran back over to the edge of the rollover and double-checked the lower mountain. The vast majority of people who survive being buried in an avalanche are found within the first fifteen minutes; after a half hour, the chances of a successful resuscitation are negligible. We didn't have time to go down and up. It was one or the other. I shouted, "I've got nothing—no clues down here. He's above us! Let's go!" I wasn't certain by any means, but we had to make a choice. If he was still alive, any indecision on our part would kill Mark in another few minutes.

With a hundred feet between us, Chadwick and I marched quickly up the slope toward another terrain roll fifty feet above. Chadwick had come to a stop. To my right, he blurted out, "Forty-eight! I've got a hit!"

Mark! We pushed harder, thighs burning, lungs stinging, legs sinking, stumbling in the debris. Mark! No time to catch a breath. I crested the rollover, and my beacon lit up—38, 37, 34 . . . 28 . . . 24. I was closing in. Then I saw a small object, a ski tip. I could discern the K2 insignia.

"I've got him! I see a ski tip!" With more ground to cover than me, Chadwick had slowed in the debris, falling farther and farther behind. I shouted out, "Mark! We're coming!"

Chadwick shouted, "Aron, take the shovel!"

I was close. 18 . . . 15 . . . I couldn't turn back to get the shovel. "No! Get your ass up here!" As I charged toward the ski tip, my beacon beeped faster and at a higher tone, like a detonator about to explode. 11 . . . 8 . . . 4 . . . Over the insistent shrill, I heard a weak moan, then another.

"Mark, I'm here!" I traced back five feet from the ski tip and lifted a briefcase-sized block of snow from the source of the moaning. A tangle of yellow hair and a red piece of cloth protruded from a pile of cementlike snow.

"Mark! Can you hear me?" Mark couldn't spare the time it would take me to be delicate with my next task. I roughly knocked his head several times while brushing the snow away from his face, quickly clearing a breathing space. When I moved the red glove bunched up in front of his mouth; Mark's leaden skin tone arrested my action. I was staring into the ashen face of an entombed ghost. Of the four dead people I've seen in my life, all had more color than Mark did at that moment.

I cocked Mark's head up and fished the icy blockage out of his mouth. It had been twelve minutes since the avalanche stopped, and Mark had been without adequate oxygen for most of that time. He was still alive but at the lowest level of alertness. I was relieved when he responded to my questions, but all he could tell me was that he was cold and tired.

I jumped up from my crouch and ran halfway to Chadwick, who threw the shovel to me. Catching it in the air, I turned and raced back to Mark. With his airway clear and him still breathing on his own, my next concern for Mark was his body temperature. Hypothermia could pull Mark from consciousness at any moment and shut down his breathing. I dug first at Mark's partially exposed left arm, then at his back and left leg, calling out my finds as I made slow progress. Mark was buried more deeply than I had been. Chadwick arrived and talked to Mark as I dug feverishly, scooping snow downhill. I needed help to move all the heavy snow. After exposing Mark's backpack, I unfastened his shovel and tossed it in front of Chadwick. "Help me dig!"

"I can't. My hands are frozen. I can't hold on to anything." Chadwick had lost both his gloves in the avalanche, and the combination of excavating me and then clawing up through the debris field had rendered his hands unusable. I had only my left glove and liner. Tearing off the outer shell, I gave it to Chadwick against his protests: "My hands are gone—save yours!"

"Take it! Turn it inside out and put it on your right hand. I need your help digging." Next I yanked off Mark's gloves, gave Chadwick the left one, and took the right one myself.

For the first time, I saw movement over at the hut, nearly a third of a mile across the mountainside to our right as we looked uphill. I cupped my hands and shouted at the top of my lungs to the people I could see milling around outside: "HELP! HELP! HELP! HELP!"

Faintly, I heard a voice reply, "We're coming!" Rescue was on its way, but Mark couldn't stave off hypothermia unless we could get him out of the snow and wrapped in more insulating layers. We swung the shovels, throwing snow, clanging the blades against each other. Chadwick missed the snow entirely on two consecutive attempts.

"Chadwick, slow down. You're not even hitting the snow." He was panicking; we were falling behind. "Here, start high and scoop the snow down—it's easier than shoveling uphill." Even with both of us toiling, Mark was slipping away. He had been repeating that he was very cold and very tired, and then about a minute of quiet passed.

Chadwick checked Mark's head again. "He's not breathing." With two rescue breaths from Chadwick, Mark resuscitated. I extracted Mark's left boot from the telemark binding and leash. Five minutes and forty cubic feet of snow later, we disinterred Mark's right leg from its encasement.

"HELP! HELP! HELP!" We shouted together to our friends at the edge of the debris field. We had done as much as we could, and we needed supplies to get Mark warmed up. Exhausted from the half-hour rescue effort and not realizing the precautions our friends were taking to ensure that they were not swept up by a secondary avalanche, I muttered in exasperation, "What's taking them so long?"

We rolled Mark onto his left side and sat him up. He lurched back and belched out the air Chadwick had blown into his belly—the rescue breaths had been partially diverted from Mark's lungs because of his head's forward position. Smothering his back and sides with our bodies, we removed Mark's pack and rooted through it for gloves and clothes. Shuddering with the aftermath of adrenaline, Chadwick and I hugged Mark and each other in a seated embrace. We smelled the raw halitosis of fear, mixed with the odors of oysters, clams, fish, and spicy hummus appetizers. Confident of Mark's survival, we broke into a gale of nervous laughter laced with relief that we were all out and stable with help arriving in minutes.

One after another, the other four members of the Albuquerque Mountain Rescue team who were with us on the trip—Steve Patchett, Tom Wright, Dan Hadlich, and Julia Stephens—skied over to the pit where we were huddled as darkness consumed the mountainside, carrying with them a down sleeping bag, a foam pad, gloves, and headlamps. We wrapped Mark in the down bag, and by the time Chadwick and I had retrieved our skis and what little of our other equipment we could find in the debris, Mark was up and mobile. It was a tribute to his strength and drive that in thirty minutes, he had gone from losing consciousness to skiing back to the hut under his own power.

We had a solemn dinner back at the hut, retelling details of the evening. Several of our friends had seen the avalanche and knew right away we were in trouble. They had gone from cooking dinner in their long underwear and socks to being fully prepared for a prolonged rescue effort and arriving safely on-scene in a half hour—a phenomenal performance. Chadwick had held himself together even through the terrifying stress of rescuing both his partners. I was proud of his fast action, and of Mark's resilience. While we had each decided to ski that slope, I felt guilty about my own decisions: decisions based on ego, attitude, overconfidence, and ambition, which overrode the combined training and experience of our group. We had survived a Grade 5 avalanche—as big as they get in Colorado. We had survived something we shouldn't have survived. We had survived, but Mark and Chadwick blamed me for pressuring them to ski the bowl. I lost two friends that Sunday because of the choices we made; Mark and Chadwick left the next morning, and they haven't spoken to me since.

Rather than regret those choices, I swore to myself that I would learn from their consequences. Most simply, I came to understand that my attitudes were not intrinsically safe. Without fully evaluating a decision for potential danger—i.e., when I had made a decision in which attitude overruled a complete understanding and mitigation of risk—I was playing the odds. I recalled an avalanche instructor's advice: "When you play the odds, you have to be able to survive not beating them." After the Resolution Bowl avalanche, I found it easier to let go of the ego and attitude that otherwise pushed me to risk more than I was comfortable with, or rushed my decision-making, causing me to skip critical steps of gathering and evaluating information. Discomfort with elevated risks was not a weakness to overcome, but a signal for me to process a decision until I could either move forward safely or choose to come back another day.

Warm weather and more storms over the next three weeks caused a rash of natural avalanche activity that diminished the likelihood of my final project for the winter—climbing the Maroon Bells, the postcard-perfect candy-striped twin pyramids that decorate calendars as the most photographed of Colorado's mountains. Every face and gully of both peaks is subject to extreme avalanche hazard. There is no low-risk route; the only way I would be able to attempt the peaks would be under stable snowpack conditions. By early March, time was running out on my winter season.

Due to my climbs through the winter, the March 15 *Aspen Times Weekly* newspaper was running a substantial article on my ascent of Capitol Peak and the Resolution Bowl avalanche. For pictures to accompany the article, I hiked out onto Highland Ridge with Dan Bayer, a photographer friend of mine. We had a bluebird day with unobstructed views of the Maroon Bells. I had said in an interview that I didn't think conditions would permit an attempt on the Bells before winter was up. But what I saw during the photo shoot led me to reconsider my chances. From 12,000 feet on Highland Ridge, I could see that the major snow chute splitting the east face of the two peaks—the Bell Cord Couloir—had avalanched repeatedly. Sometimes the safest routes to climb are the ones that have already released. Speculating that with continued warm weather, calm winds, and no more snow, the couloir would remain consolidated from the previously run-out slides, I planned an overnight trip for two days later.

On the day the *Aspen Times Weekly* cover article ran—entitled "For Whom the Bells Toll"—I skied in my randonée boots the nine miles up from the Maroon Creek road closure to 10,200 feet at Crater Lake. Directly below the Bell Cord Couloir, I crossed a half-mile-wide zone of hardened avalanche debris, the evidence of a weeklong cycle of intense avalanche activity. By one-thirty P.M., I had reached the area where I would camp and was scanning the trees past the edge of the debris for a protected campsite when a thousand-foot-long plume of snow came cascading over the lower cliffs of the East Buttress of South Maroon Peak, less than a quarter mile in front of me. On the quick draw with my camera, I took a series of pictures as the avalanche overwhelmed the forest in a cloud that rose five hundred feet off the valley floor. The sound waves hit me on a time delay. Splintering crashes punctuated the bellowing growl of the snow as it pounced from the upper cliffs onto eighty-foot-tall trees that snapped under the devastating momentum. Avalanches can travel at speeds around 100 mph, with a density four times that of air because of the suspended snow, which hits with the energy of a 400-mph wind. The pines and firs didn't have a chance. Nor would I.

As puffs of crystalline snow drifted through the valley, I chose a campsite in the trees at the farthest edge of the older debris and formulated a plan for my ascent. Avalanche threat for the couloir itself was minimal due to prior releases, but both faces empty out into the common trough. Sun exposure on the nearly vertical rock and snow faces on either side of the fifty-degree Bell Cord would put me at the greatest risk. The left face would get sun from first light until about noon, while the right face would get sun until late afternoon. Due to its longer sun exposure and more southerly aspect, the right face had already lost most of its snow and was less of a concern than the left one. I read the mountain and understood that the risk would be lowest before sunrise and just after the left face went into shadow around noon. Later in the afternoon, the right face would begin sliding, just as it did three times while I sat in my tent and prepared soup for an early dinner.

At three in the morning, I awoke and put on my cold-weather clothes, gathered my water and food, kicked my feet into my boots, and strapped on my crampons. After a quick bowl of oatmeal and protein powder, I was moving up the debris field by three-thirty A.M.

Within an hour, I was in trouble. While making my observations the afternoon before, I'd spotted a steep shortcut directly up a narrow gully. The gully would eliminate a wide traverse to the right in less consolidated snow, allowing me to enter the Bell Cord Couloir proper at 11,200 feet. Climbing on my front points in the isolated bubble of my headlamp, I was halfway up the gully when a bowling ball of ice came shooting out of the inky heavens down the tightly walled corridor and whizzed past my head. It fell with such velocity that I caught only the flash of it in my headlamp. Terror chilled my blood, but I climbed on, hoping that the twenty-pound ice cube - didn't have any friends. A few minutes later, however, another block hurtled past my right shoulder, also at high speed, and smashed into the right wall of the gully. I had to get out of the shooting gallery as fast as I could. Climbing out the top was the best option, as the blocks seemed to be leaping over a ledge that would provide cover until I left the confinement of the rock walls. The gully became steeper as I neared the top, and then my ice axe hit solid ice below the Styrofoam snow. I looked up at a forty-foot-high sheer frozen waterfall that spanned the gully wall-to-wall.

What the . . . ? Where did that come from? Why didn't I see this before? Can I climb it? Should I go down?

I didn't want to risk descending the gully—I had no idea if the bombardment was over or not—and I couldn't afford to lose the time it would take to reascend the snowy ramps. I needed to be at 13,600 feet by the time sunlight hit the mountain faces in two hours, and I - wouldn't make it if I had to give up a half hour of backtracking. If I wanted a shot at doing the climb today, I would have to climb this curtain of water ice with a single ice axe and general mountaineering crampons—not my preferred ice-climbing equipment. The crampon points on my right foot bit into the frozen glaze of the waterfall, and I swung my long-handled axe in my right hand like a shorter ice-climbing tool, until it sank to the third tooth on the pick. Finger-width cracks, shallow ledges, and inset footholds populated the rock wall on my left. Forming a right angle with the ice, the rock wall on my left allowed me to make stemming maneuvers; using counter-pressure, I could more confidently bear down on the crampon points of my right foot, where they were embedded in the ice. I surmounted two ten-foot steps in the rock using this basic technique. Trying to ignore the deathly void behind me, I continued another ten feet and ran out of ice on my right side. I was almost at the top, but now there was a small patch of frozen tundra exposed by the avalanches that had coursed through the gully. A two-inch-tall horizontal crack gave me a decent left foothold where the flat front points of my crampons could balance. My right foot could still puncture the icefall in a straight-legged stem, but the rock wall faded back from my left hand, leaving me without good holds for either hand. I was stuck.

Reversing my climb back down the mixed ice and rock dihedral would lead to a death fall. I couldn't go down; I couldn't stay. I had to go up, as improbable as it seemed. Plucking my axe from its last placement in the ice, I swung it hard into the frost-heaved earth above a grassy knob. I hardly trusted the mud to hold my weight, but my left hand couldn't pull on the last remaining rock lip—my glove was too slick. As the crampon points of my left foot skittered off their balancing point, I lunged my right hand onto the head of the ice axe. The point held fast in the frosted tundra, but I was desperate; if my axe had popped when my foot slipped, I would already be dead at the bottom of the gully.

Fraught with stress, I leaned my head to the left with my neck outstretched, and bit the cuff of my left glove in my teeth, ripping my hand free. Letting the glove dangle from its wrist loop, I crimped my fingers around the rock lip and pulled simultaneously with both arms, staring at the axe pick stabbed into the mud. It was as hard as any 5.8 rock-climbing move I've ever done, making it the most difficult free solo maneuver I'd ever attempted. Add in the altitude, remoteness, and the fact I was doing it at high exposure in the dark, and it was easy to understand why my body collapsed onto the first flat surface I could find. I was sweating so hard I needed to be wrung out, but all I could manage was to open an energy gel packet with my teeth while I reached to don my left glove. It wasn't there: My glove - wasn't dangling from my wrist.

Then it hit me that I hadn't put my wrist loop around my hand that morning. When I'd torn off my left glove to make that last move, it had dropped all the way down the gully. Damn, damn, damn! Again I debated whether or not to go down, but I knew it would mean bailing on the climb to retrieve my glove. Could I afford to risk more frostbite damage? Well, no; but I did have an extra set of liners to prevent ice-up like what had happened on Capitol. I took off my right outer shell, turned it inside out, and put it on over my spare left liner, adding my spare right liner over the one I was already wearing.

Okay, Aron, the rest of this should be easy compared to what you just did.

My heart hammered at its maximum output for the next two hours as I gained the remaining 2,300 feet to the top of the couloir just in time to watch the sun rise over the summit of Pyramid Peak three miles to the east. The shadows of the Maroon Bells swept halfway to the horizon, where Snowmass Mountain and Capitol Peak gathered their first rays of dawn under a dramatic black sky. It was an early reward for the demanding climbing I'd done in the dark, and my first winter sunrise from near the top of a fourteener. I took a long break, reenergizing with some food bars and water, then set off up the fourth-class slabs and snowfields to the summit of South Maroon, which I reached with hoots and smiles at eight-fifteen A.M. An hour later, I was back at the saddle above the Bell Cord, ready to ascend North Maroon Peak. The ridge of the Bells is one of four technical high connecting traverses on Colorado's fourteeners, the others being Blanca–Little Bear, Wilson–El Diente, and Crestone Peak–Crestone Needle. I'd climbed them all in the summer, but the Bells would be my first of the foursome in the winter. Encountering deep and fluted snowdrifts on the west side of North Maroon's south ridge, I climbed up to the snow mushrooms on the ridgetop and tunneled a hole through one of the seven-foot-high pillows clinging to the rock to make my way to the summit. I have had few mountaintop experiences when I felt the excitement and jubilation that I did on top of North Maroon. Waving my ice axe in the air, I shouted with joy at my forty-fifth winter fourteener solo, my completion of the Elk Range in a single winter and the last of the technically hard routes, and the singular experience of a double traverse of the Maroon Bells ridge. Turning to the south and a view of my tracks winding over and through the surreal snow formations of the ridge, I let loose a "Yaaahooooo!" and imagined my exuberance bouncing off alpine summits all the way to Crested Butte.

Back at the notch above the Bell Cord at noon, I felt giddy that my scheme had worked exactly as planned. I raced down the 3,400 vertical feet to my camp, picking up my left glove from the debris at the base of the "shortcut" gully, all within forty-five minutes of departing the head of the Bell Cord.

On my descent, I recalled the first time I'd rung both the Bells in a day on July 2, 2000. My best friends and closest climbing partners, Mark Van Eeckhout and Jason Halladay, and I had climbed North Maroon, traversed the ridge to South Maroon, and descended the slushy ice runnels in the East Face Couloir in a fifteen-hour round trip. Despite the gnarly descent, I remembered a moment of down-climbing blocky purple rock into the yellow-lichen-coated central notch at the head of the Bell Cord and looking out to the west over the lush velveteen green of Fravert Basin. The colors were so rich, I thought I could smell them. I felt the love of beauty to a greater extent than I ever had before. Two things became certain to me in that moment: first, that I would visit Fravert Basin and see close up the vision of nature that called to me from that rocky perch; and second, in whatever vague recess of my mind that is in charge of these life decisions, I knew that one day I would call Aspen my home. If the subject of a winter traverse of the Maroon Bells ridge had come up at that time, I would have dismissed the idea outright as an impossibility. I had done it though, not just once but twice in the same day, and five hours faster in the winter than I had done it in the summer.

SEVEN

Day Three: "Push on Till the Day"

Adversity has the effect of eliciting talents, which, in prosperous circumstances, would have lain dormant.

—HORACE

WHERE HAVE ALL THESE mosquitoes come from? I wait out two of them and return their spirits to the cosmos when they alight on my right forearm. Up until a half hour ago, I hadn't seen a single insect all day, and now a half-dozen bloodsuckers buzz around my head. Sitting in my harness, suspended from the anchor I built this morning above the chockstone, I execute them one by one until they are all gone. Bizarrely, it occurs to me that I could eat the flattened mosquitoes. It's a ridiculous and unnecessary thought: The bugs couldn't possibly sustain me, and besides, I still have most of two premade burritos. That's a good five hundred calories, and much more appetizing than dead insects.

Must be the sleep deprivation. It's making you dumb.

Yet another breeze brushes past me on its way to the Big Drop, stripping me of what little warmth I have. Later in the afternoon like this—or early in the evening, I guess—the winds come more frequently, and a crispness anticipates the arrival of night.

My gumption for chipping at the boulder is gone. I continue with the fruitless effort solely to stimulate my metabolism and push into the background the shuddering weakness brought on by the chilly winds. Even still, I work only a fraction as much as I did yesterday. I've already acknowledged the inutility of hacking at the chockstone, but some irrational part of my brain hasn't yet acquiesced to the helplessness of my situation. It insists that if I work harder and take fewer breaks, I will eventually get free. I rationalize my lethargy with the impossible thought that I don't want to get free with night approaching—I could stumble right off the Big Drop rappel in the dark, or get lost in the lower canyon.

Like you're going to get free. You're lazy and you know it. You're in the fight of your life—a fight for your life, no less—and you're too lazy to get over a little fatigue and do some work. You slothful waste. You're killing yourself here. You're going to die.

There it is, my prognosis in black and white, like an X ray held to the light. I have a terminal condition. Without being able to meet the needs of my body, I can expect to live another day and a half, perhaps. Or two days, but what would that matter? No expectation had prepared me for this tormenting anxiety of a slow death, thinking about whether it will come tonight in the cold, tomorrow in the cramps of dehydration, or the next day in heart failure. This hour, the next, the one after that. Anytime I'd come close to death before, it had been in the context of a flashing crisis, a dramatic vision. Whether the circumstance was experienced or envisioned, the chop came as an executioner's blade, fast as gravity in the form of a falling ice block, a smothering avalanche, a failed self-arrest, a peeling backflip from high on a rock face. I knew my last sounds wouldn't be any profound passing of wisdom but a muttered "Oh shit," maybe the thought "This is it," and a crushing exhale, a spattering of blood, crunching bones. I'd never imagined fading in a protracted departure. I figured I could handle just about anything that would provoke a drawn-out struggle: fighting through a storm; finding my way when I was lost;

dragging my body back from injury or illness. No, I wouldn't sit down to dinner with death, talk introspectively over a lengthy visit, and end on "Well, that's it, then, guess it's time to go."

I had been lucky so many times that even the glimpses of my final destiny had become a toy I played with to bring on a certain intense feeling, the ultimate contrast between the fear of immediate doom and the desire to live fully. I think some people would consider these the thoughts of an adrenaline junkie, but I relished more the *control* of my adrenaline than the ride it would give me if I unleashed it. On less dangerous but still adventurous trips, I pushed my limits for endurance, engaging in prolonged experiences of cathartic suffering to break down my interior walls, to cleanse my spirit for purer emotions than boredom and stress, and to surpass myself. Periodically, I would have a euphoric realization taking me beyond the filters of my brain, in which I understood that the fear and the pain existed only in the gap between a pair of neurons. I called it getting over myself. How I will get over myself now, in this canyon, is beyond any perceived powers of mind over matter I think I have—my situation is physically impossible to overcome. I am over the pain, I have the discipline to survive the fear, but I can't get over my body's need for water.

Water. I pick up my charcoal-gray Nalgene bottle and swirl the precious contents. For the last day, I've been sipping about two ounces every three hours. Hmmm. That means the ten ounces I have left will get me through tonight. I need it to last longer than that. It's after six P.M., but I haven't had any water since I put away my video camera at three-fifteen. I should skip it this time, save it for later. I feel all right, I guess. My tongue isn't unusually swollen or squishy or hard. My lips feel normal, too. I'm thinking about water fairly frequently, but maybe this stage of dehydration is like that part of fasting when I've thought I would die if I didn't eat soon, but after another half a day, the disrupting fantasies of food ceased and my hunger dissipated. Somehow I doubt thirst is like that. I bet this is just the beginning.

Whatever. Quit thinking about it; put the Nalgene away somewhere.

Stick it in the sand so you're not staring at how much you have left. Better yet, do something. Get yourself ready for night.

Yes, it's better to focus on my plan. I put my Nalgene below the chockstone in the sand and consider the coming evening. It will be pitch-black at nine P.M., and then there will be nine hours of darkness. I know it's only nine hours, but especially when I'm not producing internal heat, it will last like a polar winter. I'll sip at nine, midnight, three, and six A.M. I'll take smaller sips than last night; that will conserve more for tomorrow. I'll need it to eat the rest of my burritos. That first bite three hours ago was so dry it turned to pasty glue in my mouth; the rest will only be worse. OK, then, that's what I'll do.

That leaves me with the question of how I'll stay warm. The air seems colder than it was this time yesterday. There were a few more layers of clouds passing by today, keeping the temperature lower. But now the clouds are gone, and there's nothing to insulate me once the sun goes down. One of the few laws of heat transfer I recall from engineering classes is that radiation, or emissive heat loss, between a ground source and the night sky is proportional to the temperature difference raised *to the fourth power.* If I remember correctly, space is about 400 degrees Kelvin colder than my body. Take that to the fourth power, multiply it by a little constant I've forgotten, and that's still like twenty-five billion units of whatever. The bottom line is, I'm emitting a lot of heat into the sky. I'll need to do a better job of keeping myself warm tonight, especially since I won't be working as much. I'm just going to make it through to the morning and then worry about what's next.

Taking off my pack, I fish out the small black cloth sack in which I stowed my digital camera. Holding the sack's open end in my teeth, I take my knife in my left hand and punch out the stitched end of the bag, trying to keep from stabbing myself in the face. The lightweight material tears easily, and I thrust my left forearm into the fabric tube. Tugging with my teeth, I pull the closer end of the sack up over my elbow, creating a makeshift long sleeve for my left arm. I dismantle the runners from their spot in my pulley station and retie two more lengths of purple webbing around my right arm, pulling the strands between my forearm and the wall where I can't situate the insulated CamelBak. Also from my anchor system, I take in my teeth the extra length of yellow webbing and, applying tension against the tied-off loop, slice off a five-foot strand with my knife. I put the remaining two thirds of my first burrito in my left pocket, drop the unopened whole one into the bottom of my backpack, and wrap my right biceps in the plastic grocery sack that I was using to store my food. I tie off the plastic bag with the yellow webbing and have a long sleeve for my right arm, too.

Now to do the same for my lower half and somehow make pant legs out of the remaining 170 feet of my climbing rope. The dirty green and yellow line lies in a heap on the rock shelf in front of my knees. It takes me twenty minutes for each leg, but I manage to wrap them both from my thighs to my socks with about thirty neat loops of rope. I laugh at myself. The ropes stack like coils of potting clay; it looks like I've been attacked by two identical half-inch-thick green pythons. The coils gather and pinch at my knees when I sit in my harness, so I loosen them and make an adjustment on the daisy chain fixing me to the anchor, lifting me two inches higher in my seat. This is the most comfortable I've been since I was trapped.

With the ropes wrapped around my calves, I can lean in to the rock shelf in front of my shins—the one I was afraid I would trip over backward if I'd tried to move out of the way of the falling chockstone. Even if I had fallen, I would've been better off with a tib-fib fracture. Did I think about that, or was I worried about my head? It happened so fast, but it happened so slowly, too. How much time had I really had to react? There had been a lot to consider in that fraction of a second when I made my decision to push against the falling rock. Why did I do that? Maybe I thought I could steer the chockstone away from my head, like I had done with a similar-sized boulder on the Crestone Needle.

That time I certainly had no choice. If I hadn't redirected the boulder, it would have crushed my chest, and I would have plummeted from 14,000 feet in free fall. I had been making a traverse on the ridge between Crestone Peak and the Needle in the spring of 2000, after soloing the Northwest Couloir on Crestone Peak with hiking poles and sans crampons. I was in a ballsy mood, and instead of taking the documented and cairned route of least resistance on the traverse, I made up my own variation of adventure along which I found myself covering a considerable stretch of ground on the north side of the summit-to-summit ridge. The normal route never crosses onto the north side, and for good reason: Twice I was on-sight soloing broken and loose fifth-class rock in my mountaineering boots. I felt every inch of the three thousand feet from my position down to the Upper South Colony Lake. Cliffed out by the Black Gendarme in front of me, I knew I had to find my way over the ridge crest to the south side and easier ground. Fifty feet above me, a short and steep gully of loose rockfall debris ended in a ten-foot-high roof. It overhung a little, but the gully was only three feet wide at its head, so I figured I could stem up to the roof, chimneying myself higher until I could pull over it, probably putting myself right onto the knobby conglomerate staircase where I would finish the traverse to the - Needle's summit.

Except it hadn't happened like that. I had been four feet off the rubble in the fifty-degree gully when I yarded on the overhang and the whole roof dislodged. A thick piece of slab came unwedged from between the two towers that formed the narrow chimney. Shit! I hugged the boulder to my chest, and we fell backward as a single object until my torso twisted to the left in midair. My back hit the right-hand wall, and the boulder momentarily compressed my chest, forcing out a puff of breath. As I slid down to land in the steep scree, I shoved at the falling boulder, deflecting it away from my upper body and down into the gully just past my feet. With the wind knocked out of me, I collapsed forward, and my hands caught on the opposite wall, with my head slumped downhill. I saw the boulder bounce twice in the scree, then catapult over the lower lip of the ravine in a half-mile-long shower of crushed stone and pebbles. If my back hadn't hit the wall and kept me upright, allowing me to redirect the boulder, I would have taken a tandem ride with it. I recovered my breath but not my confidence and found myself reversing the gully to an easier crossover to the south side of the Needle.

A half hour later, within thirty vertical feet of the summit, I backed off an easy move. My head couldn't let go of the near-miss accident. I didn't even bother to switch into my rock-climbing shoes and try the final move a second time. I'd had it. I bailed off the traverse, making a heinous descent across the south face of the Needle, maneuvering down a series of four jagged rock ribs and intermediary ravines laced with rappel slings, evidence that I wasn't the first to flee from the finish to the traverse. Until my feet hit level ground at 13,100 feet, I was consumed with desperation and a wish that I had the luxury of rappelling. Back at my vehicle, I plugged my favorite Pink Floyd CD into the truck stereo and repeatedly listened to "Fearless." I sang along, the opening lines engraving themselves in my psyche: "They say that hill's too steep to climb. Climb it." Crestone Needle had beaten me down, but inspired by the music, I went back up the next morning and tagged the summit, peering down to my high point of the day before, just a few yards from the top. I learned what a fragile thing is confidence, how thin a strand it is that tethers my body to my mind through unlikely situations. What I didn't learn was that it might not always be the best plan to redirect a charging boulder with my hands.

A subtle stirring in my core tells me it's time to pray. I haven't done that yet, but I'm ready now. I close my left hand in a loose fist resting on the chockstone, shut my eyes, and lower my forehead onto my hand.

"God, I am praying to you for guidance. I'm trapped here in Blue John Canyon—you probably know that—and I don't know what I am supposed to do. I've tried everything I can think of. I need some new ideas. Or if I need to try something again, lifting the boulder, amputating my arm, please show me a sign."

Waiting a minute, with my head still lowered, I slowly tilt my head back until I'm looking up through the pale twilight, beseeching the sky itself to advise me. I surprise myself by half expecting a visual cue to lead me through my dilemma. I catch myself scanning the rock walls, looking for some supernaturally scribed hieroglyphics. Of course, there is nothing, no metaphysical counsel, no divine reply manifesting itself in the sandstone. What had I wanted? A swirl in the clouds that would tell me the time and day help would arrive? A petroglyph showing a man with a knife? In a twisted and tired effort to disguise my disappointment, I start my prayer again, sarcasm soaking each word.

"OK, then, God, since you're apparently busy . . . Devil, if you're listening, I need some help here. I'll trade you my arm, my soul, whatever you want. Just get me out of here. You want me never to climb again, I can give that up. Just show me the dotted line."

I stop and sigh. While there's anything really funny about my joke, I'm glad I haven't stopped trying to amuse myself yet.

I think that maybe this is a test, a lesson. Perhaps once I figure out the lesson, then I'll get free. Is that it? What am I supposed to get from this? What am I supposed to learn?

I think about a lesson my Aspen friend Rob Cooper and I have talked about a few times. Rob isn't a guy of many words when it comes to philosophy, but he's often proved his deeper side in a single targeted remark. Typically, our conversation patterns would start with me telling Rob about a recent adventure, and out of the blue, he would reply with his favorite non sequitur: "It's not what you do, Aron, it's who you are." Derailed from my story, I would spend the next ten minutes questioning Rob as to exactly what he meant by that. He'd repeat the axiom, and in the end, still not understanding, I would attempt to refute him. In my view, we define who we are precisely by what we do. We find our identity in action. If we do nothing, we are nothing. Our bodies even take on a look that is largely the result of our lifestyle. I never grasped what Rob was getting at. No matter how long I argued my side of the point, I never convinced him, either.

Perhaps my skewed perspective from the depth of this canyon gives me the oblique angle I need to reconsider Rob's comment. In thinking about what he has said, I have a breakthrough: Rob was sensing in the accounts of my adventures an unspoken request for his approval. More a reassurance than a challenge, his reply told me that it didn't matter to him what I had done or achieved. He deemed me a friend because of who I am—as a person, not as a climber, a skier, an outdoorsman. My confusion at his assertion had shown how right he was. I got defensive because I wanted him to respect me for my accomplishments. I had fallen prey to the mentality that places sole value on achievement while overlooking the process of achieving. Rob, along with everyone else I cared about in my life, would either respect me for who I am—as in how I treat others—or they wouldn't. My risk-taking didn't affect my integrity as a friend. Huh. I think I get it now. Maybe that's what I'm here to learn?

Well, if that was it, Aron, then the chockstone should split in two and fall harmlessly to the sand right . . . about . . . now.

Predictably, nothing happens. For another thirty seconds, nothing continues to happen, and I quit waiting. Maybe that small epiphany was an emotional table scrap, something to ease my tired conscience. I know I'm not trapped here waiting for enlightenment—I'm trapped here because there's a huge boulder sitting on my hand. How big is this thing, anyway? It's heavier than I am, but I made it move a little yesterday when I was trying to lift it. I doubt it weighs much more than a couple hundred pounds, or there's no way I could've budged it at all. With a 6:1 mechanical advantage system multiplying most of my body's weight standing in the haul-line foot loops, I should be able to dislodge the chockstone even if I lose half the lifting force back to friction. It's too late in the evening to start reconfiguring the pulley system. I'm using most of the critical pieces of webbing as limb warmers, and I don't want to give up even their slight insulation.

Night erupts from the canyon and fills the sky. Closing my eyes, I make a wish and give a visual voice to my deepest desire. I see myself catching a lift on the incessant wind, riding the tidal wave of darkness out of here, letting it carry me like a raven over the desert scrub straight up to the void. I soar over the barren buttes, maroon table-lands, and buckled mantle of central Utah, heading west over the frigid black Great Basin and Sierra Nevada Mountains devoid of city lights, the land performing a magician's trick of spectral transformation as I repeal the sunset and catch the day again somewhere over the Pacific Coast.

When my struggle feels most difficult, time swells, my agony expanding with it exponentially. I age faster, especially at night, when I lose the visual cues of time's actual progression. Three minutes of tormented shivering consume ten minutes of perceived experience, like I've fallen into a wormhole where I endure excruciating maltreatment for immeasurable eons only to return to normal consciousness. But I have found an antidote to this misery: In the hazy freedom of my imagination, I dip and weave in the whispering clouds over the sea, whitecaps changing to swells as I head still farther west. I fly higher through the atmosphere, glancing back to watch the land turn into a green frame around the cobalt ocean, islands shrinking to pinpoints. Slicing up through icy swirls of crystallized water vapor, I spiral into the vast gulf of space, jettisoning my body in a final act of evolution, metamorphosing into a splash of colored light, an iridescent cluster of hovering photons.

A bout of shivering shuts down my fantasy, the dancing particles of light dissolving to black, and I open my eyes. My mind journey felt short, but checking my watch, I see that it's nine-forty-five P.M. It was after nine when I noticed that it was dark enough to see stars. The same brilliant constellations I saw last night appear again in the narrow gap between the fissure's walls. There are two that stand out from the others, like a pair of interlaced horseshoes. I wonder if one of them is the curved stinger of Scorpio, the Zodiac sign of my birthday, October 27. Regardless of their names, the unsympathetic stars are a somber reminder that there are no lights to pollute the view. I am so far removed from civilization that I might as well be on the moon.

"Ungg-gggu-ggga-gggngh." My throat gives forth a series of unintelligible sounds as my teeth chatter, clacking spastically like a woodpecker's drill.

Trying to capture what warmth I can from the continuing shudders, I rearrange my ad hoc clothing. The top coils of my climbing rope have loosened, exposing my thighs to the cold. I cinch the wraps tighter and weave the upper end around the highest five strands, hoping that will hold the coils above my knees. I experiment with using my rope bag like a miniature bivy sack, putting my left hand and arm inside the unzipped fabric tube, then tucking my head inside the flap. The tight confines of the bag force my head forward onto my wrist, which is marginally more comfortable if I set my left hand on my right biceps, near the shoulder. Sitting in my harness with my left hip against the canyon wall, I'm stable enough that I can lean to the right, resting my head on my left hand at my right elbow, and relax my upper body. It's as if I'm putting my head down for a desk nap in elementary school.

I have produced enough warmth that I can sit in my harness inactive for almost fifteen minutes before the shivers come back. As my body quivers, the ropes loosen around my legs, and I gradually submit to fidgeting with my meager coverings for another half hour. Using my headlamp, I fuss over the ropes, fool around with the webbing looped around my right arm, adjust the punched-out camera sack on my left arm, squirm around in my harness to stimulate the circulation in my legs, and finally tuck my arm and head back into the rope bag, reassuming the position, as I have come to think of it. Another fifteen minutes of blessed idleness and then more shivers. A pattern emerges. I fidget for a half hour, raising my metabolic output enough that I can ease back in my harness for fifteen minutes. But always the cold wins, and convulsions rip through me, my jaw clenching in uncontrollable spasms until I think I'm going to shatter my teeth.

After the fourth cycle of action and repose, it's midnight, time for my designated sip of water. The hours went by quickly. Not as fast as last night, but I'm conserving my calories more than I did last night. I pick up the Nalgene from its spot in the sand and curse myself for tightening the lid too much—I can't unscrew it. Squeezing the bottle between my legs, I manage to get the lid open and bring it to my lips, tilting it just enough that a half ounce of cool water splashes onto my tongue. I crave more. The sip initiates a chain reaction of escalating thirst that culminates in a half-crazed desire to drink the entire cup of remaining fluid.

Don't you do it, Aron.

Commanding my hand to reseal the Nalgene, I recognize that I am managing to control my reactions and fight my raw instincts with a rational strategy for long-term preservation. Sometime, in the next twenty-four hours, most likely, I will run out of water. I wonder what my discipline will have me do then. Will I continue my ritual of opening the Nalgene, trying to eke the last molecule from the hard plastic bottle? I envision my tongue dryly searching the rim of the long-empty bottle, scraping over the Lexan in a deranged hope.

Returning to the pattern of fidgeting and rest, I mentally pace myself for the next six hours. Eight more cycles of adjusting the ropes and coverings, interspersed with ten- or fifteen-minute periods of stasis, and dawn will be here. I can't sleep, but sitting still helps me focus my energy. I avoid thinking about rescue or any of my self-rescue options. Most of the time, I stare at my breath, condensing on the inside of the waterproof rope bag. For some reason, it's more comforting to leave my headlamp on for a few minutes each time I tuck my head into the bag; I think it helps stave off claustrophobia. The bag is a bit bigger than a plastic grocery sack, the kind you're not supposed to let children play with. It's counterintuitive to put my head inside it, but it makes a noticeable improvement in reducing my heat emission to the night sky. Once I'm accustomed to the black-plastic-coated interior, I turn off my headlamp and listen to my breathing, feel the moisture building up inside the bag, and relax as best I can in the position, waiting for light.

It's colder now. My watch thermometer registers 53 degrees F—chilly, but I'm sustaining myself all right. As maddening as it is for my body to launch into another round of quaking tremors, I'm reassured that my involuntary reflexes are still functioning well. They could as easily have ceased to perform due to the stress and trauma of my accident. How lucky I am that the boulder didn't cause any significant blood loss. I would have gone into hypovolemic shock, my heart trying to pump an insufficient volume of blood through my body's piping. It is a meaningless reprieve. There will come a time when my body's metabolic processes no longer behave according to their operating codes, and then shapeless death will bear me away.

I decide to chip at the rock to help generate better warmth, since there's not enough work involved in adjusting my leggings. Hacking at the boulder also keeps my mind busy, though I'm no longer trying to make headway. I know the boulder will continue to settle on my arm as I remove more material from it. The area where I chipped the flakes off yesterday has already rotated down onto my right arm, eclipsing the entire night's progress. But in five minutes, I am warm and lay my multi-tool back on top of the chockstone, pull my rope bag over my head, and sit back once more. In each of the next five cycles, I include a token effort of tapping my knife blade, and sometimes the file blade, into the lopsided stone.

The sky gradually changes from black to white. My ordered regimen of fidgeting and rest has brought me through another night, though I am not thankful for the wearisome repetition of my survival. I thrive on stimulation and action, and aside from the litany of physical duress, my entrapment has brought the additional psychological curse of being unable to fully occupy my mind. I feel engaged at moments, even an hour at a time, but I can't help dwelling on the monotony of this motionlessness. If dehydration and hypothermia don't take me in the next couple of days, boredom may well dull my instincts and quash my will to live. A question haunts me: How weary will I get before suicide seems the only excitement that could relieve the ennui?

It is a colorless sunrise, too bright for stars to peek through the light. The ghost-white sky puzzles me; I can't tell if I'm still staring into the now pale heavens or peering up at a sheet of clouds. Clouds at night would be good—they help block the radiation losses that make surfaces much colder than the air temperature. But clouds during the day are less desirable. They'll keep the desert from warming up, and there's always the chance that if they bring rain, the canyon will flood, game over. Another hour passes, and the day resolves to a cloudless azure blue.

Rather than waiting for the canyon to warm up, I start the process of rerigging my boulder-lifting system. I remove the webbing from my arm. I got myself sweaty yesterday trying to lift the boulder, and I figure my exertion will warm me up. Based on my SAR training, I've envisioned an arrangement of carabiners and Prusik loops that should give me a 6:1 power ratio. Before I can attach all the loops and 'biners, I have to shorten the anchor webbing about six inches, to create more space between the chockstone and the rap ring for the expanded lifting system. I tie a series of overhand knots in the webbing above the rap ring, using up material and effectively tightening the anchor loop. As the anchor rises higher and becomes more difficult to reach, I smear the soles of my running shoes against the canyon walls, gaining almost two feet of height, but at the cost of a painful strain on my right wrist.

I remember to install a progress-capture loop from the anchor to the main line this time, so that if I am successful in raising the boulder even a few inches, I can seize the main line with the Prusik and reset the rest of the system to haul again. With a 6:1 system ratio, for every twelve inches that I successfully pull the haul line, I'll get two inches of lift on the boulder. Since my system is stuffed into a cramped three-foot space between the anchor loop and the chock-stone, I have only about a one-foot haul run until the system cinches up on itself. I need to lift the boulder six to eight inches to free the upper part of my palm, requiring at least three resets on the system. I've already decided that if one or more of my fingers are still stuck, once I get my palm free, I will do what it takes to liberate my hand, ripping off the remaining pinched digits if necessary.

With the system in place, I hoist myself up the rope until I can step into the foot loops. I notice the added spice of excitement in this at-tempt, and a hope comes that I will soon be free. But as I weight the haul loops and the rope stretches and the Prusiks grab the main line, there is no effect on the boulder. Emotionally let down but not de-spairing, I examine the system, adjust the Prusiks, and consider whether I should shorten the anchor webbing again. Because of the rope stretch, I need more space for the system to grow before it will pull on the boulder. I add two more knots above the rap ring. Trying again, I watch the system tighten, but still not even a scrape or a rum-ble from the boulder. There is no sharp attack of pain in my wrist that would certainly attend any significant movement of the chockstone. Dammit, what's going on here? I bounce in the foot loops, pulling back on the haul line with my left hand at the same time. The rope is taut in my grasp; I'm exerting as much force as I can. But as I follow the rope through the bends at the carabiners with my fingers, I feel it slacken at every turn. With my weight fully set on the system, I pluck the main line just above the boulder and realize the problem: There is no tension in the rope. It's as loose as if I had completely let up on the haul. Friction between the rope and the carabiners is dissipating every bit of force that I can apply. There are too many bends, too many losses. Maybe with pulleys I would have a chance, but not like this.

Now the disappointment settles over me. After I'd already acqui-esced to the inutility of further attempts at self-extrication yesterday, and resolved to wait for rescue, raising my hopes only to annihilate them a second time leaves me utterly dejected. My shoulders slump as I step out of the haul loops, and I tear down the haul system so I can sit in my harness and rest. I sigh disconsolately over and over again, fighting with every reserve I can to keep from crying. I am on the brink of total abdication.

I pull myself out of this wretched state by imagining my friends in Aspen getting up and going to work this morning, my housemates preparing for our roommate Leona's goodbye party. By this time tomorrow, they will know positively that something is wrong, and the search will begin. My nearly extinguished hope for salvation flickers again. I'm no worse off than I was yesterday; I'm back to waiting.

Each time I look at my watch and see it near the top of the hour, I calculate how long I've been stuck, counting down to the significant milestones. One of the effects of the sleep deprivation is that I'm unable to hold the last hour's tallies in my head, and I constantly have to start over with the math. It's seven A.M., and I have been trapped for forty hours. Forty hours without sleep, forty hours without adequate food and water, forty hours of shivering, forty hours of stress, fatigue, and agony. Exactly two days ago, I woke up in the back of my truck, where I'd slept on Friday night, and cooked some oatmeal before getting my canyoneering and biking supplies ready for the itinerary I had planned.

My thirst selectively drives my memory to focus on the five-gallon water jug bought in Moab, sitting three quarters full in the bed of my pickup. I think about the two one-liter bottles of Gatorade I bought at a convenience store late Friday night in Green River. They're spread across the floor of the passenger seat, along with some grapefruits, oranges, muffins, burritos, and snack bars that were shaken out of their plastic bags from all the bouncing and swerving on the dirt road. I hold in my mind the image of the grapefruits on the floor mat, fantasizing their juiciness. I had bought them specifically to eat after my Blue John/Horseshoe circuit, anticipating the intensifying effect a long day's journey would have on their succulence. My tongue smacks across my palate, yearning for refreshment. Before my longing can get the better of me, causing me to guzzle my six ounces of water, I shake the image out of my head.

I'm impatient with the idleness fencing me inside my head, so I evaluate my situation again. I won't have another go at the lifting system. It is as futile as hammering the rock with my multi-tool file. My options seem to have played out. I reconsider my remaining choices for the twenty-fifth time, it must be, clinging to the idea that I might have missed something.

I still haven't given amputation a full chance. I didn't even try to cut myself yesterday. I stopped short. Was it because I wasn't ready or because I was afraid it would end badly? I remember how the sight of the metal blade against my wrist repelled my hand and left my stomach heaving. I'm less than confident about the webbing tourniquet I crafted yesterday. Maybe my reticence signals a need to further prepare my strategy. Escaping this canyon on foot—scrambling the tightly twisting canyon, rappelling sixty-five feet, and then hiking eight miles—after a full-extremity amputation mandates a world-class tourniquet. In the end, I don't care if I do damage to my residual limb's tissue or remaining blood vessels with a flawless constricting device. The main problem is stopping the imminent threat to life, stanching the blood flow completely. So how can I improve my tourniquet, and thereby my plan? I've already ruled out my water-pack tubing; it's too stiff to tie a solid knot. The webbing isn't stretchy enough; it doesn't conform to my arm's contours, and I worry about getting it sufficiently tight. I need something more flexible than the tubing and more elastic than the . . . That's it! Elastic! The neoprene tubing insulation from my CamelBak is stretchy and supple but strong. It's perfect.

I'm elated at the idea. I retrieve the discarded tubing insulation from my pack, where I dropped the parts left over from yesterday's surgical prep session. Why didn't I think of this before? Using my left hand to twice wrap the thin black neoprene around my right forearm just two inches below my elbow, I tie a simple overhand knot and tighten one end in my teeth, then double and triple the knot. I take my carabiner with the purple marking tape—the same one I used yesterday, I note—and clip the neoprene, twisting it six times. Clamping down on my forearm, the material pinches my skin. I adjust my arm hairs under the band, but it still hurts. For some reason, the pain pleases me, perhaps because it reassures me that the tourniquet is working. I can see what little pink is left in my forearm fade to fish-belly white, and the flesh bunched up between my elbow and the tourniquet flashes to bright red. Oh yeah, this is way better than the webbing idea. The ache in my arm flares, but my self-satisfaction overrides it. I'm pleased with myself, and with the tourniquet's squeeze, less masochism than a renewed sparkle of hope. I'm taking action. And it feels very good to be taking action.

I'm ready for the next step. I take my multi-tool and switch it from the battered file to the longer of the two knife blades, forgetting my plans to use the sharper one. Instead of pointing the tip into the tendon gap at my wrist, I hold it with the blade against the upper part of my forearm. Surprising myself, I press on the blade and slowly draw the knife across my forearm. Nothing happens. Huh. Repeating the act, I press harder with my palm on the tool's grip. Still nothing. No cut, no blood, nothing. Extracting the short knife, I vigorously saw back and forth at my forearm, growing more frustrated with each unproductive attempt. Exasperated, I give up. This is shit! The damn blade won't break the skin. How the hell am I going to carve through two bones with a knife that won't even cut my skin? God damn it to hell.

Embittered, I set the knife atop the chockstone, unclip the carabiner, and loosen the tourniquet. After a minute, the weak blood flow in my arm raises an irritated series of red lines on my skin where I was sawing with the knife. These aggravated scratches are the sole evidence of my attempt at amputation.

That's pathetic, Aron; just pathetic.

Back to waiting.

Swoosh, swoosh, swoosh. A black raven flies overhead. I check my watch. It's eight-fifteen A.M.—precisely the same time I saw a raven yesterday morning. I wonder if it's the same one. Of course it is. It probably has a nest down the canyon someplace. How kooky is it that the bird flew off at exactly the same time it did yesterday? It seems unnatural to me that a living thing would have such a refined sense of time. The sunlight or air temperature must trigger some response that tells the bird it's time to go find some food. I don't know.

More predictably but no less punctually, the dagger of sunlight appears about an hour later, and I stretch out to it at 9:35 for my ten-minute "sun salute" break. With the twin visits of the raven and the sun dagger, I figure that my morning routines are completed. Then, for the first time, I feel pressure in my bladder. I unclip from the daisy chain, unzip my shorts, and turn around to urinate. The sand soaks up the liquid before it can puddle or splash, seemingly absorbing my urine faster than it falls. It doesn't smell as bad or look as dark as I'd have figured, seeing as how it's been two days since I peed. Feeling nature's other call, I take off my harness and drop my pants in an attempt to defecate. I don't want to stink up the canyon, but I don't have any choice. My concern quickly turns out to be moot; it's a false alarm.

Tired from the stress of the early-morning rounds of elevated and dashed hopes, I let my mind drift. I recall meeting an Australian outdoorsman, Warren MacDonald, at the Banff Mountain Film Festival last November. The festival was showing a documentary of the hiking accident in Tasmania that cost Warren both his legs above the knees. We met at a dinner where Warren filled me in on some of the details. Leaving his partner in camp to go to the bathroom one night, he crossed a nearby streambed, took care of business, and, on his way back, spent a few minutes climbing some boulders near the bank. That was when he pulled a tremendously large boulder onto himself, crushing both his legs and trapping himself in the shallow creek. By the time his partner realized something was wrong, a rainstorm had begun, and Warren found himself waiting for help in the rising waters of the stream. It took rescuers two days to free him, prying up the car-sized boulder with a hydraulic lifting jack. I saw his movie the next night, stunned at the images of Warren under the rock, and amazed by his recovery and return to the mountains. Within two years of his accident and learning to use prostheses, Warren climbed Federation Peak, one of the highest and most remote mountains in Tasmania.

From my ensnared position in the bottom of Blue John, I feel a profound level of empathy for what Warren endured. It strikes me as funny, the irony that within six months of meeting him, I would become the second hiker I'd heard of to be immovably pinned by a boulder. Maybe there have been others, too, I don't know. I wonder to myself how he went to the bathroom while he was trapped. I envy Warren's fortune at having a companion nearby to get help. If only I had been with someone . . . Warren's story inspires me to think that if I do survive this experience in the canyon, I, too, will continue climbing and enjoying the outdoors. I won't perform piano concertos like I did in college, but hey, those are the breaks.

I pass the rest of the morning and early afternoon alternating between my few activities: standing and sitting, chipping unenthusiastically at the rock, looking at the sky for early signs of flash-flood danger, swatting at insects, counting the minutes and hours until my next sip of water. Finally, it is three o'clock, the hour I've been waiting for. It's my second significant milestone, the end of my second full day trapped.

Pulling my video camera out of my backpack again, I blow the grit off the lens and align it in its spot on top of the chockstone. This is the most action I'll create for myself during the afternoon. It's uplifting to break the tedium of waiting, but unfortunately, I don't have any good news to share. I sigh and begin speaking.

"It's the forty-eight-hour mark now. It's three o'clock on Monday. I have about one hundred and fifty milliliters of water left. That's five ounces." I pause and consider my dispassionate reaction to the statement. Through the first day of my entrapment, I felt an emotional connection to the amount of water I had, the umbilical tug of its life-sustaining essence compelling me to make it last as long as I could.

Now that feeling is disconnected. Sometime in the night, my final countdown began without notice. There's so little water, it doesn't matter that there's any left at all—it can no longer affect how long I'll survive. By morning, the water will be gone. I've come to accept that fact, and with acceptance, my looming dread dissipates, leaving only emptiness.

My next thought is of my sister. I look directly into the camera lens, imagining her sitting in her living room watching this tape someday in the future. I see her face and her eyes looking back at me as though through the camera. "Sonja, I'm very proud of you. I didn't get to hear firsthand how your championships went, but I heard from Mom that you placed very well at the national competitions, that you were tenth overall in speech and debate in the nation. Hot damn, girl. I'm very proud of you. Not just for that but for who you are.

"I've been thinking about that. My friend Rob in Aspen says to me several . . . frequently . . . several times that, confusingly, 'It's not what you do but who you are.' I kind of got hung up on that a lot, because I always thought who I was, was very much wrapped up with what I did. That I was happy because of the things that I did that made me happy. If things you do make you happy, then they can also make you unhappy.

"I think that's why I found myself being as ambitious and energetic—" The wind interrupts me, and I shiver, muttering, "It's cold," then continue where I left off: "—to do all the outings that I did."

The video letter to my sister has turned into a confessional. While I don't feel regret for how I've lived, I think I'm trying to share some advice with Sonja, something she'll take from this that will help her to be happy with herself. We're similar in our assertiveness, our intelligence, and our sense of inner competition that drives us to perfectionism. I'm hoping she won't stumble into the pitfall that I have fallen into, of letting my ability to create what I want in my life convince me that "I am" only insofar as "I do." Yes, I am a mountaineer, an engineer, a music enthusiast, an outdoorsman. But I am not *only* those things; I am also a person who enriches other people's lives, and whose life is enriched by other people when I let them.

"In retrospect, I've learned a lot. One of the things I'm learning here is that I didn't enjoy the people's company that I was with enough, or as much as I could have. A lot of really good people have spent a lot of time with me. Very often I would tend to ignore or diminish their presence in seeking the essence of the experience. All - that's to say, I'm figuring some things out."

My rambling explanation eases the guilt I feel for my selfishness. Bringing to mind those memories has lifted my spirit and even made me smile despite my present circumstances. That I spent so much of my time leaving my friends behind for solo trips, or even for some alone time when I was with them, reveals a self-centeredness that displeases me. The memories evoking the most gratitude for my life are of times with my family and friends. I am beginning to understand the priceless nature of their company, and it depresses me to realize that wasn't always the focus of our time together.

I record a few snippets of my ongoing efforts to free myself. "On the situational front here, I rerigged and rerigged, even got to a six-to-one pulley system—too much friction. I wasn't even pulling the main rope taut—too many sharp bends in the rope. I chipped away some more at the rock. It's hopeless." Fatigue and sleep deprivation cloud my thinking, and I fail to mention that I tried to saw through my arm.

Now I turn toward the bleak prospects of outside intervention and rescue. "I got to the point where I was realizing the slim factors that might go into my rescue, and I don't see those happening and coming together at all in time. I'm thinking about Leona, my roommate who worries about me as much as my family does. I just told her that I was going to Utah. She'll know when I'm not back tonight that I'm overdue. Even if she immediately files a police report, it'll be twenty-four hours before they take action on anything. That said, I think there's a very slim chance that a ranger even goes by the trail-head where I parked at Horseshoe, except for weekends, to lead the walks to see the Great Gallery."

Shaking my head, I gaze at my sliver of sky, at the foot-wide bottom of the canyon, and at the rigging, anything to avoid the condemning reflection of my face in the viewfinder.

"Brad and Leah were expecting to hear from me on Saturday, but when they didn't, they probably didn't think much of it. I was supposed to meet them for the party out at Goblin Valley State Park. But I doubt they really missed me enough to take action. They didn't know where I was going, anyways. *I* didn't even know. One of the things that got me so excited was I'd crossed the state line before I knew where I was headed to, where I was going on Friday, and even then I wasn't sure about what I was going to do on Saturday. Oh, man."

I know I broke one of my rules when I left without detailing my plans in advance. Now I'm paying an overdue debt. How many times have I gotten away with making changes to my itinerary without notifying someone? It happens all the time. Not anymore.

"I also could have said something more to Megan and Kristi, the Outward Bound girls. I should have gone with them. Just left and gone out the West Fork."

Again I shake my head in self-pity and fight off a series of long blinks. I deserve all of this.

"God, I am really screwed. I'm going to shrivel up right here over the course of the next few days. If I had a way to end it, I probably would, tomorrow afternoon or so. It's miserable. It's cold. I can't keep the wind off me. It just blows. It's not even that much of a breeze, but it's cold. It comes from back there." I motion over my left shoulder with a toss of my head.

"I'm doing what I can, but this sucks. It's really bad. This is one of the worst ways to go. Knowing what's going to happen, but it still being three or four days out." My voice trails off to a hoarse whisper.

I hope I don't last for four more days. I can't imagine what shape I'll be in if I'm still alive on Friday.

Feeling the weight of my impending demise, I make a logical transition to what to do with my stuff. I can't avoid the moroseness of it, but it seems practical to advise my family about my assets, effectively recording a short version of a last will and testament.

"I did want to say, on the logistical side of things, I have some American Express insurance that should cover costs of the recovery operation when that does happen. Bank-account balances should take care of my credit-card debts. You'll have to sell my house, Mom and Dad. Possession-wise, I don't know if Sonja can use my computer and video camera . . . There are pictures on the memory stick in my pocket and in the camera. My friend Chip down in New Mexico can have my CDs. All my outdoor crap, Sonja, if you want it, if any of it fits and you can use it, you're welcome to it."

Nearly in tears, I'm finished talking. I stop the camera, fold the screen into its stowed position, and put it back in my pack. I hold my head in my left hand and dejectedly shake it, sniffling, wiping my palm down over my nose and mouth, my fingers wiping at my eyelashes and brushing the facial hair under my nose and around my frown lines.

A half hour later, around 3:35 P.M. on Monday afternoon, I have to urinate again. "How is this possible?" I wonder. That's twice today, despite the fact that I'm most certainly dehydrated. What's going on?

Save it, Aron. Pee into your CamelBak. You're going to need it.

Obeying, I transfer the contents of my bladder into my empty water reservoir, saving the orangish-brown discharge for the unappetizing but inevitable time when it will be the only liquid I have. I should have saved the first batch, I realize with hindsight. It was much clearer than this and didn't smell half as nasty. I debate whether I should drink it or not but defer that choice for later.

I eagerly dig out my digital still camera for the first time and take a series of pictures: a close-up of my arm disappearing into the rock;

a detail of my anchor system that suspends me in my harness; and two self-portraits—one looking downcanyon, and one from above my left shoulder that shows me with the chockstone. Reviewing the photos, I also flip through the ones I took during the first two days of my vacation on Mount Sopris and around Moab, then the ones of Megan and Kristi in the upper part of Blue John Canyon. The angels.

EIGHT

"I'm Goin' to Utah"

People say that we're searching for the meaning of life. I don't think that's it at all. I think that what we're seeking is an experience of being alive, so that our life experiences on the purely physical plane will have resonances within our own innermost being and reality, so that we actually feel the rapture of being alive.

—JOSEPH CAMPBELL, *The Power of Myth*

THROUGH THE WINTER of 2003, I kept my immediate attention on the nine 14,000-foot mountains that I was climbing, week by week adjusting my energy to a new route on another challenging peak. They were ends in themselves, a series of intrinsically rewarding journeys, but they also provided a winter-long training regimen that prepared me well physically for my big trip to Denali. I knew from the Stray Dogs expedition in 2002 that the 20,320-foot mountain would demand everything I had to successfully attempt back-to-back climbs, including the sub-twenty-four-hour solo speed attempt and ski descent. Once winter was officially over, I closed the books on another tremendous season with my fourteener project and turned my focus to backcountry skiing.

On an important trip that helped me regain some lost confidence in my avalanche awareness and hazard evaluation, I skied Mount Sopris near Carbondale in Colorado with Rick Inman, a friend and colleague from the Ute. We had a safe day skiing moderate slopes above the Thomas Lakes, steering clear of the steeper, more slide-prone slopes. It felt great to be free of my previous powder-hounding attitude that had gotten my friends and me in trouble on Resolution Mountain just a month earlier.

In late March, Gareth Roberts and I would be competing in the Elk Mountains Grand Traverse, a forty-two-mile backcountry ski touring race from Crested Butte to Aspen. To scout the route, I went out on a solo circumnavigation of Star Peak near Aspen, a twenty-five-mile ski trek. Wanting to test the equipment I would use in the race, I picked up some special waxless metal-edged backcountry skis from the Ute in the morning and got a crack-o'-noon start from the Ashcroft Ski Touring Center. I made the eighteen miles over the three passes before dark, but I crossed over Pearl Pass at nightfall and found myself stranded in a whiteout. I skied about halfway across the prime avalanche terrain of Pearl Basin, taking care to avoid a dozen starting zones and slide paths, but turned myself around in a circle. How many times would it take for me to learn that my compass wasn't lying to me? Lost above treeline in the dark in the middle of a storm, I decided my best option was to dig a snow cave.

It took me three attempts to find a section of the snowpack that was wind-compacted and sufficiently deep to dig out a shelter at 12,000 feet. I sat in my burrow for five hours, poking my head out every twenty to thirty minutes to check for stars, mountaintops, a valley, or trees, anything that would help me navigate with my map. There were three valleys that I could end up in from my approximate position, two of which were densely packed with trail-less dark timber. I was better off waiting to determine my exact location and then find the valley with the road cut. At around three A.M., the storm cleared enough that I could pick out a peak a few hundred feet above me, and I was on my way, skiing through the fresh snow and keeping off the steeper slopes. Home at five A.M., I showered, napped, and got to work a few minutes late, apologizing for my tardiness to my manager, Brion After, with what I felt was an exceptional excuse.

The race turned into quite the epic, with 40 percent of the teams dropping out due to bitter temperatures in the first half of the race and high winds in the second half. The cold and the storm caused serious frostbite in a dozen people, foiled attempts to stick skins on skis, broke equipment, and as my partner, Gareth, learned, froze water reservoirs solid. Not only were iced-up CamelBaks deadweight, but some competitors became dangerously dehydrated. A little under halfway through the race, Gareth and I were the last team to leave the Friends Hut checkpoint who successfully surmounted Star Pass before the turnaround time. We had raced through eight hours of negative-2-degree temperatures for eighteen miles to make the pass with two minutes to spare. Nine and a half hours later, we were the sixtieth team to finish the race, with only two other teams finishing after us (one pair of racers spent the night out when they inadvertently skied several miles off the course and couldn't retrace their mistake until morning). Skiing down the face of Aspen Mountain to the cheers of Gareth's wife and a dozen hearty race volunteers, Gareth and I dropped to our knees in free-heel telemark style just to show we were still having fun. We crossed the finish line to the flashes of cameras, bent our necks to receive our finisher medals, and smiled and laughed with chilled bottles of microbrew in our hands, feeling like - we'd won the race. In actuality, the winning teams had finished over nine hours before us, enough time to have showered and gotten a full night's rest before we tottered through the final timing gate. - That's probably why they all found their way to the awards ceremony, and we got lost and ended up celebrating on our own over burgers and beers at Little Annie's.

Two weeks later, I took a solo trip to Cathedral Peak and climbed and skied the east-facing gully on the south ridge. Once I'd finished the summertime fourteeners in 2001, I lowered my altitude bar and added another sixty peaks to my list, creating my version of what are known as the Centennial Peaks—the hundred highest peaks in Colorado, the Centennial State. I climbed fifty of those mountains in 2002, bringing my total to 109 of 119 summits above 13,800 feet. Cathedral was next on my list, and it became my 110th high summit in the state. From the top, I surveyed the length of Highland Ridge across the Conundrum Creek Valley. I was planning a traverse of the fifth-class eighteen-mile-long ridge for May, and I videotaped a scouting report to plan the trip.

Skiing off Cathedral was the most extreme backcountry ski descent I'd ever pulled off; the five-hundred-foot-long, fifty-degree east gully was only ten feet wide for most of its length. Thankfully, the snow had softened in the bright sun, allowing me to link several dozen turns down the most technical section of the couloir and relax on the lower-angled apron. I skied out past the Pine Creek Cookhouse at Ashcroft at three P.M., being one of the last people to see the unoccupied building before it caught on fire (due to a gas explosion) and burned to the ground forty-five minutes later. The fire engines blazing up Castle Creek Road puzzled me as I drove back into town, until I read in the paper the next morning what had happened.

On April 17, I skinned into Conundrum Basin near Aspen. In the morning, I climbed Castleabra Point (my 111th of the Centennial Peaks) a 13,800-foot subsidiary summit of Castle Peak and skied in the basin until noon. The best part about climbing and skiing in Conundrum Basin is coming back to the 104-degree natural hot springs at 11,200 feet and stripping down for a soak while you're still eight miles from your vehicle.

The next day, one of my Denali teammates, Janet Lightburn, and I booted up the Cristo Couloir on Quandary Peak. I skied from the summit in drop-knee telemark style on alpine-touring gear, because one of my rear bindings broke. It was a 3,000-foot joyride that tested my skiing abilities as I concocted an unconventional mix of equipment and technique. I drove home to Aspen that evening, and since

I didn't have to be at work until one P.M. on Saturday, I went out for a run in the morning. Covering an off-road marathon of twenty-six miles, I ran from my house in Aspen over to Snowmass and back in just over three and a half hours, hurtling through hip-deep snow in two separate half-mile stretches. Then I worked an eight-hour shift. Reviewing everything I'd done in the last sixty hours—over fifty miles skied, hiked, and run, and 10,000 vertical feet gained—I felt primed for my Alaska trip. The fact that I was in the best physical condition of my life would play an unexpected role on my trip the next week.

I had arranged to meet up with two friends of my climbing mentor Gary Scott. Dianne and Wolfgang Stiller wanted to climb the namesake Cross Couloir on Mount of the Holy Cross, a spectacular steep-walled gully route that ends at the 14,003-foot summit. We had planned two and a half days for the climb which had a significant ski approach of twelve miles. It would be our first outing together, and if things went well for us, we had bigger plans for Liberty Ridge on Mount Rainier. However, another late-winter storm interrupted us the day before our departure, dropping eight inches of snow on the central mountains. As the avalanche hazard rose, we knew it would be much more risky to be in the narrow couloir, completely at the mountain's mercy. A slide would rip our threesome off the slope into a one-thousand-foot-long blender of ice tools, rock walls, crampons, and snow pickets, then spit us over a cliff that intersected the couloir near the bottom. It wouldn't be a question of if we would survive, but whether our families would be able to tell who was who after being sent through the couloir's meat grinder.

It was an easy decision. Dianne and Wolfgang were in complete agreement, and we planned to try again in June. They knew I'd arranged time off from the Ute specifically to make the trip in April, and they apologized. It didn't bother me in the least.

"Actually, my manager told me yesterday that I have off until Tuesday, so now I have a five-day vacation coming. I'm skinning up Mount Sopris tomorrow with a friend. I've been thinking about the desert a lot lately. I might head over to the Moab area for some time off from the mountains."

I'd learned the year before that when you spend the month of June in Alaska, camping on glaciers, digging snow fortresses, and climbing icy headwalls, your time to enjoy the typical warm-weather activities of summer is substantially shorter. Presented with the chance to go to Utah for four days, I hoped to get in some summertime fun before the season started. Dianne and Wolfgang wished me safe travels, and I thanked them for the call. I needed to finish getting my things packed—adding my mountain-biking and climbing gear and guidebooks for the time in Utah—and go to bed. My Aspen friend Brad Yule and I had arranged a three A.M. rendezvous for our Sopris trip, and I had to get some sleep.

As I packed, Leona came home from an evening in town.

"Where're you headed off to this time?" She was happily tipsy from a few hours at the local bars.

"I'm skiing Mount Sopris in the morning."

"And you need all that?" My storage containers of climbing and biking gear, sleeping bag, and backpacks were piled in the middle of the living room.

"I'm going to Utah. I don't know what I'm doing yet. My Holy Cross climbing trip was canceled."

"Oh, bummer."

"Ehh, not so much. I've been wanting to get out to the desert and warm up a little, you know? Do some mountain biking, hit some slot canyons. Brad told me about a party at Goblin Valley on Saturday. I might try to hit that, too. I guess a bunch of people from town are going out for an all-weekend rager."

The last of the Aspen ski areas had closed on Monday, officially signaling the off-season emigration of Aspenites to exotic lands around the globe. Residents don't get out of the valley much during the busy season because of work and skiing—in fact, driving twenty miles to Basalt takes on the feel of a significant road trip. But from late April till the end of May, when the highway department opens

Independence Pass, things get real slow in town, and people flock to the warmer climes of Mexico, Thailand, the Bahamas, and Utah. It was due time for me to join the droves, right after one more ski trip.

Later that night, around four A.M., Brad bounced alongside me in the passenger seat as I busted my truck through two-foot-deep snowdrifts on the Mount Sopris access road. It was like a four-wheel-drive commercial, with snow shrapnel exploding from the wheel wells and the two of us grinning ear to ear. We were pleasantly surprised that we were able to drive all the way to the trailhead so early in the spring. Unloading our backcountry gear in the dark, we alternated trail-breaking duties up the four miles to the Thomas Lakes, the same area I'd been the month before with my friend Rick. Twilight broke over us at the frozen lower lake around five-thirty A.M., to reveal socked-in weather above treeline. Despite the weather and the increased slide potential from the previous day's snowfall, I was much less nervous about being in the backcountry on this trip. I was prepared to turn back if avalanche conditions weren't acceptable in the bowl, and I knew Brad would be, too.

Sopris has the unusual attribute of twin summits about a half mile apart, each with exactly the same elevation of 12,995 feet. We ascertained a safe ascent route to the eastern peak and skinned up above the lakes to a steep north-facing ridge. Ten-foot visibility and thin snow cover on the upper mountain precluded a summit ski descent, so we stashed our snow-riding equipment (my skis and Brad's split snowboard) at about 11,800 feet. Climbing into dense clouds, Brad and I lost our depth perception in the foggy blanket that turned ground and sky into a dingy white wall at the tips of our noses. We gave a wide berth to the precipitous cliffs on our right, which forced us to confront a cornice at 12,800 feet. I blindly led up the hard-packed snow, kicking toehold pockets into the wall with my telemark boots, the whiteout obscuring the top of the cornice. Brad had it tougher than me because he was climbing in his soft snowboard boots, but I lent him my ice axe, and he made fast work of the cornice. We reached the eastern summit together at eight-thirty A.M. I took a photo of us laughing at the frost plastered on Brad's six-inch goatee.

We returned to our skis and snowboard and, one at a time, rode the steep flank of the ridge down into the bowl, rejoining our ascent tracks. The new snow had bonded well to the older layers, and we decided that the bowl would be worth checking out. After digging a pit, we opted against skiing a gully formed by two rock outcroppings in the center of the basin, and chose instead to take a couple of laps up to the head of the bowl. With the clouds burning off in midmorning, we yo-yoed down and back up the slope, carving sweeping turns a quarter mile wide. For two hours, we painted the Thomas Lakes Bowl with the brushstrokes of skis and snowboard, lacing the mountainside before sitting down to share one of Brad's Fruit Roll-Ups. It was apropos to enjoy a kid's treat while we giggled at the good times - we'd been blessed to have that day.

Afternoon sunlight turned the snow to mush on our descent back to my truck. The day's warming temperatures had turned the parking lot and the road to mud. My truck wheels slopped around in the tracks I'd made on our way in, threatening to pitch us off the narrow road and adding more excitement to the day. Almost past the last pit of slushy snow, a steering mistake bounced us out of the ruts, and I barely brought the vehicle to a stop before sliding sideways into the sodden forest. Brad speculated that my four-wheel drive wasn't working correctly; otherwise, I would have been able to drive out of the predicament. As it was, soft mud and snow on top of thick ice left us stranded, tires spinning, for an hour and a half until—thank God for cell phones—Brad's girlfriend, Leah, arrived with a tow rope. We put my chains on Brad's tires, hooked up the tow rope, and, gunning our engines simultaneously, freed my truck.

With a plan for me to call Brad's cell phone on Saturday to get final directions to the Goblin Valley party, Brad and Leah left for Silverton over McClure Pass, and I drove down to Glenwood Springs, westward-bound. I drove three hours down the highway, reading in my canyoneering guidebook about the slot canyons near Moab and Green River. I pondered the possible itineraries and figured that I'd go mountain biking in the morning on the Slick Rock Trail down by Moab, then go for a canyon hike on Saturday that would put me in range of the desert party at Goblin Valley. Five miles along I-70 past Thompson Springs, Utah, I pulled off the interstate at a large rest area and backed my truck up into the darkest parking spot between two sixty-foot-high light poles illuminating the half-dozen landscaped mesquite trees near the picnic shelters. I laid out my sleeping bag in the bed of my pickup and crawled in, with just enough sense left in me to take out my contacts before falling into a well-earned sleep.

Friday morning, I drove the thirty miles south into Moab for an all-day mountain-biking excursion on the Slick Rock Trail. Slick Rock is one of Utah's most popular biking trails because of its twelve miles of technical sandstone challenges with only a few sand traps; its numerous viewpoints with expansive vistas of the Colorado River canyons; and its proximity to the center of Moab. I laughed at the sight of my truck in the bike trailhead parking lot, with skis on the roof rack and not a snowflake to be seen for fifty miles.

Heading out on my own, I soon caught up to a group of four proficient bikers and tailed them through the warm-up problems. Shortly thereafter, they ascended a technical challenge that was beyond my ability. Running headlong into a ten-foot-high slab of seemingly vertical rock, I toppled off the side of my bike, clipping out of my pedals in time to avoid a humiliating spill. It was my first time riding sandstone, and I found out how much I had to learn as the first dozen problems harder than a six out of ten on the local scale of difficulty thwarted me. Thankfully, each time, I safely escaped my bucking bike.

I focused on developing my skills, tackling some problems three and four times each to get them right. Mimicking some of the better bikers' techniques on a steep fifty-foot-high sandstone dome, I stood up on my pedals and thrust my weight all the way over my handlebars, compressing the shock on my front fork. I couldn't believe my tires didn't skid out and force yet another abortive dismount. Cranking hard in my lowest gear, I hammered my way up the sandstone, knowing that a slip would plant my crotch squarely on the bent neck of my handlebars. Gasping for oxygen, I felt my momentum dissipate as my legs screamed in fury, but I pumped out the last few revolutions and collapsed in my seat at the top of the dome.

By mile eight, I was able to cleanly ride the sixes, sevens, and even an eight without coming out of my toe clips. Predictably, right as I was getting confident with my riding, I got a full-on ego check in the return portion of the loop when I descended into a sand trap with my weight too far forward. I blinked, and the next time I opened my eyes, I was flat on my belly, nose deep in the sand. My bike was piled on top of my legs, back, and neck, with the handlebar pressing my head down. I squirmed and wriggled, but my legs were twisted up behind my butt, with my right foot still attached to the pedal of the upturned bike. I'd been pinned by a two-wheeled wrestling champion in a startling takedown. The airburst of my laugh blew sand up around my face, pasting grit onto my sweaty cheeks. I couldn't decide if I was more relieved that no one had seen my over-the-handlebars wreck, or disappointed that there was no one to laugh with me at my utter discombobulation. Back at the beginning of the circuit, I reattempted the problem that had first ejected me and cleaned it in front of a group of other bikers who had all dismounted to walk up the slab.

Excited and exhausted by the day, I sat at my truck and consulted my canyon guidebook about Negro Bill Canyon. A two-mile hike would take me into a natural bridge with the sixth longest span in the United States. I had enough time to drive around to the trailhead and jog in to the bridge before twilight, when the light would be best for photography.

In past excursions to Utah, I mountain-biked hundred-mile-long routes and traversed forty-mile-long canyons in a single day on foot. While I found the obvious physical challenge of these excursions an attraction in itself, I always carried my camera equipment to capture images of the Martian landscapes, surreal shapes, alluring colors, and hidden treasures of petroglyphs and kivas from cultures long disappeared. The hike in Negro Bill Canyon produced a half-dozen image sets from the streamside hiking route, as well as the natural bridge. My favorite was a picture of the azure skies and auburn desert walls reflected in a mirror-still pool surrounded by green reeds and grasses. While I was happy that I'd made the hike, my photographic appetite was only whetted. I wanted to get out to a slot canyon and see some petroglyphs.

I'd already identified the Robbers Roost area east of Hanksville for my Saturday adventure, but I hadn't picked out a specific canyon. I wanted to position myself for the Saturday-night rendezvous, and the Roost was ideal—two hours from Moab and two hours from Goblin Valley. Since I wouldn't be back in the vicinity of a grocery or convenience store for two days, I needed to stock up on water and food before I left civilization for the weekend. So I wouldn't have to carry the entire guidebook with me, I photocopied the pages of three canyons in the Robbers Roost that offered the best opportunities for narrow slots and petroglyphs. Topping off my gas tank, I was ready for an extended desert foray. I left Moab in the late evening, driving north to the interstate. I set the cruise control and read through the canyon-guide photocopies. Piecing together two descriptions of adjoining canyons, I created a unique loop that would take me on a fifteen-mile bike ride from my truck at the Canyonlands National Park trailhead to the head of Blue John Canyon, through two narrow and deep slots, over a twenty-meter rappel, and out to the confluence with Horseshoe Canyon, past the petroglyph alcoves of the Great

Gallery, finally returning to my vehicle. A thirty-mile day. I figured if I started by nine A.M., I would be out by five P.M.

At mile 162 on I-70, I exited for Green River, recognizing the sign warning travelers that the next available gas and food services were 110 miles to the west. I stopped at a convenience store in Green River and considered whether to call Brad and Leah for a final confirmation on the Goblin Valley party. Because of the late hour, I deferred the call, thinking I would get in touch the next afternoon from Hanksville. Brad would be getting up early in the morning to ski, and I didn't want to wake them. I bought two bottles of Gatorade in the store and then made a lap up and down Green River's main street until I found the Bureau of Land Management access road heading south out of town.

At the southwest edge of Green River, I pass the empty parking lot of a yellow aluminum-sided building, the Emery County sheriff's office. After hooking a right on Airport Road, I drive under the interstate into a landscape of obscurity. Not a single light perforates the absolute blackness of the San Rafael Desert.

I drive over weeds growing obstinately in the unstriped and roughly paved road, wondering if their presence is a sign of the tenacity of life or of the laxness of county maintenance. Slowing at an intersection, I turn left onto the graded dirt road leading into the Roost. It's just after ten P.M. A BLM sign indicates that the Horseshoe Canyon Trailhead is forty-seven miles ahead through the desert darkness. My truck obliterates a tumbling tumbleweed as I pass a yellow triangular sign cautioning, ROADS MAY BE IMPASSABLE DUE TO STORMS. I get the feeling I'm headed out into nowhere. Jackrabbits dart onto the road in my headlights, racing me, scurrying left then right, then heading straight down the road in front of my tires before dashing back into the hardscrabble badlands.

Cresting a swale at high speed, my headlights drop off into an arroyo, and I nearly follow the beams into the gully before I blindly swerve left and find the road cut again. The rear of my truck fishtails madly for the first of many times. Dozens of curves, swoops, and sandy washes try to catapult my truck off the road, but each time I correct my tack and make the save. I feel like I'm driving an off-road rally: skidding my tires through the corners, kicking up dust clouds, accelerating after the curves, launching over humps in the terrain. - Stuff's flying all over the place in my cab as the rock music on the stereo eggs me on. The road is like Mr. Toad's Wild Ride. I'm driving with my brights on to help me anticipate the curves hidden on the backside of the hilltops, but they barely help. I could slow down, except I'm averaging only 30 mph as it is, I'm tired, and I want to get to sleep before midnight.

I catch the distinct constellation of Perseus out my left window. Except in one ravine that I suspect is the waterless San Rafael River drainage, there are no trees and only scarce bunches of grass growing higher than a few inches. On occasion, I cross a fence line at a cattle guard—the bright yellow bars entrenched in the road have been recently painted, telling me that somebody still uses this land. Still, there are no lights to break the desolate spell that the night casts over the barren country. A beer bottle appears in the throw of my headlights; I don't swerve to miss it. My front right wheel hits the neck of the bottle, and it jumps up, bumping the bottom of my truck. I think, "Hayduke has been here," recalling the eco-protagonist of Edward Abbey's *The Monkeywrench Gang*, who protests the presence of roads by chucking his beer bottles at them.

Periodically, my truck hurtles over grooved sandstone slabs in the road tread, where county graders have scraped outcroppings flat. The graders have piled earthen banks along the roadsides, which block my headlights from reaching the desert floor. I fly over the edge of the next swale at 40 mph, to meet another curve in the road and slam my brakes hard. Dramatically reducing my speed just in time, I make the corner and shift from third into fourth on the next straightaway. I rev my truck obnoxiously through a skeletal forest of scrub bushes and rush through the night.

Another rabbit.

Another fence line.

Another curve.

Unexpectedly, a small brown sign flashes past me, pointing out the road spur to Horseshoe Canyon. I stop and reverse, then turn left down the significantly bumpier approach to the dirt parking area. There are three other vehicles and two encampments at the trailhead, despite the signs prohibiting camping in the parking area. I turn my truck around and find a flat spot near the sign board welcoming visitors to the Horseshoe Canyon quadrant of Canyonlands National Park. After organizing the splayed equipment in the bed of my truck, I roll out my sleeping bag and pad and call it a night. I drift off to sleep, thinking about the Blue John–Horseshoe circuit that I will undertake in the morning, the wind rocking my truck in the organic lullaby of canyon country.

NINE

Day Four: Out of Food and Water

I believed in belief, for its own shining sake. To believe in the face of utter hopelessness, every article of evidence to the contrary, to ignore apparent catastrophe—what other choice was there? . . . We are so much stronger than we imagine, and belief is one of the most valiant and long-lived human characteristics. To believe, when all along we humans know that nothing can cure the briefness of this life, that there is no remedy for our basic mortality, that is a form of bravery. To continue believing in your-self . . . believing in whatever I chose to believe in, that was the most important thing . . . .

—LANCE ARMSTRONG, *It's Not About the Bike*

DIFFUSE SUNLIGHT catches on the swirling undersides of thin clouds high above the Utah desert. "It's gonna be a nice sunset," I think from the bottom of the fissure. I hope that the clouds will stick around and help hold in the heat tonight. It's early Monday evening. I've been awake for fifty-seven hours. I've been trapped for fifty hours. And I've had the same song stuck in my head for forty-three hours.

Like a radio with the scan button permanently depressed, my restless and unrested mind expends its energy trolling for distraction, only to land on the same station again and again. The station has but one ten-second sample of one song. Over and over, always with the same lyric; "BBC1, BBC2, BBC3, BBC4, BBC5, BBC6, BBC7, BBC Heaven!" It's not even a real song. I feel like the antagonist Dr. Evil, my plans foiled again. I'm left shaking my fist in the air— "Why won't you leave me alone, Austin Powers? Why must you torment me?"

My fatigue has taken on the heavily drugged feel of an intense fever cooking my brain. I've fallen asleep in some odd places before—standing in front of a painting in a Paris museum; sitting at a 110-decibel Guns N' Roses concert—but I've never felt this level of sleep deprivation. It's like a disease breaking down my higher brain functions, pushing me closer to the line of irrationality. Maybe it's best that I can't sleep, lest I drift away into hypothermia. I can't sleep, but neither am I fully awake—this mental miasma has put me well on my way toward madness.

I remember a time I felt almost this way, descending the east bowl of Mount Princeton in the dark with my endurance-training mentor Theresa Daus-Weber during our first annual fourteeners bender in September 2002. We linked seven high peaks in forty-eight hours of continuous hiking, and were into the second night of the sixty-mile, 25,000-vertical-feet climbing spree when my sleep-weary mind lost its grip on reality.

I scampered across a two-mile-wide slanting boulder field ahead of Theresa. We each had a headlamp and a hiking pole to help us traverse the unstable terrain in the dark. I frequently lost sight of her behind me, since the rock flutings that featured the mountainside stood in my line of sight. Stopping to wait around each corner, I would sit and fall asleep for a moment, waking within twenty or thirty seconds to the sound of Theresa's trekking pole tapping the rocks in sync with her stride. I would see the light of her headlamp bob up in my face as she approached, and then I'd stand up without a word and scramble off over the next few dozen boulders until I couldn't see her anymore, then stop to repeat the cycle. Tick, tick, tick, her pole lightly striking the boulders. Flash, her headlamp shooting into my eyes, blinding me to the fact there was a person behind the light. Another wordless encounter, boulders zipping underfoot in the throw of my headlamp, then blessed rest.

Despite an hour and a half of movement, it never seemed like I made any progress toward the far side of the bowl, where we would intercept an access road at about 12,000 feet. Something was wrong. After the tenth or twelfth or fifteenth time I had replicated the scramble-doze-wake-tick-flash-scramble pattern, a surreal tug of insanity gave me the idea that each time I fell asleep, it reset my position on the mountainside to the same point in the middle of the boulder field. My body was somehow being transported mysteriously back uphill during my twenty-second naps, and I was reliving the same sequence over and over again.

Another five cycles, and I was sure of it: I was trapped in time, like Bill Murray in *Groundhog Day*. Somebody was doing this to me. Theresa. I convinced myself that she had put a spell on me. I was helpless against her; the only way I could break her control was by staying awake. No matter what, I couldn't help myself—when I stopped to wait for her, I dozed off instantly. The delusional paranoia was so strong that it never occurred to me to check my watch, to talk with Theresa, to create some variety to the experience, or to slow down and walk at her pace, thereby eliminating my opportunities to fall asleep. What *did* occur to me was to memorize the rocks I stepped on. If I could prove to myself that I wasn't stepping on the same rocks, that would be undeniable evidence that it was all in my head. Therein I found another problem: I couldn't remember the rocks, not even the ones I would lie on to rest.

We continued the downward traverse with my mind stuck on an infinite playback loop of rocks. After two hours, we exited the boulder field, and I told Theresa about my delusions. She told me that hallucinations are a predictable part of sleep-deprived ultra-hiking. It was nearly twenty-four hours later when I arrived at my truck, some thirty miles away, and I put an end to my delirium with a well-deserved night's sleep.

Back in the canyon, the only preoccupation that alleviates the ceaseless BBC torture is pondering the question of whether I should or shouldn't drink my urine. That subject is enough to drive everything else far into the mental background. The issue of taste doesn't really concern me; it's going to taste like piss, no matter what. The consideration is whether the urine will prolong my survival or bring on my demise. I speculate that by this point, my urine has a considerably elevated salt content, but I can't know if the salinity is greater than that already present in my blood. If my urine has fewer salts than my blood, then it won't be a problem. But at a higher concentration, it would be like drinking salt water, essentially accelerating my dehydration. I wonder, too, if the toxins and other potentially harmful contents are present at dangerous levels. This is the stuff my body is trying to get rid of, and here, I'm going to put it back in.

Sitting in front of me at eye level on top of the chockstone, my translucent blue CamelBak reservoir makes the liter of brackish orange urine look brown in the dim evening light. In the four hours since I peed into the container, the urine has separated into stratified layers: a viscous brown soup on the bottom, a dingy orange fluid in the middle, a clear golden liquid on top. A half-inch-thick accretion of yellow-white sediment collects on the liner bottom; more and more of the dregs fall out of the solution as the urine cools. I prod the CamelBak with my finger, disturbing the solids. It reminds me of the yeast in the bottom of a bottle of home-brewed beer. Of course, it's substantially less appealing.

Night falls again, presaged by the routine increase in the up-canyon breeze and another invasion of mosquitoes. Why are they so active just before dark, I wonder, and then say aloud, "And where the hell are they coming from?" There must be standing water someplace in the canyon—I didn't pass any on the way here, but maybe at the bottom of the Big Drop rappel. I think I remember something in the guidebook. I check my map. The photocopy is wearing thin along the crease lines, but I can still read the marking that calls out a pool below the rappel. It's probably a pothole, a remnant of the last rainfall, like the greenish slime on the south wall behind my feet. In fact, my map indicates that there should have been a pool in the upcanyon section, and another where I am, but they have obviously evaporated. I hope there's some kind of water supply still available at the rappel. I bet it dries up in the summer and winter, but the slime, the mosquitoes, and the gritty residue on the walls make me think there is water now. That will be very important if I get out of here—it's the only source for four miles, until Barrier Creek appears in the bottom of Horseshoe Canyon, just beyond the Great Gallery.

You're not getting out of here, Aron. You'll never see water again.

Dark.
Cold.
Stars.
Space.
Shivering.

I return to the pattern of fidgeting and rest that helped me through last night, but I can get only ten minutes of stillness from each cycle. It seems colder tonight, or perhaps I'm feeling the increased effects of starvation and dehydration on my body's metabolic systems. With the certain deterioration I've suffered since my entrapment began, I assume my body is not generating as much heat. The deeper cold increases my compulsion to retain every bit of heat possible. What else can I do to insulate myself? Unplugged from the CD player, the headphones around my neck haven't produced music for three days. I pull them over my ears all the same, like half-sized earmuffs. When I tuck my head inside the rope bag, I shut the zipper until it slides into the skin of my neck. With the bag so tightly closed around my face, I hope to benefit from my breath's warmth, letting it warm my head and preheat my next inhalation without taking me too close to the brink of suffocation.

Breath after breath fills the rope bag with moist air as I focus on exhaling against the waterproof liner. Instead of letting my breath dissipate into the chilly night air, I try to recapture some of my body's water content from the humidified exhalations. Using the rope bag like a breathing chamber seems like a sound theory, though I have no idea if it will help. I get the familiar sense that I'm prolonging the inevitable. After five or six minutes of breathing in the bag, the cold seeps up from my legs and arms into my core. Shuddering, I struggle to hold the position, sitting in my harness for another three or four minutes: left hand grabbing my right elbow, head nestled on my right biceps, knees bent into the rock shelf. But the shivers tear across me like attack dogs. I have to extract my head from the bag in order to fidget with the ropes around my legs and the coverings on my arms. I'm getting too efficient—rewrapping my leg coils takes only twenty minutes—and I have a more difficult time warming up between sit sessions. I don't even bother to take up my knife and chip at the rock; I just suffer my misery and pray that I'll live through the night.

Midnight. It's now Tuesday, April 29. After hours of debating the issue with myself, I decide to take a sip of my urine. I still have nearly a half-cup of fresh water left, but I want to find out what the urine tastes like and whether I'll be able to stomach it. With the CamelBak bite valve reattached to the tubing at the stub where I cut off the hose during my first attempt to fabricate a tourniquet, I suck two tablespoons of urine into my mouth and swallow it immediately. The night air has chilled it substantially from its initial 98 degree temperature, to maybe 60 degrees. The sharp saltiness is repugnantly tangy and bitter. My face wrinkles into a knot. Surprisingly, it's not as horrible as it could be—I don't gag or puke. My quagmire deepens. If the urine was so insufferably foul as to be undrinkable, I would have my answer—don't drink it. But because it's feasible that I could drink almost half of what I peed out before I get to the unfathomable brown filth, the question is still open. My thirst would have me drink two cups right now. That doesn't seem like a good idea, though. I think

I've heard of people undertaking some cleansing dietary program that encourages you to drink your urine, but I have to assume that you stay well hydrated at the same time. Maybe that memory is a figment—I can barely trust my brain with anything at this point—but clear pee would definitely be a better alternative than what I have available. In the end, I don't know if I should drink any more of the urine, and there's no way for me to accurately guess. I suspect it will be worth the gamble, but not yet. I'm going to keep sipping my water for the next twelve hours, until it runs out, and then I'll think about drinking my urine again.

More cycles. Three A.M., Tuesday morning, hour sixty. I mark my time trapped here at two and a half days. I've adjusted my sipping schedule to fit the shorter cycle duration. I delicately draw my water bottle from its perch and note the amount remaining: a scant three ounces. Holding the bottle between my legs, I unscrew the top with my free left hand. I hold the lid back, raise the bottle, and before I fully wet the inside of my lower lip, I force my hand to withdraw and put the bottle down, as I have done once an hour through the night.

The last mouthful of my water supply has become a sacred element. In effect, the liquid has transubstantiated from something of this earth to something holy and eternal—it has become time itself, and in time, it has become life. The longer that water lasts, the longer I will last.

Or so I tell myself. I've developed several signs that tell me dehydration has already set upon me, and even if I conserve my last water, I'll still die fairly soon. My body no longer has enough fluids to perform at an optimum level. My eyes are sunken and dry—I avoid looking at myself in my video-camera episodes because of the gaunt stretch of skin over my cheekbones. The desert air contributes its irritants to my contact lenses, but my eyes can't flush the contaminants. As the dehydration has stressed my heart muscles, my heartbeat has become weak, sometimes erratic, and fast—I time it at a resting rate of 120 beats per minute, over 60 percent faster than normal for me. Despite my elevated heart rate, my circulation has slowed over the last three days as my blood has thickened, inhibiting the delivery of nutrients to my organs and the removal of metabolic wastes. My pump is burning up as the fluid it's trying to move solidifies in my body's internal piping. With my blood pressure steadily dropping, my body temperature fluctuates unnaturally, and the slightest breeze sends me into another shivering fit. Drastically losing liquid mass, my organs suffer the brunt of the dehydration; in all, my body is losing between four and five pounds a day. The skin on the back of my hand has shriveled into reptilian crinkles; the poor elasticity allows me to form little tents by plucking at my skin with my teeth.

But for all the physical signs of my body's dire need for hydration, nothing, nothing compares to the anguish of my thirst: unslakable . . . unquenchable . . . unsatisfiable . . . insuppressible . . . inextinguishable.

I find myself wishing to get this all over with simply to bring relief to the thirst. As my end comes, it will be in cardiovascular collapse, but I wonder if the thirst won't take care of the job first.

Two hours later, it is five A.M., and time for my hourly water ritual. I place the water bottle in my crotch and again single-handedly unscrew the lid. I ease my legs' grip on the bottle and begin to raise it to my mouth. But the lid unexpectedly snags on my harness, and the bottle slips, falling to my lap. My sluggish brain responds too slowly for my hand to catch the bottle before it tilts almost horizontal, and a splash of the sacrament darkens my tan shorts, turning the red dust to a patina of shining mud.

Fuck a nut, Aron. Pay attention! Look what you did!

Water is time. With that spill, how many hours did I just lose? Maybe six hours, maybe ten hours, maybe half a day? The mistake hits my morale like a train, destroying my protective walls of discipline and meticulousness that had been keeping despair at bay. Regardless of what I thought earlier, losing half of my remaining supply

In the Grand Canyon, April 1999.

Mom and me, 1977.

My sister and me at Grandma Ralston's, 1983.

At Yellowstone National Park, 1987.

RIGHT: *My first skiing trip, 1987. Note the fear.*

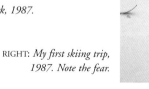

Betty Darr and me at my graduation from Carnegie Mellon University, 1997.

BELOW: *American Gothic. Mom and Dad at Lake Chelan, Washington.*

ABOVE: *With Mom, Dad, and Sonja on the top of the 14,084-foot Handies Peak, 2000.*

Sonja and me at Havasupai, Thanksgiving 1998.

My first alpine rock climb: Mark Van Eeckhout and me, in front of Wham Ridge on Vestal Peak, on Labor Day 1998.

The Grand Teton, two days before the bear stalking.

On the summit of Mount Humphreys, Arizona, March 1998.

My first solo winter fourteener—Quandary Peak, December 1998.

Ringing the Bells—South Maroon Peak, March 2003.

Steve Patchett, Jason Halladay, me, and Bob Graham,
on top of Dallas Peak, Labor Day 2001.

My footprints on the Knife Ridge on Capitol Peak, February 2003.

Maroon Bells and the Sleeping Sexton in winter.

Mount Sopris.

The equipment I carried into Blue John Canyon. All original,
except the CamelBak, webbing, and burritos.

The tourniquet, and the multi-tool.

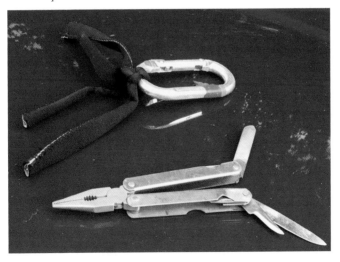

In Blue John Canyon—the last photograph of my right hand.

Megan McBride and Kristi Moore.

The S-log at the entrance to the lower slot of Blue John Canyon.

The gauntlet in the lower slot of Blue John Canyon, fifteen yards above the accident site.

Forty-eight hours into the entrapment.

Day three.

*11:36 A.M., Thursday,
May 1, 2003.*

At the bottom of the Big Drop rappel, forty-five minutes after the amputation.

At the pool of water below the Big Drop.

The rescue helicopter.

My rescuers: Mitch Vetere, Greg Funk, Terry Mercer, Kyle Ekker, and Steve Swanke.

Climbing the North Face Direct of North Maroon Peak, May 2004.

of water makes me realize how psychologically attached to it I am. Even if I have so little water left that, physiologically speaking, I might as well not have any, emotionally, I feel like I've given away half of the rest of my life.

I have been shivering in my wrappings, with my head in my rope bag, trying to push away the nagging cold, when I hear a shout in my sleep-deprived brain. It is just after six-fifteen A.M., Tuesday.

"Larry!" My mom yells out my dad's name. I see her in her bathrobe, bolting downstairs from their bedroom to tell my dad some terrible news she has just received. The image ends before I see her reach my dad. Different from a memory or a dream, the clip was more like a TV set involuntarily switched on in my mind, broadcasting from my parents' house. Was it something that already happened? Or a premonition of something yet to come? Either way, I'm fairly sure that I am the reason my mom was rushing to my dad. But was it to say she found out I'm in trouble, or that I'm found, or that I'm dead? It could have been anything.

Gradually, light resurrects the dimensions of the canyon, and I feel buoyed by the knowledge that I've survived another night. Now that there's enough visibility, I decide to update the record of my situation with another round of talking to my video camera.

Wiping at my left eye, I smear my hand across my brow and face, then sigh. I check the framing to make sure I'm at least partially on-screen, but I avoid looking at the camera as I talk.

"It's six-forty-five in the morning on Tuesday morning," I repeat to myself.

"I figure by now that Leona has missed me, hopefully, since I - didn't show up at the party last night. Another hour and a half, they'll miss me for not showing up for work. I keep thinking about it. My best-case scenario is that maybe they notify the police, and they put 'em on a twenty-four-hour hold to officially file a report, a missing -

person's report. Which makes it, like, maybe noon tomorrow that it even gets official that I'm gone."

My frustration mounts, and I'm on the verge of tearing up. "God-damn. It's really sinking in, how dumb this is. So many things about it. So many things. It's gonna be a really long time before anyone gets to me. I was thinking about it more and more. They're gonna have to pneumatic-drill this rock to pieces or amputate my arm just to get me out of here. That's when somebody finds me and then goes to get the proper tools. And then it's a haul up over two considerable staircases to get out to a helicopter landing zone, and then it's an hour flight to Grand Junction, maybe less than that. Maybe it's a half hour. What-ever."

Imagining a team hauling a pneumatic jackhammer down Blue John Canyon to break the rock apart with me still stuck under it makes the idea of rescue seem even more improbable than before. Just getting me free will be a tremendous task, and evacuating me in a litter out of the slot . . . The space is so confined, I'm not sure - there's a feasible route to use.

The logistics nightmare overloads my hope. I know it's all theo-retical, but even in theory, it sounds like a multi-day ordeal once I'm located. Moving a subject in a litter a hundred yards down a wide road grade takes five minutes with six people. Make it a narrowing winding trail, and it could be a half hour of effort. As soon as there's a haul or lowering system involved, it adds an hour or two, and that's with ideal conditions. Each level of complexity adds time and re-source demands and elevates the risk to the rescuers. For me, each one of those chockstones I crawled over or under represents a dimin-ished likelihood that I would survive the time it would take to evacu-ate my useless body. If I'm alive when a rescue team finds me, I will probably die before reaching definitive medical care. Realizing it - doesn't matter—I'll be dead before searchers get to this part of the canyon, anyway—I close my left eye in an unconscious grimacing wink and continue with the videoing. I'm exasperated.

"I tried . . . I tried cutting my arm off. I couldn't even barely break the skin with this stupid knife. I tried a couple different blades, but all I did was just mark myself up. I could barely even get any blood to draw, it's probably so thick at this point.

"I do still have the tiniest bit of water left. Well, actually, I've resorted . . . I've had a couple pretty good sips of my own urine that I saved in my CamelBak. I sorta let it distill. The sediment separated from the more liquidy stuff."

Emphasizing each word, I elaborate, "It tastes like hell," and pause, smacking my lips apart when I try to swallow. "I have about a bite of burrito left that I can barely stomach anyways.

"I tried moving the rock some more. It's not going anywhere.

"So it's been not quite seventy hours since I left on my bike from Horseshoe Trailhead, during which time I have consumed three liters of water and a couple mouthfuls of piss. Food I'm not so worried about, although I am getting too tired to the point of doing anything. I can't even chip away at the rock anymore. It's . . . I tried, and I don't have the energy and the gumption . . . It's ridiculous."

Disgusted with my impotence, I shudder and then moan, "Unaaannggh." Shaking my head, I frown and grimace, then compose myself during a long blink and look straight at the camera for what I want to say next.

"Mom, Dad, I really love you guys. I wanted to take this time to say the times we've spent together have been awesome. I haven't appreciated you in my own heart the way I know I could. Mom, I love you. Thank you so much for coming to visit me in Aspen. Dad, thank you for the time last year when we went on your trip with the Golden Leaf Tour. Those were some of my favorite times that I've had with you in a long, long time. Thank you both for being understanding, and supportive, and encouraging during this last year. I really have lived this last year. I wish I had learned some lessons more astutely, more rapidly, than what it took to learn. I love you. I'll always be with you."

Tightening my lips, I feel tears welling in my eyes. I bow my head in another long blink, then give the camera a nod, as though I'm saying goodbye, before I reach to pause the tape. A doleful breeze interjects itself in the canyon; the night's calm is at an end. When I restart the video camera, my thoughts turn to my sister and the cloud of sorrow that will cast a shadow over her graduation and wedding this summer.

"I wanted to say to Sonja and Zack that I really wish you the best in your upcoming life together. You guys are great together. Sonja, - you've got a great career in front of you. I know you guys are gonna both be very happy. I wish I could be there to see it start off. You'll graduate about a month from now. Do great things with your life— that will honor me the best. Thanks."

It makes me happy to think about my sister. Even though I got good grades in school, she came along and one-upped me in every arena, and I love her for it. She cares about learning—she's planning to be a volunteer teacher. I'm glad for her, but I'm also glad for me. - It's as though Sonja will repay the educational debt I've accrued by having taken from the system without giving back. I'm more proud of what she's done in college than of what I've done since I graduated six years ago. Even with me gone, big things will happen in our family because of her; it reassures me to know she has such aspirations.

Another breeze passes up from the unseen recesses of the canyon behind me, making me worry about a change in the weather. I can already discern a sheet of clouds thicker than any I've yet seen. No sign of thunderheads, but I wouldn't necessarily see them before they unleashed a flash flood. I'd forgotten about that risk. While I've got the camera out, I decide to record a few more video notes in case the rains come. I start the tape again, panning up to the debris over my head.

"It's also occurred to me that the flash-flood potential is still present. This stuff all up above me there, it's all been put there . . . The rocks I pulled down on top of me, it was all put there by floods. - There's four pretty major canyons upstream from me that all converge in this three-foot-wide gap where I am. Even if I'm dead at that point, it's gonna . . . it's gonna fuck things up pretty bad. This footage will be unviewable, and my body will be pretty mangled. -

That's really not here or there. I was almost wishing for it to come. In the one sense that maybe I could get a little bit of water. I don't know if that sounds ridiculous or not, but I was thinking about it last night. I guess at the point where you're sipping on your bodily waste products . . . I know I shouldn't be doing it. It's got too many salts and stuff in it, it's just gonna hasten the process.

"Three days, I've been out of water for a day and a half. That probably means I've got another day and a half. I'm gonna hold strong. But if I even see Wednesday noon, I'll be amazed."

I stop the tape. Those are tough words. Verbalizing that I'm giving myself thirty more hours to live leaves me with a sense of finality that rubs my psyche the wrong way. I put the video recorder up on the chockstone, and my body involuntarily slumps back into the harness. The words echo and rebound inside my head—"if I even see Wednesday"—until they hit a synapse holding on to a store of gumption. The next thing I know, I'm stripping webbing off my right arm and tying the purple strands into Prusik loops once again. With the practice I had yesterday, I set up the 6:1 haul-system rigging in a fraction of the time it took me to figure it out the first time, clipping the rope tied to the chockstone through the carabiners and configuring the Prusiks with a single-handed dexterity that impresses my sluggish brain. My fumbling through the night left me thinking my coordination had dried up. Stashing my water bottle, urine supply, knife, and cameras in my backpack, I clear the top of the chockstone, lastly putting my scratched sunglasses on top of my head.

"Ready for liftoff," I say to myself after double-checking the Prusiks to make sure they will lock off in the proper direction. Positioned just above my waist, the foot loops are a little higher than they were yesterday—I must have used a bit more rope in the system this time—but I mount the lower one first with my left foot and step up into the right one.

OK, now move the boulder, Aron. Do it. Bounce. Harder. Pull on the rope—yank on it. Bounce and yank. Harder! You've got to do this. Make it move!

Grunting, flailing, heaving, I bounce my weight in the stirrups and pull on the haul line. "Come on, move, dammit!"

Nothing. I am completely powerless against the mass of this stone and the friction of these walls. My feet pull themselves from the foot loops, as if they have a mind of their own that already knows I won't be giving it another go. I am defeated again. There is nothing left for me to cling to. I am violently drowning in this Gothic isolation; the more I fight it, the tighter it closes in, squeezing the life from me. Resting for fifteen minutes, I feel like crying, but my dry sobs don't produce anything. It's as though I'm too dejected even to waste my energy on tears. What good could it do me to cry? It would squander what little liquid my body has left.

Slowly, I become aware of the cold stare of my knife from inside my backpack. There is a reason for everything, including why I brought that knife with me, and suddenly, I know what I am about to do. Mustering up my courage, I dismantle a purple Prusik loop from the rigging and tie it around my biceps, preparing the rest of my tourniquet as I'd refined it yesterday—CamelBak tubing insulation wrapped twice around my forearm, knotted twice and clipped with a 'biner that I twist six times and attach to the purple webbing to secure it.

I note the time with a glance at my watch on the backpack strap at my knees: 7:58 A.M.

Folding open the shorter of the two knives, I close the handle and grasp it in my fist, the blade jutting out from below my pinky finger. Raising the tool above my right arm, I pick a spot on the top of my forearm, next to a freckle and just up from the marks I scratched into my skin yesterday morning. I hesitate, jerking my left hand to a halt a foot above my target. I recock my tool, and before I can stop myself a second time, my fist violently thrusts the inch-and-a-half-long blade down, burying it to the hilt in the meat of my forearm.

"Holy crap, Aron, what did you just do?"

My vision warps with astonishment. The light quality in the canyon bursts into beige contrast, highlights becoming bright pale tan and shadows changing to deep brown as if I've crossed over into a sepia-toned movie. I bend my head to my arm, and my surroundings leave hallucinogenic trails behind them, responding unhurriedly to my movements, as though this pseudo-film is being played at two-thirds normal speed. I was half expecting the knife to glance off my arm, but when I relax my grip, I can see the folded handle of the multi-tool thrust perpendicular into my arm. Yesterday it didn't seem possible that my knife could ever get through my skin, but it did. When I grasp the tool more firmly and wiggle it slightly, the blade connects with something hard, my upper forearm bone. I tap the knife down and feel it knocking on my radius.

Whoa. That's so bizarre.

All at once, I am curious. There is barely any discernible sensation of the blade below skin level. My nerves seem to be concentrated in the outer layers of my arm. I confirm this by drawing the knife out, slicing up at my skin from underneath. Oh yeah, there they are. The flesh stretches with the blade, broadcasting signals through my arm as I open an inch-wide hole at the site. Letting the pain dissipate, I note that there is remarkably little blood coming from the torn cells in my skin; the capillaries must have closed down for the time being. Fascinated, I poke at the gash with the tool. Ouch. Pushing the knife back into the gory hole, I probe at the inner constitution of my arm. The epidermis is twice as thick as I thought it would be, and leathery-tough. Yellow fatty tissue lies under my skin in a membrane layer around my muscle. When I root around, my view disappears as burgundy-colored blood seeps into the wound. I tap at the bone again, feeling the vibration of each strike through my left thumb and forefinger. Even damped by surrounding tissues, the hollow thumping of the blade tip against my upper forearm bone resonates up into my elbow. The soft thock-thock-thock tells me I have reached the end of this experiment. I cannot cut into or through my forearm bones.

Pushing aside that bleak conclusion for a moment, I find some levity in my situation—it's the first time in thirteen years that I have carried out a dissection, and I'm handling it much better this time around, even though it's my own arm. I recall the sheep's eyeball that stared back at me from the stainless-steel pan in ninth-grade physical science class. Cutting into the squishy orb was enough to intimidate me right out of the biology program in high school; thereafter, I stuck with chemistry and physics—anything to avoid animal parts in a nonculinary setting. That eyeball was indirectly responsible for my chosen path in engineering. It's odd that I've come back to face such an old and rooted fear in this canyon.

Sweating from the adrenaline, I set my multi-tool on top of the chockstone and pick up my water bottle. It's not time for my next sip, but I've earned this. As the first drops splash against my lip, I open my eyes and stare into the opaque blue bottom with detachment. I continue to tilt the bottle up and up, feeling a mix of deserved reward and recalcitrant spite—like I'm doing something naughty but I don't care; I'm going to do it, and the fact that I shouldn't makes me enjoy it even more.

Just do it—get it over with. It doesn't matter.

Each continued tablespoon of water satisfies me like a whole mouthful, and instantly, I'm gulping at the dribbling flow. I close my eyes . . . Oh, God. After an all too brief three seconds, I swallow the last drops of my clean water supply, and it's gone. My body wails for the water to keep coming, but there is no more. I gaze into the container poised over the bridge of my nose and shake the Nalgene, tearing free those last drops from the walls of the bottle.

Well, that's it, there's not a single drop left. I don't linger on it. Screwing the lid back on the threaded lip, I realize I've passed a moment I've been anticipating for three days. Now it's over. There's one less thing I have to worry about. I decide to disengage the tourniquet—it's making my whole arm ache, and since I won't be going any further with the amputation, there's no need to cause any excess agony. I unclip the carabiner holding the neoprene tubing and slowly unwind it, allowing my arm to regain its regular shape. At a snail's pace, my circulation returns to my arm, and I keep watch on the wound. There is no increase in the blood flow at the gash, and no pulsing at all, so I figure I have avoided any arteries. Still, the bleeding is less than I would have expected. It almost seems like the tourniquet wasn't doing anything. I make the connection that since the chockstone has pinched off the arteries and veins in my hand, it has reduced the blood flow in my arm. That would explain why my forearm is stone cold.

Pulling out the video camera, I hold it in my hand this time and begin taping the results of my surgery. My hat, webbing, and tourniquet supplies appear in the screen, on top of the chockstone.

"This next part may not be for all viewers at home. It's a little after eight. At precisely eight o'clock I took my last sip of clean water . . . and . . . hide your eyes, Mom. . . ."

Panning across the boulder, the camera comes to my arm and the gaping wound, smattered with bright red blood. My breathing becomes labored as I look at the puncture in my arm.

"I made an attempt—a short career in surgery, as it turned out—those knives are just not anywhere close to the task. I've got about an inch-wide gash in my arm that goes about a half inch deep. I cut down through the skin and the fatty tissue, and through some of the muscle. I think I cut a tendon, but I'm not sure. I tried, anyways. It really just didn't go well. The tourniquet is relaxed at this point. Which actually is a little bothersome, considering I'm not bleeding that bad, barely at all. It's so weird. You'd expect to definitely see more pulsing and bleeding, but oh well.

"I'm really fucked now. I'm out of water."

I stop the tape, more depressed than ever. With an open wound, I've introduced a new contestant in the competition to see what will kill me first—dehydration, hypothermia, a flash flood, toxins from my crushed hand, or the infection that is likely breeding in my arm at this very moment.

Stabbing yourself with a contaminated knife—that was true genius, Aron.

Surmising that the bleeding at the gash site isn't going to get any worse, I decide to cover the wound to keep the dirt, grit, and insects off it. Delicately pinching the bottom of my salmon-colored Phish tour T-shirt between my ring and pinky fingers and the palm of my left hand, I pierce the fabric with my knife, held between my thumb and forefinger. From the hole, I rip a strip of the cotton shirt from in front of my waist and wrap it three times around my forearm. There now. I have a bandage on the puncture site.

In a rush of noise, the raven's wings swat at the air seventy feet over my head—once, and twice, as it attains cruising altitude, flying its morning search route. I glance at my watch. 8:31 A.M. The bird is fifteen minutes late this morning.

The canyon behind me begins to glow in a spectrum of pastel reds as the sun breaches the depths of the upper walls. Knowing that the sun will be more punctual than the raven, I get my video camera out of my rucksack for the third time this morning, anticipating my matinal sun salute. I videotape myself stretching my leg into the dagger of sunlight as it creeps closer to me. Before the sunshine veers up the north wall, I pan the camera from the view of the bright pink and carroty-orange undulations twenty yards downcanyon, to my calf absorbing the precious warmth of my only direct sunlight.

"It's so pretty back there. For a . . . about twenty minutes, it's actually possible for me to get a little direct sun on my leg if I try really hard."

Like a prisoner with a pretty view beyond the bars of his cell window, I'm not sure whether the beauty of the canyon in the morning light inspires my tenacity or erodes my resolve. I yearn even more for freedom.

With the tape paused, my thoughts radiate out from the canyon to my friends all over the United States, readying for another workday. I wonder if any of them are thinking about me. I highly doubt the alert of my absence has gone any further than the upstairs office at the Ute Mountaineer, but at least somebody knows for sure that I am officially overdue. Theoretically, my manager is at least wondering what has happened to me, if not actively searching. I begin reminiscing about my friends, our favorite trips, and the places we have experienced together. For being just twenty-seven, I feel like I've had the adventures of someone twice my age, and the fortune to have had so many caring and fun people share their time with me on trips, at concerts, and in the outdoors. Thinking about my family and friends makes me smile. Memories bring me a tidal change of morale, absolving me of my preoccupation with the agony of my crushed wrist under this boulder. My mood shifts from one of speculation on the dim hopes of my rescue to a highlights reel of my life. This uplift is something I definitely want to record on the video. I wonder if my friends will get to watch it at my funeral, and that morose thought actually makes me happier—I can picture a church full of my friends in black, watching what I'm about to say on a big-screen television positioned near the altar. Getting ready, I adjust my hat, clear my throat, and try to swallow, which makes my lips smack at the dryness of my mouth.

"I was thinking about what I was talking about earlier, about my regrets about not focusing on the people enough. And I don't know. I was thinking maybe that's not totally true.

"I was thinking about some of my favorite trips that I've done with some of my favorite folks. Erik and Jon, going to Winter Park during those Jazz Fest trips, and everything from building the Dr Pepper can stacks on top of the refrigerator, to sticking noodles on the ceiling, to watching television late into the night and getting so jazzed up on sugar and caffeine, man, just having a fun time. Making those heinous—they were really good—peanut-butter sandwiches with honey. Jon, when we climbed Longs Peak, our first fourteener together, and that road trip we did last year out through the East Coast, so many states, just buzzing around. That was really fun, to be out there with you and Chrystie. Seeing you guys put your life together there, building it, that's really cool.

"Erik, I was remembering many times about Maui with Matt and Brent. That was such a fun week. So many good trips to see String

Cheese shows, like down at the Wiltern Theatre, and that whole run when we did most of that Winter Carnival two years ago. When we went to Jazz Fest with KPat. Oh my gosh. I've never been so belligerently wasted at eight in the morning as when we were sitting on that boardwalk by the Mississippi River. Man, it was crazy—going back to sit in the hot tub, getting up a couple hours later to go do it all again, five days in a row. Amazing."

I squint in a smile. Images come to me of that wild week in New Orleans when we saw twenty full-bore concerts in five days on an average of three hours of sleep—usually between nine in the morning and noon. By the end of it, I was so exhausted that I fell asleep on a N'Awlins barroom floor in the middle of a beer-swilling crowd while one of the bands was in the throes of a second set. You'll never find your limits until you've gone too far.

"I was thinking about a trip I did with Erik Zsemlye and Rana—I'm thinking about you—when we went up to Denver from Albuquerque and we opened the windows up in a storm and this whiteout blizzard came into the car and it was a whiteout in the vehicle as we were driving up toward Antonito. How beautiful Rana looked in her snow-ice-princess costume.

"Sonja, I was remembering the trip to Washington, D.C., and the high-point trips that we did that time. When we went down to Havasupai and I fell off a cliff into a cactus and I almost drowned in the Colorado River. I was thinking about another time with Jean-Marc and Chad in Phoenix, we went down to Mexico and Margaritaville our butts off, sailed around the horn down at Rocky Point and back after loading up on Coronas and tequila on the beach. Jamie, when you and I went to Havasupai—that was beautiful. Down at the camp, it was so awesome, waking up together on New Year's morning. Wow."

Laughing a laugh of utter exhaustion, I recall the irony of the memories that involved a close brush with death. I've listed several times when I almost died as some of my favorite memories, times when I had fun via the intensity of the experience. Regardless of the psychological implications, I find a certain comedic relief for my current situation, wondering if I'll feel the same way if I survive my entrapment in Blue John.

"It goes without saying, all the fantastic trips I've done with my family, but Dad, you and I have done some special ones to see Gettysburg, the history of Virginia and Pennsylvania, we did that one back in college. The first time we went to Canyonlands, Zion, Bryce, Capitol Reef, Arches, all these places that draw me back to the desert each time. Thanks for those. So many special times with great people in my life."

I shake my head in amazement at my fortune. My memories overrun my ability to keep them sorted, connected, or ordered, and they begin tumbling out in chaotic ramblings.

"I was thinking, too, Erik, that first road trip to see music when we went to see the Grateful Dead over Fourth of July weekend in 1995.

"Gary Scott, our trip up Denali—that was the whole catalyst for me leaving my job. Thanks. Good luck on Everest, man. I know you're up there high right now, probably Camp Three or so. Be safe, come back.

"I was thinking, too, about when Judson came up from Phoenix to climb Mount Rainier together in this blitzkrieg event. Taking a nap on the Disappointment Cleaver at twelve thousand five hundred feet, at three o'clock in the afternoon after summiting, when we started at two in the morning. 'Five more minutes to Camp Muir!' And it wasn't."

My smile grows even wider. Judson kept asking me how much farther the milestone camp was; I could see where we were going, but the moonlit night distorted my sense of distance, and I made earnest prediction after earnest prediction that we would be at the huts in fifteen more minutes, then five more minutes, until, after a dozen estimates of "five more minutes," we finally tromped into camp just in time for sunrise. I was lucky Judson didn't drop me in a crevasse for my lousy guessing.

"I was remembering, Chip, when you and I drove to Flagstaff and back for Keller Williams. That was another blitzkrieg. Oh, man, so many incredible times. Places I went with my friend Erik Kemnitz—to his house in Rochester one weekend in college. When I went out to California a couple times and met up with Soha and Craig and Buck, I think I even got a couple of you guys to your first Phish show."

I'm feeling my tiredness delaying my efforts to speak coherently. Simply being awake seems to be fully taxing my brainpower. I need rest, but I can't sleep. Bracing my left elbow against the southern canyon wall, I hold my head up with my hand and continue.

"Bryan Long, that one we did last year. Mountain biking and hiking and hot springs, then two Cheese shows, and another two Cheese shows. Zach, thanks for being my friend, we got to go hiking up on Sandia Peak with Erik that day. Ahhh, fun. I do appreciate all those times, so many good folks in my life. Rana, our trip to Telluride to see the Cheese. That was my best 'last day' ever, skiing in the full-blown pigtails, tie-dye shirt, pink fluorescent boa, our flags flying high that day."

My smile is cracking my dry lips. I need some lip balm, but I'll wait to get to it in a minute. Even the pain of my lips makes me feel thankful for the people I love.

"So thanks, everybody. Thanks for the good times. I do appreciate each and every one of you. Norm and Sandy, you guys are like my folks away from home. All my friends' parents, too, for bringing up such wonderful people who have participated in my life, thank you. My friends in Aspen that I got to stay with over the last six months, beautiful, beautiful people, all of you, thank you. Bryan and Jenn Welker, Bryan Gonzales and Mike Check, thanks. Rachel, you're a wonderful woman, thank you. I could say the same thing about a lot of people in my life. Thankfully, I'm getting to say it now. I love you all. Hugs."

Wow. How good do I feel now? I wonder if this is a bit like my life flashing before my eyes, but on a slower time line. What makes the human brain respond to death with reflection? I always figured people saw images of their family as a way of saying goodbye, but considering what the memories have done for me—giving me a surge of positive energy, smiling, feeling happy—I ruminate over an ulterior purpose. Perhaps the whole life's highlights reel thing is a survival instinct, something engrained in our subconscious, the brain's final trick in the bag to continue its own existence. I imagine that once adrenaline has failed to engage a successful fight-or-flight impulse, the flash of memories acts as a secondary reflex, motivating us to keep fighting even when we don't think there's any fight left in us. In the face of an imminent demise, the medulla oblongata kicks into involuntary overdrive and says, "You think you're done? How about all those people who care about you? How about all those people you care about?" and bam! you've got a little more spunk. Maybe that's why suicide seems most tempting when you don't have people telling you they love you, or when you don't care if they do—there is no flash, the backup system fails. Maybe that's why our brains store memories in the first place, to spur on a stubborn body when the endgame has begun. Well, whatever. I'll take the happiness and uplift and leave the psychobabble. I feel good, that's the important thing.

Come noon, I am biding my death, shackled to the canyon wall. With so much practice sitting in my harness, I have found the most comfortable angle for my knees, the best height for my daisy chain, and the perfect edge location for the rope coiled like a pad in front of my shins. I have taken care of my body to the best of my faculties with the available resources. Strangely, I have to pee again. I decide I will decant my current stash before I unzip, but pouring off the clearer top part of the liquid in my CamelBak will be quite the coordination challenge. I grip my empty Nalgene between my thighs and hold it steady while I bite the upper end of the blue CamelBak water bag in my teeth. I keep the reservoir tilted, one bottom corner lower than the other, and the sediment settles off to one side of the outlet. I pinch the bite valve with my fingers, slowly letting the liquid run out into the Nalgene as the salt silt stays behind. With only the dregs left in my CamelBak, I close the Nalgene lid, set it on the chockstone, and dump out the leftovers from the blue reservoir into the sand behind my feet. Ewww. That shit stinks.

Good, that means you got rid of the worst of it.

I pee into the CamelBak and close the lid tight, setting it back onto the chockstone next to the Nalgene. This fluid is the darkest yet, pungent and warm. I'll let it cool off and settle before I decant it again—the taste isn't so ripe when it's colder.

At about one-thirty Tuesday afternoon, I decide to pray once more. This time, I already have my answer as to what I should do. There's only one thing left—wait for death or rescue, more likely the former. So instead of asking for guidance or direction, I ask for patience.

"God, it's Aron again. I still need your help. It's getting bad here. I'm out of water and food. I know I'm going to die soon, but I want to go naturally. I've decided that regardless of what I might go through, I don't want to take my own life. It occurred to me that I could, but that's not the way I want to go. As it is, I don't figure I'll live another day—it's been three days already—I don't figure I'll see Wednesday noon. But please, God, grant me the steadfastness not to do anything against my being."

I am going to see this through, whichever way it ends.

The third twenty-four-hour period of my entrapment is done. There is no water left to conserve, no potentially liberating trial left to complete. At three P.M., with nothing left to decide, my existence comes down to this: Take care of myself as best I can, physically and mentally. Physically, there is nothing I need to do until nightfall—the afternoon is the warmest time, so my only need is to adjust my body position to keep my circulation somewhat active.

The lack of demands from my body leaves nearly my full attention on sustaining my mind. Without sleep, external stimuli barely seem real, and some of them aren't. I've heard voices twice more since I solved the mystery of the kangaroo rat's nest, but they weren't real sounds, just fabrications that my brain conjured to fill the audio void of the canyon. There is only the thinnest thread connecting my conscious thoughts with reliable reason. I'm wary that something will slip past and trick me into a rash or dangerous decision. Time passes most quickly when I am recounting memories. I return again and again to them. I realize I've left out a very close friend from the videotape; it's time once more for filming.

My labored, shallow breathing resounds in the canyon. I try to settle it before I begin, but it forces me to pause every few words. Fatigue has overcome my neck muscles, and I have to prop my head with my left hand, as I did before.

"Continuing with the theme. I was thinking about Mark Van Eeckhout, all the great times we've had together. Back from our trip to Aravaipa, driving out there when I sat in the back of your truck, listening to cheesy eighties music with Angie. To when we skied little Williams Peak near Flagstaff. And our big-powder day at Wolf Creek, still one of the greatest days ever in my skiing life. All the great days at Pajarito together and coming up to visit in Los Alamos, and mountain biking, and climbing. To getting out on Baldy, my first back-country trip. All the trips we did with Patchett over those Labor Days, man, so many great times there. Four Labor Days in a row, I think, we made it out. I loved every one of them. Vestal Peak and that trip up Wham Ridge, Pigeon the next year, Jagged the year after that, Dallas the year after that. Man, some of my favorite mountain trips there with you guys. Oh, wow."

My exhausted smile allows a soft moan to slip out of my mouth. After a pause, I change tack, remembering a few of my financial holdings that my family will likely have to sort through.

"Logistics for a second. I've got stocks with CompuServe, UBS PaineWebber, the briefcases under my clothes rack in Aspen have the information about the stocks. I got rid of the Delphi stock, still have the GM stock. Those can go for Sonja or Mom and Dad, if you have another use for them. For the search-and-rescue folks who do execute the body recovery, it'd be appropriate to give them a donation for their efforts, too."

I feel good that I've covered just about all the bases to make it easier for my parents to close out what small estate I have. But really, what is on my mind is food and drink. Chilled, succulent nectars, fruits, cold desserts, all things moist and yummy.

"Man, I can't stop thinking about grapefruit juice, a margarita, or an OJ, or a Popsicle, all these great things I'd love to have. An orange, a tangerine. Oh, I can't think about that stuff.

"I'm thinking that in the best of all possible situations that - someone's gotten ahold of Mom and Dad by now, that you guys are at least aware I'm missing, um, yeah, I don't know."

I want my parents to know that when they found out I was missing, I was still alive.

About forty minutes later, before four o'clock, I remove the final bite of my last convenience-store burrito from its plastic wrapper. The pale white flour tortilla has desiccated around the softer bean interior. Moist it is not. The bite I had at noon was cardboard, primed to absorb any remaining fluids from my body. Once again, I debate the merits of my next action. Will the last chunk dry me up more than it will provide sustenance? I don't know. I do know I'm hungry. The - wrapper's nutritional information tells me I have eaten a total of five hundred calories in the two burritos over the last seventy-two hours, and I guess I have about fifty calories left in this last bite. When I'm active, I eat twice the recommended daily average of food, between four and five thousand calories a day. Going since Saturday without substantial food, my body is consuming itself to make up the difference. As little as I have left, it won't matter much if I do or don't eat the burrito, but it will put something in my stomach.

I pop the dried-out bite of burrito in my mouth and chew on it for twenty seconds, then take a sip of urine from my Nalgene to soften the mash. Ugh, it's nasty. I grimace as I chew for another ten seconds, then swallow the disgusting mess, chasing it with another bitter swallow of urine. I should have dipped the bite in the urine and used what saliva I had left to swallow it; it might have saved me from that extra swallow of piss at the end. No matter, I won't have to go through that again, because now I'm out of food. I've licked and re-licked my candy-bar wrappers, scavenged for crumbs from my muffin bag, and polished off the burritos. That's it. I'm on the urine diet now.

Returning to the video camera, I figure I'll occupy myself a bit more and document that I just finished my food. Taking several long blinks, I film myself speaking very slowly, with long pauses between each sentence. I notice my voice is getting higher and wonder if that's because of the dehydration tightening my vocal cords.

"Tuesday at four o'clock. It's about sixty-five, sixty-six degrees out. Just running through the numbers again in my head. There's very little hope for this kid. I just tried to eat my last bite of burrito and had to wash it down with a slurp of the top part of the bottle of urine, anyways. It seems to leave the denser part at the bottom, but - it's no Slurpee. I could use one of those. I didn't want to sign off without saying 'I love you' to Grandma and Grandpa—both pairs, Anderson and Ralston. Grandpas, I'll be seeing you soon here. Grandmas, I love you both, proud matriarchs. All my relatives in Ohio, I love you. I'm privileged to be a part of this family."

I long to see my family again, but I know I've entered the protractedly dismal final countdown to my death. This is going to be a hard night.

TEN

Stirrings of a Rescue

dum spiro, spero
—*Part of the official state motto of South Carolina. Literally, "While I breathe, I hope." Or more loosely, "Where there is life, there is hope."*

SATURDAY AFTERNOON, Kristi and Megan left the confluence where they last saw me, hiked up the West Fork of Blue John Canyon, and sat down to have lunch. The two young women relaxed and chatted for about a half hour then packed up their trash and started on their journey up the wash. Sometime during the next hour, they became disoriented and weren't able to interpret their map to navigate around the dead end below a fifteen-foot cliff rising up from the canyon floor. Backtracking, then returning upcanyon, pacing around below the cliff, they spent an hour trying to figure out the instructions that called for them to bypass the cliff on the right side of the canyon.

"If we go up the right side, it looks like we'll have to go out the right-hand canyon. I don't think that's the way to go." Kristi pointed at the two conjoined branches of the canyon upstream from their vantage. "And it's sketchy-looking, trying to cross that ledge over to the left canyon."

"Yeah. I'm not climbing up this overhang, either. But how else do we get up there?" The sandstone slab in front of Megan was discouragingly steep, even curling back over itself in a lip at the top. Flipping open the guidebook, Megan found the page marker for Blue John Canyon. "OK, here. The book says, 'Walk along the right (east) side on a little trail, then route-find down two steep sections.' Are we sure that side is east?"

"I don't think either side is east. East is down the canyon, where we came from. We're hiking up the West Fork, so we're going west. I don't get it; there is no east side. Can I see the map again?"

"Yeah, sure—here." Megan handed the map over to Kristi, running her finger over the guidebook page again and again.

"Man, I wish Aron were here—he'd have this figured out in no time." She sighed and started the route-finding process over again. "OK, so we put my bike up here, at the head of the West Fork. And we're here . . . or somewhere around here. We haven't left the main drainage. Yeah, we have to go left. Why does it say right?"

"Oh . . . my . . . God," Megan blurted out. "Kristi, we are total idiots. It's on the right on the way *down* the canyon. But we're going *up*. The 'little trail' is on our left. It's gotta be up *there* somewhere." She pointed up to the left.

"Oh, man—you've got to be kidding me. That's ridiculous. How did we miss that?" Kristi felt crushed that they had duped themselves with such a rookie mistake (akin to holding the map upside down).

Megan quickly found a sandy ledge on their left that cut back and forth up the canyon wall like a wheelchair ramp. They followed it up and over the cliff, where they continued up the wash until the footprints petered out into sandy hillsides textured by miniature ravines and water drainages. Two hours later, well after five P.M., they arrived at the main dirt road where Kristi's bike was locked to a pine tree. Kristi lost the rock-paper-scissors toss to see who would ride the bike back to get her truck at the Granary Spring Trailhead. On the ride, Kristi searched the plateau for my red mountain bike. Had she known where to look, she would have seen it still leaning against a juniper tree a hundred yards off the left side of the road when she was about halfway back to the trailhead. By the time she mounted her bike on the roof rack of her 4Runner at the Granary Spring Trailhead and drove back to pick Megan up, Kristi had decided that they'd taken so long in the canyon that I must have come around to meet them already, and they'd missed the rendezvous.

Pulling over to the side of the dirt access road in front of her friend, Kristi rolled down her window and joked, "Hey there, you need a lift?"

Resting in the seats, the women filled their water bottles and drank up, rehydrating after the tiring hike up the West Fork. Megan asked Kristi, "Should we go back to the Granary Spring Trailhead and wait for Aron?"

"I think he made it out before us, actually."

Megan didn't believe it. "No way, he had like ten miles left to hike. There's no way he already got out and came to look for us."

"But I looked for his bike, and I didn't see it. There aren't that many places to hide a bike out there. I think he's gone. He probably went to Goblin Valley to get to the party."

Megan figured Kristi had missed seeing my bike and that I would be around in another hour or two. "Should we go back just to see if he shows up?"

Kristi was concerned about her fuel situation, knowing it would be twenty-five miles to the nearest gas station. She hesitated. "If we drive around much more, we won't make it to Hanksville. We've got maybe thirty miles left—we should really go and get gas and just meet him at Goblin Valley before it gets dark."

Not feeling strongly about it one way or the other, Megan acquiesced, and the friends drove to Hanksville for gas and a hamburger and milk shake at a greasy spoon called Stan's.

An hour later, around the same time that Brad and Leah were roving the desert back roads at Goblin Valley, Kristi and Megan turned off the highway into the state park, looking for the same party. A large sign indicated that the campground was full. Kristi stopped the vehicle to consider their next move.

"Should we go to the campground and try to find the party?" Megan asked.

"I don't know." Kristi laughed at herself, then explained, "It's funny, this whole day has been so indecisive. 'Should we wait or should we go get gas? Should we go this way or that?' "

"It'll be fun, but I'm tired."

"Me, too." Then Kristi reconsidered. "But it'll be fun."

Megan said, "You know what's going to happen? We go in there, and everybody'll be drinking, and then we'll drink. And then it will be dark, and the campground is full, and we'll be drunk and have to go drive around the desert looking for a place to camp."

Figuring they would find me over at the Little Wild Horse Canyon the next morning, Kristi and Megan turned around and drove down the highway on the way to Little Wild Horse until the pavement ended. They pulled off on a spur road, where they camped out that night. Sunday morning, they took their time getting ready and then drove the short commute, parking next to a Toyota Tacoma at the parking area for Little Wild Horse. Kristi noticed the vehicle first.

"Hey, do you remember what kind of truck Aron has?"

"Uh-uh. I don't think he told us," Megan said, still feeling tired from the previous day's effort in Blue John.

Kristi said, "That Toyota looks like it could be his. It's got skis and a bike. And it's got Colorado license plates. I bet that's his truck."

"He's probably already in the canyon," suggested Megan.

Kristi agreed. "Yeah, it's already eleven-thirty. He probably went in."

"We should put a note on his windshield with our e-mails, in case we don't see him in the slot."

"But what if it's not his truck?"

Megan was used to exchanging e-mail addresses with people, to arrange future trips and invite them to visit Moab. She was surprised she hadn't done that with me the day before. "Well, if it's his, he'll have our e-mails, and if it's not, they'll just throw it away."

"It's an out-and-back canyon, though. If he's in there, then we'll see him on his way out."

"OK, then. Should we have lunch before we go and see if Aron shows up here?"

"Hmm, I'm not really hungry yet." Kristi was ready for some hiking and exploring.

While they were walking, Megan continued speculating about whether they would see me at Little Wild Horse. "Do you think he came and went already?"

Kristi pondered the question for a few seconds. "I guess he either got up really early and went through it already, or he's so completely hungover that he decided not to go hiking today at all."

"Why didn't we get his phone number?"

"We were just going to see each other again."

"Yeah, but that's weird. I'd usually have exchanged numbers or e-mails or something, and we didn't. He was really nice. That was so cool that we met him in the canyon, and he hiked with us and didn't just blow by us."

The pair enjoyed themselves through the morning, exploring the narrow slot of Little Wild Horse. In the end, they doubled back on their entry path, coming out the same slot to the parking area. After packing Kristi's white 4Runner with the remnants of a weekend of off-road adventuring, they drove back through Green River to Moab on Sunday afternoon. Megan wondered what had happened to me, but neither thought about something out of the ordinary. There were too many rational explanations. They didn't worry about whether they would see me again; they talked about how much fun they'd had over the weekend and about how refreshing it was to get away from work for a change. They agreed it was too bad that they had to go back to the Outward Bound warehouse the next day to prepare supplies for another set of upcoming trips. They were hardly ready to trade their carefree desert explorations for their indoor offices, but they decided they would go out again soon, and with that promise, the shock of returning to civilization lost some of its sting.

*   *   *

After helping me get my truck unstuck from the ice and mud on Thursday afternoon, my friends Brad and Leah Yule left the Mount Sopris area near Carbondale, Colorado, and drove the scenic highway over forested McClure Pass on their way to the southwest part of the state. It was well after dark when they pulled off Highway 550 into the scenic mining town of Silverton, where they slept in the back of Brad's truck right on Main Street. Leah was already four months pregnant so the next day, she caught a ride with her mom and went shopping in Durango while Brad skied Silverton Mountain with some of his colleagues from Aspen's Incline Ski Shop. Brad and his coworkers had saved up their tips for the entire season to pay for a trip to the recently opened experts-only ski mountain; lift tickets were over a hundred dollars each, but that included a guide and a unique in-bounds backcountry experience that powder junkies lust after. That evening, Brad and his friends stayed in a Silverton hotel room to sleep off the aftereffects of a local brewer's festival that had included topless sledding at the base of the ski area. After a late start the next morning, Brad went down to Durango and met Leah. They drove the Devil's Highway, Route 666, into the Utah desert. Late Saturday afternoon, Leah monitored their cell phone as they drove north on Highway 95 across the upper arm of Lake Powell, waiting for me to call and finalize our rendezvous plans for Goblin Valley that evening.

By seven P.M., they were heading into the San Rafael Swell, traveling west off of Highway 24. Leah watched the signal indicator bars on the cell phone's screen disappear as they drove along the flat stretches of pavement. They got a usable signal only when the vehicle crested small bumps in the terrain.

"Why don't we call him?" Leah inquired.

"He doesn't have a cell phone. He said he would call to get directions."

"You know what? Before we get so far out here that we lose the reception entirely, we should check the messages. Go back to that bump where it was higher. I got four bars there." Brad made a U-turn to swing back into range. The homemade wood camper shell rocked the vehicle slightly to the passenger side as Brad pulled the turn tight on the two-lane highway.

"OK, stop right here, on this little hill." Leah checked the three messages on the phone, but none of them was from me. "That's weird that he didn't call. Did he say for sure he was going to come?"

Brad answered, "Well, he never really said so. I told him about the party, and that we would be there, and that there were going to be people from Aspen there that he knew. He sounded interested, and he said he was going to call and get directions."

"Maybe he decided not to. Should we wait here to see if he calls?"

"He didn't have much of a clear plan before he left—he just wanted to go climbing and hiking and get the heck out of Dodge. You know, off-season stuff. I didn't ask him to sign in blood that he was going to come. I think we should get going so we can find that billboard." One of Brad's friends had promised to leave more specific directions stuck to a billboard at the entrance to the state park, to cover for any last-minute changes.

Within five minutes of departing the hump in the road, the truck's left rear tire went flat. Brad discovered that the spare was dangerously low as well. Moving at a sluggish 5 mph, the couple continued on toward Goblin Valley State Park. Brad retrieved the directions, the main navigation being to turn left at the Scooby-Doo stuffed animal stuck in a juniper tree. The evening sun hammered straight into Brad's eyes, turning the dust-frosted windshield into a glass curtain. They missed the turnoff for the party and drove around for an hour as the sun went down and the desert sank into darkness.

Exhausted from a full day in the truck, they quickly lost interest in cruising the back roads of the state park at 5 mph, so Brad pulled over in a finger canyon off a spur road, found a flat parking spot, and they retired into the camper for the night. It was not a big loss to them to have missed the party—they were an easygoing couple out on a road trip for whatever fun they found, and there'd be plenty more parties through the off-season. With daylight aiding them on Sunday morning, Brad and Leah puttered around until they found the aftermath of the party—friends lying about the desert as if a plane had crashed into a nearby ravine. One friend revived enough to take them on the hour-long drive into Green River to repair the tires. They returned in the early afternoon.

Assuming that I had either found the party or come up with something more interesting to do, Brad and Leah were unalarmed that they didn't see me in Utah. With only two days back in Aspen before their honeymoon trip to the Bahamas, they had pressing preparations on their minds, though they figured they would see me at the Spruce Street party on Monday night.

Monday was hectic at my house. My roommates were getting ready for our first party of the off-season, a big blowout to rejoice in the transition of seasons and of roommates. With the four Aspen ski areas closed, the season was officially over. After working with me at the Ute all winter, Leona Sondie was leaving for Boulder, where she planned to work as a landscape gardener for the summer. Elliott Larson was moving in to join his mountain-bike–racing teammate Joe Wheadon, rounding out the foursome with Brian Payne and me. Brian was back in town after a two-month absence—his January ski accident had forced him to move in with his parents in Ohio for recovery and rehab—and I would be back from my vacation. It would be a rare occasion that we'd all be together. That it was a workday night was inconsequential to the scale of the party; few of the attendees would have serious responsibilities the next day, off-season bringing with it a respite from significant duties on the job. Party planning included getting a keg, stocking up on grilling supplies, stringing decorative lights around the house, inviting fifty people to come over, and rolling up the living-room-wall garage door to add some extra party space to our thousand-square-foot home.

Typical of older buildings in the Smuggler Mine area of Aspen, 560 Spruce had gone through several renovations throughout its 115-year life. Consequently, the house had a funky character, including a roll-up garage door installed in the west wall of the living room. The Smuggler Mine Company had built the house as an assay office where assessors weighed silver ores and measured their purity. In 1894, when the largest silver nugget in the world was extracted from the mine, it most likely passed through 560 Spruce, though no one at the time was much excited by the find, since the silver crash of 1893 had dropped the bottom out of the silver market. As it sat on the assessor's scales, the largest nugget in the world held little more value than a decorative rock.

In the postwar era of Aspen's history, 560 Spruce was reincarnated as a fly-tying shop that added the roll-up garage door to the west wall of the first floor and remodeled the assay office into a one-bedroom apartment. Later renovations and additions divided the two-story barn-style building into two apartments, one studio unit upstairs and a four-bedroom place downstairs. In the lower unit, the kitchen surrounded an afterthought of a bathroom, with two entrances into the shower, one from directly behind the kitchen sink. The garage/shop space became the living room, with the remnant roll-up door still in place. With a deck installed outside the garage door where the driveway had been, the warm weather of spring and summer brought the opportunity to roll up the wall of the living room and enjoy the sun and breeze in the house, or push one of the house's beat-up couches onto the deck for an outdoor nap.

Friends started showing up on Monday evening, including Brad and Leah and Rachel Polver, and before the sun had set in a dazzling light show over Mount Sopris, the food from the grill-your-own potluck was gone. Rachel thought it was odd that I hadn't shown up for a grubfest, given my seldom satisfied appetite, but Leona reassured her that I'd be back from Utah in time for the main party. As more friends and acquaintances gathered and the party rocked on into the night, music blared out the open wall, and my roommates shouted over the stereo regarding my nonappearance.

A cupful of beer in his hand, Elliott raised the question: "Hey Bri-guy, have you seen Aron yet? I thought he had to work tomorrow."

"He's probably still out on his trip. I haven't seen him since Wednesday. Does he know about the party?" Brian asked Leona.

Leona repeated what she'd told Rachel earlier. "Yeah, when he left, he said he'd be back here for it. I told him I was leaving on Tuesday, and it'd probably be our last chance to hang out, and he said he'd be here. It's my going-away party. He better not miss it. I'll be pissed."

"What time is it? If he's real late coming back, he's probably gonna be ready to walk in and crash." Elliott was concerned that - they'd have to tone down the party if I came home wanting to go to bed. "He's gonna have a hard time getting to sleep with the party raging. Maybe he figured that and stopped to sleep someplace."

"That'd be better than having to kick everybody out. It looks like this could go on a while."

Brian was right—it did go on a while. Though he went to bed shortly before midnight, by the time Joe and Leona ushered the last partiers out to catch buses and walk home, it was well after two A.M.

However, come eight-fifteen Tuesday morning, I hadn't shown up at the Ute Mountaineer for work. My manager, Brion After, called the house at Spruce. Leona had just woken up and was stumbling around in her room, groggy-eyed and hungover.

"Hey, Leona, it's Brion. Is Aron there?" Brion sounded more hopeful than curious, and slightly anxious.

"What? No. Isn't he there?" Leona was instantly awake with worry.

"No, he hasn't come in or called. I was thinking he might be sleeping off his vacation. Is his truck there?" Leona roamed around the house with the cordless phone in her hand, peeking out through the kitchen window to see if my truck was in one of the parking spaces in front of the wood-slat fence. Knowing my habit of stuffing a vacation to the chockablocks, she thought I might have driven through the night and rolled straight to work that morning. She checked my room for any indication that I'd been there and left, but there was nothing. Something wasn't right.

"Did he pull a Leona? Maybe he forgot his shift changed."

Brion and Leona chuckled at her self-effacing joke. She had gained a reputation after she'd missed a shift she was supposed to cover, and then compounded the goof-up a week later when she came in to work and wasn't even on the schedule.

"It's possible, but he said 'See you Tuesday' on his way out the door. He knew today was his project day."

"He must still be on his way home from Utah, then," Leona said. "Maybe he'll be there in an hour or so."

"Maybe. I'm gonna go, but I'll check back. When do you leave?"

"In an hour, once I get the car packed."

"OK, call me if you see him."

"I will. Bye." Leona hung up and paced around with a heavy heart. She started packing her aunt Leslie's Subaru with her belongings, readying for the drive down to Boulder, but the more full the car got, the more worried she became.

Aware that I had never been over fifteen minutes late in the past, Brion was also starting to get concerned. He went down to the sales floor around eight-thirty A.M. to talk the matter over with another employee and climber, Sam Upton. "Have you seen Aron come in yet?"

Sam looked up from organizing the trail-running shoes in the display room. "Uh, no—he's supposed to be redoing the camping wall this morning, right?"

Ignoring Sam's question, Brion pressed. "He hasn't called or anything?"

Sam sensed the tension in his voice. "No. Is something wrong?"

"I don't know. I just talked with Leona, and he wasn't home. She said it didn't look like he'd been there at all. It's eight-thirty now. The only time Aron's ever been more than a few minutes late was when he had that epic up on Pearl Pass." Remembering the time a month earlier when I had spent the night bivouacking in a hand-dug snow pit at 12,000 feet, Brion had confidence that I would show up unless I was in serious trouble.

Understanding the implications, Sam asked, "Do you think he's had an accident?"

"Aw, I don't know. The only thing I know for sure is he's not ditching work. It's possible something bad might have happened."

"He could be lost or hurt. But I doubt he's lost—he's always wearing his compass and altimeter watch, and he's good with it," Sam said.

"No, I know. Even if he were fifty miles out in the middle of nowhere, he could cover that in a day. It's not a panic situation. I mean, he's strong enough that if something happened, he'd get himself out. Anything short of a broken leg wouldn't even slow him down. And if he broke his leg, he'd crawl back. It'd take him awhile, but he'd get out. We have to give him twenty-four hours," Brian concluded, and Sam agreed.

Leona called in to the Ute once an hour, speaking with Brion and Paul Perley, the general manager. She recounted the last time she'd seen me, on Wednesday night almost a week before. "He had his boxes of climbing equipment out and his biking stuff. He said he was going to do some climbing, some canyoneering, and maybe some mountain biking. He was packing like 'Oh, I should take this just in case I go biking,' and 'Oh, I should take this in case I want to do some climbing.' He usually would have it all figured out ahead of time, but this time I don't think he knew where he was going. He said he was going to Utah, to the Canyonlands area. The question is, did he make it to the desert?"

As the afternoon slipped away, Brion reiterated his decision with Paul. "We have to give him until nine o'clock tomorrow morning.

Any mountaineer would want the chance to get himself out of trouble before the helicopters start flying. If he isn't here at the start of his shift tomorrow, I'll call his parents and get the ball rolling."

Tuesday evening around six-thirty P.M., right after their shifts, my roommates Brian and Joe were sitting in the living room at Spruce Street, relaxing with the garage door rolled up, testing the quality of the beer left in the keg.

"Hey, what's the story with Aron?" Joe inquired.

"He's still gone," Brian replied. "I think Leona called the Ute this morning. He didn't go in to work."

"What do you think we should do, call the cops or something?" Joe wasn't sure that was the right thing to do, but it struck a chord with Brian.

"You know, we probably should," he said after thinking about it for a long moment. He pulled the phone book out from under the coffee table at his feet and leafed through the pages for the number of the Aspen police department. He dialed the nonemergency number and spoke with the dispatcher after the first ring. "A friend of ours was due back from a trip last night, and he hasn't come home, and it's been a day. I just wanted to let you know we think he's missing. It's pretty low-key—we're worried about him, but we're not freaking out. What can we do about it?"

"We can file a missing person's report. You said it's been twenty-four hours?"

"Yeah, he was supposed to come back from Utah yesterday, and he missed work today."

"What's his name?"

Brian provided my name, age, approximate height, weight, and description to the dispatcher, who typed the data into the police computer system.

"Do you have his license-plate information?"

"Uh, yeah, hold on, I think I can get it for you." Brian went in my room and found an old climbing itinerary from when I had soloed the Bells two months earlier. It listed my license number—NM 846-MMY—and the year and model of my truck.

"Where do you think he went? You said Utah?"

"I know he was heading out to ski Mount Sopris on Thursday, but he was all packed up for a trip. I think he said he was going to the Moab area in Utah."

"Anything more specific than that, or just the Moab area?"

"That's it. He usually leaves itineraries, but he didn't leave one this time."

"All right. That's a start." They hung up.

What the dispatcher didn't tell Brian was that I hadn't been missing long enough for the police to do anything yet.

ELEVEN

Day Five: Trance Sanctuary

The real test of any choice is, "Would I make the same choice again?"
No one can see beyond a choice they don't understand.
—THE ORACLE, *The Matrix Revolutions*

BEATIFIC IVORY FACES SMILE AT ME. They are half protruding from red womblike walls, surreally pale and bald, like contenders in a Patrick Stewart look-alike contest who have been doused in flour. The walls seem to form a scarlet tube of organic tissue, a fibroid tunnel pulsing in waves that could be an eight-foot-tall empty blood vessel, except that I'm inside it. In my dreamy vision, I reach out, brushing the tissue's sponginess with my fingers. It responds to my touch with welcoming caresses. As though I've triggered a release, I sense I have begun moving along the tube, passed along by the wave motion. Stringy pulp drapes cling to my face and arms with the invisible softness of a wildflower petal as I float through the veiled twists and turns of the passage. Passing the saintly faces one at a time, I am vaguely aware of their blurred animations, like adoring mimes calling out to me, but I can't hear their voices. An uncertain familiarity compels me to look more closely at the faces, but I can't pause long enough in the tube, and they continue to drift past me before I can place any particular one. I can't quite tell their sex, either, but they seem to be about my age or maybe a little older. In any case, I feel comfortable here, like the faces are my friends—or, more exactly, like the faces are the faces of my friends—but I can't tell.

The forward movement continues for some time, relaxingly passing me along the placenta-like corridor. I feel like I'm enjoying a gentle crowd surfing, but I'm worried, too. What's happening? What is this stuff around me? Where am I? Is this a dream? Where's the canyon? My surroundings seem to respond by supporting me more firmly, and then the tube slopes up in front of me. Until this point, my journey has been strictly horizontal. I couldn't feel the pull of gravity before, but now it's like I'm riding the uphill portion of one very bizarre roller coaster. There are no more faces, just the lining of the walls slipping by in monotonous progression minute after untold minute. How high have I gone? Several hundred feet, I imagine. The grip of the fleshy waves on my body becomes subtler, with the exception of slight vibrations that add to the roller-coaster sensation, tugging at my legs, waist, torso, and back.

Intensifying, the vibrations shake me more and more, distressing me. Now I want to find out what's at the end of this incline. I get the feeling there will be some kind of gateway. I want to see it, perhaps pass through it, but I somehow know I will shake free of the delicate wall lining before I make it to the end. Vibrations cause me to have tumultuous spasms. I won't make it to find out what comes after the incline. I peel free of the lining, seizures ripping me away from the vanishing walls of the vessel. Without their support, I somersault backward in suspended slow motion, shuddering violently, as though I am about to detonate. Blackness eradicates the tunnel, and the dream-state quaking resolves into real shivers, my body trying to free itself from the tenebrous clutches of the canyon night.

It's Tuesday night, just after sunset, and my sleep-deprived mind is fabricating delusional flight from my entrapment, if not for my body, at least for my spirit.

Distracted by fatigue and the relative warmth of the day, I haven't yet redonned my Lycra shorts, but the evening's oncoming chill signals another nine hours of weary battle. I had removed the shorts prior to my surgical attempt this morning. Thinking I might succeed, I was planning to use their padded liner as an absorbent bandage on my stump, but of course I hadn't needed it. For never having been formally trained in backcountry medicine, I'm proud to have covered so many medical needs with my improvisations. I'm almost disappointed that I won't get a chance to test their efficacy, but I have resolved not to make another attempt at amputating my arm. I've proved to myself it's infeasible to cut through the bones. Bound by my own disintegrating capacities, I know any further efforts to cut off my arm will be certain suicide.

Death by dehydration is turning out to be even more psychologically grueling than I was anticipating on Saturday. Waterlessness stalks me, the indomitable leviathan of the desert drawing in closer every hour. Enforced insomnia compounds my body's anguish, loosing a fourth-dimensional aberration in my head. I no longer exist in a normal space-time continuum. Minute by minute, my sleep deprivation dismantles yet another brain function. Considering my deteriorated state, seeing Wednesday morning will be another accomplishment altogether. I've outlasted my first predictions that I wouldn't live to see Tuesday evening. Maybe I'll outlast myself again.

Just hang on. That's all you can do.

I decide to put my Lycra shorts back on under my thin tan nylon shorts. The act engages me for nearly ten minutes. I unclip my harness from the supporting rope system, unthread the waist belt from its double-back safety ring, and drop the harness around my legs to my feet. Removing my shorts, I marvel for a moment at the scrawny appearance of my pasty legs in the light of my headlamp. I've lost a lot of weight, maybe twenty pounds or more, and I was no chub when I walked into this canyon. I've got a long way to go till I use up all that body mass, but the sad part is, most of it will become fodder for the insects and scavengers of this desert environment. I haul up my biking shorts, catching my shoes on the stretchy fabric as I poke each leg through its hole. The tan shorts slide back on easily, followed by the twisted mess of the harness. Getting my legs through the appropriate loops takes three attempts before I get all the tangles worked out. Weaving the belt through the slotted ring is simple enough with one hand, but reversing the webbing to complete the double-back cinch is more difficult, and after five minutes, I leave it unfinished, as it was before.

Blackness inters me in the canyon. Another night of hypothermia's depredations awaits me. I'm fitful and restless as I resolutely cycle through a dozen repetitions of retightening the rope around my legs, often drifting away on another extraordinary trance fantasy in the ten-minute reprieves I earn between bouts of shivers. My spirit yearns for its freedom, and I leave myself a half-dozen times. Sometimes the voyages are psychedelic dream-trips, like the journey through the blood vessel, and other times I see myself from above on an out-of-body vacation where my soul can leave the canyon, like it did on Sunday afternoon when I flew over the Pacific Ocean and turned into a photon shower in the vacuum of space.

Still other experiences begin with seeing my friends, whole-bodied yet transparent, ghosts who temporarily inhabit the canyon with me until we leave together to go to a familiar setting. They never communicate with words, only with gestures, and by somehow transmitting emotions across nonverbal wavelengths; if they want me to feel safe and reassured, then that's what I feel. If they wanted me to be frightened, then I would feel fear, but I don't—I am totally comfortable in the trances. Regardless of the location or the company in these visionary experiences, there is always a mute voice that reminds me when I need to resume taking care of myself. I inevitably delay my return until my body is convulsing from hypothermic shivers, but I always know when it is time.

In real space, confined between the chockstone and the canyon wall, I intermittently pour off the top layer of my urine from the CamelBak into the Nalgene bottle, leaving the unsavory sediment to dump in the sand behind my feet. I repeat this activity more often than needed, just to break the tedium. Oh, what I would give for a crushed-ice strawberry daiquiri, a margarita, a malted milk shake, a tall glass of grapefruit juice, a cold bottle of Budweiser. Every thought is preceded and followed by a thought about a beverage of some kind—drinks that my memory produces in vivid projection when I close my eyes, floating in a spot two feet in front of me and about six inches above eye level. It's peculiar that no matter what the drink, it always appears to me in a form from my past, and in the same elevated space, within reach but not there. I'm not sure if letting my imagination entertain itself sustains me or makes me thirst more for the drink. It's the same debate I've held with myself about the last of my food, the last of my water, drinking my urine, all the most important choices of my entrapment: "Is this good for me, or will it make things worse?" I have been careful to deliberate over every choice. But here I remain.

Confusion, delirium, and ruthless cold compete for equal time through the night, warping even small segments of time into compounding infinities of struggle against the cruelty of the elements. The same horseshoe-shaped constellations that I first noted on Sunday night center themselves over Blue John Canyon, their march across the sky following my sight line of the heavens between the blinders of the walls. I wonder who else is up there on the desert plateau, looking at the same celestial ceiling, and if they, too, are noticing the stars' rotations. I don't get far with the thought. In fact, my thoughts rarely finish themselves. My mind sputters as though it has run out of fuel, getting only two or three words into a question or a resolution before it drifts into silence or another pressing input. I - can't keep my focus.

My brain has put itself out to pasture. It is unmotivated to accurately track time, either consciously, with my watch, or by the subconscious instincts on which I usually can rely. Typically, my mind has a very precise ability to assess time. For example, earlier during my entrapment, if I looked at my watch, then thought about my sister's wedding, fidgeted with my headlamp, and tucked in the webbing around my right biceps, I had an intuition that it had been about two minutes. Whatever I did, I had a sense of the appropriate duration, and that estimated time correlated closely with the real progress of my watch.

But presently, that correlation is gone. With fatigue causing so many clipped thoughts, things seem to take longer than they actually do. I'm having a difficult time understanding why only two minutes have passed, according to my watch, when it feels like ten. Another bout of paranoia strikes me, and I clutch tight the idea that my watch was damaged in the chockstone accident and is no longer truthfully telling the time. Maybe it's closer to dawn than I had figured; maybe - it's even a day further along. (Or maybe I'm completely unhinged.) It takes me awhile to deduce that my Suunto is functioning just fine—how else could it predict the coming of dawn, the daily appearance of the raven and the sun dagger, and the fall of night so accurately? OK, OK, so it really is only one-thirty A.M.

I have a half hour till my next sip of urine. At least the piss is chilled now; I'm glad for that. But I'm even happier for the beverage memories that mesmerize me from time to time, complete with life-like projections.

I close my eyes, and I am an eight-year-old sitting on the back porch of my grandparents' house in the central Ohio countryside, playing gin rummy with my grandpa Ralston. We beat the heat with a 7-UP, poured from a refrigerated two-liter bottle into a white Styrofoam cup with five cylindrical ice cubes, the carbonation tickling my nose as I lift the cup for a sip. Just as I can taste the clear sweetness, the memory changes to a vision, and there in front of me is the Styrofoam cup in a halo of light, glowing like the Holy Grail, atomized fizz popping up over the cup lip in the backlighting. I shiver and open my eyes, and though the inside of my rope bag is perfectly dark, the vision blinks out.

Again I shut my eyes, and it is a late-summer afternoon in 1987.

Deep in a childhood memory, I am taking a break from baling hay with family friends on a rolling green hillside field in eastern Ohio. The view to the north is open and lush; a pocket of uncleared forest cuts the southern horizon two hundred yards away. We are sitting on the rear of the baling trailer's bed, taking turns chugging ice-cold sun tea thick with sugar from a red and white thermos. When the jug comes to me, I raise it up, and condensation drips onto my cheeks from the lid. I pause to wipe the humidity away from my eyes, then I shudder and lose the vision before I can gulp down any of the syrupy tea.

A serial succession of visions takes me around the world and traverses most of my life. I take my first sip of beer from a pull-tab can of Budweiser on my family's back porch with my dad and uncle in 1985. I drink warm sake with my friends Jon, Erik, Moody, and Chrystie in our hotel room in downtown Nagoya, Japan, before a Phish show in June 2000. I sip on a double-length straw stuck in a Slurpee wedged in the triangular hole in the handlebars of my bike as I ride back from a 7-Eleven near my parents' house in suburban Denver, on a July afternoon in 1991, before I had my driver's license.

One beverage in particular surfaces repeatedly in my mind, its salted rim cloaking the sweet taste of a blended mixture of ice, tequila, triple sec, and lime. I imagine that I'm slobbering over myself, foaming at the mouth in lust for a margarita, but my tongue adheres to my cotton-dry palate. My breath rasps through my desiccated throat, and I wheeze then choke on my vocal cords, and I am reminded of a fact that the beverage memories have pushed aside: I am dying.

At three A.M. I apply more lip balm to my lips, hoping to seal in any last moisture they might have, and it occurs to me that I might likewise be successful in sealing my tongue. Painting the petroleum wand across my tongue makes me salivate, and I suck on the lip balm, curious about its caloric content. If it gets my body excited for food, maybe it will be worth a shot to eat some of it. I bite off a small hunk, about a tenth of the total stick, and mush it around in my mouth. It coats my teeth and my tongue, and minute amounts of saliva ooze through the layer of tasteless jelly. The resulting goo gobs up around my molars, and I decide not to swallow it. The fact that I am still producing saliva encourages me; I'm not yet into the most severe stages of dehydration. Aside from that inferred conclusion, I gain nothing from the effort. My hunger remains unabated.

Without physical activity to keep me busy, I spend cold hours recounting dozens of my favorite trips with family and friends. From Japan to Peru to Europe, from Alaska to Florida to Hawaii, from climbing mountains to seeing our favorite bands, I call up my fondest memories. I have fulfilled my purpose in life by exploring so much of the world, bringing myself happiness and inspiring others with my adventures. I have met my calling at every opportunity and lived an intense and dramatic life.

Still, I'm not ready to die. I drop into a series of trances. In one, an unidentified male friend appears in front of the chockstone wearing a heavenly white robe, and soundlessly beckons for me to follow him. We turn to the wall of the canyon, just to the left of the ledge where my rope anchor is set. I press on a panel of sandstone, and the wall hinges back on itself, swinging open to the right. We leave together, him first, walking through the door frame that has miraculously appeared, and we step from the sandy canyon bottom into a carpeted hallway in a house. My friend leads me into a living room that is full of more of my friends relaxing on couches and easy chairs. I feel an immediate surge of cheerfulness, as if I've arrived home after an extended journey. I still can't distinguish the friends, but they chat together like we're at a dinner party, the voices murmuring and swooshing in my ears at an indecipherable level.

I stand in the doorway, feeling at ease, but I cannot engage anyone. They exist on a different plane, and though we can see each other, I am different—somehow, they aren't real. My friends look up from their conversations as if to let me know they heard me think that and respond in unified thought, "We're here when you need us. When you are ready, then we will be real."

I'm affronted. "What's going on? What's happening to me here? Am I inside my head? Am I dreaming? How can that be, if I'm not sleeping? But how is this possible if it's not a dream?" I debate whether or not I'm sleeping. I'm pretty sure I don't lose consciousness or fall asleep during these episodes. My muscle control seems to stay intact, because otherwise my body would recoil from the violent pain of the weight on my right wrist. No, this mental retreat center is someplace more abstract than my everyday consciousness, but it's not exactly a dreamworld, either. Somehow, I am maintaining my body in the canyon while simultaneously departing it.

Most of all, I clamor for some verification of what is real, but before I can reach a decision, my mind forgoes the questions it has just asked. My senses are feeding me realistic information that this trance world does in fact exist. I can reach and touch the walls and furniture in this roomful of friends. I can smell the scented candles burning on the end table. I feel the breeze when someone opens the sliding glass door to the patio and walks outside. While much of the atmosphere presents itself convincingly, it is as though I am watching from the dark side of a one-way mirror. There is action, but I can't participate in it. I find I am no longer moving anything other than my head and arms; my legs have locked at the knees. And that business with the canyon wall opening up? That's just crazy.

Eventually, I come back into my body, predictably finding my core convulsing in cold spasms. I spend another hour fidgeting with my wrappings and the rope bag before I leave the canyon again, but this time I follow a friend whom I identify at first glance. It is my best friend from high school, Jon Heinrich, and I watch my spirit float up out of my cloaked back and head inside the rope bag. We walk through the hinged canyon panel as I've done twice already, and we enter a small, dark, tightly packed square room with barely enough space for the two of us to stand without bumping into each other. The room is pitch-black except for a line of bright light reflecting off the unpolished concrete floor. Jon has apparently misplaced the key that presumably would open the door. He flicks on a light switch, and thin metal shelves full of cleaning supplies appear on three sides of us, an industrial mop sink in the corner to my left. We're in a - janitor's closet. Somehow I know it is located in a hospital, as opposed to an office building or a school, and my hopes dart wildly.

Bang on the door, Aron! Get help! You need medical attention, and these people can get it for you.

But Jon won't let me rap on the hollow metal door, as if to tell me it won't do any good to cause a ruckus—the hospital and the canyon are a world apart. Minutes pass, I slowly understand that the help here are not the doctors and nurses on the other side of the door who will respond to my body's needs but my friend Jon, who reinforces my courage and bolsters my strength with grace, empathy, and gratitude. I realize how lucky I have been to know him, and my emotions rally around his presence. However, an unspoken voice breaks the - trance's spell: "It's time to say goodbye."

I don't want to go. Once again, more insistent now, reality nudges me: "It is time to say goodbye." I signal my need to Jon with a jerk of my thumb and nod in appreciation for his blessed visit. I am on the verge of tears, having to leave him, but I know better than to stay. My departure takes a strange effect, as though my consciousness is a ball of solidified energy that suddenly melts like a scoop of ice cream, pooling on the closet floor, then dripping from the vision world back into the space between the canyon walls. Gradually filling my body from the legs up, I reenter my cold-stiffened body.

The shivers begin, wracking my core with furious vengeance, and I wonder if the voice let me elope too long this time. There is always that noiseless voice. It stays in my real body, the watch-keeper that calls me back before I quiver over the invisible brink into hypothermic sleep. In the trances, I don't feel the cold, the pain, the hunger, the fatigue, the thirst. Whether the destination is a janitor's closet or a living room, and not some expansive vista of bucolic hills or the cloud thrones of angels, each experience is comforting, and I don't want it to end. Indeed, Jon's visit has given me a boost of courage and hope, and through my tremors, I say out loud, my voice echoing in the dark canyon, "I've got a few more days left in me." If I can keep going into the trance world and feel the presence of my mom, my dad, my sister, and my friends, then I may have found my strategy for surviving longer than even my latest prediction of Wednesday noon.

The trances give me hope, but I know, too, that each one will end with the same diving despair that accompanies my return to the canyon, where I feel the cold and thirst and all the other debasements of my entrapment. For the boost they provide, the trances only reinforce that I am not actually free. I may have passed ten minutes more of a heartless night by escaping into an out-of-body experience, but it is ten minutes that push me on toward my indelibly prescribed fate. Even if I last a few more days, it won't be long enough for rescuers to locate and save me.

In the piercing brutality of night, I repeatedly escape into trances, but they melt from my memory the moment I return to the canyon. If heaven turns out to be as comfortable as the trances, then what I return to in the canyon is nothing short of hell. Hell is conventionally portrayed as a crowded, infernally hot place—Milton's Pandemonium—ruled by a horned devil overseeing the torture of lost souls. I know better now. Hell is indeed a deep, chthonic hole, but hot? No. It is a bitterly dark and unbearably cold place of lonely solitude, an arctic prison without a warden and but one abandoned inmate, forsaken even by the supposed ringleader of the underworld. There is no other spiritual energy, good or evil, on which to project love or hatred. There is only one emotion in hell: unmitigated despair wrapped in abject loneliness.

Twilight eventually disperses the bleak spell of Blue John Canyon. A dozen mosquitoes and a mild but gritty downcanyon breeze usher in the morning, and after two hours of both ignoring and swatting at the nagging insects, I have daylight to console me. I am not so alone; the sun has arrived to join me for another journey. Glorious torrents of gold light splash on the walls thirty feet behind me, flushing the oppression from the canyon. For the first time in two days, I get out my digital still camera and take a picture of this flash flood of light. When I gaze downcanyon over my left shoulder at the heavenly array, the colors seem to radiate from the sandstone surfaces, not just reflect off of them. I cannot fathom that a more exalted display would accompany anything less than the Rapture. My eyes begin to water. Before I stow the camera, I set up and take a self-portrait, the glowing brilliance floating behind my head like an aura. With the light, the natural activities of desert life resume: The kangaroo rat sketches around in his nest, and more bugs revive to fly around my head.

Another part of my morning ritual is the daily update for the video camera. Just before nine o'clock, I dig the little unit out of my backpack. Why I don't leave it out, I'm not sure. Maybe it's one more way to keep myself busy, always unthreading and rethreading my right shoulder strap through its buckle.

I wonder if my parents are involved in any theoretical search. The only way I can be traced is for the authorities to obtain my debit- and credit-card purchase histories, which would lead them to Glenwood Springs, Moab, and then Green River. No, wait: I paid cash for those Gatorades in Green River. Damn. The investigators will really have to get lucky to find my truck. If all they know is that I was in Moab on Friday, with four days and a vehicle, I could be anywhere in the U.S. by now. When the waiting period is over and the police start actively looking for me, they'll have to first deduce that I'm not trying to evade them, ruling out the possibility that I've run off. Then they'll have to decide that I'm still in Utah, and get the National Park Service and local sheriffs to check out the most probable locations around Moab.

The really depressing news is that I'm in one of the most unlikely places in a five-county area. There are easily two dozen more popular areas closer to Moab that the NPS and sheriffs' offices will want to check before they would branch out to such a remote trailhead as Horseshoe Canyon. With limited resources, the NPS will follow the historical data of where people get lost most frequently and focus there first. Some three hours away from the town, Horseshoe will be one of the last places the NPS will check, possibly a full day into their initial involvement.

On the improbable shot that the NPS finds my truck, their next step will be to send out strike teams to sweep Horseshoe Canyon. If they encounter my truck anytime past early afternoon, it will be the following morning before they send out a team to clear the upper reaches of Blue John Canyon, fifteen miles farther down the road. Seven miles into the canyon, they would find me, but a hasty team - won't have anything close to the gear that they will need to free me from the boulder. I estimate an additional twenty-four-hour period from the time I am found until I could be freed and transported by helicopter. But at least they'd have water. Just a liter or two and I could go on another day easily. I bet they'd have more than that, as much as I can drink. Daydreams of clear fresh water distract me from thinking about the search.

Finally, I turn on my video camera. Before I start taping, I look at myself in the screen. I seem extraordinarily alert, considering my situation, and I am surprised to see that the redness is gone from my conjunctiva. Counterbalancing that small piece of good news are the hollows in my cheeks. From over my right shoulder, the light from downcanyon dances on the screen, a comely canary-yellow glow. Clearing my throat, I press the record button and begin speaking, immediately noticing that my voice has raised half an octave since yesterday, higher yet again as my vocal cords tighten due to the dehydration.

"Wednesday morning at nine o'clock. I'm curious how the sleuthing is going for everybody out there. Hopefully, somebody figured out how to pull the credit-card report and figure out where I've been, like to Grand Junction and Moab and from there." I involuntarily dart my eyes back and forth, up and down, then stare blankly down to my left foot. Tilting my head, I speculate, "Maybe the NPS ranger at Horseshoe made a report about my truck being there, I - don't know," and conclude with a shrug.

I remember that a couple of items back in Aspen will need to be sent to other people, so I give a few more directions for my parents.

"Anyhow, the bike in my room in Aspen belongs to John Currier, who lives just a few houses up the street from Erik Zsemlye. All these addresses and names you should be able to find on my PalmPilot, which is in the glove compartment of my truck. Also, the sleeping bag that's in my cubby at work belongs to Bill Geist, he's paid for it, so maybe you can get it to him, part of the Denali thing."

Last on my mind for this go-round with the tape are a few of my favorite memories. "I'm thinking about 7-UP in a Styrofoam cup," I explain, and take a long blink to conjure up the image one more time. I let out a tiny moan, then move on with another drink memory. "Five-Alive at Grandma Anderson's house. Some of my favorite beverages going down on the list now. I'm thinking through it."

I am gasping for breath between sentences and decide that I've had enough stimulation for now. Once I have shut down the video camcorder and stowed it on the chockstone shelf, I update my hour tallies in my head: 96 hours of sleep deprivation, 90 hours that I've been trapped, 29 hours that I've been sipping my urine, and 25 hours since I finished off the last of my fresh water.

While I am running the numbers, the raven flies over my head. I seethe with envy for the bird's freedom.

On a lighter note, I count up that it's been four days since I used toothpaste or a toothbrush. What I wouldn't give to break that sabbatical. With a week passed since I last shaved, my whiskers are a quarter inch long. Rubbing my hand around my chin and neck, I wonder how long my beard will be by the time I'm found—it'll keep growing for a day or two after I die—maybe a half inch or more?

* * *

Time has lost its meaning. Counting up the hours and days is now simply record-keeping. The exercise evokes no emotional response, only a matter-of-fact acknowledgment: "Oh, OK, so that's how long I've been here." By midmorning, I am not checking my watch anymore. I don't want to see how quickly the day is passing, because I know what will come tonight, and I'm hardly looking forward to it. It seems best that I ignore time. I can't speed it up or slow it down; I can only absorb the surreal impressions that swirl in my head, delayed imprints of the walls, telltale trails of the mental claustrophobia that comes with such a long time without sleep, constricting my thinking and shutting down my rational processes one by one.

Suddenly, I have a new idea—what about using a rock as a wrecking ball to smash into the chockstone and potentially remove more of the sandstone from above my hand? Or maybe this is an old idea. Have I thought of this already? I can't remember. It is brute force compared to the tactical precision with which I could peck at the boulder with my multi-tool, and that lends a positive angle to the theory. At least it's something different.

I extract a melon-sized rock from the pile at my feet. While supporting my body with my left arm pressing against the escarpment of the canyon wall, I use my legs to roll the bowling ball up onto the ledge at my knees. Once I realize its awkward mass, I'm hesitant. If I lose control of the stone, it will fall directly into my lap or even onto my foot. At twenty-plus pounds, it's unreasonably large for the job, but I make an attempt, first hoisting it onto my left shoulder and then heaving it forward onto the chockstone in a pulverizing explosion of grit and chalky sandstone. Sure enough, the rock bounces off the chockstone and lurches with the push of gravity for my feet. I jerk my legs out of the way, and it falls back into the pile. The smart thing is probably to leave it there. The stone's impact did little to demolish the chockstone; the majority of the dust raised by the collision came from the rock I threw, not from the boulder. I need a rock of harder composition than the chockstone. I hunt around and discard from contention each of the remaining rocks near my shoes. This is the obstacle that halted my brainstorming efforts three days ago.

Sometimes when I am climbing, I get stuck at a difficult section because I keep trying the same move the same way and, not surprisingly, keep failing. At that point, I often realize I'm not seeing all my options—I seized upon an obvious choice without taking in the full spectrum of possibilities. Looking around, I might see a foothold that allows me to position my body higher, or a handhold that was previously out of my field of vision.

What am I missing here? What have I ignored because it wasn't obvious? Arching my head back until I'm upside down, I can see several palm-sized stones lodged over my head in the debris compacted around the large chockstone behind me. There, slate black with a slight reddish tint, an egg-shaped stone stands out from the others; it doesn't seem to be sandstone but a mineralized layer. Though it may not be harder than the chockstone, it's more likely to be of similar hardness, and there's the chance it will be the break I need. Reaching up above my head into the kangaroo rat's chockstone nest, I pull out the rock. Another stone falls and almost hits me on the head, glancing off my shoulder.

Damn falling rocks. There should be a sign.

The black rock in my hand is the weight of a shot put. It's perfect. I can lift it without straining myself, and smash it into the boulder without letting go of it. Why it took me so long to turn around and look in the nest for such an opportunity, I can only attribute to the lethargic numbness that diverts and confounds me. Still, taking new action is an accomplishment in itself.

My left hand quickly bruises from absorbing the recoil of each blow of my handheld hammer. After dozens of hits, I have to stop. The damage to my left hand is too great.

Calculating that the diminishing likelihood of my survival has reached its bottom limit, I pick up my video camera to tape my last requests. I begin speaking, my voice taut; I can hear the exhaustion plaguing my efforts to remain coherent.

"It's two P.M. on Wednesday afternoon. It's getting close to four days since I dropped in this hole. Some logistics still to talk about. Cremation is probably a good idea, considering what will probably be low-quality remains after this is over. If it's still appropriate to have pallbearers, I'd like for my friends Jon Heinrich, Erik Johnson, Erik Zsemlye, Brandon Rigo, Chip Stone, Norm Ruth to be pallbearers, and Mark Van Eeckhout as well." I have named most of my closest friends, more than will be necessary to carry me to my final resting place, but I want to include as many as I can.

While I'm considering whether I have anything else to say, the tape runs out. I rewind it and then start it playing from the beginning. The images enthrall me, and I enter a rapturous state, like a child watching *Sesame Street*. I have a miniature television in my hands! I entertain myself for an entire hour with the tape that I've made. The subject matter is rather dismal, but I enjoy watching the moving pictures of myself, though for some reason my mind critiques my messages to my family, correcting and editing as though I'm going to do a second take. What an inane concept. I image directing myself: "OK, that was good, Aron, but this time say it with *feeling.*" Ridiculous.

I stop the unit and then rewind it a second time so I can record again, taping over my footage from Mount Sopris with a more urgent message about dividing my remains to be scattered at some of my favorite and special places across the United States.

"I was talking about a ceremony and a cremation, and I'd like to do ashes spreadings among destinations that have been dear or special places. I know that, um, I'd like if it's possible for my family to have some. And then for—I haven't got this figured out yet—I'd like for some of it to go with Erik back to California and maybe even take it to the coast, Big Sur, where we had that great trip where we went down to Santa Barbara and that was excellent. Some of it can go maybe with Jon to the East Coast, and if there's places out there, maybe at Mount Greylock in the vicinity where we almost hit that porcupine, just to spread me around out there. Sonja, if you take a little bit of me to Havasupai, if you ever go there again, that would be really special. Mark, for you to take some of me and do a little spreading ceremony at the top of Sandia Peak, that would be cool.

"So, um, last requests, I guess, oh, that . . . Actually, Chip and Norm, maybe you could take some of me with Erik and take it down to the Rio Grande in the Bosque, in the river, flowing. That covers kind of the oceans and rivers and forests and hilltops.

"I haven't mentioned Dan and Julia, they've been really special to me. And if Dan and you and Mark and Jason and Allison and Steve Patchett and the guys from search and rescue, on a powder day, maybe there's a little left of me to spread around at Pajarito or Wolf Creek."

Realizing I haven't spoken of my all-time favorite concert experiences, I push past my labored and shallow breathing to say, "I don't think I could let it go without mentioning Japan 2000 and Bonnaroo and Horning's, some of the best times I've ever had with my friends seeing music. There's so many that are up there, too. New Year's with Phish at Big Cypress, New Year's with String Cheese in Portland—night of the space cowboy. Thanks for all those."

Wrapping up once more, I feel somewhat more upbeat about my longevity, but I know I'm on my last legs. Looking straight into the lens, I bid one last adieu: "I'm holding on, but it's really slowing down, the time is going really slow. So again, love to everyone. Bring love and peace and happiness and beautiful lives into the world in my honor. It would bestow the greatest meaning for me. Thank you. I love you."

A rack of light clouds moves in through the afternoon, muting the normal ten-degree rise in temperature in the canyon. My watch indicates that the day's high temperature so far has been 57 degrees. The clouds spread out across the Robbers Roost plateau and then disappear as evening comes around. With the lowest high temperature of the past five days coming today, tonight promises to be the coldest and most difficult night. My strength is diminished, and my body's resources are utterly depleted. Even in the early evening, I can't keep from shivering. I cut off a strand of my anchor webbing from behind the knot and wrap it loosely a half-dozen times around my neck, just to add some fabric to cover the exposed skin. Maybe that will keep me half a degree warmer, I figure.

I want to keep smashing at the chockstone with my hammer rock, but I can't bear the suffering it imposes on my left hand. It's like punching a brick wall again and again. I have an idea to use my left sock around the rock as a pad between it and my hand. Each smashing impact still damages my left hand, but I am making tremendous progress compared to hacking with my ineffective knife. With the series of attacks I've made over the course of the afternoon, I have removed more material from the boulder than in the first four days put together. The debris is plentiful enough that I've laid the black camera sack I was using as a long sleeve for my left arm over the bandage on my right arm to protect my knife wound from the pulverized grit. Just after six P.M., I take a break to relax my aching left hand and pull out the digital camera again. I take a picture of my right forearm covered with the debris of my effort—an inch-thick layer of sand and rock chips. Putting the camera down, I brush off the rubble, trying to keep the day-old stab wound clear of dirt. A rushing sense of hopelessness overtakes me. Even at this accelerated rate, I can't possibly obliterate the chockstone to the point where it will release my hand. Not before I die. And that's even assuming that I could keep up the demolition, which has already caused enough pain in my left hand that I think I might have broken my pinky and ring fingers, or perhaps a bone in my palm above their highest joints. I look forlornly at the hammer rock, wearing my gray SmartWool sock like a stocking cap, and decide to abandon the effort yet again.

Let it go, Aron. Leave the rock there. Why cause yourself any more pain when it's a futile endeavor to begin with?

I put my sock back on my foot and pull it as high as it will stretch on my calf, knowing I can't afford to lose any of its insulating effect during the coming night. Somewhere inside my mind, I know I - won't survive tonight in Blue John Canyon. It's not something I debate or internally discuss, but when I consider that I am going to die in a matter of hours, it rings true. Contrasting my burst of anger earlier during my entrapment, when I lashed out and hit the boulder with the palm of my hand, I accept this statement with a peaceful sense of acknowledgment that I am not in control of this situation. If my time is up, then it is up, and there's not a thing I can do to stave it off any longer. And if my time isn't up, then it's not, and there's nothing further I need to worry about. But I think the former is much more likely than the latter. I understand that this is the end, that I - won't survive the night, and the thought does not stir me, because I have stopped fighting for control. Letting go of my desire to dictate the outcome of my entrapment releases a disconnected feeling of lightheartedness that vaguely approximates bliss. I wonder if this is what rapture feels like, that mystical experience when each soul relinquishes its earthly embodiment and connects with the divine. It's not the same as when I have my out-of-body trances, and it's not apathy or resignation, it's more like I've let go of a spiritual burden. I feel like I've recognized a great truth: Some other marvelous force is in control, and has been all along. Give it whatever name I want, all I know for sure is that I don't have to sweat it out anymore, because I'm not in charge.

Clammy supernatural breezes suck the heat from my body, and my shivering escalates intensely. The canyon is an ice box. Each night has been progressively harder, but these are the killing winds.

Counting from dusk till dawn, I get through only two of the painfully frigid nine hours before I decide it is time to make a final annotation. My watch confirms that it is April 30, for another hour, at least. I had lost interest in time during the afternoon, but now every minute seems important, as any one of them could be my last. I re-etch my name in the sandstone wall over my left shoulder, tracing over the letters I carved with my knife on Saturday after I wrote "Geologic Time Includes Now." Above the four capitalized letters of my first name, "ARON," I scratch into the red rock, "OCT 75." Below my name, I make the complementary scratching "APR 03." It doesn't occur to me to write "May," as I am certain I won't see the dawn at the far end of this hideously cold night. I finish the epitaph by carving "RIP" above my name and birth month, then I lean back in my harness and set the knife on top of the chockstone before I slip off into a trance.

Color bursts in my mind, and then I walk through the canyon wall on my own this time, stepping into a living room. A blond three-year-old boy in a red polo shirt comes running across a sunlit hardwood floor in what I somehow know is my future home. By the same intuitive perception, I know the boy is my own. I bend to scoop him into my left arm, using my handless right arm to balance him, and we laugh together as I swing him up to my shoulder. This interaction is a powerful departure from the previous trances; in the others, I was spellbound and restrained from engaging other people. But now I am actively participating in the action. I'm mobile and free.

The boy happily perches on my right shoulder, holding my arms in his little hands while I steady him with my left hand and right stump. Smiling, I prance about the room, tiptoeing in and out of the sun dapples on the oak floor, and he giggles gleefully as we twirl together. Then, with a shock, the vision blinks out. I'm back in the canyon, echoes of his joyful sounds resonating in my mind, creating a subconscious reassurance that somehow I will survive this entrapment. Despite having already come to accept that I will die where I stand before help arrives, now I believe I will live.

That belief, that boy, changes everything for me.

TWELVE

Firestorm

Knowing is not enough; we must apply. Willing is not enough; we must do.

—JOHANN WOLFGANG VON GOETHE

BY NINE A.M. on Wednesday, April 30, my twenty-four hours were up. Brion After walked across the sales floor at the Ute Mountaineer, brooding: "Where the hell is he?" He paced among the racks of skiwear, snowshoes, and camping supplies, his concern mounting. My shift had started at nine o'clock, and for the second day in a row, I hadn't shown up or called. At nine-fifteen A.M., Brion looked at his watch and decided he had waited long enough. He went upstairs to the office. First he called the house on Spruce Street to check if I'd come home yet, but no one answered. Brion knew what he needed to do next, but he was interrupted by Leona's phone call from Boulder.

"Did he come in?" Leona's directness barely disguised her fear. Despite her effort to keep herself collected, her voice wavered. She was taking an emotional brunt from my disappearance, and it had worn on her through her first night back in the Front Range.

"No, he's not here. He was supposed to start twenty minutes ago, at nine." Brion's anxiety over my whereabouts was straining his voice. "He's so diligent, I know something's really going on."

Leona was also certain something was wrong. "This has gone on long enough. We need to get his parents involved."

"I was just thinking about that. There's an outside chance that he called them to tell them what's going on. Would you mind calling them? I need to get the shop ready to open here in the next half hour."

It was more than Brion's sense of duty to the Ute that motivated him to ask for Leona's assistance. Neither he nor Leona wanted to be the person to tell my mother and father that their son had gone missing and was most likely in a lot of trouble. Leona found a way to avoid the messenger's job. "I don't have their number. But you do, Brion."

"I do? Where?"

"In his paperwork. I bet you he put his parents as his emergency contact on his application. Do you have his file?"

"Oh. Yeah, just a second . . . it's in my drawer . . . here." Brion pulled my manila employment folder from his file drawer and flipped the cover open. There, on top of the thin stack, was my employment application, with my parents' names and phone number, as Leona had predicted.

At nine-thirty A.M., Brion called my parents' house in Denver. My dad was in New York, leading a group on the fourth day of their tour of the city. My mom was just back from an errand to the post office and was sitting in her upstairs office, in the room I'd used as my bedroom until I went to college and my parents converted it for my - mom's management consulting business. She answered the home line with a smiling greeting: "Hello, this is Donna."

"Donna, hi. This is Brion After calling from the Ute Mountaineer in Aspen. I'm Aron's manager."

"Oh, yes, good morning, Brion. How are you?" My mom had met Brion the week before on her trip to Aspen to visit me.

"I'm fine, thanks," Brion replied. Knowing that he was about to unload a tremendous bomb on my mom, he hesitated, then let the words drop. "I was calling to find out if you know where Aron is." After pausing, Brion continued, "He hasn't come in for work in two days. He hasn't called, and no one has seen him in almost a week."

Brion's words left my mom shell-shocked. She sat in her swivel chair silently absorbing the significance of what he had told her. It was finally that horrendous day she had hoped would never come.

Brion knew that the hushed phone line meant she hadn't heard from me, but he had no idea if she was going to start crying, get upset, or explode. It relieved him when she firmly asked, "You realize what this means?"

Brion said, "We think something has happened."

"Yes. The kinds of things he does are very dangerous, and he goes out by himself a lot. He wouldn't miss work without calling in if he could. Something terrible has happened. We have to find out where he is. What have you done? Have you talked with his roommates?"

Brion was impressed at my mom's response and instantly felt some of the psychological weight of responsibility lift from his mind. He had found the ally he needed to move forward with the search, and quickly brought my mom up to speed on the developing situation.

My mom thought it was odd that I hadn't told my roommates about my plans, but it didn't completely surprise her. She had coached me during my early seasons of winter climbing to always leave a note on my desk at Intel, or with one of my friends, so that someone would know where I was. At first I left notes on the dash of my vehicle at the snowed-in trailheads, but once I started visiting more and more remote areas, I realized I needed a better system. It could be weeks if not months before someone would happen upon my vehicle at a given trailhead, so I followed my mom's suggestions and made it a habit to tell at least one person about my plans. One winter climbing season, in 2000–2001, I had called my mom before and after each fourteener I attempted, but she didn't much like hearing the details of my hair-raising adventures, so I went back to leaving word with my friends.

Terrified about what might have befallen me, my mom struggled to concentrate on what they should be doing. Pushing aside the fear that gnawed in her gut, she was able to carry on with her discussion with Brion: "Have you talked with the police yet?"

"No, I haven't. I was going to do that next."

Never having been trained in search and rescue, my mom knew very little about missing person's reports. She was uncertain about what the police would need to get the search going, but she understood emphatically that was what needed to be done. Speaking almost more to herself than to Brion, my mom said, "Missing person's reports have to be filed in the jurisdiction where the person lives, I know that much, so it should be with the Aspen police. I'm not really sure what the process is, whether the county sheriff needs to be involved, but they'll know what to do next. Will you go to them and file the report?"

Brion agreed. "I'll call them right now and call you back as soon as I'm done."

"Thank you, Brion. I have to go." My mom's world was caving in around her. She immediately phoned her longtime friend Michelle Kiel, who was coming over later that morning to discuss plans for the neighborhood garden club, and asked her to come right away and hurry. "Aron is missing," she stammered.

Minutes later, Michelle opened the front screen door to find my mom involuntarily rocking back and forth on a stool at the kitchen counter, clutching her heaving stomach and sobbing in grief-stricken terror. My mom's wail overwhelmed them both. They hugged for several minutes, crying together, and then my mom drew on her own courage and Michelle's comforting presence to gather herself and start talking through the options of who might know something about my plans.

For my mom, this was the most emotion-wrought hour of her life, all the unspeakable what-ifs floating through her mind one after the other, but still she managed to reason through the puzzle. "He's usually very good about telling someone where he's going. If he didn't say anything to his roommates, or leave a note there at the shop, I - don't know. Maybe he wrote an e-mail to somebody, telling them what he was going to do."

Michelle's face lit up. "We could check that. Does he have Internet e-mail, like Yahoo! or Hotmail or something?"

"I know he has a Hotmail address. Why?"

"Do you know his password?"

"No, I have no idea."

"We can go online and see what we can do." Michelle knew that at the least, they could try resetting my password, accessing my files, and seeing what my friends and I had written about most recently.

At the account log-in page, Michelle pointed out the link that suggested, "Forgot your password?" They encountered a screen requesting my e-mail address, home state, and zip code. My mom ran downstairs and pulled out her address book. Back at the computer, she and Michelle tried entering my Aspen zip code but were denied access.

Stumped for twenty minutes, my mom tried using the zip code for her house before she remembered that I'd set up my e-mail account when I was still living in New Mexico. Checking her address book again, she typed in my old Albuquerque zip code, and the site finally responded with the password reset page, asking, "High school?" My mom exclaimed, "Oh—I know the answer to that! Maybe this will work." However, because the site demands that the spelling match the preregistered answer perfectly, the two amateur hackers had to blindly come up with the exact combination of abbreviations I'd used. Time and again, the site replied in bold red type, "Please type the correct answer to your secret question." So close and yet so far. Michelle and my mom were guessing at variations on my high school's name when the phone rang.

Back at the Ute, events snowballed after the first conversation with my mom. Brion called Adam Crider with the Aspen Police Department just after ten A.M. and reported me missing. He explained that I had gone on a weekend trip and hadn't returned for a party on April 28, and that I'd subsequently missed two days of work without calling. Adam began filing the report, noting that Brion was "very concerned," and logged the statement into the department's Law Incident Table at 10:27 A.M. Adam asked Brion to keep compiling information on where I might have gone, and said that he would stop by the Ute in a few minutes to see what Brion had collected.

At 10:19 A.M., Brion called Elliott, who was alone at our house on Spruce Street, to have him look for anything that might indicate where I'd gone. Brion explained that he'd filed a missing person's report and needed some more specific information about where I had been headed that past weekend. Brion was especially keen on finding out anything related to my Alaska expedition. He told Elliott, "I need your help. Somebody said Aron was supposed to be meeting his Denali team for a training climb. Can you check around in his room for anything that says who they are?"

"Yeah, sure." Elliott wasn't in any rush with his cleaning, moving, and unpacking. He didn't have a job to go to, since he'd left his mechanic's position at a local bike shop. He walked into my bedroom, off the living area, and looked for paperwork. He found it in abundance, but the first thing that caught his eye was a stack on one of my shelves with travel itineraries and folded photocopies of maps. While the stack looked promising at first, Elliott quickly determined from the water wrinkles and worn-through folds that they were all from past trips, most of which he'd heard about from me during his frequent visits to the house.

Elliott rifled through a dozen files stashed randomly about my room, folder after folder full of personal correspondence, old bills, and tax returns. A half hour passed before he found an orange folder in the back of a satchel under my clothes rack that said "Denali '02" on the tab. Names and phone numbers appeared on old e-mail printouts, but Elliott dismissed calling any of my old teammates after he found the climbing permit application I had submitted in April 2002. Thinking, "Ahhh, the Park Service would have Aron's new team information," Elliott pulled his cell phone from the pocket of his worn-in pumpkin-colored Carhartts and dialed the number, which rang through to the Denali National Park and Preserve ranger station in Talkeetma, Alaska. Despite Elliott's best assurances that he was honestly trying to help his friend who was missing by getting in touch with the expedition teammates, the rangers at the climbing registry desk were set against giving out any names or phone numbers. (Policy disallows the distribution of private information to non-government parties.)

Elliott understood their position but wanted to leave the issue open so that he might call back with some higher authority. He thanked the rangers for considering his request and hung up, debating whether to have the Aspen police call the Talkeetma station. First, though, he wanted to check in with Brion. Time was slipping by, but in the hour since they'd spoken, Brion had hit pay dirt. "Don't worry about searching anymore. I found Aron's folder in his locker, where I should have looked in the first place. Anyway, I've got their information." On the printouts of e-mails to my teammates, he had found the addresses he needed. At twelve minutes before eleven, Brion had sent an e-mail to Team Green Chili Winds, alerting them to my absence and asking for information.

From: Brion After
Sent: Wednesday, April 30, 2003 10:48 A.M.
To: Janet Lightburn, Bill Geist, Jason Halladay, David Shaw
Subject: Looking for Aron Ralston

Hello,
I am Aron's manager at the Ute Mountaineer in Aspen Co., and surprisingly he has not arrived to work in the last 2 days. We are getting very concerned about his well being, and I am wondering if any of you would know where he may be, or can give me any information on his most recent trip. None of his friends/roommates are sure where he went, but we do think he went to Utah on April 24th or 25th. Possibly to meet some of you for Denali training. If you have any information on Aron, please Email me back at this address. Or you can call me at the Ute. We have contacted the Police, and his

family, as Aron is usually very diligent on arriving on time and
keeping in touch with us and his friends.

Best regards,
Brion After

At that point, although he had done some excellent sleuthing,
Brion was getting ready to leave for Australia for a few weeks' holiday
and was a little behind in wrapping up business at the shop. He
needed to pass the baton to someone who would be around, so he cir-
cuitously asked Elliott for backup: "What are you doing today?"

Sensing the loaded question, Elliott said, "Uhh, I was cleaning out Leona's room, getting ready to start moving my stuff in, unpacking, like that. You need me to do something else? I'm glad to
help."

"Well, yeah. I'm starting to get e-mails back, and I'm getting
swamped. I'm supposed to be leaving tomorrow for two weeks.
Would you be able to come in to the shop and make some calls and
watch for e-mails?"

"Sure thing. I was going to come in anyway and bug you some
more about giving me a job. I'll be there in ten minutes."

A few minutes before eleven-thirty A.M., Brion was on the phone calling my mom. His call interrupted my mom and Michelle's efforts to
crack my password protection. My mom was happy to hear back
about the progress Brion had made with the police and the e-mail to
my Denali teammates. She spoke with him about the additional data
the police needed while she continued to hack away. Brion asked if
my mom had my license-plate information. She went downstairs to
the drawer where she had tucked half a sheet of white paper on
which she'd written the make, model, year, and license number of my
pickup truck. She had asked me for the vehicle description when I
was home at Christmas in 2000, prior to a winter solo fourteener

climb, in case she needed it in an emergency. I had hastily told her the vehicle information from memory, so she unknowingly passed along to Brion an error I'd made.

As my mom finished confirming the truck description and license, she hit enter on the most recent attempt to guess the answer to my "secret question" and gave a gasp when the computer screen changed for the first time in a half hour. Michelle and my mom shouted in unison, "We got it! We got it!" and hugged each other.

"What's going on? What happened?" Brion asked when my mom came back on the line.

"We've been trying to get into Aron's e-mail for the past hour. We just figured out how to change his password. We're going to read his mail and see if there's anything about where he went."

Brion could hear the pick-me-up effect that the success had on my mom. "Are you into his account now?" he inquired.

Scanning through the most recent e-mails from my friends, my mom explained, "Yes, we're looking at his in box. If we don't find anything in his messages, would you be able to send a big e-mail to all his friends and find out what they know?"

"Sure, that's a great idea," Brion replied. My mom gave Brion the new password, and they agreed he would carry out the mass e-mailing while she and Michelle read through the two dozen e-mails I'd received since I had last checked my messages on Wednesday the week before. After hanging up, Brion immediately phoned Adam Crider over at the Aspen Police Department to relay the truck description and license number.

After my mom had transferred the password to Brion, Michelle had to leave to go home and pack for a trip with her husband. Alone again just before noon, my mom called my sister in Lubbock, who was working on her senior thesis for the Honors College at Texas Tech. Her voice raw from the crying and upheaval of the past two hours, my mom spoke softly: "Sonja, I just found out this morning that your brother is two days overdue for work. Do you have any idea where he was headed or what he was doing?"

Sonja was calm, but she didn't have much information on my recent travels, since we hadn't spoken in a couple of weeks. "I have no idea where he's at. I'm sorry, Mom. Are you OK? Do you want me to come home?"

"No, stay there and finish your paper. I'll let you know what happens. Try not to let it distract you."

Despite my mom's wishes, life would not go on without distraction for either her or my sister. Even though Elliott was at the helm of the e-mail search, passing leads along to the Aspen police, who were fully engaged once Brion phoned in my vehicle information, my mom could not go back to working without becoming fraught over what might have happened to me.

Minutes after twelve o'clock, Elliott arrived at the Ute, leaning his silver road bike against the bike rack in front of the store. Elliott rarely drove around town, as he could usually bike to the Aspen core in less time than he could drive and find a parking spot. After Elliott jogged the stairs up to the office, Brion handed him the '03 Denali folder and summarized his most recent activities. "Here's the file of people - he's going to Denali with. I've been getting replies from a few of them, and I've talked with one of them, Jason Halladay. His - number's on a piece of paper in the folder. Aron's mom's number is there, too. Also, this is his e-mail address and password. His mom wants us to send an e-mail to everyone in his address book." Brion was going full speed, and yet he was barely keeping his head together in the midst of the most hectic firestorm he'd ever experienced.

"Who's the contact at the police?" Elliott asked.

"Oh yeah. I've talked to them a couple times. Here's the number of the guy over there, uh, Adam."

"What have you told them?" Elliott was thorough and wanted to know everything that everyone involved knew.

Brion gave him a pass-down of the information he'd told Adam up to that time. Elliott sat down at Brion's cluttered desk and pondered what he was going to do next while Brion walked through the shop to check on the shorthanded staff.

Amid the stack of e-mail printouts Brion had made that morning and handed to Elliott was the response from Jason Halladay. Jason had replied fifteen minutes after Brion's initial e-mail, clarifying about our May 1–4 Denali training trip. At 11:03 A.M., he had written, "We have not heard from him since last week. The last e-mail I have from Aron here at work is from April 22 but he did not mention his upcoming plans." Jason was going back to his town house for lunch and had typed out, "I may have a more recent correspondence from him at home and I will check on that as soon as I get home." Just over a half hour later, Jason had sent in another message, with excerpts from the seminal e-mail I'd written to him in January, inviting him to join me for any of a slew of slot canyons, as well as the climbing expedition to Denali. Sitting at Brion's desk, Elliott read this e-mail:

From: Jason Halladay
Sent: Wednesday, April 30, 2003 11:40 A.M.
To: Brion After
Subject: RE: Looking for Aron Ralston

Brion,
Hello again. I checked my home e-mail and last I heard from Aron was April 23rd reporting on his trip on Quandary. He didn't mention plans for the upcoming weekends but earlier this year he mentioned the following canyons as trips he'd like to do in Utah:

Canyons:
Black Box of San Rafael;
Virgin River in Zion;

Cable/Seger canyons (San Rafael area);
And any other technical slots listed as "best of" in Kelsey's books
(do you have the San Rafael Swell book?—it's excellent).

You're right, he may just not have known about his work schedule and hopefully we see him tomorrow night in Georgetown but it would be out of character for him to forget his work schedule and not keep in touch with at least someone.

Thank you, again, for contacting us,
Jason

Brion came back in the office and discussed with Elliott whom to call next. Brion offered, "From what I know, Brad Yule was the last person who saw Aron. But I don't know how to get ahold of him."

Elliott exclaimed, "You gotta be kidding me. I've got his cell-phone number right here." Whipping his cell phone out of his pocket, Elliott looked up Brad's number and then called him on one of the office lines, catching him at the Denver airport, ready to board the connecting leg of his flight to Atlanta.

"Hey, Brad. I've got a question for you. Aron didn't show up for work yesterday or this morning, and we're really starting to worry about him. We're trying to get information to give the police so they can start a search. It seems like you were the last person to see him. Do you know where he went? What's the best information you have from him when you talked?"

Brad recalled the ski trip on Mount Sopris for Elliott, including the information that we'd gotten my truck stuck on the drive out, and that I'd departed for the desert but I hadn't been specific about my destination.

"We thought we were going to hear from him before the party Saturday, but he didn't call, and then we didn't really make it to the party, either."

"OK. Do you remember what he had in his truck?"

"He had his mountain bike and his skis on his roof rack, and he had his climbing stuff with him and his skiing stuff and camping gear."

"Was he going out for more skiing?"

"No, I'm pretty sure he was going to do some canyoneering."

"Oh, OK. The police want to know what his stuff looks like. Like his backpack and jacket."

"I don't remember, exactly, but hey, Elliott, I'm on the plane, and I have to go. I'll think about it and call you when I get to Charlotte."

On the plane, Brad got out his digital camera and reviewed the pictures from Mount Sopris, double-checking which backpack I'd had with me that day and which jacket I had been wearing, making some mental notes to share with Elliott when he landed in North Carolina.

Just before talking with my sister, at 11:43 A.M., my mom sent a message to the Denali team members from her account. Using the addresses from an e-mail she and Michelle had found in my in box, she requested any info they had, as Brion had already done. Jason Halladay called her from the Los Alamos National Lab, where he had returned to his job as a computer technician, to give her the same information he had sent to Brion. My mom went down to the basement and retrieved a road atlas, marking down the locations of Zion National Park and the San Rafael Swell on the map. Jason tried to help her as best he could, but he didn't know the exact locations of a few of the canyons. He needed his canyoneering guidebook, but that was back at home.

Elliott relayed my last known point and subsequent direction to Adam at the APD, who asked if there was a more specific location other than simply the Utah desert. Elliott pulled out the list of possible Utah destinations provided by Jason and read that to Adam. Crider recognized Zion National Park from the list and located the San Rafael Swell on a map of Utah. Although the lead was from an uncorroborated three-month-old e-mail, it was the only specific information collected up to that point in the investigation, and Adam followed through as best he could. Just before one P.M., he issued a teletype message to the Washington, Grand, and Emery county sheriffs' offices and followed up with phone calls to Grand County and Zion, to ensure that the national parks received the information.

Grand County is home to Canyonlands and Arches, two of the most popular national parks in the western United States. Because of the concentration of agencies managing public lands in Grand County, it's possible to cross three, four, or even a half-dozen boundaries on a single bike ride, four-wheel-drive outing, or day hike. To better coordinate incident response and provide a greater quality of service to the public, the Park Service, Forest Service, Utah State Parks, and Bureau of Land Management share a unified command and visitor information center in Moab. With Adam's action, nearly every public resource agency in the southeastern quadrant of Utah had my vehicle information. While none of them was actively searching yet—it would be too costly to track down every vehicle that might or might not be in the state—they were on the lookout and would call the Aspen police if they happened upon my truck.

Elliott began an intense process of notifying my friends across the U.S. that I was missing. From Brion's desk, Elliott monitored my Hotmail account, Brion's Ute account, Brion's EarthLink account, and his own Yahoo! account, scrolling through message after message from my disconcerted friends. By trading e-mails through the afternoon, Elliott collected a few leads but mostly just waded through replies that said, "I have no idea where Aron is, but I'm worried for him." Standing out from the other e-mails was one from my friend Dan Hadlich, which pointed Elliott to Mount Sopris and Mount of the Holy Cross in Colorado, but not to Utah.

From: Daniel Hadlich
Sent: Wednesday, April 30, 2003 12:27 P.M.
To: Brion After, Jason Halladay
Subject: RE: Looking for Aron Ralston

Brion and Jason,
I do not believe Aron was heading to Utah this past weekend.
I've enclosed the following information I received from Aron on
April 20th via e-mail:
>I'm headed out to skin up to Conundrum Hot Springs and climb
>Castleabra tomorrow. Maybe soak in the pools a little too! Then
>climbing the Cristo Couloir on Friday with Janet, skiing Sunday to
close
>down Ajax for the season, and starting all over next Wednesday
with a
>trip to ski Mt. Sopris, climb the Holy Cross Couloir on
Friday/Saturday,
>and who knows what else from there! Spring may be here, but I'm a
>long way from hiking anywhere when I can ski or climb snow!
>
>Cheers,
>Aron
That would mean that Aron would have been on Mt. Sopris on
Wed-Thurs (4/23–4/24) and the Holy Cross Couloir on Fri–Sat
(4/25–4/26). Has anyone searched those areas for his vehicle?
Please contact me ASAP if you hear from him. Also, let Julia and I
know if additional folks are needed to drive around and look for him
or his truck this weekend.

—Dan.

Although it counterindicated what I'd said to Brad, Dan had provided the only itinerary I'd left in writing, and Elliott knew he needed
to follow through on the Holy Cross lead with the Aspen police.
When they talked just after one P.M., Adam said he would call the police department in Minturn, the town nearest the access for Mount

of the Holy Cross, to have them check the Tigiwon Road for my vehicle.

"However," Adam informed Elliott, "the license information you gave me is invalid. We searched the computer records, and that New Mexico plate number 888-MMY doesn't exist. I put Eagle County on the lookout for a maroon 1998 Toyota Tacoma, but we need to get the correct plate."

Elliott said he'd call my mom and double-check the number.

Unable to eat lunch, my mom returned to her upstairs office, where she sat at her desk, organizing some papers while terrifying thoughts of my undoubtedly dire situation maddened her to the edge of a breakdown. Then she fought back. Nipping off another upwelling of helplessness, my mom threw down her papers and said aloud, "I have to do something to help Aron." For my mom, it was as though my life now depended on her actions. She was not going to sit tight and wait to hear back about how things were progressing. That just wasn't her style.

My mom twice tried calling my dad in New York to let him know what was happening and ask for his ideas on what to do, but he didn't have his cell phone turned on, and he was out of his hotel room, so my mom left messages for him to call her as soon as he got back that evening. On her own, with the info she'd received from Jason, my mom brainstormed a short list of groups to contact: the Aspen police, Brad Yule, the Utah Highway Patrol, and Zion National Park.

Before my mom could contact the first name on her list, her cell phone rang. It was Elliott, calling to notify her that my license information was incorrect. She pulled out the note she'd referenced previously and read the number to Elliott one digit at a time.

After the third digit, he interrupted her. "Wait, eight-eight-*six*, you said? OK, Brion had written down eight-eight-eight. The rest is 'M-M-Y'? I'll get this to the police."

Just over a half hour later, Elliott called my mom back. The Aspen police had told him that wasn't my license number, either—it belonged to a Chevy Blazer registered to an Albuquerque woman. Taking the initiative, Elliott had called the New Mexico Department of Motor Vehicles and tried to get them to search for my proper license number using the truck description and my name, but they weren't able to help him. Unfortunately, my mom didn't have any better information, so they hung up without any further plans for how to get my correct license information.

Minutes later, at three-forty-five P.M., the home line rang again. It was my dad calling from New York. My mom was now in the same position of delivering the terrible news as Brion had been that morning.

"I got a call from Aron's manager this morning. He missed work yesterday and today, and no one's seen him since last Friday. No one knows where he went."

Shocked for a moment, my dad instantly began pondering what might have happened to me. He was disturbed that I hadn't left word with anyone. Alarmed as he was, though, he knew they needed to address the immediate problem. There would be ample time later for emotions to play themselves out.

My mom told my dad what was going on. For each thing she told him she'd done, he asked a few questions to clarify whether there were any unchecked leads, but each time, they determined that she had done everything they could think of. Still, my dad wanted to come home immediately. "Do you think I should make arrangements?"

My mom replied, "No, it's a short tour, you'll be home in three days. By the time they get someone in there to take your place, it'll be Saturday night, and you're coming home Sunday. There's nothing else you could do here, anyway."

Comforting my mom as best he could from across the country, my dad knew she needed someone to be there with her, especially as things slowed down. "If I'm not coming home, then you have to promise me that you'll call the church and ask for someone to come and stay with you."

My mom resisted the idea of asking for help, saying, "I really don't think that's necessary." But my dad finally convinced her to call Hope United Methodist Church, our family's congregation in Greenwood Village, a southeast suburb of Denver. My mom agreed, then said - she'd contact the sheriffs' offices and the National Park Service.

Lastly, my dad advised, "If you haven't done it already, you need to write everything down so you can refer back to it when you make the follow-up calls."

"Yes, I've started making a phone log," my mom told him. From their combined experience working with bureaucracies, they knew the importance of keeping track of who said what, when, so the next time, when my mom called and someone different answered, she could still be effective.

By the end of the conversation, all the other possible explanations for my disappearance—that I might be out camping along a stream with some friends, or that I'd been irresponsible and not called to let anyone know I'd decided to extend my vacation—were exhausted. There was no Pollyanna rationalization, no easy dismissal that could explain my prolonged absence. With the alarm mounting to the level of a terrible ache in my dad's stomach, by the time he said "I love you" to my mom and hung up, he felt like he'd been shot in the gut.

Things weren't any easier on my mom, since ringing up the church turned out to be the most emotionally challenging call she made all day. As strong-willed as she is, she wasn't used to asking for help for herself. However, when a good friend, Ann Fort, called back a few minutes later, saying she would be over to the house by seven P.M., my mom was glad she'd made the request.

At 5:23 P.M., starting with the Aspen police, my mom began calling the names on her yellow legal tablet. She told the same story a half-dozen times in a series of twenty-minute conversations. She talked with law-enforcement representatives across Utah for two hours, beginning at five-forty-five P.M., speaking first with two state patrol dispatchers within the Department of Public Safety (DPS) and then with another two dispatchers from the Zion National Park police, submitting request after request for urgency in their assistance on my case. Each time before she hung up, she finished with the question, "Who else should I call?"

Via our network of climbing friends and search-and-rescue colleagues, Steve Patchett had received a forwarded copy of the e-mail I'd written to Jason designating the four Utah canyons I'd wanted to visit. As a rescue leader with the Albuquerque Mountain Rescue Council and one of my many mentors, Steve was acutely aware that time was of the essence in the developing situation. The first twenty-four hours of a search are often the most critical. From his house in Albuquerque, Steve called Mark Van Eeckhout in Los Alamos, and they spoke about the canyon list at 3:38 P.M. on Wednesday, trying to figure out where some of the more obscure canyons were located. Mark typed "Seger Canyon" into a search engine that found "Tom's Utah Canyoneering Guide." Clicking on the link, Mark read through a full guidebook-style description, complete with driving directions and topographic maps for the canyon. On the other end of the phone, Steve marked an "X" in central Wayne County on his Utah road atlas, following the driving directions that Mark read to him off the Web page. They found Cable Canyon adjacent to Segers Hole, at the southern end of the San Rafael Swell.

Steve then called the Ute Mountaineer, responding to Elliott's e-mail and volunteering his time. Steve and Elliott talked for almost twenty-five minutes, and Steve said he would contact the various authorities in Colorado and Utah. Elliott had received an e-mail from my climbing friend Wolfgang Stiller, and confirmed in a short phone conversation that we had canceled the Mount of the Holy Cross trip due to avalanche conditions. However, Wolfgang had acknowledged that it was possible I'd gone ahead with the attempt by myself. Elliott passed this along to Steve, who said he would call the Eagle County sheriff to close out on the Mount of the Holy Cross lead. He told Elliott his next efforts would focus on the Utah locations.

Between four-fifteen and five P.M., Steve called the Zion National Parks police and the Emery County sheriff's office (ECSO), headquartered in Castle Dale, Utah, to initiate searches at the trailheads for the Virgin River and the Black Box of the San Rafael, respectively. The Zion police indicated that they would check for my vehicle during their evening sweeps of the trailheads. Steve spoke with Captain Kyle Ekker of the ECSO at 5:19 P.M. in his Castle Dale office. Captain Ekker took the information from Steve and then had his ECSO dispatcher enter the missing person's report, including issuing an all-points bulletin for my truck. Additionally, Captain Ekker asked local search-and-rescue volunteers to drive out to various trailheads. By 6:07 P.M., deputies and SAR folks were en route to Swinging Bridge, Joe's Valley, and the Upper and Lower Black Boxes. By 6:51 P.M., all four field units had reported back to the ECSO dispatcher that they were searching the outlying trailheads of the San Rafael region for my vehicle. Volunteers Russell Jones and Randy Lake of the Emery County search-and-rescue team met in the area of the Lower Black Box and took all-terrain vehicles in to check the most inaccessible trailhead that normally can be reached only by mountain bike or on foot.

After filing reports with the other counties, Steve got through to my mom at 6:38 P.M. and let her know about the trailhead sweeps. Additionally, Steve was mobilizing a group from Albuquerque to go to Utah as early as the next day. My mom said she would keep in touch with DPS and a half-dozen contacts Steve provided, to keep tabs on the leads. As Steve read off his list of names and phone numbers, my mom recognized Emery County from the list she'd made after compiling the canyon information with Jason earlier in the afternoon. Once she got off the line with Steve, she was impatient to know if they'd found anything. When she called Emery County at 7:20 P.M., the dispatcher was in the process of receiving the calls from the field deputies and asked my mom to call back just a minute later. During the second conversation, my mom learned that the posse had "negative contact with the missing person or his vehicle."

My mom pressed the searchers to keep going after dark, but the dispatcher indicated that was unlikely, as most of the deputies were going off-shift. It seemed reasonable to the dispatcher to suggest, "Sometimes hikers get disoriented and become lost. A lot of times, they find their way back after a few days."

"This person clearly does not know my son," my mom thought, and she replied in a stern assertion, "He is not *lost*. Something has happened to him." But she acknowledged that the manpower situation was not going to permit these rural county sheriffs to dedicate all of their night-shift patrols to the hunt for my truck. She ended the conversation politely, then considered what to do next.

In the next ten minutes, she talked with Eric Ross of the Aspen police, who had taken over from Adam at the shift change. They decided he should go to my house in town and gather my credit-card numbers. My mom called and asked Elliott to help Eric, who was on his way to Spruce Street. Once the officer arrived, he and Elliott sat down in the living room and went over what had been going on at the Ute all afternoon. Elliott had left the shop when the doors closed at six P.M., bringing the files back to the house but suspending the e-mail routine until the morning, as we had no Internet connection at the house. Elliott took Eric into my room and showed him the files with my credit-card and bank statements. Eric made notes of the numbers while Elliott looked for my checkbook, which he found on my shelves. Voiding check number 1066, he tore it out and handed it to Eric. Eric told Elliott he would call the credit-card companies to track my purchases and then go to my bank when it opened in the morning to track my debit-card transactions.

Ready for bed after an emotionally and mentally exhausting day, Elliott wrote out a note that he affixed to my room door: "Aron, - you're missing. Everybody's looking for you. Knock on my bedroom door or call my cell phone the minute you see this note." Then he retired for the night.

*   *   *

My mom spoke again with my dad at nine P.M. to tell him about the search activities. This second conversation left my dad pacing in his hotel room, certain there was something keeping me from coming back. He knew I hadn't simply taken off or gotten lost; the only things he could think had happened were that I'd fallen and broken my leg, or I was stuck under a rockslide on the side of a mountain. Praying to me, "Hang in there, Aron, stick with it," he fought back other, more distressing thoughts. My dad knew, or wanted to believe, that I was alive, but that meant I was injured. It hurt him to know I was suffering; however, that was better than the alternative. There was no way he was going to find enough peace to sleep—grief kept him up and moving—so he busied himself preparing notes for the rest of the New York tour, in case he did need to leave and hand over the reins to someone else.

Up in Boulder, my friend Leona was riding back with her aunt from a meditation session that hadn't helped ease her anxiety over my disappearance. She closed her eyes and felt a connection, something beckoning to her, and then a fuzzy vision appeared, like a dream. She saw a spirit that was clearly me, visible from the waist up. She recognized me but couldn't tell where I was. She could tell I was alive and mostly OK, but frightened. I was holding my arm tight to my chest, as if I had injured it, and I was standing in a tight, dark place, wearing a green shirt. She sensed that I was conscious of her presence and scared, not of her but of my surroundings. She saw her arms reach out to reassure me with a comforting touch, but she was petrified herself—she couldn't reach me. I had a decision to make. And it seemed I would have to make that decision on my own. Her empathy strengthened the vision's accompanying physical sensations: She felt cold chills, a parching thirst, and deep exhaustion. She came out of the trance and was spent, as if she had just run ten miles. Sitting in the passenger seat of her aunt's car, she realized they were home, but she couldn't remember any of the fifteen-minute trip since they'd left the group session. Leona followed her aunt into the house, drank three liters of water, and went to bed, praying with her hands clasped that she wouldn't dream about the vision. She knew she was power-less to help me, and she didn't want to have another dreadful episode when there was nothing she could do.

After talking with my sister at 10:20 P.M., my mom went to bed. She slept about an hour, then grew restless. After midnight, she lay in bed with her eyes open, thinking about me. At two A.M., having waited edgily for the shift change ever since she'd woken up, my mom called the Aspen police. She learned that the search was slowing down due to a lack of information from my credit-card use—apparently I - hadn't used any of my cards since Thursday, April 24, in Glenwood Springs, to buy gas. There was no indication that I'd gotten any far-ther than Eagle County. But the biggest sticking point was the license plate; none of the numbers had generated the correct vehicle descrip-tion when the police had done a records search. My mom knew that, but apparently Eric had tried again. What he said next gave her a pleasing lift: He had looked up the number for the New Mexico state police on their twenty-four-hour DMV assistance line, but without knowing the registration address, which obviously wasn't in Colorado, he couldn't perform the inquiry himself. My mom told Eric she would make the call and get the correct license-plate in-formation; she was excited and relieved to once again have something to do.

At two-forty-five A.M., she got through to an officer in Santa Fe who was able to manipulate the computer file systems and perform a rough search based on the vehicle make and the registered address, which my mom correctly deduced was my town home in Albu-querque. Within ten minutes, she had confirmed my license number was NM 846-MMY and relayed the information to Officer Ross. It was the best feeling she'd had since she successfully reset my e-mail password over sixteen hours earlier. As soon as the sheriffs' offices opened in the morning, she would start through her call list for the third time. Walking across the kitchen from her station at the phone, my mother sat down on the carpeted steps leading upstairs to where her friend Ann was sleeping in the guest bedroom, and for the next three hours, she held a solitary vigil, praying to me, "Hold on. We're coming, Aron, we're coming. Just hold on."

THIRTEEN

Day Six: Enlightenment and Euphoria

It's only after we've lost everything that we are free to do anything.
—BRAD PITT, *as Tyler Durden, in* Fight Club

PEEKING OUT from the inky confines of my rope bag, I watch dawn pushing its way into the canyon. The fresh daylight reduces the visions that dominated my night. However, my brain is so twisted around from 120 hours without sleep that the new day's reality feels like a hallucinatory fabrication itself. The ugly chockstone on my arm is hardly discernible from the imagery generated by my delirious mind. With five days of gritty build-up pasted to my contact lenses, my eyes hurt at every blink, and wavering fringes of cloud frame my dingy vision. I can't hold my head upright anymore; it lolls off against the northern canyon wall, or sometimes I shift and allow it to fall forward, where my left forearm braces it. I am a zombie. I am the undead.

It is Thursday, May 1. I cannot believe I'm still alive. I should have died days ago. I don't understand how I lived through last -night's hypothermic conditions. In fact, I'm almost disappointed that I've survived the night, because now the epitaph on the wall is incorrect—I didn't "rest in peace" in April, after all. For a short moment, I ponder whether to fix the date, but decide not to bother. It -won't matter to the body recovery team, if they even notice it, and the

coroner will be able to discern my death date from the extent of de-
composition within a day or so. That's good enough, I figure.

Where is the confidence I felt during the vision I had of the little
blond boy, my future son? Psychologically, I thought I had hit bottom the night before, when I carved my epitaph, only to then find as-
surance in picking up that toddler. But my buoyancy has been
enchained by the stoic might of the boulder and the bitterness of the
piss that etches ridges into the roof of my mouth. Drinking sip after
sip of urine from my grotesque stash in the Nalgene has eroded the
inside of my mouth, leaving my palate raw, reminding me that I am
going to die. The piss's acidity dissolves any remaining self-belief I
found in the middle of the night. If I am going to live, why am I
drinking my own urine? Isn't that the classic mark of a condemned
man? I have been sentenced and left to decay.

It's eight-thirty A.M., but the raven hasn't flown over me yet. I wonder
after it for a time but lose my thoughts to the insects that are swarm-
ing with all-time intensity around the chockstone. After I swat a few
of the flying bugs with my left hand, killing them to entertain myself,
I look at my yellow Suunto, which says 8:45. Even the bird has forsaken me—it has not been later than 8:30 for its daily flight, but
today, nothing, no raven. In its absence, I feel that my time draws
nearer, as though it was a totemic deity sustaining me.

A desire bubbles up: I want to die with music in my ears. Somewhere along the days, even that dreadful BBC song from *Austin Powers* lost its hold on my psyche. But I can't bring a single melody to
mind. All I have is the awful hush of the canyon; silence maddens me.
I need my CD player. The headphones haven't left my ears or neck in
five days, but the player and two CDs are in the main compartment of
my backpack. I sling my sack off my back with three easy movements
and rest it on my raised left knee, my fingers diving to the bottom,
where they find the Discman and discs . . . and a half inch of sand.

Before I extract the equipment, I know it's a hopeless cause. The discs are scratched beyond playability. Five days in the desert have left their plastic coatings looking like I took a belt sander to them. No matter. The Discman won't even spin the disc that's in it already. It tells me NO DISC each time I push play. I swap out the batteries, but only to be thorough. I must have bashed the unit against the wall at some point over the last five days and whacked the laser out of alignment.

The camcorder, however, has survived the sand and havoc in my pack. Giving up on the music, I decide to video another bit. It occurs to me that I've entered the time of highest probability that I will be rescued while I'm still alive. I put my backpack back on and resecure the shoulder strap for the fiftieth time. Resting the video unit on the chockstone, I get myself settled and try to collect my thoughts. When I first speak, the thinness and elevated pitch of my own voice startles me. Another reminder that I am nearly dead, just waiting for the Reaper.

"I was just thinking . . . It's Thursday at about nine o'clock in the morning. I'm entering the highest probability of time that will interface . . . that someone will actually find me, and that I'll still be alive."

"That's almost good news," I think. But considering that I've established the rescue window to start anytime today through Sunday, - it's not cause for hope of imminent help. My chances have upgraded from "ridiculously improbable" to perhaps "totally unlikely." I don't dwell on the issue. In fact, because my mind is confounded by a persistent and deepening daze, I couldn't dwell on something if I wanted to—I don't have the mental stamina. Somewhat randomly, I think about my sister and her wedding. She and Zack had asked me to play the piano for a few minutes during their upcoming ceremony in August, and I said I would. But obviously, I won't; I won't even be there. It disheartens me, but I realize there may be something I can do.

"Sonja . . . if you still want me to play at your wedding . . . there's a tape in a box in the basement of Mom and Dad's house. The box is labeled, I think, 'My Piano Stuff,' or 'My Music,' maybe. There's a tape in there. It's me, playing mostly music audition songs from about 1993 or 1994."

I immediately imagine her inserting the tape into a cassette deck, listening to the songs at our parents' home with my mom. I know it will be an ultimate effort for them to listen to the music I played so studiously ten years ago: Mozart and Bach, Beethoven and Chopin, my favorite. Another image jumps into my mind, this time from the wedding. I can't place the exact setting, but it is pastoral and out-doors. The same piano music wafts broodingly from a speaker sys-tem, churning into a menacing cloud that breaks to drench the assembly of our extended family in a downpour of tears. My death will cast blackness over Sonja's wedding, but I know she will carry on with it. There will be no question and no reason to postpone. Life moves on for the living.

I move on and scatter the images of my mother and sister in my mind, leaving a broken trail of thought to pick up again later. Realiz-ing there was one more thing I forgot to mention about my financial assets, I start to explain my wishes for my retirement planning ac-counts.

"Also, obviously, my Schwab IRA accounts can go to Sonja if - there's . . ."

I don't finish the sentence. Disjointed thoughts spasm, my mind is adrift. Where there was previously a concept I was attempting to express, I don't have even a memory. I float, expressionless, lost, then stumble upon another fleeting thought, but I can't connect with it fast enough to bring it to words. It sinks back under the surface of my mental ocean, then bobs up again. This time I seize it. It has to do with my cremation and the distribution of my ashes.

"Oh . . . um . . . clarifications . . . Knife Edge peak . . . For the part of me that goes back to New Mexico. The Bosque and Knife Edge—the Knife Edge being one of my favorite climbs ever. So maybe that would be what Dan and Willow and Steve DeRoma, Jon Jaecks, Eric Neimeyer, and Steve Patchett would go and do."

Clearing my throat once again, I press the silver record button on the back of the unit. I hope what I've said on the tape will serve both as an appropriate goodbye to my loved ones and as my last will and testament. I've covered what to do with my possessions and finances, and I've tidied up my estate, as much as I have one to tidy, hoping to benefit my sister. While I could have been more organized, I am drained from the effort involved in thinking through all this and have no wish to edit or redo any of the video. For what will be the last time, I fold the screen of the recorder flush against the camera body and tuck the unit into its notch between the left side of the chockstone and the canyon wall.

Miserable, I watch another empty hour pass by. At least I don't have to fight to stay warm. The cold bite of the outer atmosphere no longer sucks off my body heat as it did throughout the night. But by removing the need to reconfigure the ropes around my legs and the cloth and plastic wraps around my arms, daytime has removed the last bustle from my experience in the canyon. Without even that minimal distraction, I have nothing whatsoever to do. I have no life. Only in action does my life approximate anything more than existence. Without any other task or stimulus, I'm no longer living, no longer surviving. I'm just waiting.

Since the recoiling blows of the hammer rock tenderized my left hand, all I've had left to do is wait. For what, though? Rescue . . . or death? It doesn't matter to me. The two endings represent the same thing—salvation and deliverance from my suffering. I can't stand the inactivity that breeds such apathy. At this point, the waiting itself is the worst part of my entrapment. And when I'm done waiting, all there is, is more waiting. I can touch the face of infinity in these doldrums. Nothing gives even a slight hint that the stillness will break.

But I can make it break. I can ignore the pain in my left hand and resume smashing the chockstone with the handheld wrecking ball. I can continue hacking away at the rock with my knife, despite its inutility. I can do everything I've done in the past five days for the sake of motion. I reach for the rounded hammer rock, then realize I'm going to want my left sock for a pad. Off with the shoe, off with the sock, and I have the cushioning for my battered palm. The bruises on the meaty pad of my thumb are the most sensitive to the impact, and they scream for reprieve from the first blow through the fifth, when I pause. Adrenaline channels into anger, and I raise the hammer again, this time in retribution for what this wretched piece of geology has done to my left hand. Bonk! Again I strike the boulder, the pain in my hand flaring. Thwock! And again. Screeaatch! The rage blooms purple in my mind, amid a small mushroom cloud of pulverized grit and the burning smell of the sock that comes between the rock and the chockstone, melting with the friction heat of each strike. I bring the rock down again. Carrunch! With animalistic fury, I growl, "Unnngaaarrrrgh!" in response to the throbs pulsing in my left hand.

I force myself to stop, and can't release my grip on the hammer rock. My fingers have been paralyzed in their clench.

Whoa, Aron. You might have taken that too far.

Gradually, my shocked nerves relax, and my digits extend until I can let go of the rock, which I set on the chockstone. I've created a mess once again. I want to brush the collected dirt off my arm, away from the open wound. I take my knife and begin clearing particles from my trapped hand, using the dulled blade like a brush. Sweeping the grit off my thumb, I accidentally gouge myself and rip away a thin piece of decayed flesh. It peels back like a skin of boiled milk before I catch what is going on. I already knew my hand had to be decomposing. Without circulation, it has been dying since I became entrapped. Whenever I considered amputation, it had always been under the premise that the hand was dead and would have to be amputated once I was freed. But I hadn't known how fast the putrefaction had advanced since Saturday afternoon. Now I understand the increase in the interest of the indigenous insect population. They could already smell their next meal, their breeding ground, their - larvae's new home.

Out of curiosity, I poke my thumb with the knife blade twice. On the second prodding, the blade punctures the epidermis as if it is dipping into a stick of room-temperature butter, and releases a telltale hissing. Escaping gases are not good; the rot has advanced more quickly than I had guessed. Though the smell is faint to my desensitized nose, it is abjectly unpleasant, the stench of a far-off carcass.

On the heels of the odor, a realization hits my brain—whatever has started in my hand will shortly pass into my forearm, if it hasn't already. I don't know and furthermore don't care if it's gangrene or some other insidious attack, but I know it is poisoning my body. I lash out in fury, trying to yank my forearm straight out from the sandstone handcuff, never wanting more than I do now to simply rid myself of any connection to this decomposing appendage.

I don't want it.

It's not a part of me.

It's garbage.

Throw it away, Aron. Be rid of it.

I thrash myself forward and back, side to side, up and down, down and up. I scream out in pure hate, shrieking as I batter my body to and fro against the canyon walls, losing every bit of composure that I've struggled so intensely to maintain. Then I feel my arm bend unnaturally in the unbudging grip of the chockstone. An epiphany strikes me with the magnificent glory of a holy intervention and instantly brings my seizure to a halt:

If I torque my arm far enough, I can break my forearm bones.

Like bending a two-by-four held in a table vise, I can bow my entire goddamn arm until it snaps in two!

Holy Christ, Aron, that's it, that's it. THAT'S FUCKING IT!

I scramble to clear my stuff off the rock, trying to keep my head on straight. There is no hesitation. Under the power of this divine interaction, I barely realize what I'm about to do. I slip into some kind of autopilot; I'm not at the controls anymore. Within a minute, I orient my body in a crouch under the boulder, but I can't get low enough to bend my arm before I feel a tugging at my waist. I unclip my daisy chain from the anchor webbing and drop my weight as far down as I can, almost making my buttocks reach the stones on the canyon floor. I put my left hand under the boulder and push hard, harder, HARDER!, to exert a maximum downward force on my radius bone. As I slowly bend my arm down and to the left, a Pow! reverberates like a muted cap-gun shot up and down Blue John Canyon. I don't say a word, but I reach to feel my forearm. There is an abnormal lump on top of my wrist. I pull my body away from the chockstone and down again, simulating the position I was just in, and feel a gap between the serrated edges of my cleanly broken arm bone.

Without further pause and again in silence, I hump my body up over the chockstone, with a single clear purpose in my mind. Smearing my shoes against the canyon walls, I push with my legs and grab the back of the chockstone with my left hand, pulling with every bit of ferocity I can muster, hard, harder, HARDER!, and a second cap-gun shot ends my ulna's anticipation. Sweating and euphoric, I again touch my right arm two inches below my wrist, and pull my right shoulder away from the boulder. Both bones have splintered in the same place, the ulna perhaps a half inch closer to my elbow than my radius. Rotating my forearm like a shaft inside its housing, I have an axis of motion freshly independent of my wrist's servitude to the rock vise.

I am overcome with the excitement of having solved the riddle of my imprisonment. Hustling to deploy the shorter and sharper of my multi-tool's two blades, I skip the tourniquet procedure I have rehearsed and place the cutting tip between two blue veins. I push the knife into my wrist, watching my skin stretch inwardly, until the point pierces and sinks to its hilt. In a blaze of pain, I know the job is just starting. With a glance at my watch—it is 10:32 A.M.—I motivate myself: "OK, Aron, here we go. You're in it now."

I leave behind my prior declarations that severing my arm is nothing but a slow act of suicide and move forward on a cresting wave of emotion. Knowing the alternative is to wait for a progressively more certain but assuredly slow demise, I choose to meet the risk of death in action. As surreal as it looks for my arm to disappear into a glove of sandstone, it feels gloriously perfect to have figured out how to amputate it.

My first act is to sever, with a downward sawing motion, as much of the skin on the inside surface of my forearm as I can, without tearing any of the noodle-like veins so close to the skin. Once I've opened a large enough hole in my arm, about four inches below my wrist, I momentarily stow the knife, holding its handle in my teeth, and poke first my left forefinger and then my left thumb inside my arm and feel around. Sorting through the bizarre and unfamiliar textures, I make a mental map of my arm's inner features. I feel bundles of muscle fibers and, working my fingers behind them, find two pairs of cleanly fractured but jagged bone ends. Twisting my right forearm as if to turn my trapped palm down, I feel the proximal bone ends rotate freely around their fixed partners. It's a painful movement, but at the same time, it's a motion I haven't made since Saturday, and it excites me to know that soon I will be free of the rest of my crushed dead hand. It's just a matter of time.

Prodding and pinching, I can distinguish between the hard tendons and ligaments, and the soft, rubbery feel of the more pliable arteries. I should avoid cutting the arteries until the end if I can help it at all, I decide.

Withdrawing my bloody fingers to the edge of my incision point, I isolate a strand of muscle between the knife and my thumb, and using the blade like a paring knife, I slice through a pinky-finger-sized filament. I repeat the action a dozen times, slipping the knife through string after string of muscle without hesitation or sound.

Sort, pinch, rotate, slice.

Sort, pinch, rotate, slice.

Patterns; process.

Whatever blood-slimy mass I fit between the cutting edge and my left thumb falls victim to the rocking motion of the multi-tool, back and forth. I'm like a pipe cutter scoring through the outer circumference of a piece of soft tubing. As each muscle bundle yields to the metal, I probe for any of the pencil-thick arteries. When I find one, I tug it a little and remove it from the strand about to be severed. Finally, about a third of the way through the assorted soft tissues of my forearm, I cut a vein. I haven't put on my tourniquet yet, but I'm like a five-year-old unleashed on his Christmas presents—now that I've started, there's no putting the brakes on. The desire to keep cutting, to get myself free, is so powerful that I rationalize I haven't lost that much blood yet, only a few drops, because my crushed hand has been acting like an isolation valve on my circulation.

Another ten, fifteen, or maybe twenty minutes slip past me. I am engrossed in making the surgical work go as fast as possible. Stymied by the half-inch-wide yellowish tendon in the middle of my forearm, I stop the operation to don my improvised tourniquet. By this time, I've cut a second artery, and several ounces of blood, maybe a third of a cup, have dripped onto the canyon wall below my arm. Perhaps because I've removed most of the connecting tissues in the medial half of my forearm, and allowed the vessels to open up, the blood loss has accelerated in the last few minutes. The surgery is slowing down now that I've come to the stubbornly durable tendon, and I don't want to lose blood unnecessarily while I'm still trapped. I'll need every bit of it for the hike to my truck and the drive to Hanksville or Green River.

I still haven't decided which will be the fastest way to medical attention. The closest phone is at Hanksville, an hour's drive to the west, if I'm fast on the left-handed reach-across shifting. But I can't remember if there's a medical clinic there; all that comes to my mind is a gas station and a hamburger place. Green River is two hours of driving to the north, but there is a medical clinic. I'm hoping to find someone at the trailhead who will drive for me, but I think back to when I left there on Saturday—there were only two other vehicles in the three-acre lot. That was a weekend, this is midweek. I have to accept the risk that when I get to the trailhead, there won't be anyone there. I have to pace myself for a six-to-seven-hour effort before I get to definitive medical care.

Setting the knife down on the chockstone, I pick up the neoprene tubing of my CamelBak, which has been sitting off to the top left of the chockstone, unused, for the past two days. I cinch the black insulation tube in a double loop around my forearm, three inches below my elbow. Tying the black stretchy fabric into a doubled overhand knot with one end in my teeth, I tug the other end with my free left hand. Next, I quickly attach a carabiner into the tourniquet and twist it six times, as I did when I first experimented with the tourniquet an eon ago, on Tuesday, or was it Monday?

"Why didn't I figure out how to break my bones then?" I wonder. "Why did I have to suffer all this extra time?" God, I must be the dumbest guy to ever have his hand trapped by a boulder. It took me six days to figure out how I could cut off my arm. Self-disgust catches in my throat until I can clear my head.

Aron, that's all just distraction. It doesn't matter. Get back to work.

I clip the tightly wound carabiner to a second loop of webbing around my biceps to keep the neoprene from untwisting, and reach for my bloody knife again.

Continuing with the surgery, I clear out the last muscles surrounding the tendon and cut a third artery. I still haven't uttered even an "Ow!" I don't think to verbalize the pain; it's a part of this experience, no more important to the procedure than the color of my tourniquet.

I now have relatively open access to the tendon. Sawing aggressively with the blade, as before, I can't put a dent in the amazingly strong fiber. I pull at it with my fingers and realize it has the durability of a flat-wound cable; it's like a double-thick strip of fiber-reinforced box-packaging tape, creased over itself in quarter-inch folds. I can't cut it, so I decide to reconfigure my multi-tool for the pliers. Unfolding the blood-slippery implement, I shove the backside of the blade against my stomach to push the knife back into its storage slot and then expose the pliers. Using them to bite into the edge of the tendon, I squeeze and twist, tearing away a fragment. Yes, this will work just fine. I tackle the most brutish task.

Grip, squeeze, twist, tear.

Grip, squeeze, twist, tear.

Patterns; process.

"This is gonna make one hell of a story to tell my friends," I think. "They'll never believe how I had to cut off my arm. Hell, I can barely believe it, and I'm watching myself do it."

Little by little, I rip through the tendon until I totally sever the twine-like filament, then switch the tool back to the knife, using my teeth to extract the blade. It's 11:16 A.M.; I've been cutting for over forty minutes. With my fingers, I take an inventory of what I have left: two small clusters of muscle, another artery, and a quarter circumference of skin nearest the wall. There is also a pale white nerve strand, as thick as a swollen piece of angel-hair pasta. Getting through that is going to be unavoidably painful. I purposefully don't get anywhere close to the main nerve with my fingers; I think it's best not to know fully what I'm in for. The smaller elastic nerve branches are so sensitive that even nudging them sends Taser shocks up to my shoulder, momentarily stunning me. All these have to be severed. I put the knife's edge under the nerve and pluck it, like lifting a guitar string two inches off its frets, until it snaps, releasing a flood of pain. It recalibrates my personal scale of what it feels like to be hurt—it's as though I thrust my entire arm into a cauldron of magma.

Minutes later, I recover enough to continue. The last step is stretching the skin of my outer wrist tight and sawing the blade into the wall, as if I'm slicing a piece of gristle on a cutting board. As I approach that precise moment of liberation, the adrenaline surges through me, as though it is not blood coursing in my arteries but the raw potential of my future. I am drawing power from every memory of my life, and all the possibilities for the future that those memories represent.

It is 11:32 A.M., Thursday, May 1, 2003. For the second time in my life, I am being born. This time I am being delivered from the -

canyon's pink womb, where I have been incubating. This time I am a grown adult, and I understand the significance and power of this birth as none of us can when it happens the first time. The value of my family, my friends, and my passions well up a heaving rush of energy that is like the burst I get approaching a hard-earned summit, multiplied by ten thousand. Pulling tight the remaining connective tissues of my arm, I rock the knife against the wall, and the final thin strand of flesh tears loose; tensile force rips the skin apart more than the blade cuts it.

A crystalline moment shatters, and the world is a different place. Where there was confinement, now there is release. Recoiling from my sudden liberation, my left arm flings downcanyon, opening my shoulders to the south, and I fall back against the northern wall of the canyon, my mind surfing on euphoria. As I stare at the wall where not twelve hours ago I etched "RIP OCT 75 ARON APR 03," a voice shouts in my head:

I AM FREE!

This is the most intense feeling of my life. I fear I might explode from the exhilarating shock and ecstasy that paralyze my body for a long moment as I lean against the wall. No longer confined to the physical space that I occupied for nearly a week, I feel drugged and off balance but buoyed by my freedom. My head bobs to my right shoulder and dips to my chest before I right it and steady myself against the wall. I stumble as I catch my left foot around the rocks on the canyon floor, but I get my legs under me in time to prevent a hard fall onto the southern wall. It is beautiful to me that I could actually fall over right now. I glance at the bloody afterbirth smeared on the chockstone and the northern canyon wall. The spattering on the chockstone hides the dark mass of my amputated hand and wrist, but the white bone ends of my abandoned ulna and radius protrude visibly from the gory muddle. My glance lingers and becomes a stare. My head whirls, but I am fascinated, looking into the cross section of my forearm.

OK, that's enough. You've got things to do. The clock is running, Aron. Get out of here.

FOURTEEN

Homing In: "We Have His Truck"

You must believe it before you can imagine it.

—MARK TWIGHT, *signature inscription in my copy of* Kiss or Kill

F OR THREE HOURS, my mother sat in the dark on the aspen-white carpet of the upper stairway in our family's home in Denver. These were the same stairs I bounded up and down two at a time for six years in middle and high school, earning uncountable reprimands from my parents. She was unable to relax, worst-case-accident scenarios chasing one another through her mind. The intense anxiety in her stomach forced her to crunch her body into an upright fetal position, her knees tucked in the crooks of her crossed arms, her forehead resting on the bend of her left forearm.

She was waiting for land-management personnel to return to work in the morning. Like me, my mom is not very good at waiting. She prayed, but even after she had prayed dozens more times, she was restless and unsettled. Needing to do something, at about five-forty-five A.M., she got up from her vigil and started to wade through her list of federal and state agencies that administer the public lands in central and southern Utah. My mom called a half-dozen groups in those early hours of Thursday morning. First she phoned the Hanks-ville branch of the Bureau of Land Management (BLM) and left a message; then she called the St. George police and filed a report. Next she filed the missing person's information with the Department of Public Safety (DPS) dispatcher in Cedar City and, minutes later, with the DPS dispatcher out of Richfield. Her voice was exhausted and tattered with emotion when she spoke with Georgia, the Richfield dispatcher of DPS, at a quarter to seven. In explaining that I would not have much money and would therefore be camping out of my truck, my mom called me a cheapskate, but followed that by saying that I was very responsible and would not have failed to call in to work unless something disastrous had happened that kept me from reaching a phone.

Georgia sent a statewide "Attempt to Locate" notice over the radio at 6:52 A.M. with the information my mom had provided:

All cars, Richfield, attempt to locate missing person. He should be in the Utah, possibly the Parks areas.

All cars, Richfield, attempt to locate missing person out of Aspen, Colorado, traveling to Utah, for a backcountry trip. He was last seen April 24th, last Thursday, in Aspen. Advised he was going to go somewhere in Utah where it was warm to hike.

His vehicle is maroon '98 Toyota Tacoma, has New Mexico plate, Eight-Four-Six-Mike-Mike-Yankee, New Mexico Eight-Four-Six-Mike-Mike-Yankee, will have a topper and ski racks on top.

All call, continuing, subject is Aron Ralston, twenty-seven-year-old white male, six-foot-two, a hundred-and-sixty-five pounds, brown eyes, brown hair. He is alone, he is an experienced hiker, search and rescue, and mountain climber, also a skier. Very responsible person.

Subject failed to return to his work Tuesday as expected. He has not been heard from. He should have ski racks and ski equipment on his truck. He had advised a friend that he was going to Utah backcountry, on a hiking trip. Would have been traveling I-70, unknown from there and he should be camping in his truck. Would have very little money.

At the BLM office in Salt Lake, Larry Shackleford spoke with my mom at eight A.M. Immediately upon hanging up, he sent a "Be On the Look Out" notice for my vehicle to the BLM and Utah State Fish and Wildlife offices, then called a half-dozen of his personal acquaintances in those bureaus to follow up and make sure they received the action request. It reassured my mother that Georgia and Larry had taken direct action to help move the search along. She was tired of hearing from the police and some of the dispatchers that "this happens all the time" or "he'll eventually show up someplace." These actions were two rays of sunshine for my mom through that darkest morning. She was anxious for Captain Kyle Ekker, the most cooperative and helpful of the many contacts she had established and maintained over the past twenty-four hours, to resume his shift so she could speak with him about the investigation's progress.

At nine A.M., Adam Crider walked out of the Aspen Police Department with a voided check from my checking account and headed over to the U.S. Bank. First thing on a Thursday, the bank was empty of customers, and he approached the first window and interrupted the teller preparing her drawer for the day.

Upon hearing his spiel, the teller summoned the bank manager to get his approval to access my debit-card history. The small group peered at her computer screen as she entered the digits of my account.

"It looks like the last transaction was on the twenty-fifth, in Moab, at a City Market."

"How much was it?"

"Twenty-two thirty-one was the charge . . . no cash back." (I had stocked up on water, juice, fruit, candy bars, and burritos.)

"What's the one before that?"

"Twenty-nine twenty-two at Clark's here in town on the twenty-fourth." (I had bought groceries on the evening of the twenty-third, before going home to pack for my ski day with Brad and the subsequent Utah vacation, but the supermarket had not processed the transaction until after midnight.)

"And that's it? Nothing after the twenty-fifth? How frequently is this updated?"

"It's immediate, at least within a few hours, depending on how the merchants submit their batches."

Crider already knew from the phone work he and the other officers had done the night before that my last credit-card transaction had been on the twenty-fourth, gassing up in Glenwood Springs, the city at the intersection of the Roaring Fork River and the Colorado River. From Glenwood, it's possible to head east or west on I-70, which didn't tell the officers much except that I hadn't used my credit cards for a week. With the information from the bank, Adam knew I'd arrived in Moab and probably departed from there on Friday the twenty-fifth. But where had I gone?

At 9:07 A.M. on Thursday, Steve Patchett sat in the kitchen of his Albuquerque home and considered what needed to be done next with the search. As a union electrician, Steve was presently without a job—which usually happened for four to six weeks every six months or so—so he had time to dedicate to the search planning. He first dialed the Emery County sheriff's office on his home line and was transferred to Captain Kyle Ekker. The two men reviewed the status of the search initiated by their conversation the previous afternoon. Kyle explained that the first search hadn't turned up any clues.

"We had our guys out at the Black Box with some of the search-and-rescue team on off-road vehicles, but they didn't find anything. Two deputies went out to Joe's Valley, which I don't think was on your list, but there's a lot of hiking out there. Nothing there, either, though. We called everybody back in just before dark."

Steve asked, "Did you get anyone down to Segers Hole?"

Segers had been next on Kyle's list, but he hadn't dispatched anyone, because it was nearly a three-hour drive from Castle Dale, in the
northwest part of the county, down to the remote and unpaved
southern region. With the increased manpower of the day shift, Kyle
could afford to send a deputy with some volunteers from the county's
search-and-rescue team down to the Muddy. He said, "It's a long way,
but we're going to check there. I was waiting for daylight and a couple more pairs of eyes, but that's next. Is there anything else you can
tell me?"

Steve paused and considered all the information he'd reviewed. It
was mostly a hunch, but he told Kyle, "I'm pretty sure he's in your
county."

Kyle promised to update Steve when the reports came back from
the more far-flung locations, and thanked him for his involvement.
After hanging up, the captain looked at his maps and thought
through a short list of other places he would have his deputies and the
SAR volunteers check while they were on the way out to Segers. -
"We've already covered the upper corners of the county," the captain
thought, "and most of the trailheads in the central part of the county.
If he's in the county, he's down south. Where do people go down
there? There aren't even any roads." But one dirt road, the Lower San
Rafael Road, cuts a sidewinding curve through the southern section
of Emery County, down into a no-man's-land at the fringes of
Canyonlands. "Maybe there, over in the Robbers Roost area," he
thought as he pored over his enlarged map of the county. There are
dozens of canyons and dry washes out in the Roost, most on BLM
land accessible from the Lower San Rafael Road and its continuation,
the spur that dead-ends in the Maze. Kyle knew the Maze drew considerable numbers of people through Emery County down into
Wayne County. It'd be worth a call, he figured, even if he didn't send
his guys over the county line.

Kyle dialed the Hans Flat ranger station at the entrance to the
Maze District of Canyonlands, inquiring about a red Toyota Tacoma
truck at nine-fifteen A.M. Ranger Glenn Sherrill answered the phone

and immediately recognized the vehicle description. That truck had been at Horseshoe Canyon since the weekend.

"I was just there. I saw that vehicle, oh, three days ago, and it's still there," he told Kyle.

Typically, fewer than ten people visit Horseshoe Canyon each day, with maybe a few more on the weekends. Nearly everyone hikes in and out of the canyon in half a day. The National Park Service posts rangers in the canyon every day at the Great Gallery to monitor visitors and protect the five-thousand-year-old petroglyphs. Since they are typically the first to arrive and the last to leave the trailhead each day, the rangers are accustomed to finding the dirt parking lot empty, or with one or two vehicles and tents set up nearby. They are certainly attuned to notice when one vehicle sits in the parking lot for the better part of a week. Because my truck obnoxiously blocked the welcome sign directly across from the entrance road (I'd parked to make the rear bed level for sleeping), it was all the more conspicuous.

Even feeling 90 percent certain, Glenn paused and hedged his assertion. "Well, I think it's the vehicle."

Kyle asked, "Do you have anybody who can go check the license plate?"

"Yeah, will do. Let me call you back."

Glenn signaled over the radio to his rangers in the parking lot who were preparing to hike into the canyon. They confirmed that the truck was still there and verified the license plate. Glenn phoned Kyle and reported the positive identification. "We have his truck."

"Thank you for your help. We're going to get somebody on-scene."

The captain dispatched Sergeant Mitch Vetere to drive out to the trailhead and then had his dispatcher try to get Sheriff Kurt Taylor from Wayne County on the radio. Sheriff Taylor was off-duty until the afternoon, but his chief deputy, Doug Bliss, called back within the hour.

Since the trailhead for Horseshoe Canyon resides just over the county line in Wayne County, the search had potentially moved beyond the purview of Kyle and his deputies. Although my vehicle was sitting in Wayne County, if I had gone to the north in the canyon, I would be in Emery County; if I went to the south, I would be in Wayne County. With Doug's permission, Kyle continued as commander and began the process of initiating the Park Service's incident-response command. He had already called the DPS dispatcher in Price, Utah, to ask for helicopter support.

The news of my truck's discovery at Horseshoe Canyon reached Elliott at 9:37 A.M. He spent the next hour on his cell phone to spread word of the breakthrough. It was the focal point of new hope for my friends around the country. In Aspen, Rachel sent e-mails to my friends in the Roaring Fork Valley in 48-point font. Down in New Mexico, Steve Patchett talked with Jason Halladay on the phone at 10:31 A.M. Within the hour, they had coordinated two groups of my friends, search-and-rescue colleagues, and climbing partners in Albuquerque and Los Alamos who were making immediate plans to drive to Horseshoe Canyon. Steve called Kyle Ekker to let him know a team from the Albuquerque Mountain Rescue Council was responding. Captain Ekker assured Steve they would be welcome to participate in the search.

At our home in Denver, Ann Fort and my mom were working on a different plan. They were creating a missing person's poster to send via fax to a list of United Methodist churches in the Grand Junction area, asking them to take the flyer to gas stations around town and find out if anyone had seen me on my way to Utah. My mom had dug out the *Aspen Times* article from back in March, and cut out the self-portrait I'd taken on Capitol Peak. She taped the picture onto a piece of copier paper and, below the four-by-six picture, wrote out my physical description and the best information that she had regarding my whereabouts:

> Aron Ralston, 10/27/75, age 27. 6'2", approx. 175 lbs., brown unkempt hair. Last seen Thursday 4/24 approx. 6pm near Carbondale, COL. Used credit card at a gas station in Glenwood Springs early evening 4/24. Very athletic—possibly headed to Utah camping, biking, or skiing.

Adding my truck description and the correct license-plate number, my mom finished the poster with the phone number for the Aspen police. She and Ann were at the copy machine when the doorbell rang.

"I wonder who that is?" my mom inquired aloud. Without crossing the room to peek out the window, she went downstairs and answered the door. It was Sue Doss, another friend from church. Sue and her husband, Keith, had been the codirectors of the high school youth programs at Hope when I was at Cherry Creek. I had spent dozens of weekends with them and traveled to Wyoming on two trips with the youth group to volunteer at church camps; I had even given their daughter Jamie her first lessons on the piano. After I graduated and went on to college, the Doss family had remained close to my parents.

Sue had come directly from Hope UMC, where she heard about my mom's request for support during the crisis. My mother quickly told Sue the limited amount she knew about my situation. There were more tears and hugs and sobs, but shortly, Sue, Ann, and my mom were ready to get back to work.

The threesome began a long-distance distribution of the freshly made poster. My mom asked the office administrator at Hope Church to fax over a phone list of United Methodist churches in Grand Junction. Juggling two phones to collect fax numbers, my mom also got the fax machine warmed up. At nine-forty-five A.M., they were about to go into high gear when my mom's cell phone rang.

The voice on the other end belonged to Acting Chief Ranger Steve Swanke of Canyonlands National Park. It was the first time my mom had spoken with Ranger Steve, as he introduced himself—he had just become involved in the investigation within the hour—but she was ecstatic to hear his startling good news.

"Mrs. Ralston, we have located your son's vehicle," Steve said in a friendly drawl honed by a career of interacting with the public.

With a gasp, my mom relayed the news in an escalating din of excitement just short of a scream: "They found his truck! Thank God! They found his truck!" After Steve gave my mom the full situation update, she and her friends hugged, then they sat on the back porch, knowing that now there was nothing more they could do but pray the rescuers found me and that I was alive and OK.

In a coordinated effort between the NPS and the Emery County sheriff to command the incident response, Ranger Steve Swanke and Captain Kyle Ekker requested helicopters, search dogs, a climbing team, ground personnel, and horse-mounted search teams for the effort in Horseshoe Canyon. At the Unified Command Headquarters in Moab, Swanke assigned two investigators to research a subject profile on me. One of their first actions was to go on the Internet and enter my name in a search engine. They immediately turned up my website, with links to my mountaineering projects, canyoneering trip reports, and photo albums of rock art panels in New Mexico. They deduced that I was an experienced outdoorsman but not necessarily familiar with the area around Horseshoe Canyon, providing one of nine factors that go into the subject profile evaluation.

The National Association of Search and Rescue (NASAR) guidelines help incident commanders assess the relative urgency of a - subject's absence, based on the number of subjects and their age, medical condition, equipment, and experience, along with factors for the weather, terrain, and history of rescues in the area. Assigning values of 1, 2, or 3 to each factor, search leaders can measure their response appropriately. A 1 indicates a higher urgency than a 3. A very old (1) and inexperienced (1) subject with a history of heart disease (2) who is lost by himself (1) in a storm (1) with only the clothes on his back (1) in a region of steep, rocky terrain (1) that has a history of incidents (1) with a low probability of a bogus search (1) would earn a total profile score of 10. Any score of 9 to 12 dictates a first-degree emergency response.

From the information available on me, the relative urgency worksheets in the incident command guidelines suggested a second-degree measured response, which differs from an emergency response only in the speed and number of people and equipment initially committed to the field. However, because of my extensive experience with solo-climbing winter fourteeners and the nearly weeklong duration of my absence, Ranger Swanke increased the urgency to an emergency response.

On Swanke's request, New Air Helicopters, a charter service out of Durango, Colorado, launched a helicopter for Horseshoe Canyon just before noon on Thursday. Subsequently, the NPS requisitioned a another bird from a Forest Service firefighting crew in southern Utah, effectively commandeering it for assistance with the search mission. In the mission objectives, Swanke declared that his second-priority goal, behind ensuring the personal safety of search-and-rescue personnel, was to "Locate, access, stabilize, and transport Ralston by 20:00 hours on 05/01/03." It was a by-the-book statement for which search-and-rescue leaders sometimes use the acronym LAST—for locate, access, stabilize, and transport—with a necessarily ambitious time frame to have me out of the wilderness in the first ten hours.

Captain Ekker conferred with Wayne County's commanding officer, Chief Deputy Doug Bliss, who agreed to call out his county's search-and-rescue group, including a horse team for faster ground-searching capability. Even though it was his request to deploy the mounted searchers, Captain Ekker joked, "Well, with the helicopter in the air, by the time you pull those horses down there, we'll have found him. But bring 'em out, and be ready to stay the night."

At 11:25 A.M., Chief Deputy Bliss paged the search-and-rescue group with the message to rendezvous in Hanksville: "Meet at Carl - Hunt's for search in Horseshoe Canyon area. Bring horses, be prepared to be out all night."

Terry Mercer, a pilot with the Department of Public Safety, had just been canceled for a flight, and had left his DPS helicopter fueled and sitting on the helipad at the Salt Lake City International Airport, when he got a call at ten-forty-five A.M.

Within twenty-five minutes, Terry was airborne and communicating with Captain Ekker, who asked him to pick up one of his officers at the Huntington airport in the northwest part of the county, some seventy air miles from Horseshoe Canyon. By twelve-fifty P.M., Terry had landed and brought on board the aircraft bush-bearded Detective Greg Funk, fresh from an undercover assignment in the Emery County sheriff's narcotics division. They departed for the canyon, just thirty-five minutes away by air.

Even with the two-hour flight from Salt Lake, Terry's DPS chopper was the first to arrive at Horseshoe Canyon, landing in the dirt parking lot. Sergeant Mitch Vetere showed Terry my maroon truck, and they looked through some of my hiking and camping gear in the pickup bed. After a quick discussion with the BLM and NPS rangers gathered at the trailhead, Terry and the two officers decided that the best place to look for an experienced hiker would be to search the northern end of the canyon, toward its intersection with the Green River. When the next helicopter arrived, it would fly over the upper half of the canyon, to the south of the trailhead.

With their flight plan identified, Mitch joined his colleague Greg in the backseat of the helicopter as a second pair of onboard eyes, even though he was particularly averse to flying. Federal regulations prohibit BLM and Park Service employees from boarding any aircraft that does not have a green-card registration. Since the Utah DPS officials have a primary focus of aiding the counties, they don't let their pilots have green cards, and thereby avoid any obligation to help with federal requests. While this policy usually works in DPS's favor, conserving the department's limited resources for local and state needs, it removed the dozen BLM and NPS rangers assembled at the trailhead from the pool of available air searchers. Thus, as much as Mitch disliked flying in general, and despite the special anxiety he reserved for helicopters, he was the only person at the trailhead who could ride.

At 1:56 P.M., Terry lifted the DPS chopper in a swirling cloud of red dust, and flew into Horseshoe Canyon on a northeast bearing toward the confluence of Barrier Creek and the Green River. For twenty miles, he steadily piloted the helicopter below the rim rock, following the meanders of the dry Barrier Creek streambed at the bottom of the canyon. Greg and Mitch watched for footprints in the sandy canyon floor and kept an anxious eye on the unnervingly scant distance between the helicopter's rotor blades and the sandstone walls. With the smell of jet fuel reminding him that he was riding on an airborne gas tank, Mitch wondered repeatedly, "Gawd, what am I doing here?"

Terry spent about an hour flying down the canyon, until they reached the Green River. Greg and Mitch hadn't seen any sign of a hiker, though they figured they only would have seen someone who was out in the open or up and walking around. There were too many boulders, trees, and shadows for them to have a high probability of detecting me if I were injured and unable to signal the helicopter or slightly hidden from overhead view.

At 2:50 P.M., Terry turned the helicopter around and started quickly working back up Horseshoe Canyon to the trailhead. He had about a half hour of fuel left and would have to land and take off, dropping the officers at the trailhead, before making a twenty-minute dash over Canyonlands to refuel at Moab. It would be a close call to get to the helipad within the time limit.

For the time being, Terry had done all he could do. As he pulled the helicopter up out of the canyon, Mitch took his first easy breath in an hour, looking forward to putting his feet on terra firma once again.

FIFTEEN

A Date with Destiny

It was like having sex with death.

——BARRY BLANCHARD *on his team's attempt to climb
the 15,000-foot-high Rupal Face of Nanga Parbat, in Pakistan*

IT'S 11:34 A.M., Thursday, May 1, 2003. I set my knife on top of the chockstone and package my stump in the plastic grocery sack that had been stuffed between my right arm and the wall. Wrapping the white sack with the yellow webbing I have around my neck, I stuff my arm into the empty CamelBak backpack, throwing the tightened straps over my head to hold my amputated arm to my chest in a makeshift sling. It doesn't cross my mind to stop and remove my biking shorts for additional absorbent padding; at this point, I just need to get moving. I clean two carabiners out of my pulley rigging and clip them to a loop on my harness, then frantically toss a few necessary loose articles into my pack—the empty water reservoir, the mostly full bottle of urine, the video camera, my pocketknife—and pause as I pick up my digital still camera. Some instinct inside me pulses, and I turn on the camera. In five seconds, I take two close-up photos of my severed hand. It is an unsentimental goodbye. Turning off the camera, I replace the lens cover, stuff it in the pack, and carefully cinch the cord shut. After a brief survey of the chockstone vicinity to make sure I'm not leaving anything critical behind, I sloppily grab two dozen coils of my climbing rope in my left hand and stumble off down the canyon.

After careening from wall to wall continuously for the first fifty feet, I have to stop and restore my calm. My heart is raging, beating three times its normal resting rate, but with only a fraction of its regular pressure. I'm in danger of blacking out.

Settle down, Aron. You can't pass out now.

It will do me no good to rush and overexert myself. First I have to get to water. I deeply inhale and exhale three breaths, compose myself, and go on, dragging the rope behind me in an ever tangling mess. It takes me twenty minutes to cover the next 150 yards. What light was here two hours ago, when the sun dagger made its appearance, is gone, but my eyes are used to the dimness, and I don't bother to turn on my headlamp. The serpentine slot canyon is less than shoulder width for most of the distance; I carefully scoot sideways through the passage so I don't bump my right arm. In at least ten different places, I have to single-handedly perform an intricate series of semi-technical scrambling maneuvers, first tossing the rope through each narrow twist in the canyon and then clawing my way through after it. I slide on my butt down into a toilet-bowl feature where water has scoured out a round pothole at the bottom of a pair of S-curves. Thankfully, it is a shallow bowl, with an easy shelf to clamber over at the exit. I worry that a smooth-walled pothole even just a few feet deep could be an insurmountable obstacle for me now. My mood is frenetic; I'm trying to move as quickly as I can, but at the same time, adrenaline and endorphins are warping my mind. This hundred yards of slot stretches out to twice its actual length, and I expect to exit the narrows four or five different times before I finally burst into the sun on a rock shelf midway up a sheer-walled amphitheater some 150 feet deep. I walk out into the middle of the shelf and look around. The position is spectacular, like in *The Temple of Doom,* when Indiana Jones rides the railcar out of the underground mine and he's cliffed out halfway up an unscalable face. Fortunately,

I am prepared for this: I have my harness, rappel device, and a sufficient length of beefy rope. To my left are two bolts drilled into the rock with a recently tied-off loop of webbing threading through the bolt eyelets, and a floating rappel ring that drapes down to a point some three feet back from the edge of the rock shelf. This is the Big Drop rappel.

Standing in the sun for the first time in six days makes me slightly light-headed. I wobble to the leading edge of the queen-bed-sized shelf to peer down the Big Drop. There, in the sandy bottom of the amphitheater directly below the Drop, is a bathtub's amount of water in a shallow and turgid pool. My head is baking in the sun, and at the enticing sight of water, I swoon and almost lunge headfirst over the precipice, but catch my balance before I fall over the edge.

Whoa, Aron, slow down. No stupid mistakes.

I hastily clip myself into the anchor with my daisy chain and set to work untangling the 170-foot remaining length of my originally 200-foot rope. Using my left hand and my mouth to shuttle-feed the sandy rope, I tediously work one end at a time back through the knots I've unintentionally formed over the past five nights of coiling the rope loops around my legs, and then dragging the whole mess behind me through the slot for the last twenty minutes. Out of sight to my left, little by little, one end of the rope inadvertently slides over the lip of the rappel ledge until its mass has enough tension to tug the rest of the rope precariously close to the shelf's edge. I hear the distinctive zip-zip of the slinking rope and turn to watch it slithering out of sight over the edge. Instinctively, I jump on the tail of the rope with my left foot, pinning it tight to the sandstone shelf with my running shoe. If I drop the rope, the game is over. This ten-and-a-half-millimeter-diameter lifeline is a sine qua non of my escape from Blue John Canyon. Without it, I would be forced to exit up the canyon, where I know there is no water, journeying in my handicapped state up rough terrain for four hours until I could theoretically flag down assistance on the dirt Maze road. That is, if I lived that long, which I - wouldn't. If I drop the rope, I might as well chuck myself off the ledge and follow its free-falling arc in a terminal swan dive into the shin-deep puddle sixty-five feet below.

Don't drop the rope, Aron. No stupid mistakes.

I tie a figure-eight on a loop near the middle of the rope and clip the knot into the anchor. This second potentially fatal near-miss in under five minutes has me sharply focused on setting the rappel and getting to that pool of water. Every minute I've spent untangling the rope has parched me more and more. Now that I'm fully exposed to the sun's warmth, I feel the dehydration accelerate threefold; with each pass of the gritty rope through my lips, my tongue and palate increasingly turn to grating sheets of sandpaper. One knot extracted from fifty feet up the rope requires three dozen bites. Finally, I figure out a better method—to hold the knot in my mouth and reverse the rope through the loop. I still have to hold the cord in my lips and override my tongue's instinct to lick at it every few seconds. My respirations strip the last moisture from my body, and though I'm only five minutes away from the puddle, I have to drink something immediately.

Spitting out the rope, I pinch it between my knees and sling my backpack off my left shoulder, then carefully lift the right strap off the end of my padded stump. Down in the bottom of the main compartment is my charcoal Nalgene bottle, three quarters full of piss. Whereas I previously have only sipped or taken a mouthful at a time of the decanted orange urine, now I gulp three, five, seven ounces down in ten seconds and retch violently at the foul taste of the repugnant liquid. But the sensation that I am shriveling up on this ledge abates, and I can continue preparing the rope.

After fifteen minutes of sorting the rope into two knot-free stacks, it is ready to go over the edge. I check the knot, clipped into the single carabiner secured on the purple webbing of the anchor, and, one at a time, toss each pile of rope over the cliff. Ordinarily, I would remove the knot and let the rope dangle from the anchor. This would allow me to pull the rope down once I reached the bottom;

today, however, I intend to abandon it. I won't need it after this, and right now I'm truly unconcerned about littering.

Standard practice would have me back up the anchor carabiner with a second one, the gates opposite and opposed, but I'm not worried that this one will accidentally open or fail. There is nothing the 'biner can catch on, and its rating is strong enough that I could hang two pickup trucks off of it. The webbing is new within a month, and I'm satisfied with its strength as well; it hasn't been chewed on or chafed or significantly degraded by the sun. If I didn't trust the webbing, I could clip my rope on a 'biner directly into one of the bolt eyelets, but I decide the setup is plenty sufficient to hold my weight on the descent.

Next, I take my Air Traffic Controller (ATC) rappel/belay device and bend each rope strand through one of the twin slots in the mouth of the device. Once they're through, I clip my main carabiner through the rope loops. After I tighten down the lock on the carabiner gate, I'm finally on rappel. I unclip my daisy chain from the anchor webbing and back up until my weight comes onto the rope and anchor system. Checking my harness, I see that I haven't doubled back the waist belt through the D-ring that holds it in place. Theoretically, the belt could pull through the ring, and then my weight would be suspended entirely by my leg loops. If I had two hands and weren't in the process of bleeding to death, I would double back the belt, but right now, with water waiting below, it's a risk I'm willing to take.

Looking down at my feet, I back up in jerking motions, feeding six inches of the ropes through my ATC with each stuttering step. At the edge, I can peek down between my legs at the dizzying six-story drop and see that the ledge I'm departing hangs out over the rest of the cliff. I'm slightly nervous about doing this rappel with just my left hand. If my grasp slips or for some reason I let go, I have no backup; I'll accelerate down the rope, only slightly slower than in free fall, and take a hard landing next to the pool, probably breaking my legs or worse. It's very important that I take the overhanging section slowly.

Just ease back. Little more. Little more. That's it, Aron. Step down onto that block. No, left foot first. Good. Steady. Now your right foot. Excellent. Lean back on the rope. Trust it. Push your butt out. Straighten your legs. Now feed a little more rope out. Slowly. Sloooowly. Good. Now hold on tight.

The pucker factor is high on the upper part of the rappel. With the rope's weight putting additional friction on my rappel device, I have to fight and pull the strands to feed them through the device bit by bit—a significant effort that saps my remaining strength—but not so much that I slide down the rope and lose my balance. It's like trying to drive a car in 5-mph stop-and-go traffic while pressing the accelerator to the floor and controlling the vehicle's speed by releasing the hand brake. I have to let off the brake to get going, but it's dangerously easy to release it too far and lose control. Doing it one-handed means I don't have any way to reach out and stabilize myself when I start to swing one direction or the other as I move my feet over the awkwardly uneven lip of the shelf. I'm most worried that I'll let too much rope through, fall off the lip, and hit the edge of the shelf with my shoulder or my head, then let go of the rope. The poached air sucks my pores dry, and I'm tortured for three minutes as I make a prolonged series of infinitesimal adjustments and maneuvers to get my body under the shelf. Finally, I let a little more rope through the ATC, my feet cut loose off the lower edge of the shelf, and I'm dangling free from the wall on my rope, some sixty feet off the ground. A moment of giddy delight replaces my anxiety as I spin around to face the amphitheater, floating comfortably in midair. Gliding down the rope, moving faster as I get closer to the ground, I notice the echo of my ropes singing as they slide through the ATC.

Touching down, I pull the twenty-foot-long tails of my ropes through my rappel device and immediately lunge for the mud-ringed puddle. I move out of the sun and into the cool shade, brusquely swing my pack off my left side and then more delicately over my right arm, and once again retrieve my Nalgene. When I open the lid this time, I toss its contents into the sand off to my left and fill it in the puddle, scooping up leaves and dead insects along with the aromatic water. I'm so parched I can taste the elevated humidity around the pool, and it piques my thirst. I swish the liquid to rinse out the bottle and then dump that to the side as well.

Scooping the bottle through the pool twice, I again fill it with the brown water. In the time it takes me to bring the Nalgene's rim to my lips, I debate whether to sip it slowly or guzzle away and decide to sip then guzzle. The first droplets meet my tongue, and somewhere in the heavens, a choir strikes up. The water is cool, and best of all, it's brandy-sweet, like a fine after-dinner port. I drink the entire liter in four chugging swallows, drowning myself in pleasure, and then reach to fill the bottle again. (So much for sipping.) The second liter follows in the same manner, and I refill the bottle once more. I wonder if the water would taste as wonderfully sweet to a normally hydrated person. If the water really is this delicious, what makes it that way? Are the dead leaves stewing the liquid into some kind of desert tea?

I sit at the edge of the puddle, and, for the moment, I am enjoying myself, as though my thirst is all that really matters, and now that it's taken care of, I am totally at ease. Everything disappears. I even cease noticing the pain of my arm. I daydream as if I'm on a picnic, sitting in the shade after a long lunch, with nothing left to do except watch the clouds roll by.

But I know the relief will be short-lived. As relaxed as I am, I have eight miles of sandy hiking in front of me to reach my truck, and I need to steel myself for it. I notice several sets of hoofprints in the sand off to my right. Someone, or a group of someones, has ridden up into and out of this box canyon since the last storm. My heart leaps to think I might come across a party of cowboys somewhere along my hike, but I know better than to yell out or hold those hopes too closely. The dried-out road apples dotting the wash for fifty yards downcanyon tell me it's been over a day since those horses came through here. And tourists on horseback aren't likely to spend the night.

I quaff the third liter more conservatively, even nestling the hard plastic bottle in the sand for a minute or two to rummage through my pack and sort out what I can leave behind. I set aside my broken Discman and the two scratched CDs, and decide that everything else will come with me. With my digital still camera, I take a picture of my doubled rope hanging down the Big Drop and then hold the camera out in my left hand for a self-portrait with the pool in the background. It's 12:16 P.M. I am elated to have come this far, but the photo records a grungy eight-day beard, specks of gore from the operation, and a haunted grimace. After putting the camera and the video camcorder in the outer mesh pouch of my backpack, I work at fitting the bite valve back on the tubing stub at the bottom of my CamelBak reservoir and then fill up the container with two liters of the syrupy water.

Still drinking my third liter, I get out my folded guidebook photocopy and measure the distance to the first landmark on my journey, the confluence of Blue John with Horseshoe Canyon. The map is delineated in kilometers, and doing the conversion I estimate it's a solid two miles from where I'm sitting to the confluence. After that, a short half mile will bring me to the boundary of Canyonlands, and two miles after that, I'll pass the Great Gallery, which the caption under the photo on the left side of my photocopy describes as "probably the best [pictograph panel] in the world." Another three quarters of a mile, or maybe a mile, and I will come to the first water seep in the Barrier Creek drainage. That means it will be at least two hours until I get to the next place that could possibly have water. I don't know for sure if there will be anything there—it will depend on the water table and any rains that came the week before I arrived in Utah—but I'll need water by then, whether it's there or not.

The best I can do to prepare for the coming march is fill my CamelBak and Nalgene and seal them closed. I'm as ready as I'll ever be. I stand up and feel the water sloshing in my stomach. I wish I could rest and let the water enter my system, but I'm slowly bleeding out, and I have three, maybe four hours to go from here. I made my choice an hour and forty-five minutes ago when I cut into my arm. Now I resolve to follow that choice through to its conclusion—

reaching my truck and then getting to a clinic or, failing that, a phone.

Marching into the wide-open, sunny, sandy canyon bottom, I start my eight-mile trek. The heat instantly saps what little rehydration I accomplished at the pool, and within two hundred yards, I have to take a sip of water. After going through the rigmarole of digging my Nalgene out of my pack, I take my last remaining nonlocking carabiner off my harness's gear loop and clip the gate through the bottle's cap loop, then snap the metal link onto a strap hanging off the left side of my backpack's padded waist belt.

Continuing on, I walk past several large cottonwoods and a thicket of tamarisks that testify to the substantial runoff that passes through this part of the canyon. In another hundred yards, the brush subsides. I tire of walking in my harness, with the belay device and daisy chain dangling in front of my thighs, so I tear the belt back through the safety ring and wiggle my legs out of their loops one at a time until the harness and the attached accoutrements drop behind me to lie in the sand like a pile of dead snakes. "That'll be someone - else's little score," I think, "some fine canyoneering booty, that." Through the first meanders of the canyon, I find myself crossing the fifty-yard-wide floor to take advantage of the shade at the edges of the wash, but still, the effort of walking at even a moderate pace leaves me parched within a minute of sipping at my water. After a single mile, I'm as thoroughly dried up as I was at the top of the rappel, and I've already drunk a full liter, a third of my water supply.

Not ten minutes after leaving the puddle, my bowels wake up for the first time since Saturday morning. I know what's coming, and I know it's coming quick. I rush over to an alcove along the edge of the wash where the occasional flood action has carved out a bench on the outside curve of the stream course, and hurry to undo the belt on my shorts. I strip down my three layers of shorts, biking shorts, and underwear just in time as I desecrate the slickrock. The water I've drunk has spilled over out of my stomach and flooded my bowels.

Oh, dude! Jeezus! That's horrendous, man!

As if I weren't in enough distress already, now I have to try and clean myself up. It's pointless to try to wipe; I have nothing except my clothes, and I kind of need those. I pull up my underwear but take off the biking shorts and stuff them in the top of my backpack. I put my tan-and-blood-colored shorts back on and feel ten degrees cooler without the black padded shorts. No time to dwell; the episode is past.

Hiking again, just before the canyon swerves to the right in a sweeping gooseneck bend, I take a left into a side canyon, thinking it to be the main drainage, but within forty steps, I feel an added strain on my debilitated system and realize that I'm actually walking upgrade and turn around.

No stupid mistakes, Aron. Pay attention here. You knew this wasn't Horseshoe Canyon. It'll be obvious when you get there. Keep track with your map. You know how to do this.

Suddenly, I feel a wetness spreading across my lower back. My CamelBak is leaking. I stop and drop to my knees, swinging my backpack around to the front. Sure enough, the bite valve is leaking water out of the bottom of the CamelBak. It's not designed to hold back pressure at the bottom of the reservoir, and since I sliced away the tubing that would usually connect there, I have a problem. I open my empty Nalgene and squeeze the bite valve into its mouth, pouring half the remaining contents of the reservoir into the bottle. "Now what?" I wonder. If I leave the water in the CamelBak, it'll leak out and be gone before I get to Horseshoe. I screw the lid back on the Nalgene, clip it on my backpack strap, and decide the best thing I can do now is drink the rest of the water in my CamelBak and go the rest of the way on what's in the Nalgene. It's not ideal, but it's better than wasting the water.

Now my new reality sets in. I have drunk five liters of water in under an hour and covered only a mile of the canyon. I have one liter of water left, six miles to go, it's only going to get hotter, and I'm only going to get weaker. I have to figure out a better way to do this, or I'll be dead before I get halfway to the Great Gallery. A memory comes to mind, a story I read in a running magazine maybe a few years ago, about the legendary Mexican Indian tribe of the Tarahumara. I remember being impressed not just that the tribesmen would run distances of fifty miles in a day, often in their bare feet, and through the heat of the desert, but that they would undertake these ultramarathons without any support—they wouldn't even carry any food or water. Their trick was to take in a mouthful of water at the start, not swallowing it but rather carrying it in their mouth, allowing that single swallow to humidify the air going into their lungs. As long as they kept their pace below their sweating threshold, they would lose only the humidification that they exhaled. I decide it's worth a shot and take two ounces of water in my mouth and hold it there while I walk myself closer, yard by yard, to my truck hidden somewhere up on the tablelands to the north.

I immediately sense that the trick is working. Although I'm still thirsty, I'm breathing well and don't feel a tenth as parched as I did when I was drinking the water outright. This might just help me conserve the rest of my water supply.

At mile two of my march, at 1:09 P.M., I come to the confluence of Blue John and Horseshoe canyons and take a left toward the Great Gallery without missing a stride. However, in another five minutes, the sand in my left shoe builds up enough that I decide to stop and take it off. It's been grating my sole raw, and I can't stand it anymore. My left foot is much worse off than my right because I left the tatters of my left sock at the chockstone, stretched over the hammer rock's top. Getting my shoe off and emptying it are the easy parts. I still cannot tie the laces, so I pull them tight and tuck the loose ends into the sides of my shoe next to my bare foot. Good enough. From here forward, I am as diligent with my steps as I can be to avoid the sand, both for ease of travel and to avoid getting more grit in my shoe.

At mile two and a half, I come across a barbed-wire fence hanging across the wash, suspended by burly cables sunk into the rock on either side of the streambed. This must be the boundary for the national park, I figure, as I duck through a cutaway section in the middle of the fence where the boards are loose at the bottom. Right after I step through the fence line into the Horseshoe Canyon District of Canyonlands, my bowels start shouting, and my sphincter clenches. I charge over to a suitable spot in the shade of another shelf where I can lean and purge my intestines. Diarrhea won't usurp blood loss as the primary threat to my life, but if it keeps up, it could dehydrate me even more. Round two over, I hike up my plaid boxers and shorts and march onward. The water trick continues to help me hike briskly while minimizing my intake. I swallow every five or ten minutes, but the good news is that I still have over twenty ounces left in my Nalgene.

At mile four, I pass a three-hundred-foot-high wall on my left with dozens of broad-shouldered figures painted to enormous scale in all shades of tan and maroon. These are the pictographs of the Great Gallery, which I acknowledge now merely as a milestone on my march. Just down the canyon, amid a small coppice of reeds, cattails, and bulrushes, I step into soft waterlogged ground covered by a thick growth of grasses. A few paces farther through the marsh, I push aside some sedges and find a short stretch of open water. Hallelujah! It's 1:55 P.M. when I stoop over a muddy rivulet six inches wide and two inches deep and try to refill my water containers. It's a frustrating enterprise but worth every effort; I was down to just five ounces in my bottle, and now I can stock up again. I have to build a small mud dam so I can scoop my CamelBak reservoir through the muck. I kidnap a pair of tadpoles in my water bottle, but I figure why bother trying to get them out? I've probably consumed several hundred thousand invisible swimmers up to this point. What's the difference of two more, just because I can see them?

The blood from my stump is dripping quickly now, despite my tourniquet and wrappings, and several dozen red splotches appear in the sandy mud as I try to get more water into my CamelBak. The pain in my arm aches insistently around the tourniquet, and it takes on a mountainous presence of its own in my mind, repeatedly sending its single-minded message: "Your arm is severely injured; you need to make it better." The pain tempts me to sit and regain strength, but I know I have to press on. At least I have more water now.

Other footprints join together to form a gradually more distinct path through the sand dunes and tunnels of cottonwoods in this part of the canyon. Cairns appear beside the path. It makes sense that this part is more traveled, since it's the approach to the Great Gallery. I can't discern the age of any of the footprints, only that there have been dozens since the last rain or flood. Still, following the lesson I learned during my entrapment, I decide not to yell out. If there are people in this canyon, I'll find them, but it's best not to elevate my hopes.

At mile six, I make a left turn heading toward a colossal alcove that must be a hundred yards wide and at least that tall, overhanging a good hundred feet at its deepest point. Nearing the mammoth roof, the streambed turns to the right, and an unexpected sight shuts down my motor system as if the main breaker tripped in my head's fuse box. There, seventy yards ahead of me, walking side by side by side are three hikers, one smaller than the other two. Other people! I can't believe it. Up until this moment, I wasn't at all certain I would see another person in the canyon. I swallow the water in my mouth and shake my head, trying to determine if they are heading toward me or not. For the briefest moment, I wonder if they are really there. They seem to be walking away.

Quick, Aron, call to them. They'll help you.

I have to signal them before they get too far off. I try to shout, but my voice catches in my throat once, then twice, and I merely gargle the remains of my last mouthful of water. Finally, I manage a feeble "Helllp!" After a deep breath, I make another, stronger shout: "HELP!"

The group stops and turns back to face me. I keep walking and shout again, "HELP! I NEED HELP!" All three of them start running toward me, and I feel as though I am about to cry. I'm not alone anymore. This thought is a major relief, and while I still have a good reserve of gumption left, I feel a boost of confidence: I'm going to make it. I know now that I won't have to drive myself anywhere once we get to the trailhead. These people are going to help me.

I'm going to make it.

We close the distance, and I see what I presume is a family: a man and a woman in their late thirties, and a boy who I guess is their son. They're all dressed in shorts, T-shirts, hats, and tall hiking boots. The woman has a fanny pack around her waist with two water bottles in the side holsters. The man has a midsize backpack on, nearly the same size as mine, but it looks light and is probably mostly empty.

As we get close enough that I can talk to them, I begin telling them, "My name is Aron Ralston. I was trapped by a boulder on Saturday, and I've been without food and water for five days. I cut my arm off this morning to get free, and I've lost a lot of blood. I need medical attention."

I finish my announcement, and we come to a stop, face-to-face, a few feet away from each other. I'm coated in blood on my right side from my shirt collar to my shoe tip. I look at the boy—he can't be more than ten years old—and fear that I've just scarred him for life.

The man speaks, his single short sentence coming through to me as through a mental fog until something clicks in my mind. Realizing he has a Germanic accent, I decipher the six words:

"They told us you were here."

It takes me a good five seconds to process the full meaning of his statement, and the next thing I know, I'm hiking at full speed down the canyon, barking at this innocent family to start hiking. "We have to get moving. We'll talk while we walk. Can you understand me all right?"

The dad nods but protests, "You should stop and rest."

I reiterate my command—"No, we need to keep hiking"—and then begin barraging them with questions: "Who are 'they'? Who told you I was here? Do you have a phone of any sort that works down here?"

The family trots to catch up to me as the dad replies, "There are police at the parking. They told us to keep an eye out for you. We told them we would."

"Do you have a phone?" I ask again. They do not. The dad has a GPS on a string around his neck. "Can you tell me how far is it to the trailhead?"

"It is, ahh, three kilometers."

Oh, man, how can that be? I check my map, and it looks much closer than that, maybe a mile to where the trail leaves the canyon bottom and another mile of steep hiking. "Are you sure?"

He shows me the GPS screen. He's benchmarked the route, and the display indicates that we are now 2.91 kilometers from and 220 meters below the trailhead. The elevation will be the devastating part. I can feel the strain that comes with hiking up over the ten-foot-high sandbars where the trail cuts the corners off the meandering wash channel. I start to have doubts that I will make it to the trailhead after all. Maybe it is the knowledge that there are rescuers there, and that they might be able to come get me, but I begin to understand my body is failing. I've lost too much blood. Even minor obstacles cost me a great deal of energy and cause my heart rate to skyrocket.

Thinking through the sequence of events that will most quickly lead to definitive medical care, I ask the hikers for their names so I can plan what I'm going to ask them to do.

"I am Eric, and this is Monique and Andy," the dad replies. "We are the Meijers, from Holland." (That explains the accent as well as the excellent English.) I haven't yet heard Monique or Andy speak, but I can safely assume their English is just as good as Eric's.

"OK, Eric, you guys look pretty fit. I need one of you to run ahead and get to the police at the trailhead." I am fairly certain that the people there aren't actually police, but that's what he called them. "I need them to send down a litter and a team of people to help carry me out. I don't think I'm going to be able to make it out of the canyon. Will you do that?"

"Monique can run—she is fast."

Still hiking along, I look to his wife, and she nods. "Do you understand what I need?" I ask.

"Yes, a litter and a—"

I interrupt her. "Wait. Did the police have radios and phones?" The two adults nod. "OK, I need you to ask them for a helicopter." Why I didn't think of this first, I don't know—maybe because of my fatigue—but a helicopter will be much better than a litter team. All I'll have to do is get up to a place where a helicopter can land, and then wait. I think I can manage that. I look at Monique. "Please, now, go fast."

[The following passage is from a letter from Eric Meijer, giving his account of our unplanned rendezvous.]

> On Thursday May 1st, our family [my wife, Monique, our son, Andy, and myself, Eric Meijer] planned a trip to the Horseshoe Canyon, a remote section of Canyonlands N.P. in Utah. At the start of the trailhead we talked to a ranger who told us about a car that was parked in the area already for several days and that the owner might be missing in the canyon. We joked that we would keep our eyes open and that we would try to find him.
>
> After a hike of 3.7 miles to the Great Gallery (Indian rock art) where we took some pictures, we returned and suddenly heard a noise behind us, and after that a voice that cried "Help, I need help!"
>
> Monique and I immediately realized that this had to be the missing person. We didn't find him, he found us! A bit unstable but pretty quickly he walked nearer and we saw that the right-hand side of him was full of blood.
>
> His arm, or better what was left, hung in a self-made sling. We ran towards him and he spoke clearly: "Hello, my name is Aron. A boulder fell on me on Saturday. I have been stuck for five days

without food or water. I cut off my hand four hours ago and I need
medical attention. I need a helicopter."

We decided that my wife and our son would try to get out of the
canyon ASAP to get help, whilst I remained with Aron to move with
him in the same direction, giving him food and water and
supporting him mentally at the same time. Aron asked me to carry
his backpack and by continuous talking I tried to find out as much
as possible about his further well-being. It was important to direct
him ASAP out of the narrower part of Horseshoe Canyon towards
the wider area near the climb out where a heli could possibly
land.

As Monique takes off at a jog, Andy follows her. I almost ask the
boy to stay with us so Monique can go faster, but more immediately,
I think of asking Eric if he has any food. He thinks and calls out to
Monique, and she stops. "We have a couple Oreos left, but Monique
has them," Eric explains to me, and shouts to her to get out the cookies as we catch up to her. She hands over the clear plastic sleeve that
held fifteen cookies with an apology that she and Andy ate most of
them already. She and the boy turn and run off again.

There are only two Oreos left, but they are heaven-sent, and I dis-
pose of them in a single chomp each, pausing after the first one to unscrew the lid on my water bottle and take a swig of tadpole water to
wash it down. After I munch the second cookie, Eric hands me an
unopened half-liter bottle of distilled spring water. It doesn't taste as
good as the Big Drop puddle water, but it's a vast improvement over
the sandy sludge currently in my Nalgene. I thank Eric for the water,
and I ask him if he will carry my pack. He says certainly, and I shrug
it off, lightening my burden by a few pounds.

Eric talks with me and asks a few questions about what happened.
I'm trying to walk with the water in my mouth still, but each time I
reply to one of his questions, I swallow the water. When I finish talking, almost always keeping my answers short, I take another few

ounces into my mouth and hold them there. After a half-dozen rounds of inquiries, I let Eric know that I need to stop talking and focus on hiking.

About five minutes after Monique and Andy leave us the second time, Eric and I come across another hiker, in his early forties, headed in the opposite direction with an older woman who looks to be his mother. He asks if we need any assistance, and I reply with a question: "Do you have a cell phone or a satellite phone?" He does not have a phone of any kind, but he offers that he is medically trained. Relieved to have come across someone with more medical knowledge than my meager education by osmosis from search-and-rescue missions, I ask him to join us as we hike. He leaves the woman who continues hiking and introduces himself as Wayne, and I engage him in a back-and-forth to double-check that I'm doing everything I can at the moment to help myself. We walk together through endless stretches of tamarisks that whip at my arm and face, as I ask questions like "Is it OK that I eat?" ("If it doesn't make you throw up, sure") and "Should I worry about drinking too much water?" ("If it doesn't make you throw up, you'll be OK.")

I assume that Monique and Andy Meijer are running farther ahead to climb out and ask for a helicopter, but I haven't seen them for about ten minutes. As we come up on yet another long sandbar covered in brush and a few scattered trees, I have to stop to empty the sand in my shoe again. The grating friction on my bare left foot is so intense that it pushes the agony of my arm into the background. I find it ironic that my foot is distracting me from the fact that I've cut off my arm. I think it's doubly ironic that now, when I tell Eric I'm going to stop, he is the one who protests, "No, you must keep going."

"No, listen, I am going to sit down and empty the sand out of my shoe, and then you are going to help me retie my shoe when I'm done." I can be a bossy SOB when I'm tired and in pain, but Eric takes it in stride, and after I find a seat on a downed tree trunk and dump half a sandbox out of my sneaker, he ties my shoe for me.

I tried to imagine what Aron must have gone through over the past few days. I was really impressed by his physical, as well as mental, power. He exactly knew what he was doing, what he wanted and where his limits were even after going through all this.

Despite all the loss of blood, his walking pace was remarkably strong, until sand in his shoe started to irritate him and he just stopped in a shady part to get that out of the way before he wanted to continue. He asked me to fasten the lace of his shoe.

It is mile seven, and a few minutes after three P.M. The sun is beating down hard on the shadeless sand at the bottom of the eight-hundred-foot-deep Horseshoe Canyon. Eric and Wayne and I have just come around a wide bend in the open canyon, and I see what must be the beginning of the exit trail that leads to the parking area, zigzagging up the steep hillside ahead on the left. Somewhere on the rim, some seven hundred feet above me, the rescuers are waiting. Oh, how I wish I were a raven and could simply open my wingspan and, with a husky-voiced ca-caw, catch a rising thermal current in the air; I'd be at that trailhead in two minutes.

It will kill me if I try to hike out of this canyon. I've lost too much blood; I'm on the verge of deadly shock. I contemplate sending Eric up to get help as well, but before I can spit out the idea, the rapid stutter of a booming echo interrupts my thoughts.

Thwock-thwock-thwock-thwocka-thwocka-thwocka.

Two hundred yards in front of us, the metallic body of a wingless black bird rises over the canyon wall.

The sight shocks me into an abrupt halt and then inundates me with emotion. In disbelief, I try to sort out how Monique and Andy got to the trailhead and the rescuers brought in a helicopter so quickly, but I then understand that this bird was already here. My astonishment yields to immense relief, and it's all I can do for the moment to remain standing in the sand. Also stunned to a standstill, Wayne and Eric begin waving their arms over their heads, trying to signal to the helicopter. We are in the middle of the canyon, the tallest, darkest

shapes in a hundred-foot-diameter area on a flat sandbar that is
sparsely covered with short grasses and stunted rabbit brush, but even
still, I'm not sure the helicopter's occupants see us until the bird banks
at low altitude and loops back to soar over our heads a second time. I
look around for the best landing zone and decide it will be in the wash
in front of us. I hastily hike the fifty yards to the edge of the sandbar as
the helicopter banks into another U-turn and hovers two hundred feet
above the dry streambed. Eric catches up to stand beside me, and we
watch the helicopter begin its descent. I take ten short steps into the
streambed and turn my back to the landing zone, anticipating that the
rotor wash will kick up a bunch of sand. I bring my remaining energy
to bear on keeping my legs strong. My knees are weak, and every instinct tempts me to drop and kiss the earth to praise my deliverance,
but I am well aware that my brain is tired of supporting the burden of
my pain and the demands of the discipline that has sustained me. It
wants to abdicate, but I cannot let it, not until I am in a hospital.

The engine whine falls, and the dusty wind at my back dies to a
breeze. I turn around to see a stiff-legged passenger hop awkwardly
out of the rear door of the helicopter. The figure motions for me. I
walk briskly in a wide curve to where the man is standing at the side
door of the chopper. He yells, "Are you Aron?"

I nod and shout into his ear, "Yes. Can I get a lift?" and turn to
find a uniformed officer of some type sitting at the far side of an all-
leather backseat, gaping at me. There are no paramedics wielding IV
bags, nobody has latex gloves, and there's not a single piece of medical equipment in sight. I wasn't expecting a medevac flight, but I -
wasn't expecting full leather, either.

For some reason, the urgency of my own situation dissolves, and
I want to give the pilot or officer a fair chance to put down a cloth or
jacket before I stain the leather red. I shout into the helicopter over
the engine and rotor noise to no one in particular, "I'm bleeding—it's
gonna make a mess of your backseat!"

A voice booms, "Just get in!" and I clamber across two stacked
backpacks to the middle of the backseat. I shout to the man who

motioned me to the door, "Please get my backpack!" and nod to where Eric is standing with my pack in his hands some eighty feet in front of the helicopter. Running out from under the rotors and around to Eric, he then races back with my nearly empty backpack in his hands. The only contents are the water bottle and CamelBak, with a few ounces of mud in each, my headlamp, multi-tool, and two cameras, a measly five pounds total. Yet its weight had felt five times that in the last two miles before I found the Meijer family. "After carrying it all that way," I think, "I'd hate to leave it behind." All aboard, we fasten our seat belts, and the pilot brings the engines to full power, kicking up the dust of the canyon floor.

Someone hands me a headset to put on, and the officers help me get it on over my blue Arc'teryx ball cap. The pilot asks if I can hear him, and I respond, "Yes," as I settle into the leather seat, lifting my injured arm above my head. Elevated, the insistent throbs are a little more bearable. I watch droplets of blood slither down the dangling strand of webbing at my elbow. One by one, they reach the end of their rope and drip onto my already soaked shirt.

We lift off, and my attention lifts from my shirt to the canyon. We fly higher and higher, and my gratitude again brings me nearly to tears, but dehydration has sealed shut my tear ducts. Although I'm wedged between the two passengers in the backseat, I can still see out the windows of the aircraft quite clearly. Staring straight ahead, I watch the twin black figures of Wayne and Eric recede to small blotches on the red canvas of Barrier Creek's gravel streambed until the chopper's window frame blocks them from view.

As we crest the rim of the canyon, my mind fumbles when it tries to comprehend the sudden shift of the horizon. The line demarcating the edge of my universe had been claustrophobically penned in for the past six days, trapped as I was, but now it leaps a hundred miles in a single moment, receding over the magnificent landscape of Canyonlands into the haze surrounding the La Sal Mountains in the east. My vision reels.

The vibrations of the helicopter engines mount to a dull roar, only barely muted by the headphones. "How long until we get to Green River?" I ask, unnecessarily straining to raise my voice.

Be strong, Aron. You're almost there. Hang on.

The pilot comes back, clearly audible over the scratchy background static: "We're going directly to Moab. It'll be about fifteen minutes."

Oh, wow, good. "Is there any water I can have?"

Both of the officers scramble, as if my request has shaken them out of their astonishment. I can't blame them. If a blood-soaked guy came and sat next to me, it'd be a few minutes before I would think to offer him a drink, too. The man on my left turns up a screw-top bottle of spring water and hands it to me. After I've held it for a second staring at it dazedly, he realizes the top is still on, so he unscrews it and gives it back. We shift around, and the uniformed officer on my right moves a jacket under my arm to soak up the bloody runoff.

In just two minutes, we come to a massive river below us, and from its color and our position, I'm certain it is the Green River. The pilot says over the headsets, "Keep him talking."

I reply, "I'm still drinking the water." I can hardly believe I'm still able to stomach any more liquid, or that I still feel thirst. Including what I've got in my hand now, I've drunk over two and a half gallons of water in the past three hours.

"Don't let him pass out," the pilot warns the officers. I'm not worried I'm going to pass out, as the pain won't even let me rest, but I do want to get to a hospital as soon as possible.

"How much longer do we have?" I inquire, sounding to myself like a whiny kid pleading for a bathroom break on a road trip with his family.

"Twelve minutes from here," the pilot says. We follow the river north for a minute or two in silence as I take another three gulps of water, finishing the bottle. When we bank to the right, I see a winding dirt road that drops over a canyon wall to the river. "See that road?" I ask.

The man on my right looks out the window and nods. "Yeah?"

"That's the beginning of the White Rim, uhh, Mineral Bottom, - it's called. I biked that with some of my friends a couple years ago. It's over a hundred miles." The officer seems slightly slow to absorb what I'm saying. Perhaps it's all in my perception of him, or perhaps it's his disbelief that I've turned the flight into a scenic tour. We're over the Island in the Sky district of Canyonlands, heading northeast. I know this area well enough to judge our progress. I ask the pilot, "Will we go by the *Monitor* and the *Merrimac?*"

"I don't know what those are," the pilot explains.

The officer on my right asks me what happened, and I begin to tell him about my week. I wriggle around enough that I can get the map out of my left pocket, and I show him where I was stuck. I explain about the chockstone, how it moved and I became trapped, how I shivered through five nights, how I ran out of water and drank my own urine, how I finally figured out how to amputate my arm. In recounting the story, I begin to wonder about the timing of the helicopter and how it found me in the canyon at the perfect moment when I needed it. If it had been an hour later, I would have died waiting for help. Or, if I had figured out how to cut off my arm two days earlier, when I stabbed myself, there wouldn't have been a helicopter, and I would have bled out before getting to my truck, let alone Green River. I had been right on Sunday when I said on the videotape that amputating my arm would have been a slow act of suicide.

After six minutes or so of explaining my story, I see two thin sandstone buttes out the front window. The formations of eroded rock resemble two submarines engaged in battle, and I declare, "Look, that's them, the *Monitor* and the *Merrimac*." I know we're getting close, but we seem to be banking to the right again when I was thinking town should be straight ahead. "How much farther?"

"Less than five minutes. We'll fly over that drop-off, and we'll be right over town."

A question digs at me. "How did you find my truck? I mean, I could have been anywhere."

"Your mom called our dispatcher yesterday and had us searching all the trailheads."

Four minutes later, the helicopter bursts over the rim rock, leaving Canyonlands behind, to reveal a lush valley, green with fields, and a forest of trees engulfing thousands of buildings. We cross the Colorado River and slow down as we approach the center of Moab, Utah, passing row upon neat row of houses and streets, ball fields, stores, schools, parking lots, and parks.

Circling around once, I see an open green lawn that we're apparently going to use as a landing zone. As the pilot touches the bird gently down on the vibrantly green grass, I notice that the building off to the right of the lawn is a hospital.

Oh my God, you made it.

There is a man in a Park Service uniform standing on an asphalt driveway off the right side of the helicopter. Next to him are two women in white coats at opposite ends of a wheeled stretcher. On the pilot's signal, the officer on my right swings the helicopter door open and hops out, holding the door for me to follow his lead. I undo my seat belt and carelessly let the headphones rip themselves off my head, then jump down onto the grass. Ducking my head, I take half a dozen long strides under the rotors, heading toward the asphalt. I approach the uniformed man who seems to accept my gruesome appearance with an expectant air, and without introducing myself, I announce in an urgent voice, "You need to know that I've lost a lot of blood, that I had to amputate my arm this morning after being trapped for six days without food or water, and that I'm wearing a tourniquet that I applied today. It's around my arm inside this packaging."

Seemingly impressed at my self-assessment, the man replies, - "Let's get you inside," as he turns to the women, who present the stretcher. I sit my rump on the gurney, lie down on my back, and swing my legs up. Bliss. I haven't been prone in six days, and I immediately begin to relax. If it weren't for the throbbing pain of the tourniquet on my stump, I could fall into a seven-year sleep.

The nurses push me through the automated doors of the emergency entrance and into an empty hospital receiving area. Another woman shuttling supplies into an emergency room looks at me with surprise, as though I've caught her in a compromising situation. Recognition follows her shocked stare, and I understand why there is no one at the reception desk or in the seating area. This is not a major metropolitan hospital where critically injured patients walk in off the street every few minutes; this is a quiet rural hospital on a Thursday afternoon in the early season. These three women probably constitute a significant portion of the present hospital staff. The trauma team is most likely on call; hopefully, they aren't far away. By current appearances, the hospital staff probably realized they had an inbound patient only a few minutes before the helicopter landed on the front lawn. One of the women tells the Park Service man to follow us into the emergency room as they cart me inside the sterile room and park the gurney next to the ER table under a large circular lamp hood in the middle of the room. The nurse at my head asks me if I can transfer myself to the table on my left side, which I manage while holding my right arm steadily off my chest.

Except for the Park Service man, the others disperse. One woman returns in a minute to tell the others who have brought in more supplies that "the anesthesiologist will be in in five minutes." The nurses remove my shoes, sock, and hat, then cover me with a gown. Next, the man speaks to me. "Aron, I'm Ranger Steve with the Park Service. Is there anything I can do for you?"

It isn't the question I am anticipating, but I think first of my mom. "Can you let my mom know that I'm OK?" Thinking of how she must have been involved in this and what it's done to her, my voice is but a tremulous whimper.

"Yes, I have her phone number. I'll call her as soon as we're done."

"Thank you." I pause and recompose myself, continuing, "I left a lot of stuff in the canyon. My ropes, my CD player, my harness, a lot of stuff. Would you be able to send someone in to clean up my stuff?"

"We'll certainly do that," Steve answers.

"Some of it's where I was trapped, some of it's below the rappel. My bike"—I pause, reaching under the gown for my pocket—"is by a juniper a hundred yards from the east side of the road, one mile south of Burr Pass." I pull out the folded-up map and hand it to Steve. Digging into my zipped pocket, I retrieve the bike-lock keys as Steve orients himself with the bloodstained map. "Here, these are the keys," I say, handing the small ring and twin keys across my body to Steve. "I locked the bike to itself, not to the tree, so in case I lost the keys, I could still get the bike back, but it will be easier to get the bike back to the road if the tires roll freely."

"Can you point to where your bike is?" Steve inquires, holding the map in front of me.

"Yeah, sure," I say, rolling over a little to extend my left hand. "Oh, no, I can't; it's off the end of the map. But it's right where I said, the last tree for a mile, a mile south of Burr Pass, which is a rise just off the edge of the map."

"Can you point to where you were trapped?"

"Yeah, it's the only east-west section of the canyon just above the Big Drop rappel. Do you see it there?" I point to the mark that reads, "Big Drop, 1550, Short Slot."

"OK, anything else?"

"Just keep track of my backpack, please, it's very important—it's on the helicopter—and get my truck and stuff. Thank you." I'm alert but exhausted, and I want to close my eyes, but I know I can't sleep. Then a woman in a white smock and face mask enters the room and introduces herself as the anesthesiologist, asking what happened. I tell her the short version, and she scoots off through a side door of the ER, promising she'll be back with some drugs.

Steve says, "Aron, I'd like to get as much information from you as I can. How big was the boulder?"

"I think it was two hundred pounds. I budged it just a little right after it first fell on me, but I couldn't lift it with my rigging, so it had to be at least that, I guess."

"And when did it fall on you?"

"It was about two forty-five Saturday afternoon."

"How did it happen?"

"I pulled it loose. It was stuck—it was a chockstone—and I stepped onto it, then climbed down off it, and I pulled it. It bounced back and forth, smashed my left hand a little, then caught my right hand. I was trying to push away from underneath it when my hand got caught." I can hardly believe I'm telling this story. I'm dumbfounded that I'm lying on this table, given the odds that I would survive six days of dehydration and hypothermia, then survive cutting my arm off, rappelling, and hiking seven miles through the desert. And that helicopter. That was a miracle.

Before Steve can ask any more questions, the anesthesiologist returns, this time carrying a loaded syringe and a needle that looks to my eyes like it's big enough to inoculate a horse. I know what she's going to do, and I interrupt her in a firm voice. "Whoa, I need to tell you something. Sometimes I have reactions to needles. I've passed out from shots, and I fell out of a chair once after having my blood drawn. My doctor told me to tell people that before I get a shot. In my condition now, I don't know what might happen to me. I could go into shock."

The doctor, stopped cold in her tracks at my first words, absorbs what I am telling her with a fixed stare. All I can see are her eyes, which are wide open with disbelief, even as she says, "You mean - you're *not* in shock?"

"I don't know, clinically, maybe, I don't—"

She shortcuts my wavering with a direct question: "I've got this morphine ready. Do you want it or not?"

"Oh hell yes!" I exclaim. "Give it to me. Just hold me on the table if I start slithering around, OK?"

I look over at Ranger Steve as the doctor injects the needle. A mild burning courses up my arm as the narcotic enters my vein, but I never lose consciousness. Steve and I resume our debriefing as I describe my intended route from the Horseshoe Canyon trailhead down the Maze road, through Blue John Canyon, over the Big Drop, and back to my truck via Horseshoe Canyon. Explaining the dimensions of the section of slot where I was trapped, I reiterate the size of the rock and tell Steve how I was stuck in a standing position but that I rigged up an anchor so I could take the weight off my legs. I fill in the time line as best I can before I get drowsy from the morphine, outlining when I ran out of water, when I ran out of food, and when I figured out how to break my arm bones and amputate my arm. Then, as I hear a new voice, a man's baritone, asking what the items are covering my right arm, I feel someone tugging at the CamelBak pack that I used as a sling, and I hear Ranger Steve say, "There's a tourniquet or two under there. The rest is just padding." With the world diving into a tunnel, I manage to slur, "Juss one, on my forearm," before my streak of 127 hours of uninterrupted experience ends at three forty-five P.M., Thursday, May 1, 2003.

Ranger Steve Swanke takes my map and the notes from our discussion and walks into the reception area. After he collects himself from the surreal twenty-minute conversation he just had with me, his first action is to unclip his Park Service–issued cell phone from his belt and call my mom. She answers on the second ring, "Hello, this is Donna," her voice stronger and more hopeful than the first time Steve heard her answer the phone with those words.

"Donna, hello. It's Ranger Steve again. I have some good news and some bad news. We've found your son; he's alive and he's going to live." Steve pauses and then issues the more difficult half of the update: "He was forced to amputate his arm to get out of the situation he was in. He's in Moab now, but I'm sure he'll be headed to Grand Junction shortly."

My mom exhales heavily, as if she had been holding her breath for the last two days. "Thank God." She instantly feels the relief of a mighty burden lifted. Her prayers have been answered: Her son is alive, and he's going to be OK.

Still holding the phone, she turns to Sue Doss, who is at the kitchen table. "Sue, they found him! He's going to be OK!" Never in her life has she been more full of joy than in that moment. For my mom, even the bad news is a blessing in that it isn't any worse. She gathers herself, and the words rush out to Steve: "Oh, thank you, thank you. Thank you for bringing him back. We'll leave right away."

"Is there anything I can do for you?"

"Please be in touch as you know more."

"I'll do that. Anything else?"

A second request forms slowly in her mind, and she teases it out. - "You'll probably have to file a report or talk to the media about Aron. Please don't be judgmental."

Taking a few minutes to assess his notes, Ranger Steve sorts through the facts, looking for causes and contributing factors. As an experienced outdoorsman himself, he reflects for a few moments about how many times he has gone out hiking and kayaking by himself. "What is this all about? I go out and engage in risk activities by myself without always telling my wife where I'm going. It's happening in Canyonlands today. There are people out there on their own involved in risk activities, solo, without anyone knowing where they are." He fingers the map, knowing from my website that I am an experienced canyoneer and that Blue John Canyon is not a difficult canyon. Usually, Steve expects that an accident's severity will be proportional to the terrain—extreme consequences befit extreme environments—but this event was catastrophic relative to the ease of the topography. "This is five-one canyoneering; it really doesn't get any easier than this. I move rocks hiking in the canyons all the time, I can relate to that. We dance with these canyons with white gloves on, like we're walking on eggshells. That's what canyoneers do. We're always conscious of it: 'Is this rock going to move?' or 'Is that rock going to move?'"

Steve peers through the window in the door of the ER, watching the nurses and the doctor bustling around my unconscious body, thinking about what makes the difference in those thousands of decisions on any given outing. "Most of the time we judge it right, and on occasion we judge it wrong," he deliberates, "and most of the time when we judge it wrong, the consequences are pretty inconsequential. On occasion, the consequences are pretty significant." He concludes, "This was someone being in the wrong place at the wrong time, an extreme case of bad luck. It's just bad luck."

After talking with Captain Kyle Ekker, my friend Rachel Polver calls Elliott, her voice ringing with excitement. "They found Aron! Are you sitting down?"

"Yeah, sure," Elliott lies, pacing around the living room of the house at Spruce Street.

"He's alive . . . but he cut off his arm."

Elliott's muscles stop propelling him around the room. His stunned reaction is "Holy cow, I should have been sitting down for that."

Immediately after landing, pilot Terry Mercer calls in a fuel truck from the Grand County search-and-rescue group. DPS flies for enough rescues in the Moab area that the local SAR team has access to a small tanker. One of the team's rescue leaders, Bego Gerhart, drives the truck to the hospital, since Terry doesn't have enough fuel left to take off and fly to the airport just ten miles north of town. As the helicopter refuels, Ranger Steve asks Detective Funk and Sergeant Vetere to pick up a soft-sided cooler from the hospital and fill it with ice. The ER doctor, Dr. Bobby Higgins, wants to see what he can do to save my hand for a possible reattachment. Greg and Mitch's next assignment is to return to Blue John Canyon, find the place where I had been trapped, and retrieve my severed right hand. Mitch doesn't want to fly any more than he has to to get back to his vehicle at the trailhead, so Terry yells over to Bego at the fuel truck, "Hey, you wanna go for a ride?"

Bego is up for the trip and joins Greg in the back of the helicopter for the fifteen-minute flight back to Horseshoe Canyon. Terry drops Mitch at the trailhead at four-thirty P.M., and then Terry, Greg, and Bego take off to find the slot. With the map I gave Steve, and with - Bego's knowledge of the area, they are able to land precisely on a sandstone knoll above the hidden slot. Once in the canyon, Terry is out of his element, but as a more experienced canyoneer, Bego coaches him along. They figure they'll need all three men to roll the boulder off of my hand. They scramble down past the entry drop-off, run the chockstone gauntlet, twist through the meandering narrows, and in five minutes, come to an installation of ropes and webbing hanging from the point of a ledge at their feet. This must be the place.

Climbing down from the lip of the drop, the trio easily determines that they will not be able to move the chockstone without significant mechanical aid. It's not sitting on the ground, as they imagined, but wedged between the walls, and they estimate it to be closer to half a ton than the two hundred pounds I reported. For the time being, the decomposing remains of my long-dead hand cannot be retrieved. After Greg takes a few photographs for evidence, they collect the yellow webbing, green and orange rope, and other artifacts of my six-day tenure in that hole, and scramble back up the slot to the helicopter, leaving behind the fresh smear of blood on the canyon wall where my hand is crushed beside the fallen chockstone.

After untold hours of unconsciousness, I come to. I'm lying in a dark hospital room, with fluorescent light from the nurses' station filtering through the translucent drapes pulled across the window to my left. My vision is blurred, but I can see that I am alone. Before I pass out again, my single thought is "I am *alive*."

* * *

Sometime later, I wake up again. A nurse walks into my room and says in a cheery voice, "I thought I heard some rustling."

"I'm alive," I say to her in a gasp. I know I'm alive because I am in pain. My right arm aches, my legs ache, my left hand aches; in fact, there is nary a part of me that doesn't ache.

"Yes, you are alive. Your mom will be happy to know that when she comes back."

"Mom?" I say, my voice rasping just above a whisper, delicate and weak. The word releases an internal torrent of love that courses through me, overwhelming my drugged brain and loosing a deluge of sobs.

Mom.

It hurts my body to cry, but I have no control. As the tears recede, I see a clock on the wall but I can't read the time. Someone has taken out my contacts. I squint and make out both clock hands pointing somewhere to the left of down. It's shortly after seven- or eight-thirty, only four hours since I was rescued. Moab is at least a seven-hour drive from Denver. Despite the sedation, my mind works well enough to know the math doesn't add up.

"She'll be back. She was here last night after your surgery. She's probably having breakfast, and she'll be in in a half hour or so."

Last night? Breakfast? I ponder those concepts for a long moment, perplexed in my fatigue. It must be morning. "What day is it?"

"It's Friday morning," the nurse explains while finishing up her duties, moving precisely about my bed.

"Oh," I say, but it comes out as a soft moan. I am stumped by my inability to link together any experience since I lost consciousness on the table in the ER. It seems like I just blinked, and now I'm in a different room. Moab is a long way from Denver. Did my mom fly here? "How did she get here so fast?" I manage to ask, my throat chafing with dryness.

"Where did she come from?"

"Denver."

"It's only about four and a half, five hours to drive here."

Five hours? That can't be. "Five hours to get to Moab?"

"Oh, you're not in Moab, dear, you're in Grand Junction. They flew you over last night."

"Oh," I mutter, trying to orient myself. I have no recollection of another flight after that amazing helicopter ride. But Grand Junction, I understand that. I'm in Colorado.

I am immobilized by exhaustion, which is a good thing, considering I have a full octopus's compliment of tubes, insulated wires, and other unnatural tentacles running across the sheets into various parts of my arms and head. Before I can entertain any further explorations of my environment, I pass out again.

When I come around the next time, Sue Doss is at my bedside. I am pleased and comforted to see her. In her soft Texas twang, Sue says, "Your mom is right outside," and she steps out the door to get her.

My mom walks into the ICU room. The harsh light of the fluorescent boxes embedded in the ceiling bathes her in a glorious glow. I can't distinguish her features—but I can see her take two steps to stand beside me on my left side. I lift my left hand, and she takes it in both of hers. Her hands are cool, soft, and trembling ever so slightly. She bends down and kisses my forehead. At close range, I can see how much worry I've caused my mom, and though I can barely speak, I scrape out "Mom, I'm sorry I scared you. I love you." She shakes her head, and before either of us knows it, we are crying together.

Regaining her ability to speak as the sniffles subside several minutes later, my mom tells me, "Sue and I were joking that if it wasn't a broken leg that had kept you from coming home, you were going to have two broken ones by the time we got done with you."

We both choke out a laugh and smile at each other. Love passes between us, reaching that spot that can be touched only by the reunion of a son with his mother, a mother with her son. I know we both want it to be a long time before we leave each other's side again.

Epilogue:
A Farewell to Arm

You've got to love the life you live, and live the life you love.
—JERRY GARCIA BAND, "(I'm a) Roadrunner"

THE DAYS AND WEEKS following my rescue were nothing short of extraordinary. Even before my dad arrived in Grand Junction, my story was headline news across the globe. I had lost forty pounds and a liter and a half of blood in the canyon and had a long recovery ahead, the progress of which I could watch on the CNN scrolling news ticker: "Colorado climber who amputated own arm in critical care." After three surgeries in five days and more pancakes than had ever been consumed by a patient in the St. Mary's intensive care unit, the floral arrangements and I outgrew the ICU and had to be moved to a room upstairs, where, during my brief episodes of consciousness, my dad read to me from stacks of letters that came from my friends and from strangers, from just around the corner and from all the way around the world. One woman from Salt Lake City sent a card telling me she had flushed a stockpile of her deceased husband's sleeping pills down the toilet. She wrote, "Your act of bravery has inspired me to hold on more dearly. I had promised myself that I would end my life if things had not gotten better one year after my husband's death. I know now that suicide is not the answer. You inspire me to stay strong, remain brave and to fight for life." My parents and I wept over that letter every time we read it; it was a reminder in difficult times of the greater ripple effects that my rescue and recovery were having on people.

Throughout that week, there were few moments when my parents left my side. With their love, the encouragement of thousands of prayers, special stealth visits by many of my friends, and the excellent care of the St. Mary's doctors and nurses, I slowly regained enough mobility that by Wednesday, May 7, I was ready for my first journey outdoors since my accident. The hospital's recreational therapist would have taken my dad and me to the park across the street, but because an armada of journalists and photographers guarded the hospital doors around the clock, we instead enjoyed a commanding view of Grand Junction's greenery and canyon escarpments from a couple of folding chairs perched on the hospital roof. The air and the colors held a sweet vibrancy throughout the half hour we spent swapping outdoors stories and talking about baseball. It was one of my favorite memories from a lifetime of special moments with my dad.

Also that afternoon, I received a package in the mail: a gift from my friend Chris Shea, who lives in Portland. Opening the box and unwrapping the tinfoil coverings, I found a chocolate cake slathered with icing—in the shape of my right hand. When a group of my Aspen friends drove out to see me that night, bringing binders full of music for me to enjoy while I was laid up, my mom cut the cake and served it up with milk from the hospital cafeteria. It was an oddly funny moment, watching my friends smile and laugh as we joked, "Take this, eat; do this in memory of my hand." We named the reunion the Last Dessert.

Thursday, I donned my own clothes for the first time in a week and borrowed my mom's camera for a special occasion. Heavily stoned on three prescribed varieties of the best narcotics known to mankind, I rode with my parents in a hospital car to an auxiliary building half a block away and walked into a room filled with some five dozen reporters and possibly twice that many camera crews and photographers. I couldn't help myself—I had to take a couple of snapshots. This was the way the world met me, and I guess a lot of first impressions were made during that twenty-minute news conference. I'd just like to say, in my own defense, that I was higher than a lost kite in a hurricane. When a reporter asked me what three things I was most looking forward to and I said, "Going home with my parents, taking a walk with my friends, and sipping back on a tall, cold, salted, frosty margarita," that's because it was the truth. I can't say how many times I thought about margaritas when I was trapped—probably not as much as I thought about my family and my friends, but it was a lot.

Immediately after the press gathering, I talked with my photographer friend Dan Bayer, who had come to Grand Junction to take pictures for the *Aspen Times*. Earlier in the week, he had gone into Horseshoe Canyon and hiked the seven miles to the rappel site at the Big Drop. Along the way, he had found my harness and belay/rappel device where I'd abandoned them, and he returned them to me. He told me he had seen the pool of water at the bottom of the rappel, the one I drank from, and he asked me, "Did you see the dead raven floating in it?"

Once I was off the most potent narcotics, St. Mary's released me. My parents and I drove home to Denver, where friends from six states had flown in for a surprise reception. In one weekend, I fulfilled two of the three things on my "looking forward to" list. It wouldn't be until I weaned myself off the eighteen pills I was taking each day that I would be able to enjoy a big ol' salty marg.

By Thursday, May 15, I was in the hospital again, this time St. - Luke's Presbyterian Hospital in Denver. Only two days earlier, my doctors had discovered a potentially lethal bone infection in my right arm. The same dirty knife that had saved me was now killing me. After yet another surgery, I was put on the strongest intravenous antibiotics available (needles), and then had battery after battery of blood tests (more needles) to check that the drugs were fighting the infection. The next day, Friday, was to be my sister's graduation from Texas Tech University. With more tests and another surgery pending, I cried with my parents as it became clear that I wouldn't make it to Texas to see Sonja receive her diploma. Then, just twenty hours before the ceremonies in Lubbock, my doctors and nurses came up with a plan that would allow me to leave the hospital for three days. With intricate instructions on how to inject the intravenous antibiotics ourselves, my parents and I sped off on a ten-hour midnight drive to Lubbock, Texas. While my dad steered us down the two-lane highways of the Texas panhandle at 70 mph, my mom ran my IV system from the backseat, hanging the drip bags on the coat hook above the side window. By the time we arrived in Lubbock, the car looked like a MASH unit, littered as it was with spent supplies and torn packaging, but we were in time for the Honors College awards banquet where Sonja was honored as the Texas Tech Outstanding Student of the Year. Once all the weekend festivities were over, my parents and I helped my sister pack up her belongings, and then we sat down with my grandma Ralston for a family tradition: playing round after round of euchre. It was just like old times.

Back in Denver, I had one last surgery, and an interesting one it was. I needed an angiogram, which is not, as one might think, a message personally delivered by a singing cherub, but a procedure that started with a curiously smiling prep nurse shaving off the right half of my pubic hair, and then inserting a catheter into my femoral artery until it slid up into my chest. The nurses used the catheter to pump X-ray-sensitive dye into my bloodstream, whereupon I could watch the veins of my right arm appear periodically on a television screen. That was just the warm-up round. Once the results from the angiogram were in, the plastic surgeon knew which of the three retracted arteries to go after in my arm. My tourniquet had damaged one, but the others were in good shape. This was important, because subsequently, the surgeon transplanted a four-inch-long segment of muscle from my inner left thigh onto the end of my right stump, and after fishing out the arteries in my arm, he connected their blood supplies to the slab of raw meat stitched onto my forearm. For the finishing touch, he sliced a rectangular section of skin from my right thigh and patched over the whole end of my arm. This little ten-hour surgery I did not get to watch on television. (It was preempted by the war in Iraq.)

The hours after I came up from the anesthetic proved to be the lowest point of my recovery; I hit bottom that night. I had seven tubes running in and out of me, three new sources of pain from the donor sites as well as my right heel (pressure from my foot's weight had pinched a nerve in my heel during the surgery); I couldn't sleep, and wasn't allowed to eat or drink, so I complained mercilessly. How was it that I had cut off my arm without so much as a whimper, and yet now all I could do was whine? The nurses upped my narcotics hour after hour, but they couldn't touch the pain. Eventually, though, I couldn't put three words together to form a sentence; I wanted to tell my mom and dad I was sorry for being such a bitch, but it only frustrated me more to try and talk. My mom sat through it all for six hours until dawn, forgoing sleep and trying to comfort me, though my suffering was relentless despite the drugs. When the morning light came through the drapes, it illuminated her face in a saintly glow, and I cried at her beauty until I finally passed out.

By May 25, I had spent seventeen days in the hospital, but at last I went home for good. I was fixed up, I'd put on almost all of my lost weight, and the bone infection was retreating. However, being on the IV antibiotic program meant that once every eight hours, I had to lie down and get connected to a drip bag for half an hour. This went on for six weeks. Even when it meant getting up in the middle of the night, my mom and dad were always there to make sure I got my medications at the right time. All I had to do was sit still, but I hated that IV system and the weakness that it represented, and I rarely let an opportunity to complain about it pass me by.

Convalescence was hard on me. Not just the drip-bag routine but the whole thing. I hurt all the time from both phantom and real pain, even with the drugs. While I was continuously medicated, I never rested well. Usually, I would lie in bed all night semi-comatose—not really awake, but not sleeping, either. Narcotic stupor doesn't allow your mind to reset properly. As each dosage came on, I would involuntarily crash—in doctors' offices, between occupational and physical therapy sessions on a bench in the clinic's workout room, or while sitting in traffic as my mom shuttled me home. When I revived, it was because the drugs were wearing off, and then all I had was anguish. My frustrations and the drugs turned me into such a bossy and grouchy snot that even I was sick of hearing myself.

My being at home again was difficult for all of us, too. Though we were thankful to have one another and felt blessed to be together as a family, the workload took its toll. My parents each had their businesses to tend to besides looking after me. Add in my appointments, drugs, and insurance issues, and on top of it all, the media and public attention—we had to leave the phone off the hook for almost two months, and called the local authorities to fend off the television station vehicles that staked out the house—and we were all worn threadbare.

For the first four weeks, I was as dependent as a toddler. I found myself easily fed up by the effort involved with my new life, in which rest, recovery, and rehab had replaced skiing, mountaineering, and concerts. Everything was so time-consuming; one clinic appointment occupied an entire morning of preparation and commuting for my mom and me. And there were a hundred appointments, all of which had to be coordinated around my drug schedule. I didn't get out of Blue John Canyon to spend my life in a groggy blur of structured confinement perforated with agony. Yet that's what my life had become.

The challenge in the canyon had been severe but straightforward. Once I was out, the challenges became more complex, and at first, I felt unprepared to adapt to my new circumstances. I wanted to get my life back, but that meant I had to learn how to cope with my frustrations and turn them into motivation for action. The drugs were my first targets. In June, with most of the post-operation pain fading, I gradually weaned myself off the painkillers. I could once again enjoy a few choice freedoms—driving my truck, going running with my friends, enjoying a big ol' salted margarita. I regained more and more of my self-sufficiency and "grew up" again in a process akin to a second adolescence. My mom didn't want to let me go, and I couldn't blame her, but I had to get my independence back, for both our sakes.

Once I was off the narcotics, things got better quickly. I learned how to tie my shoelaces and even tie a necktie one-handed. Improving rapidly, I practiced my left-handed print and cursive (I had been a righty prior to my accident) and began typing on my laptop with just five fingers. My occupational therapist got me a rocker knife so I could cut meat. With either adaptive equipment or new techniques, I relearned how to do just about everything I needed. I figured out how to put on my watch and fasten that tricky left wrist button on my dress shirts using my teeth. Still, there were things I needed help with. Sometimes my independence drove me not to ask. Other times, though the offered help was well meant, I wanted to figure things out for myself. In the kitchen one afternoon, I caught my sister trying a little too hard to be sensitive while watching me start to peel an orange.

"Do you need a . . ." She let the question die.

"Do I need a *hand?*" I finished for her. "Of course I do, silly; I've only got one now." I smiled at her, and she blushed. Getting out my rocker knife, I cut the orange into unpeeled eighths, just like I used to eat at Little League soccer. I secretly stuck a slice in my mouth so it covered my teeth and started hopping around doing my impression of a gorilla. Just at the moment my sister thought I'd totally lost my marbles, I flashed my goofy grin at her, revealing the orange peel. It caught her right as she was taking a sip of water, and she snorted back into her glass, splashing her face. After that, it was a joke for us, her asking me if I needed a hand even when I wasn't doing anything.

Because of my margarita comment at the press conference, people sent me all sorts of related gifts: twenty-dollar bills with yellow stickies labeled "Margaritas," gift certificates to Mexican restaurants with reputations for making good margs, even bottles of tequila. Periodically, I got large packages that usually turned out to contain margarita supplies. When I opened one particular box, the contents briefly stunned me. I called my sister into the kitchen. There, besides the bottles of tequila, triple sec, and margarita mix, was a box containing a Black & Decker rechargeable-battery-powered blender. No way. My sister and I became giddy imagining the possibilities—hiking up high peaks, pulling out the backcountry blender, and making margaritas right from the snow. How cool was that? I called out, "High five," and raised my arms, facing my sister. She put her hands up, ready for contact, and at the last split second, as we both realized the problem, she redirected to give my left hand a high ten. "Ha-ha! You totally forgot!" I teased her. "No, you put it up there, you forgot, too." She was right, I had. We still laugh about our whiffed high five.

Highlights from the next few months sound so improbable that I can barely believe they happened to me. Four of my friends and I were invited to dinner with our rock idol, Trey Anastasio, and his eight-piece band before their June performance at the Fillmore in Denver. Another of my favorite bands, the String Cheese Incident, ran a major benefit auction and poster sale at Aron's Incident, a July concert held in my name in Santa Fe, New Mexico, that raised seventeen thousand dollars for the five volunteer search-and-rescue groups in Utah, Colorado, and New Mexico that assisted with my rescue. Kristi and Megan, the two women from Moab whom I met in Blue John Canyon, came to the concert, as did my sister and my parents, and about two gazillion of my friends.

I made my return to the mountains with a visit to the avalanche site on Resolution Mountain, where we recovered the belongings Chadwick, Mark, and I lost in the Grade 5 slide in February, including my Sony digital camera, which, when I changed out the battery—despite the shock of the avalanche and the facts that it melted through a ten-foot-deep snowpack, was exposed to four months of rain and sun, and got chewed on by marmots—started working again on the spot. It's still taking great pictures. (Well done, Sony.)

In July, I went on David Letterman's show, met a dozen of the biggest names in broadcast journalism, saw five concerts around the West with my friends, went rock climbing with my new prosthetic arm in Castlewood Canyon near Denver, and hiked a contiguous series of five fourteeners in thirty hours in central Colorado. August saw me rock climbing with my fellow amputee and friend Malcolm Daly in El Dorado Canyon near Boulder, pacing my friend Rich Haefele to his first ultramarathon finish in the Leadville Trail 100, and surviving two hair-raising back-to-back days of intense photo shoots for *GQ*'s "Men of the Year" issue and *Vanity Fair*'s "People of 2003" issue.

On August 31, I gave a reading at my sister's wedding, about how love is like a dance. She looked more beautiful than I'd ever seen her as she said "I do" to her husband, Zack Elder. During the reception, Sonja and I boogied together to "Climb," her favorite String Cheese Incident tune, laughing and smiling as we let our freak flags fly in front of all our relatives.

Four days after the wedding, I climbed the standard route on Mount Moran in Wyoming with a team of eight of my friends. The special treat for me was leading the majority of the difficult sections of climbing using the one-of-a-kind prosthetic device that I designed with the production help of three amazingly generous companies: Hanger Prosthetics, Therapeutic Recreation Systems, and Trango (a climbing equipment company). Two weeks later, I competed in Minnesota's Adventure Duluth race with my two teammates, finishing in the middle of the pack after twelve miles of sea kayaking, four miles of white-water canoeing, and twelve miles of trail running.

In September, my mom and I watched the video I'd made in the canyon. We cried together—it was hard for my mom to see my suffering on the tape, but it made us both thankful to still have each other in our lives. We sat on the couch and held hands, saying "I love you," over and over.

And then there was the return to Blue John Canyon. I took four of my friends, Mark Van Eeckhout, Jason Halladay, Steve Patchett, and Kristi Moore, as well as an entire team from *Dateline NBC,* through the slot where I was trapped from Saturday, April 26, until Thursday, May 1, 2003. In one of those odd synchronicities of life, I stood on top of the boulder that had crushed and pinned my hand exactly six months *to the minute* of when it fell on me. Once everyone else cleared out down through the canyon, I held a solitary ceremony in which I distributed the cremated ashes of my hand in the accident site and rubbed out the visible remnants of the "RIP OCT 75 ARON APR 03" inscription on the southern wall, two days before my twenty-eighth birthday. Later that night, back at our helicopter-supported encampment, I dropped a plastic cup of red wine on Tom Brokaw's shoe.

Over the course of the summer, my sister and I had joked repeatedly about my new status as a pirate, practicing our "arrs" and our "me-hearties" together. Imagine our amusement, then, when we discovered that September 19, 2003, had been officially designated as "International Talk Like a Pirate Day." A month later, I went as Captain Funhook for Halloween in Aspen, and was delighted when I ran into a fellow climber dressed up as Aron Ralston, post-self-surgery.

Through the fall and winter, I returned to lead climbing on rock, mountain biking, ice climbing, backcountry telemark skiing, cross-country skate skiing, and solo winter mountaineering. I solo-climbed Mount Wilson and El Diente Peak on March 17 and 18, 2004, in official winter, making my first solo winter fourteener ascents since my accident and bringing my project total to forty-seven of fifty-nine. In the next two seasons, I plan to finish the project, potentially becoming the first person to solo-climb all fifty-nine of the Colorado 14,000-foot peaks in winter. By the end of the season, I was performing at, near, or even in some cases, above my ability levels prior to my accident. My roommate and friend Elliott Larson and I raced together in the Elk Mountains Grand Traverse, the ski race from Crested Butte to Aspen, and took six hours off the time Gareth Roberts and I set in 2003, when I had both my hands. Next year, I'm going to cut off my left arm and see how much faster I can go.

For all that has happened and the opportunities still developing in my life, I feel blessed. I was part of a miracle that has touched a great number of people in the world and I wouldn't trade that for anything, not even to have my hand back. My accident in and rescue from Blue John Canyon were the most beautifully spiritual experiences of my life, and knowing that, were I to travel back in time, I would still say "see you later" to Megan and Kristi and take off into that lower slot by myself. While I've learned much, I have no regrets about that choice. Indeed, it has affirmed my belief that our purpose as spiritual beings is to follow our bliss, seek our passions, and live our lives as inspirations to each other. Everything else flows from that. When we find inspiration, we need to take action for ourselves and for our communities. Even if it means making a hard choice, or cutting out something and leaving it in your past.

Saying farewell is also a bold and powerful beginning.

BIOGRAPHICAL CHRONOLOGY

1987 Moved to Englewood, Colorado; started middle school; went skiing for the first time

1988 First overnight backpacking trip, in Rocky Mountain National Park

1990 First trip to Utah; visited Arches, Capitol Reef, Bryce, and Zion national parks and monuments

1993 Graduated from Cherry Creek High School; rafted Cataract Canyon in Canyonlands National Park, Utah; moved to Pittsburgh, Pennsylvania, to attend Carnegie Mellon University

1994 Hiked first fourteener, Longs Peak, in Colorado

1995 Was a raft guide on the Arkansas River in Colorado for the summer; moved to Lausanne, Switzerland, for a year of study abroad

1997 Graduated from Carnegie Mellon University; stalked by a black bear in Grand Teton National Park; started working at Intel in Phoenix, Arizona

1998 First winter climb on Humphreys Peak, Arizona; first alpine rock-climbing trip on Vestal Peak, Colorado; backpacked into Havasupai Canyon with my sister for Thanksgiving; climbed first winter solo fourteener, Quandary Peak

1999 Moved to Tacoma, Washington; climbed Mount Rainier and Mount Shuksan in Washington; moved to Albuquerque, New Mexico; joined the Albuquerque Mountain Rescue Council

2001   Climbed in the Cordillera Blanca in Peru; finished hiking the Colorado fourteeners in November

2002   Left Intel; climbed Denali in Alaska in June; moved to Aspen, Colorado, in November

2003   Climbed Pyramid, Holy Cross, Longs, Capitol, and the Maroon Bells as winter solo ascents; got caught in a Grade 5 avalanche on Resolution Peak, Colorado; visited Blue John Canyon, Utah

GLOSSARY

anchor: To fix a rope to the mountain by any of a variety of means, including: placing removable or permanent climbing gear into tapered cracks; looping webbing around a thick tree trunk, or around a large rock or chockstone; or drilling bolts into the rock.

ATC: Air Traffic Controller, a brand name of a belay/rappel device.

belay/rappel device: A variable-friction device that controls the speed a rope passes through it, used both to belay another climber or to rappel.

BLM: Bureau of Land Management, the government agency responsible for managing some federally controlled public lands; separate from national forest, monument, or park lands.

CamelBak: A company that makes water reservoirs and backpacks for outdoor sports; especially useful for hands-free drinking. The user sucks water through a tube connected to the reservoir.

carabiner (also 'biner): A metal link with a gate that opens and closes, allowing a climber to clip the link to an anchor, the rope, webbing, or a belay/rappel device. For better security, some carabiners have lockable gates.

chimneying: A climbing technique that uses the counteracting pressure of feet and hands on opposite walls to move up or down a chimney-width rock feature such as in narrow slot canyons. Also known as stemming.

climbing rope: A special design of rope with a core and sheath that stretches when dynamically loaded, absorbing a significant amount of the energy generated when a climber falls, as opposed to static ropes that do not stretch.

cornice: A snow feature usually found on summits and ridges where wind blows and compacts the snow into an overhanging bulge, like a frozen wave curl.

couloir: A funnel- or hourglass-shaped snow-filled gully, usually exposed to rock and ice falling into it.

crampons: Metal spikes, often arranged ten or twelve per foot on boot-length metal platforms that are strapped to mountaineering boots for climbing snow and ice.

daisy chain: A six-foot-long sewed loop of half-inch-wide Spectra webbing that is stitched to itself every five inches along its length, creating a series of load-bearing fabric links in a "chain" of webbing. Typically, at exposed rappel anchor sites, with one end of the daisy chain hitched to his climbing harness, a climber clips a carabiner through one of the links to a solid anchor to prevent a fall while working near the edge.

downclimbing: Descending steep terrain using climbing techniques, as opposed to rappelling or using anchors.

DPS: Department of Public Safety; in Utah, the DPS oversees the state highway patrol.

ECSO: Emery County sheriff's office.

ICS: Incident Command System, the command structure and guidelines used by most government agencies and search-and-rescue teams to manage large-scale emergency operations.

Lexan: Trade name of a type of hard plastic, used in some outdoor recreation water bottles.

mixed: Combination of ice, snow, and rock terrain; also mixed climbing, climbing on mixed terrain, using crampons and ice tools on rock.

Nalgene: Brand name of a company that makes outdoor recreation water bottles.

NPS: National Park Service, an agency within the Department of the Interior that administers national monument and park lands.

progress-capture loop: A knot, such as a Prusik knot, used in lifting systems to hold the load in place while the haul system is reset for a subsequent lift.

Prusik knot: A special friction knot useful for ratcheting operations such as ascending a rope or in pulley systems. When loose, the knot can be slid up a rope but locks when tightened under downward force.

randonée (also alpine touring, or A/T): Backcountry skiing equipment similar to downhill ski equipment but with rear binding components that allow the boot heel to lift for uphill travel, then lock the heel down in ski descent mode. Unlike telemark skiing boots, A/T boots can be used with most crampons.

rappelling: Descending a cliff using a rope and a special friction device.

rappel ring (also rap ring): A welded aluminum ring that links a climbing rope to an anchor for rappelling, allowing a climber to pull the rope down from the anchor more freely, once the rappel is completed.

SAR: Search and rescue.

Spectra: Trade name for a type of synthetic fiber used in climbing ropes and webbing, stronger for its weight than traditional fibers.

stemming: See "Chimneying."

telemark: Backcountry skiing equipment with a single free-heel mode that allows for both uphill travel and downhill skiing; named for a region in Norway. Downhill technique on telemark gear uses an alternating dropped-knee stance that advances one ski in front of the other to execute a turn. Telemark boots have a toe baffle that flexes, which is necessary for the telemark ski stance, but which makes them incompatible with most crampons.

travertine: A type of rock formed by water with high concentrations of lime that are deposited wherever the stream flows or splashes. As the creek changes course or water levels drop, lime residue solidifies into travertine and changes from white to burgundy as other minerals in the accretion, notably iron, oxidize and turn red.

webbing: Flat or tubular strips of closely woven high-strength fabric, useful for building climbing anchors. Usually used in three-quarter, one-inch, and one-and-a-half-inch widths.

yarding: In climbing, to pull hard on a handhold.

ACKNOWLEDGMENTS

Dedication

This book is a testimony to the love of my parents, Donna and Larry Ralston, and my awesome sister, Sonja Marie Ralston Elder. For the memories we've had together and for the ones we have yet to create, I got out of that canyon.

With special love for Marjorie Ralston and Grace Anderson, and in memory of my grandfathers, P. K. Ralston and Karl Anderson, and our family friend Betty Darr—I think of you every time I see a sunrise. To the hundreds of friends I met through my time at Cherry Creek High School, Carnegie Mellon University, Intel, and in Aspen, it was all of you who sustained my spirit in the canyon.

For the awe-inspiring power of the greater spirit, I am here to bear witness that there are energies larger than we are that surround us everywhere, and when the times are right, we can connect with those energies. Those times of connection are the spiritual structure of miracles.

For their friendship and help in my rescue: my roommates Leona Sondie, Brian Payne, Elliott Larson, and Joe Wheadon; my best friend in Aspen, Rachel Polver; my colleagues and managers at the Ute Mountaineer, most notably Brion After and Bob Wade; Steve Patchett, Mark Van Eeckhout, Jason Halladay, Dan Hadlich, and Brad and Leah Yule; and all my friends who helped by phone and by e-mail to create the chain of events that led to my rescue. To Michelle Kiel, Ann Fort, Sue Doss, and Dave Brush, my thanks for your support of my parents in those most terrifying days.

To my rescuers, what you do day in and day out can hardly be appreciated enough: Rangers Steve Swanke and Glenn Sherrill and the National Park Service; Captain Kyle Ekker, Sergeant Mitch Vetere, and Detective Greg Funk and the Emery County sheriff's office; Chief Deputy Doug Bliss and the Wayne County sheriff's office; pilot Terry Mercer and the Utah Department of Public Safety; the volunteers of the Grand, Emery, and Wayne counties' search-and-rescue teams, Mountain Rescue Aspen, and the Albuquerque Mountain Rescue Council; the Aspen police; the Meijer family; Wayne Marrs; and Spanish Valley Mortuary.

Thank you to the staff of Allen Memorial Hospital in Moab, St. Mary's Hospital in Grand Junction, St. Luke's Presbyterian Hospital in Denver, the Colorado Amputee Rehabilitation Management Team, and the Limb Preservation Institute; as well as to my surgeons and doctors, Dr. Bobby Higgins, Dr. Jeffrey Nakano, Dr. Michael Rooks, Dr. Arline Burnell, Dr. Cynthia Kelly, Dr. Gary Snider, and Dr. Rebekah Gass; and also, Dan Prinster, vice president of planning and business development at St. Mary's, the day and night nurses at St. Mary's—with special love for Renae Mason and Kelly Owens—occupational therapist Gary Saunders, and recreational therapist James Tanner, for my first journey outdoors after my accident, to the rooftop of the hospital.

I also thank Dr. Skip Meier with the Amputee Services of America, who coordinated my rehabilitation with the help of Erin Cantwell; Dr. Howard Belon, occupational therapist Julie Klarich, who coached me to eat crackers with my prosthetic until I got it (it takes the finesse of an egg juggler), physical therapist Carol McGowan and her colleagues, who challenged me to beat the clinic records on the balance balls, and my fellow patients in Dr. - Belon's support group.

My appreciation to Paul Poister, for volunteering his time to field media requests for my family during my hospitalization.

Support, Inspiration, and Encouragement

Thank you to my friends who flew and drove from around the country to visit me during my convalescence in the hospital and at home.

Thank you to everyone who wrote my family and me an e-mail, called to see how we were doing, or sent CDs, gifts, margarita supplies, donations, and hundreds of letters of well wishes and encouragement after my accident. I'm sorry I couldn't write all of you personal thank-yous.

Thank you to Troy Farnsworth, Jack Uellendahl, and Branden Petersen at Hanger Prosthetics, Malcolm Daly at Trango, Bob Radocy at TRS, and Dr. Will Craig for the prosthetic equipment that has enabled my independent return to rock climbing, ice climbing, solo mountaineering, canyoneering, kayaking, canoeing, cross-country and telemark skiing, mountain biking, and volunteering with search and rescue.

Thank you to my inspirations: the mellifluous Luke Dempsey, for his editing; Dr. Harry "Show, Don't Tell" Kelleher and Bill Bradley, my high school English teachers; Sharon Carlson, for the title idea; Ron Elberger, who embodies the fact that tenacity comes in small packages; my fellow FOCs and the String Cheese Incident; Norm and Sandy Ruth, the soul parents of my New Mexico family; Trey Anastasio and Phish; the authors and subjects of my favorite outdoors literature: John Fielder, Lou Dawson, Gerry Roach, Michael Kelsey, Edward Abbey, Warren MacDonald, Mark Twight, Erik Weihenmayer, Joe Simpson and Simon Yates, Chris McCandless, Anatoly Boukreev, Neal Beidleman, John Muir, Jon Krakauer, Jon Waterman, Timmy O'Neal, Douglas Mawson, and Papillon; Quentin Tarantino, from whose work I found the inspiration for the story outline; the NBC documentary group—Tom Brokaw, Colleen Halpin, Karen Epstein, Rich Platt, Craig White, Paul Thiriot, and the Shermanator; and the Landmark Forum.

Outdoor Teachers and Partners

For everyone who has ever been tied to me by a rope, you have taught me about not just the mountains and the skills to move among them, but also trust, beauty, friendship, and that soloing isn't the only way to have fun in the outdoors: Mark Van Eeckhout, Steve Patchett, Gary Scott, Jason Halladay, Marshall and Heather Ulrich, Tony DiZinno, Theresa Daus-Weber, Rich Haefele, Dawn Baker, Dan Hadlich and Julia Stephen, Steve De-

Roma, Jon Jaecks, Eric Niemeyer, Kyu Park, Pam Pelky, Bob and Yvonna Graham, Howard Huang, Bill Hemmen, Paul Budd, the Misiuks of Washington, Jamie Laurens, Jon Heinrich, Scott MacLennan, Jim Dennis and the NMMC, Rick Inman, Dave Johnson, Dave Benjes, Jeff Herd, Greg Jackson, Aaron Blawn, Judson Cole, Jamie Stoutenberg, Angie Kokjer, Mike Michalek, Guido Bender, Carl Drew, Megan Simon, Sarah Hall, Chewy Hoover, Tony Angelis, Suwei Wu, and Jackie Blumberg.

RECOMMENDED READING

For the stories and history of Blue John Griffith, I used Pearl Baker's book and recommend it for an entertaining look into the lives of the anti-heroes who populated the backcountry of southeastern Utah in the late 1800s and early 1900s.

Baker, Pearl. *The Wild Bunch at Robbers Roost*. Abelard-Schuman, New York, 1971.

Additionally, I recommend the following books for the influence they have had on my life.

Abbey, Edward. *Desert Solitaire: A Season in the Wilderness*. Random House, New York, 1968.

———. *The Monkeywrench Gang*. Avon Press, New York, 1975.

Bickel, Lennard. *Mawson's Will: The Greatest Survival Story Ever Written*. Dorset Press, New York, 1977.

Boukreev, Anatoly, and G. Weston DeWalt. *The Climb: Tragic Ambitions on Everest*. St. Martin's Press, New York, 1997.

Dawson II, Louis W. *Dawson's Guide to Colorado's Fourteeners, Volumes 1 and 2*. Blue Cover Press, Monument, Colorado, 1994.

Kelsey, Michael R. *Canyon Hiking Guide to the Colorado Plateau, 4th Ed.* Kelsey Publishing, Provo, Utah, 1999.

Krakauer, Jon. *Into the Wild*. Villard Books, New York, 1996.

———. *Into Thin Air: A Personal Account of the Mount Everest Disaster*. Villard Books, New York, 1997.

Pirsig, Robert. *Zen and the Art of Motorcycle Maintenance: An Inquiry into Values*. William Morrow and Company, New York, 1974.

Roach, Gerry, and Jennifer Roach. *Colorado's Thirteeners, 13,800 to 13,999 Feet: From Hikes to Climbs*. Fulcrum Publishing, Golden, Colorado, 2001.

Simpson, Joe. *Touching the Void: The True Story of One Man's Miraculous Survival*. Harper & Row, New York, 1988.

Twight, Mark F. *Kiss or Kill: Confessions of a Serial Climber*. The Mountaineers Books, Seattle, 2001.

Twight, Mark F., and James Martin. *Extreme Alpinism: Climbing Light, Fast, & High*. The Mountaineers Books, Seattle, 1999.

TEXT PERMISSIONS